'By the end of the next decade we will be the world's largest nation. We already are the world's largest multicultural, multi religious, multiethnic, multi linguistic democracy. The success of the Indian experiment in nation building and on the social and economic empowerment of a billion people is vital for the future of mankind in the twenty first century.'

Manmohan Singh Prime Minister of India
Source: India, the Next Decade
edited by Manmohan Malhoutra (2007) Routledge

'This riveting collection of essays on popular culture in a globalized India represents a rich tapestry of colors, patterns, and textures, woven by a team of expert weavers.'

Arvind Singhal, Ph.D.
Samuel Shirley and Edna Holt Marston Endowed Professor,
University of Texas at El Paso

'Over the last two decades, Moti Gokulsing has been tireless in his efforts to widen the understanding of popular media in South Asia, particularly Indian cinema, in the global academe. His new effort and that of his co-editor Wimal Dissanayake are an imposing effort to combine scholarship with new perspectives on the changing landscape of the popular modes of self-expression in the region. It is bound to attract the attention of both academics and general readers.'

Ashis Nandy
ICSSR National Fellow
Centre for the Developing Societies, India

'This edited collection presents some of the most exciting interdisciplinary scholarship on popular culture in contemporary India. For over two decades, Indian popular culture has undergone rapid and decisive changes resulting from the liberalisation of the economy and the influx of transnational media. These developments have had profound consequences for the lives and aspirations of many Indians, particularly those residing in urban areas. The essays in this volume track some of the shifts that have occurred, with a sensitive eye to how these changes have implicated social and cultural life in contemporary India: its large canvas encapsulates topics ranging from food culture and cyber culture to print culture and fashion, in addition to film and television. One of the most remarkable features of this collection of essays is its sensitivity to the nuances of local specificities even as it keeps in mind the bigger picture of some of the larger changes taking place on a national and global scale. I cannot wait to read and teach this book, and draw on it for my own research.'

Associate Professor Purnima Mankekar
University of California

Popular Culture in a Globalised India

As India celebrated the 60th anniversary of its independence in 2007, much praise was lavished on its emergence as a major player on the global stage. Its economic transformation and geopolitical significance as a nuclear power are matched by its globally resonant cultural resources.

This book explores India's rich popular culture. Chapters provide illuminating insights into various aspects of the social, cultural, economic and political realities of contemporary globalised India. Structured thematically and drawing on a broad range of academic disciplines, the book deals with critical issues including:

- Film, television and TV soaps
- Folk theatre, Mahabharata, myths, performance, ideology and religious nationalism
- Music, dance and fashion
- Comics, cartoons, photographs, posters and advertising
- Cyberculture and the software industry
- Indian feminisms
- Sports and tourism
- Food culture

Offering comprehensive coverage of the emerging discipline of popular culture in India, this book is essential reading for courses on Indian popular culture and a useful resource for more general courses in the field of cultural studies, media studies, history, literary studies and communication studies.

K. Moti Gokulsing is Senior Visiting Research Fellow at the University of East London. He is the co-founder and co-editor of the journal *South Asian Popular Culture* (SAPC) published by Routledge. His *Illusions of a South Asian Identity* was published in the April 2008 issue of SAPC.

Wimal Dissanayake is a Professor in the Academy for Creative Media at the University of Hawaii. He is the founding editor of the *East–West Film Journal* and the author and editor of a large number of books including *Global/Local: Cultural Production and the Transnational Imaginary*. He is also a distinguished creative writer who has won Sri Lankan national awards for his poetry and literary writings.

Popular Culture in a Globalised India

**Edited by
K. Moti Gokulsing and
Wimal Dissanayake**

 Routledge
Taylor & Francis Group

LONDON AND NEW YORK

First published 2009
by Routledge
2 Park Square, Milton Park, Abingdon, Oxon, OX14 4RN

Simultaneously published in the USA and Canada
by Routledge
270 Madison Avenue, New York, NY 10016

*Routledge is an imprint of the Taylor & Francis Group,
an informa business*

© 2009 Editorial selection and matter; K. Moti Gokulsing and
Wimal Dissanayake; individual chapters the contributors

Typeset in Times by Keyword Group Ltd
Printed and bound in Great Britain by Antony Rowe Ltd., Chippenham,
Wiltshire

British Library Cataloguing in Publication Data
A catalogue record for this book is available from the British Library

Library of Congress Cataloging in Publication Data
Popular culture in a globalised India / edited by K. Moti Gokulsing and
Wimal Dissanayake.
    p. cm.
  Includes bibliographical references and index.
  ISBN 978-0-415-47666-9 (hardback : alk. paper) –
  ISBN 978-0-415-47667-6 (pbk. : alk. paper) 1. Popular culture–
  Social aspects–India. 2. Globalization–Social aspects–India.
  I. Gokulsing, K. Moti. II. Dissanayake, Wimal.
  DS428.2.P67 2008
  306.0954–dc22   2008029016

ISBN10: 0-415-47666-6 (hbk)
ISBN10: 0-415-47667-4 (pbk)
ISBN10: 0-203-88406-X (ebk)

ISBN13: 978-0-415-47666-9 (hbk)
ISBN13: 978-0-415-47667-6 (pbk)
ISBN13: 978-0-203-88406-5 (ebk)

Contents

Cyberculture – the software industry   205

14 **India goes to the blogs: cyberspace, identity, community**   207
    PRAMOD K. NAYAR

15 **The Indian software industry: cultural factors underpinning**
    its evolution   223
    FLORIAN TAEUBE

PART VI
Sports – tourism   237

16 **Opiate of the masses or one in a billion: trying to unravel**
    the Indian sporting mystery   239
    BORIA MAJUMDAR

17 **Going places: popular tourism writing in India**   252
    ANNA KURIAN

PART VII
Food culture   265

18 **The discreet charm of Indian street food**   267
    BHASKAR MUKHOPADHYAY

    Conclusion   274
    Bibliography   280
    Index   282

Map of India

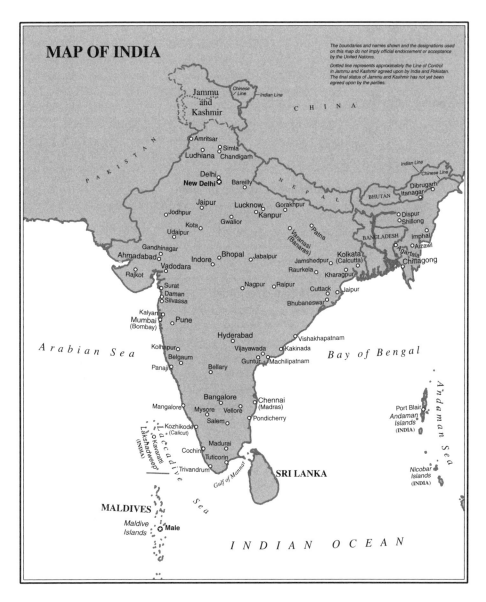

MAP OF INDIA

The boundaries and names shown and the designations used on this map do not imply official endorsement or acceptance by the United Nations.

Dotted line represents approximately the Line of Control in Jammu and Kashmir agreed upon by India and Pakistan. The final status of Jammu and Kashmir has not yet been agreed upon by the parties.

Adapted from UN Department of Peacekeeping Operations Map No. 4140 rev.3

Illustrations

Figures

Tables

Notes on contributors

Christiane Brosius is Assistant Professor at the Department of Anthropology, South Asia Institute of the University of Heidelberg in Germany. Her book Empowering Visions was published by Anthem Press in 2005. She is co-founder of Tasveer Ghar/House of Pictures: A Digital Network of South Asian Popular Visual Culture (www.tasveerghar.net). Her recent manuscript on globalisation, urbanisation and the new middle classes in India will be published by Routledge, New Delhi. cbrosius@hotmail.com

Lynne Ciochetto is an Associate Professor at Massey University, New Zealand. The main focus of her research is the visual documentation of international advertising and signage. Publications include studies of global advertising, specific target audiences and case studies of contemporary advertising in Russia, Vietnam, India, Thailand and China. L.M.Ciochetto@massey.ac.nz

Wimal Dissanayake is a Professor in the Academy for Creative Media at the University of Hawaii. He is the founding editor of the *East–West Film Journal* and the author and editor of a large number of books including *Global/Local: Cultural Production and the Transnational Imaginary*. He is also a distinguished creative writer who has won Sri Lankan national awards for his poetry and literary writings. ddissa@yahoo.com

Shehina Fazal was Senior Lecturer in Media and Communications in the Department of Applied Social Sciences at London Metropolitan University until July 2008. Her research interests focus on the media, the diaspora and transnational communications. Her latest book *Television in India* will be published in 2008 by Palgrave Macmillan. shehinafazal@hotmail.com

Geetanjali Gangoli is Lecturer in the School for Policy Studies at the University of Bristol. She has worked on violence against women and feminist movements in India with a special emphasis on legal activism. She was a Visiting Research Fellow at the London School of Economics (1999–2000) and her latest book is *Indian Feminisms: Campaigns against Violence and Multiple Patriarchies* published by Ashgate in 2007. G.Gangoli@bristol.ac.uk

K. Moti Gokulsing is Senior Visiting Research Fellow at the University of East London. He is the author of *Soft-Soaping India: The world of Indian televised soap*

operas (2004), co-author of *Indian Popular Cinema a narrative of cultural change* (1998, 2004), and the co-founder and co-editor of the journal South Asian Popular Culture (SAPC) published by Routledge. His *Illusions of a South Asian Identity* was published in the April 2008 issue of SAPC. gokulsing@ntlworld.com

Angma Dey Jhala is an Assistant Professor of History at Bentley University. She was trained at Harvard and Oxford universities and her book, *Courtly Indian Women in Late Imperial India*, was published in 2008. She is also a published fiction writer and is presently working on a novel. angmajhala@gmail.com

Jayasinhji Jhala is Associate Professor of Anthropology at Temple University. He was trained at Harvard University and Massachusetts Institute of Technology. He is a Documentary Filmmaker and his films of Bhavai theatre: *ShaktiMa Noh Veh-The drama of ShaktiMa* **and Tragada Bhavai** are distributed by Documentary Education Resources, Watertown M.A. jayasinhji@gmail.com

Anna Kurian teaches at the Department of English, University of Hyderabad, India. Her interests include children's literature, Shakespeare and early modern culture and popular culture studies. Her recent work includes essays in Indian writing in English and entries in the *Oxford Encyclopaedia of Children's Literature* (2006). epikurian2005@yahoo.co.in

Peter Kvetko is an Assistant Professor of Music at Salem State College. He has studied Hindustani classical music as a student of Stephen Slawek and Shamim Ahmed Khan and directs the sitar and tabla ensemble at Salem State. He also performs traditional Indonesian music with the Boston Village Gamelan. His research concerns popular music and transnational ideologies of class and power. pkvetko@salemstate.edu

Pamela Lothspeich is an Assistant Professor of Hindi–Urdu at the University of North Carolina at Chapel Hill. She received her Ph.D. in Comparative Literature from Columbia University in 2003. Her research interests include 20th-century Hindi literature, and the Indian epics in modern literature and theatre. Her book, *Epic Nation: Reimagining the Mahabharata in the Age of Empire*, is to be published by OUP India in 2008. ploth@email.unc.edu

Karline McLain is Assistant Professor of South Asian Religions at Bucknell University. She is the author of the book *India's Immortal Comic Books: Gods, Kings, and Other Heroes* (Bloomington: Indiana University Press, 2009), which was awarded the Edward Cameron Dimock Jr Book Prize in the Indian Humanities by the American Institute of Indian Studies. kmclain@bucknell.edu

Boria Majumdar a Rhodes Scholar, is a Research Fellow at La Trobe University, Melbourne. He is the Executive Academic Editor of 'Sport in Society' and joint General Editor of the Routledge Series 'Sport in a Global Society'. He has published widely on the history and politics of sport in South Asia and his latest book is *Olympics: The Indian Story* (with Nalin Mehta) published by Harper-Collins in July 2008. cristorian@yahoo.com

Nalin Mehta is Honorary Research Fellow at La Trobe University, Melbourne, and Visiting Fellow at Australian National University, Canberra. He has over ten years of experience as a broadcaster, most recently as Deputy News Editor with Times Now. He is the author of *India on Television: How Satellite News Channels Changed the Way We Think and Act* (New Delhi: Harper Collins, 2008) and has edited *Television in India: Satellites, Politics and Cultural Change* (London: Routledge, 2008). He now works for UNAIDS. nalinnikki@gmail.com

Anna Morcom is RCUK Academic Fellow in the Music Department of Royal Holloway College, University of London. Her research interests centre around music/dance in the context of a rapidly changing world with a particular focus on Tibet and India. She is the author of *Hindi Film Songs and the Cinema* published by Ashgate in 2007. Anna.Morcom@rhul.ac.uk

Bhaskar Mukhopadhyay teaches Cultural Studies at Goldsmiths, University of London. He has published numerous articles on India in international journals and has edited a six-volume compendium, *Britain in India 1757–1905* (Pickering & Chatto) with Partha Chatterjee. His monograph, *The Rumour of Globalization: Decentring the Global from the Vernacular Margins* comes out in 2008. privatemiaaow@gmail.com

Pramod K. Nayar teaches in the Department of English at the University of Hyderabad, India. His interests include postcolonial studies, English writing on India and cultural studies. His recent publications are *English Writing and India* (Routledge 2008), *Postcolonial Literature* (Pearson 2008) and *Reading Culture* (Sage 2006). *An Introduction to Cyberculture* and *The Cybercultures Reader* are forthcoming from Blackwell. pramodnayar@yahoo.co.uk

Ram Puniyani is a Former Professor of ITT Mumbai, and has written widely on the threat posed by religious nationalism and terrorism. His recent books *Communal Politics: Facts versus Myths* was published in 2003, Second Assassination of Gandhi in 2006, Terrorism: Facts versus myths 2008. He is the recipient of many awards, the most recent being the Indira Gandhi Award in October 2006 for furthering the cause of communal harmony through his lectures and writings. He is currently engaged working on books, videos and posters to promote communal harmony and to dispel the myths about minorities. ram.puniyani@gmail.com

M. K. Raghavendra is a National Award-winning film critic. He was awarded a two-year Homi Bhabha Fellowship in 2000 to research into Indian popular film narrative and his book *Seduced by the Familiar: Narration and Meaning in Indian Popular Cinema* has just been published by Oxford University Press in 2008. mkragh54@gmail.com

Florian Taeube is Assistant Professor at Strascheg Institute for Innovation and Entrepreneurship (SIIE), European Business School (EBS), Germany. Previously, he was Post-Doc at Imperial College London and, during his PhD, Visiting Scholar at the Wharton School and Indian Institute of Science. His research interests are in international business, entrepreneurship and organisation theory. Out of his thesis on Indian IT, he has published several articles and book chapters. florian.taeube@ebs-siie.de

Acknowledgements

In editing this volume of essays, we have incurred a huge debt of gratitude to the eighteen contributors, spread across the globe, whose diligence, competence and professionalism have made what is undoubtedly a challenging project an exciting and learning enterprise.

We are also indebted to a number of people, too many to mention individually. But the following deserve special mention:

- Dorothea Schaefter at Routledge for her support and encouragement and to Tom Bates, Vicky Claringbull, Madhavi Bhargava also at Routledge and Rahul Raj Raghavan for advice and help
- The three anonymous referees who provided constructive comments which have helped us to shape the book
- Ashis Nandy, Rustom Bharucha, Bhaskar Mukhopadhyay, Boria Majumdar, Nalin Mehta, Rajinder Dudrah, Pramod Nayar, Lionel McCalman, Ann Slater, Gillian Klein and Cornel DaCosta for intellectual support during the planning of this book
- Neeraja Sundaram for help with the T&F House style
- Chris Folorunso, Web Operations Manager, at the University of East London for help and advice on computer issues
- Our respective families for moral support while we were working on this book.

While every effort has been made to trace copyright holders and obtain their permission for materials used in this volume, if there are errors or omissions, the publishers will, if notified of any corrections, incorporate them in future editions of this volume.

Permission to reprint copyright materials from the following sources is gratefully acknowledged.

The Viveka Foundation for images published in the chapter 'Gods, Kings, and Local Telugu Guys: Competing Visions of the Heroic in Indian Comic Books' by Dr Karline McLain of Bucknell University.

Shyam Benegal's permission to Pamela Lothspeich to publish the stills from the film 'Kalyug' in her chapter 'The Mahabharata's Imprint on Contemporary Literature and Film'.

Varsha Kale, Hon. President, Bhartiya Bargirls Union for permission to Anna Morcom to publish the photograph of the Bar Girls Union Publicity Poster in her chapter 'Indian popular culture and its "others": Bollywood dance and anti-nautch in twenty first century global India'

R.S Iyer, Photographer, for permission to Christiane Brosius to use the photograph of Gurgaon in her chapter 'The Gated Romance of "India Shining": Visualising Urban Lifestyle in Advertisement of Residential Housing Development'.

Permission to quote from Bounds, P. (1999) 'Cultural Studies- A student's guide to culture, politics and society' was sought from his publishers who have reverted rights of this title back to the author but so far no reply has been received from him. However, the publishers have stated that under fair deal there should be no problem (emailed correspondence dated 11 August 2007 refers).

Note on transliteration

We have retained the various forms of transcription adopted by the individual authors.

Glossary and acronyms

This glossary, compiled from a variety of sources, is highly selective, but it contains much of the basic terminology used in this book.

Achkan: a long jacket worn in South Asia

Acharya: Clergy and God men

Adivasi: The original inhabitants, tribal

Ashoka: The great third-century BC Maurayan emperor

Astha: Faith

Avatar: Incarnation

Babas: The God men

Babri Masjid: The mosque at Ayodhya demolished by right-wing Hindus in December, 1992

Backward Classes: Members of the Scheduled Castes and the other low-ranking groups (sometimes referred to as Other Backward Classes – OBCs)

Bharatiya Janata Party (BJP) is a Hindu Nationalist political party and represented the first unified party in opposition to the Congress Party

Brahmin: A member of the priestly caste, the highest caste

Brahminism: The most elite stream of Hinduism, based on caste and gender hierarchy

Chattris: elevated, dome-shaped pavilions used as an element in Indian architecture

Chudidars: tightly fitting trousers worn by both men and women in South Asia and Central Asia

Darshan: means seeing and being seen by the deity

Dharma: has a variety of meanings-may mean religion, duty, law morality, a divinely ordained code of proper conduct

Cow Slaughter: One of the political campaigns taken up by RSS combine to browbeat Muslims

Dalit: Ex-untouchables, the low castes amongst Hindus

Eklavya: English translation – The Royal Guard

Gaghras: is a flowing skirt-like garment tapered at the waist with drawstrings which flares out from the body. This garment is traditionally worn in western India in the regions of Rajasthan and Gujarat.

Gazal: a poetic form consisting of rhyming couplets and a refrain

Ghats: a series of steps leading down to a body of water in many parts of South Asia

Haveli: a term used to describe private residences in North Indian architecture. Ordinarily it is an enclosed space with a courtyard in the centre.

Hinduism: the religion has many streams, not founded by any prophet

Hindutva: literally 'Hindu-ness'(Hindu cultural identity) a political ideology of Hindu nationalism propounded by V.D. Savarkar in 1923

Hookah: a single or multi-stemmed (often glass-based) water pipe for smoking

Jati: caste in the sense of named 'birth group'

Jazia: a tax levied by some Muslim Kings for non-Muslims

Karma: one's actions, duty. Related to the idea of heaven and hell as well as rebirth

Karva Chauth: A fast done by wife for the long life of her husband

Kathak: The major form of North Indian classical dance

Kotha: the salon of the courtesan

Kumbh Mela: Mass religious congregations

Mahaarti: Mass religious invocation

Mahabharata: epic tale of the battle of the Kauravas and Pandavas, two royal clans

Masjid: Mosque

NCERT: National Centre for Education Research and Training

Odhanis: scarf-like garment worn over the *gaghra*, often used to cover the head and upper body. It is traditionally worn in western India in the regions of Rajasthan and Gujarat.

Paan: Betel leaf (Piper betel) combined with areca nut. It is chewed as a palate cleanser and breath freshener. A dash of tobacco gives it a mild intoxicant effect.

Pakeezah: Pure one

Qawwali: Sufi devotional songs

Ramjanmabhoomi: a political movement to build a temple in honour of Lord Ram at the site of Babri Masjid in Ayodhya (the alleged site of Ram's birth)

Raj Nartaki: The court dancer

Rakhi: the thread tied by sister on brother's wrist

Raksha Bandhan: A popular Hindu festival of north India where sister ties a thread on brother's wrist, seeking protection

RSS combine: Diverse organisations formed and controlled by RSS – it is popularly known as Sangh Parivar

Saffronised: Saffron is the political symbol of RSS combine

Salwar kameez: A traditional dress worn by women (and men) in South Asia

Sangh parivar: the RSS 'family' of organisations

Sanskar: The cultivation of religious norms

Savarkar: The Hindutva ideologue who gave the political definition of Hindus

Scheduled Castes: (SCs) – the official term for Untouchable castes

Scheduled Tribes: (STs) – the official term for India's 'tribal' or adivasi populations

Shakha: Branch, the morning assembly of RSS

Shudras: Untouchables. Lowest caste in Hindu hierarchy

Syncretic: The traditions (religious/cultural) deriving from diverse roots

Tawaif: a courtesan who often catered to the Muslim nobility of the subcontinent

Varna: the four categories (or colours) which traditionally define and divide Hindu society (Brahmans; Kshatriyas; Vaishyas; Shudras)

Yatra: pilgrimage or religious procession

Zamindari: land owning and revenue collecting classes

Zenana: architecturally the female quarters of the palace or home where women lived behind seclusion

Introduction

K. Moti Gokulsing and Wimal Dissanayake

Rationale

As India celebrated the 60th anniversary of its independence in 2007, much praise was lavished on its emergence as a major player on the global stage. Its economic transformation, its nuclear arsenal, its emphasis on cyberculture, its international reputation for outsourcing facilities and its popular tourist destination are some of the main factors accounting for India's present rise to power. Comparatively little attention has been paid in the West to its incredibly rich popular cultural traditions.

This edited volume is a contribution to the emerging discipline of Popular Culture in India[1] – 'Cultural Studies is still an infant discipline in India and it is not very clear which sector of life it should take up for study' (Mukhopadhyay, 2006: 284). The contributors to this volume have taken up this challenge and provide illuminating insights into various aspects of the social, cultural, economic and political diversity of a globalised India. The strength of the volume resides in the fact that it represents some of the best thinking of the rising generation of Indian scholars and draws on a broad range of academic disciplines which address the issue of popular culture.

There is, however, a vast and contentious literature on both popular culture and globalisation (see e.g. Barker 2008; Jones 2006), and a comprehensive discussion of the main arguments is beyond the scope of this introduction. Consequently, we are opting for a particular version of popular culture and globalisation consistent within the accepted meanings of both popular culture and globalisation.

In order to contextualise the version of popular culture and globalisation we are opting for, we start with a summary of the British-inflected notion of popular culture via Hoggart, Williams, Thompson, Hall and others and the theoretical approaches underpinning the development of Popular Culture/Cultural Studies in Britain. This account is intended as points of reference rather than framing devices for a contextually nuanced study of popular culture in a globalised India. We then provide a brief account of Globalisation and Popular Culture in India, focusing on traditional popular cultural topics as well as on new areas such as Cyberculture and the Software Industry. Finally, we choose the concept of *relationality,* borrowed from Rao and Walton (2004) and situate its relevance to this book.

Introduction

The aim of this book is to gather together in one volume some of the most insightful writings on popular culture in a globalised India and contextualise them in a way that would promote a fruitful discussion.

What exactly is Popular Culture and how should we approach it? What insights does it provide for an understanding of India that other disciplines do not? These are some of the issues which we explore in this introduction.

At one level, it is easy to talk about popular culture. In the words of O'Sullivan *et al.* (2001: 231), Popular Culture is 'of people in general, for people in general; well liked by people in general ... usually synonymous with "good" in ordinary conversation'.

At another level, Popular Culture is also synonymous with what is gross, vulgar and cheap – unworthy of serious study. Both of these definitions co-exist within Popular Culture, particularly in its early days as a discipline – an issue we take up a little later.

But these definitions of Popular Culture mask its substantial growth as an inter-disciplinary subject, drawing its strengths from a variety of theories and methods from the Humanities and Social Sciences.

Popular Culture is generally considered as a combination of communication studies and cultural studies. According to Milner and Browitt (2002: 7) 'Cultural Studies is an entirely new discipline defined in terms of a new subject matter: that is the study of popular culture'.

There is a substantial literature on the concept of culture and the emergence and growth of Cultural Studies as a distinct field of academic inquiry since the 1950s (see e.g. Fiske, 1989; Hall, 1981; McQuail, 2005; Storey, 1993; Strinati, 2004; Turner, 1996).

The seminal contributions of Hoggart (1957), Thompson (1963) Williams (1963) and Hall and Du Gay (1996) are crucial to our understanding of Cultural Studies and the emergence of Popular Culture as a most significant concept in cultural analysis.

Yet, for an academic discipline that has seen a phenomenal growth globally, there is hardly any agreement among the academics as to what exactly culture means. It is not our intention in this Introduction to focus on the debates about the definitions of culture – one of the two or three most complicated words in the English language according to Williams (1976); rather, we will select aspects of culture to contextualise popular culture within a cultural studies framework.

One non-controversial aspect of culture is that it is 'the ensemble of social processes by which meanings are produced, circulated and exchanged' (Thwaites *et al.* 1994: 1).

Following the arguments in Thwaites *et al.* (1994), we agree that culture is the site of the production of meanings, not the expression of meanings which exist elsewhere and by calling it an ensemble of processes we are saying that it is not a unified process.

This view is supported by Clifford who in his writings (see e.g. his book *The Predicament of Culture: Twentieth Century Ethnography, Literature and Art* 1988) is critical of the idea of cultures as coherent and unified. One of his arguments is that culture is contingent, syncretic and historical, a view relevant to this book.

Cultural Studies, then, is not a coherent and unified discipline with clear-cut substantive topics, concepts and methods which differentiate it from other disciplines. Likewise, Popular Culture reflects neither a unified way of thinking nor an easily mapped path of development (Gains and Cruz, 2005: 2).

What then is Popular Culture about?

Building on Williams' (1965) arguments in *The Long Revolution* that culture encompasses three related elements:

- A 'lived' element – focusing on the lived experience of people;
- A 'documentary' element – dealing with the transmission of meaning;
- An 'ideal' element – a sceptical attitude towards received ideas and high culture (Bounds, 1999: 14–15),

we note that these complex processes are produced and consumed within particular material circumstances.

> Text and practices are both products of and constitutive of the social world. This is made up of a whole range of organisations from, for example, institutions of the media and other cultural producers, the family, education and various agencies of civil society to everyday practices within specific social groups ... Questions of power and access (are also crucial...).
>
> (Gray, 2003: 12)

Who has access to, who is excluded from, who excludes himself/herself from (social exclusion) and who engages actively in the uses of cultural artefacts in making sense of their own and others' lives are political issues. All these come together in producing, disseminating and consuming popular culture. It is important to note that the meanings associated with popular culture which are produced, circulated and exchanged are complex and not simply accurate and efficient transmission of messages – they are never entirely fixed and, although not lost in transmission (to adapt a popular phrase), are 'never wholly determined by the original context' (Thwaites *et al.* 1999: 2). Thus Cultural Studies and its subject matter Popular Culture have a continually changing agenda.

According to one of the founding fathers of Cultural Studies in Britain, it was literary studies which were the single most important element of this new discipline. Hoggart with the other two founding fathers of British Cultural Studies – Williams and E. P. Thompson – focused on the creation of a common culture in Britain rooted in the distinctive values of working-class life.

The focus, however, was on working-class youth. The emergence of feminism, multiculturalism and anti-racist approaches led to the exploration of ways in which relationships between age, race, gender and sexuality play out in the making and consuming of popular cultural forms.

In recent years, issues of difference, identity and hybridity have become important to popular culture studies. With the impact of globalisation, knowledge-based economies and rapid technological changes, other issues such as cyberculture, the software industry which we discuss later are taking centre stage in debates about popular cultural issues, thus confirming the point we made earlier that popular culture has a continually changing agenda. At the heart of this changing agenda are the concepts and theoretical approaches which have underpinned the discipline of Popular Culture and to which we now turn for a brief description.

Theoretical approaches

Given the complex conceptual and theoretical frameworks which underpin the disciplines of Cultural Studies / Popular Culture, it would be foolhardy of us to provide a summary. The intention in this section is to give a brief description of some of the basic trends in Popular Culture from its early days to the impact of globalisation for the benefit of readers who may not be familiar with this development.

Responding to societal changes such as the development of the mass media, the founding fathers of British Cultural Studies developed some of the main theoretical strands which have shaped Cultural Studies / Popular Culture since their emergence in the 1950s. They critique the existing disciplines such as English and Sociology for their limitations, their modes of analysis and theories and argue for ethnographic approaches to deal with the concerns of everyday life:

> Culture, if it is to be understood in its broadest sense, is not just the property of the powerful and the elite, but is produced through interactions and encounters within daily life. Here the notion of lived cultures is crucial.
>
> (Gray, 2003: 39)

Williams's vision for reform was the creation of a common culture in Britain – a whole way of life shared by everyone – 'a culture is not only a body of intellectual and imaginative work; it is also and essentially a whole way of life' (1963: 311). This meant a rejection of the common culture envisaged by Leavis who argues that the rise of industrialism and commercial forms typical of industrial society were destroying the literary inheritance of an 'organic community' leading to the culture wars between the 'canonical high culture of established academic tradition' and the lived cultures of the people:

> What ... Leavis diagnosed cultural decline, Williams, by contrast, discerned a long revolution leading towards, rather than away from the eventual realisation of a socialistic, common culture.
>
> (Milner and Browitt, 2002: 34)

Williams, Hoggart and Thompson were members of the New Left – 'a new form of socialist politics ... they were less interested in abolishing capitalism than in humanising it through radical reforms'. Here they were keen to revive the idea that socialism could only work effectively if (a) ordinary people ran it for themselves and (b) a cultural dimension in which working-class ways of life would be more highly valued is restored (Bounds, 1999: 18).

In the 1970s, a significant number of studies focused on working-class cultures, theoretically informed by Marxist ideas. Aided by Althusser's concept of ideology, Gramsci's concept of hegemony and Barthes's semiotics, the focus was on working-class culture and subcultures. In much of

> subcultural theory, the question of resistance to the dominant culture comes to the fore ... for Cultural Studies writers of the 1970s subcultures were seen as magical or symbolic solutions to the structural problem of class.
>
> (Barker, 2004: 193)

Unlike the earlier phase of Cultural Studies/Popular Culture, the writers favoured the abolition of capitalism and the establishment of a socialist society, characterised by 'the common ownership of the means of production, distribution and exchange' (Bounds, 1999: 20). The studies during that period were overwhelmingly on male subjects – the lads – and as McRobbie (1980: 37) suggests 'women and the whole question of sexual division have been marginalised'.

The arrival of Stuart Hall as director of the Birmingham Centre for Contemporary Cultural Studies (CCCS) in 1968 marked a shift in the CCCS's focus on Popular Culture. He emphasised the political centrality of culture and pointed out that we misunderstand modern societies if we think of culture as mere leisure or entertainment. He views culture as one of the sites where the struggle for and against a culture of the powerful is engaged. With the increasing importance of new social movements in the 1970s such as feminism (e.g. McRobbie), anti-racism (Gilroy, 1982 *The Empire Strikes Back*), the racialised Other and gay liberation movement (e.g. Queer Theory), issues of gender, race and ethnicity as well as the role of the mass media took centre stage in theoretical formulations.

The contributions of Stuart Hall and his team at the University of Birmingham are well known and well documented.

For the purposes of this Introduction and its relevance to popular culture in a globalised India, Debord's arguments:

> In societies where modern conditions of production prevail, all life presents itself as an immense accumulation of spectacles. Everything that was directly lived has moved away into a representation ...
>
> The spectacle is not a collection of images but a social relation among people mediated by images. (Debord, 1984 paragraphs 1 and 4)

encapsulate some of the objectives of this book.

Globalisation and popular culture

Here too, as we saw in the development of Cultural Studies/Popular Culture, there is a vast literature on globalisation. At least, two aspects of globalisation and their implications for Popular Culture concern us:

- how technologies can overcome global distances and we appear to live in a borderless world where images can be relayed instantaneously;
- one particular economic system – the free market or global capitalism – now pervades most of the globe

(Branston and Stafford, 2006: 47).

It is useful to see globalisation as an umbrella term involving knowledge-based economies and technological changes as two of its key parts.

We are all familiar with the notion that the economic revolution we are now witnessing worldwide is driven by rapid technological changes. Some writers such as Castells (1996) have defined the knowledge economy in terms of 'knowledge as the key factor of and technology as the key resource for production'. These technological/information technologies have been characterised by Castells (2000: 28) as aspects of a network society. In his view there is now a transformation of the labour market, a structural divide between 'programmable labour' that is capable of reskilling itself and adapting to rapid change and 'generic labour' that is more disposable and can be replaced by machine technology. In addition to this structural divide, there is also a digital divide in which nations which do not have access to this speed of communication will find themselves left behind.

Enter India and its popular cultural traditions

Where does India find itself in this digital divide?
As Sen has observed,

> It is not easy to think of another country that has as many flourishing languages and literatures. What is central to our present turmoil is, of course, religious diversity, and there again our position is unique. The vast majority of Indians may be Hindus, but we have more than a hundred million Muslims (India has the third largest Muslim population in the world), we have more Sikhs than any other country, more Jains too, more Parsees as well; India has had Christians for over fifteen hundred years (much longer than Britain has had any) and while the number of Indian Buddhists today may be small, ours is the birthplace of Buddhism. I don't believe there exists another country the religious diversity of which begins to match ours (1993: 39–40).

In 1977, on a visit to India, E. P. Thompson remarked that India was not an important country but perhaps the most important country for the future of the world. Few countries are larger than India, only one more populous, none more diverse (confirming Sen's observations above) (Guha, 2007b: 14).

Does Thompson's judgement sound hyperbolic, particularly as a decade earlier when India was due to hold a general election in February 1967, *The Times* ran a series of articles under the title 'India's Disintegrating Democracy – Indians would soon vote in the fourth – and surely last general election'?

Thirty years after E. P. Thompson's observations, India's journey to the centre stage of a globalised world is well known and well documented. India is being courted by all the major powers as it emerges as a major player on the global stage.

A number of articles and books by Western commentators as well as by diasporic Indian scholars have sung the praises of India. For example, in December 2003 *Business Week* published a cover story entitled, 'The rise of India' and in 2004 *Newsweek* published its 'Asia's powerhouse, a good place to do business where the individual is king'. In 2005 Friedman's 'The world is flat' spoke of how 'a country of snake charmers, poor people and Mother Teresa had been recalibrated – it is now also a country of brainy people and computer wizards'. This view is shared by Jeffrey Sachs, the internationally known Economics Professor as well as the 2007 Reith Lecturer who in his 'The end of poverty' spoke of how 'the return of China and India to global economic prominence would reshape global politics and society in the 21st century' (see Guha 2007a for a fuller and insightful discussion). The recent India's nuclear deal with the USA has confirmed India's membership of the elite club.

Popular culture in India

But, as we stated earlier on, this discourse is mainly about the economic transformation of the largest democracy in the world, its nuclear arsenal, its emphasis on cyberculture, its international reputation for outsourcing facilities and a popular tourist destination. Of India's popular culture, only the Indian Popular Cinema (frequently referred to as Bollywood) is now part of mainstream cinema. India presents us with a unique site in terms of the dynamics of popular culture.

Indian society, like the rest of South Asia, is multiethnic and multilingual and this complicates every aspect of daily life and culture. As Dharwadker (2007) has pointed out, India has

> 125 major languages belonging to four different language families, they are written in a dozen script systems and according to the 1961 Census of India (the last report to record such data) the country uses some 3000 speech varieties on a daily basis. … The scale of India's multilingualism makes many forms of high and popular culture extremely complex …

While multilingualism and multi-ethnicity in India increase India's cultural diversity, this volume focuses on such traditional popular cultural topics as,

(a) Cinema
(b) Television
(c) Theatre/Folklore

(d) Religious Nationalism
(e) Sports
(f) Music
(g) Dance
(h) Fashions
(i) Advertising
(j) Comics/Cartoons
(k) Photographs/Posters
(l) Tourism
(m) Food

Globalisation is having both positive and negative effects on India's popular cultural traditions.

On the positive side, there is now greater transparency in government to be more responsive to 'the needs and concerns of its citizens'. India is liberating its trade policies and opening its markets to the outside world. The increasing economic growth of India has led to the growth and spread of a consumer middle class so that far more people have access to cable and satellite television, video, computer, the internet and to buy fashionable clothes, watch sports, live concerts and 'even to collect art and rare handicrafts'.

On the negative side, globalisation is benefiting only a minority of the population – the 200/300 million labelled middle class – leaving the majority of its 1.2 billion people in India who are the poor, the disadvantaged and the voiceless in unhealthy and high-risk working conditions.

What prospects are there of popular culture shedding some light on a globalised India?

Earlier on, we mentioned Bollywood as the best-known popular culture of India. But Bollywood is only one of a number of regional and linguistic cinemas and centres of film production. Other aspects of Indian popular culture can be found in a variety of writings (not always easily accessible in the West). Of India's incredible social, cultural, economic and political diversity, this book has selected some of the most traditional categories of popular culture ('the usual suspects' mentioned above) for critical examination. Additionally, the book tries to move the discipline of Popular Culture forward by including some aspects of what is often referred to as the cultural studies of cyberculture.

In this respect recent developments in the social sciences provide helpful insights into some of the ways in which Popular Culture is moving forward. What has been the preserve of anthropologists, sociologists and cultural studies analysts – folk and oral cultures, local resistance, 'symbolic violence of dominant discriminatory ideologies', the construction of identity of the marginalised and their representations – in fact the lived experience of nearly half a billion people in the case of India – has now become the focal concerns of economists. Thus, they are now increasingly focusing on how social and cultural factors shape human behaviour – in line with Landes's (*The Wealth and Poverty of Nations*, 1998) statement 'if we learn anything from the history of economic development, it is that culture makes all the difference'. And while there is a relationship between culture, power and the economy, this relationship is all the more complex in India since, as we mentioned earlier, there are so many regional languages as well as a number of oral, visual and written cultures (Kasbekar, 2006: 10). Consequently, in selecting the topics for this book, much consideration has been given to covering the various regions of India.

A recent publication *Culture and Public Action* (Rao and Walton, 2004) brings together a collection of essays by some of the leading economists and anthropologists such as Amartya Sen, Mary Douglas and Arjun Appadurai who examined the complex interaction between culture and development with case studies that ground their observations in the everyday life of the disadvantaged.

The approach adapted by Rao and Walton is one where culture is inherently dynamic, always in process, always subject to contestation. And since their view of culture is one that informs our view of popular culture in this book, we quote the relevant part:

> Culture is concerned with identity, aspiration, symbolic exchange, coordination and structures and practices that serve relation ends, such as ethnicity, ritual, heritage, norms, meanings and beliefs. It is not a set of primordial phenomena permanently embedded within national or religious or other groups, but rather a set of contested attributes, constantly in flux, shaping and being shaped by social and economic aspects of human interaction.
>
> (Rao and Walton, 2004: 4)

Although the chapters in this book can 'stand alone', the thread that binds them together is the concept of *relationality* – the relationships among individuals within groups, among groups, between ideas and perspectives and how meaning, power, practices and institutions help the forms that frame the whole way of life of people in India (see Harriss, 2005 for a useful discussion).

Overview of the sections

Where relevant, we have grouped the topics together to provide some sort of logical sequence:

Part I: Film/Television/TV – Soaps/Indian Feminisms
Part II: Folk Theatre/Myths – Mahabharata–Ramayana/Religious Nationalism
Part III: Music/Dance/Fashions
Part IV: Comics – Cartoons/Photographs – Posters/Advertising
Part V: Cyberculture/The Software Industry
Part VI: Sports/Tourism
Part VII: Food Culture

Of the topics grouped in Part I, the cinema, in particular Bollywood, is by far the best known of India's popular culture. Ignored by academics until two decades ago as pointed out by Mira Reym Binford (1989) 'It (Indian Popular Cinema) is little known in this country (USA)', Bollywood has generated a substantial literature as it has gone global. But Bollywood is only one of a number of film industries in India – So Many Cinemas as Garga (1996) categorised the Indian Film Industry. The Regional Cinemas of India produce a substantial number of films, but they do not have Bollywood's global reach.

Raghavendra provides some interesting insights into how the Kannada popular film articulates the concerns of the locals in Bangalore which has recently emerged as the key hub of global enterprise in India. He examines local responses to global Bangalore and how Kannada language cinema tends to resist global Bangalore.

Much has been written about the impact of television in India and its phenomenal growth in the last two decades. Mehta explores the rise of the 24-hour news channels in India and their impact on politics. He argues persuasively that Indian television thrives on programming genres that marry older argumentative traditions with new technology and notions of liberal democracy to create new hybrid forms that strengthen democratic culture. Furthermore, Mehta suggests that political leaders and parties adapt their daily practices of politics to the 24-hour publicity satellite television provides.

Television also screens soap operas which, as Gokulsing (2004) has argued, have become more popular than films. Fazal critically examines gender issues from the soap operas and states that although there is greater representation of women on television, their images are bounded by national as well as by patriarchal considerations. She argues that contemporary representations of women in soap operas are replacing the emancipated role models seen in earlier soap operas with those that focus on the traditional cultural values.

Gangoli uses a study of feminist campaigns against sexual harassment and in favour of sexual freedoms to explore meaningfully the diverse responses of Indian feminisms to shifting patriarchal challenges in the context of globalisation, the role of law within these discourses and the effectiveness of women's legal rights in the Indian context.

In Part II, Jhala draws upon his anthropological background and filmmaking skills to give a fascinating picture of the Muslim Tragada Bhavaiya role in the making of Hindu identity. What Jhala seeks to demonstrate is that the Muslim Tragada Bhavaiyas of Kankavati village are exemplary champions of the Hindu ethos in the towns and villages of Saurastra and that their performances made a vital contribution in the forging and maintenance of a tradition that welcomes difference.

Popular/Folk theatre enjoys a huge audience in India and nothing is more popular than the retelling of India's sacred epics: the Mahabharata and the Ramayana. Lothspeich provides an insightful approach into how the two epic narratives – previously conceptualised as national history or national allegories – are often strategically used in cultural production to meditate on as well as to critique the [post-1947] nation.

While religiosity is an integral part of India's culture, the recent ascendance of Hindu Nationalism has had a damaging effect on the fabric of the nation of India.

Puniyani charts skilfully the rise of Hindu Nationalism and how during that period Muslim and Christian minorities were demonised and presented as a threat to Hindu religion in various ways. He suggests that the impact of Hindu Nationalism on popular cinema and television serials has been immense since they now propagate conservative values.

In Part III, through ethnographic and textual analysis, Kvetko demonstrates how Indipop has struggled to achieve widespread success and remains largely a product of urban-, middle- and upper-class experience. With roots in the cosmopolitan, Westward culture of Mumbai (Bombay) English-educated middle classes, Indipop music cannot merely be dismissed as an example of Western imperialism in India. Kvetko shows skilfully how the sound of Indipop evokes a practice of individualised consumption that, although connected to global capitalism, is thoroughly tied to the unique histories and experiences of professional musicians and music marketers in Bombay.

Focusing on Bombay but this time on the Bombay bar girls, Morcom looks back at the anti-nautch campaign that saw the banning of temple dancers and courtesans and examines clearly the struggle over public morality, national identity and female respectability as they are manifested in the new post-liberalisation phase of India's modernity where the terrain is now popular/mass rather than classical/elite culture.

Harking back to how Bollywood has reflected the pageantry and theatre of royal visual splendour from the intricate zari work of silver and gold thread to opulent textiles, Angma Jhala critiques the influence of royal India on contemporary Bollywood fashions and Indian popular culture more generally.

In Part IV, McLain provides a fascinating angle into the competing visions of the Heroic in such comic books as the *Amar Chitra Katha*. The goal of these comic books is to immortalise Indian heroes, including deities such as Krishna and Ram. McLain states that in the past decade a new generation of comics creators has arisen in India. Focusing on Vivalok Comics which provide an alternative to the *Amar Chitra Katha*, she examines the competing visions presented in the Amar Chitra Katha and *Vivalok Comics*.

Using a case study located in New Delhi, Brosius examines real estate advertisements and hoardings of New Delhi, enriched with ethnographic data from interviews with real estate developers or architects. The author suggests that the returning non-resident Indians (NRIs) enforce what she calls an 'enclaved gaze', a perspective that corresponds to the gated communities, the integrated townships and shopping malls and the club house culture that become increasingly available to the new middle classes. Brosius argues that this view of India and on the cosmopolitan Indian is based on postcolonial mimicry and auto-orientalism or colonialism.

In 'Advertising in a globalised India', Ciochetto explores meaningfully the profile of contemporary advertising in India in the wider context of trends in international advertising, the recent changes in Indian economy and society and issues concerning the cultural impact of foreign advertising in India. Ciochetto demonstrates that in recent years the massive expansion of advertising by foreign companies has played an important cultural role as the Indian economy increasingly becomes part of the globalised marketplace.

In line with recent developments worldwide, Nayar examines, in Part V, a new form of Indian popular culture: the blog. He focuses, on the one hand, on the blog as essentially a personal space whose 'spirit' involves the construction of the hyperlinked, augmented private self for public consumption and on the other hand, Nayar looks at the blog as a mode of community building. Nayar explains clearly how blogs enable the marginalised to have a voice and thereby possess a certain degree of agency, even as the use of this voice helps build links with others.

Another recent development in India is the software industry and Taeube charts its successful development. He draws attention to two phenomena in his analysis. He demonstrates how the south of India exhibits a more intensive regional culture not only of learning but also of innovation and how the contributions of Brahmins, traditionally the priestly and knowledgeable caste group, are crucial.

In Part VI, Majumdar draws attention to the lack of serious academic study of sport. Drawing upon his specialist knowledge of cricket, he shows how all modern sports came to India as part of the 'Games Ethic' during the colonial period but they were all subverted, used and adapted to Indian conditions, becoming vehicles for identity formation and politics. While cricket is by far the most popular Indian sport, Mazumdar looks at how hockey and soccer too offer equally illuminating case studies to understand the progress of wider political and social process in India from the colonial period to the age of globalisation.

In her chapter on tourism, Kurian looks at the key discourses and visible ideologies of tourism in its most popular form in contemporary India: travel columns and essays in print journalism – what Kurian labels 'tourism writing'. In identifying the emergence of a new kind of traveller: the global Indian, at home in the world, she argues persuasively how the exotic is no more truly exotic for the Indian traveller and how exoticism – as transculturation is to her the most striking feature of popular tourism writing.

Finally, in Part VII, Mukhopadhyay examines the historical (re)construction of taste in postcolonial India. As the tempo of urbanisation reached a certain momentum in postcolonial India, the author suggests that there emerged the category of anti-food or junk food. He provides a fascinating historical ontology of food by analysing this process and the theoretical core of his argument derives from the recent Foucaultian and post-Foucaultian attempts to revive the problematique of 'manners' by rethinking it in the wider canvas of government. In linking food with politics, Mukhopadhyay wants to rethink the wider implications of modernity in a non-Western state.

Note

1 Unless specified otherwise, by India we mean the Republic, not the subcontinent.

Part I

Film–Television–TV Soaps–Indian Feminisms

1 Local resistance to global Bangalore

Reading minority Indian cinema

M. K. Raghavendra

Regional popular cinema and 'Bollywood'

Indian cinema has attracted much attention globally as a body to have withstood the commercial onslaught of Hollywood but, for some reason, the popular variety is considered synonymous with 'Bollywood' or Hindi cinema from the city of Mumbai, the former Bombay. Only around a third of the cinema made in India is in Hindi and it has been suggested[1] that the 'cinemas of India' is a more appropriate way to regard the body as a whole because of the varieties of film that 'Indian cinema' has traditionally included.

There are different ways in which Indian cinema can be categorized and if one of the earliest was to regard it in terms of its commercial appeal ('popular', 'art' and 'middle' cinemas), it is also possible to identify the categories on the basis of the regional constituencies they address. Such identification is useful when our interest is in understanding the preoccupations of a constituency by interpreting the respective regional language cinema, and it is apparent that only 'popular' kinds of cinemas address sizable constituencies.[2] While 'Bollywood' has as its constituency audiences dispersed across the length and breadth of India and including Indians from the diaspora, the regional cinemas address largely local constituencies[3] based on the languages they are made in. Hence, while Hindi cinema may be said to be pan-Indian, articulating 'national' concerns and addressing the 'Indian' identity, popular films made in the regional languages appear to articulate vastly different concerns and address local identities within India. That the different regional cinemas narrativize visibly different experiences from those narrativized by the Hindi film suggests that the regional cinemas have access to levels of local experience not available to mainstream Bollywood cinema. Globalization is an issue that Bollywood more or less endorses today but some local cinemas are not comfortable with its effects. Bangalore (being renamed Bengaluru), being the hub of the IT industry, is progressively an emblem for a globally resurgent India, but to local (Kannada language) cinema in Bangalore (as we shall see) the city is an increasingly dark and sinister space. This chapter proceeds on the hypothesis that interpreting a few highly successful Kannada language films of the past year or two (in which Bangalore is a key motif) will indicate what the city means to the local Kannada-speaking populace (or *Kannadigas*), the constituency that Kannada cinema addresses. This is expected to help problematize some issues about Bangalore that have not yet received widespread notice. Of course its 'global importance' is only one aspect of Bangalore but this role has seen the city being transformed beyond recognition. When I speak of 'global Bangalore' therefore, I do not refer to its position in global enterprise but to the transformed city as experienced by the people inhabiting it.

'Bollywood' and globalization

An examination of mainstream Hindi cinema is necessary before we interpret the recent discourses in Kannada cinema. It is in contrast to those of 'Bollywood' that the motifs in today's Kannada language cinema gain most significance. Mainstream Hindi cinema has tailored itself to play a pan-Indian role[4] and, it is now acknowledged, undertake a key function in creating and sustaining the nation as an 'imagined community' after India's independence in 1947.[5] The actual mechanism by which this is achieved has not been studied closely but it involves Hindi cinema's narrativization of social history. The use of types (e.g. character types) enables mainstream Hindi cinema to allegorize[6]/represent implicitly the political/social developments within the nation. In Mehboob Khan's *Andaz* (1949), for instance, the dangers in the modernization process are allegorized as the trials undergone by a young woman on account of her being too 'modern'. State authority is usually represented by police officials and courts, which is why surrendering to the police – for example, Zia Sarhadi's *Footpath* (1953) – is an admission of moral guilt in the 1950s and why the courtroom scene often featured as a key ingredient in film stories after 1947.

An important trend seen in cinema after 1947 is the strengthening of the figure of the mother. The mother has been and remains a site of virtue in Hindi cinema[7] but the attachment between mother and son becomes stronger in the Hindi cinema after 1947 – *Awaara* (1951) and *Mother India* (1957) – and this is interpreted as 'oedipal'.[8] But the strengthening after Independence suggests that psychoanalytical interpretations are inadequate and that the motif has a covert political significance. Since the figures of the mother and father are often aligned along contentious planes, oedipal conflict could be a way of allegorizing a political discourse. In *Awaara*, it can be argued, the mother allegorizes the impoverished land while the hated father (a judge) represents state authority unmindful of the land and those dependent on it. More often, the mother is a useful way of allegorizing the nation. This conclusion is important and I will draw upon it while discussing Kannada cinema. The assumption is that the same codes operate overall because of the underlying cultural homogeneity.

Until the early part of the 1990s, 'Nehruvian socialism' was India's official ideology[9] and this finds correspondence in class/social conflict of various kinds in Hindi cinema, the poor being morally favoured over the rich. This continues until 1992–93 but we detect a transformation with Suraj Barjatya's *Hum Aapke Hain Koun..!* (HAHK [1994], Who I am to you?), the first of the films to evict the poor from the narrative, providing spaces for them only as servants of the rich.

Globalization was viewed with some alarm initially and the notion was perhaps imagined in the same way that modernization was in the 1950s – as something immensely attractive but still fraught with grave hazards for traditional ways of life. In the Hindi 'noir' films beginning with *Jism* (2003, Body), the adulterous/murderous woman acquires her behavioural vocabulary in a global milieu, a space from which tradition has been evacuated. It is significant that mainstream Hindi cinema has since films like *Jism*, *Aitraaz* (2004, Objection), *Jurm* (2005, Crime) and *Zeher* (2005, Poison) looked at marital infidelity more evenly in Karan Johar's *Kabhi Alvida Na Kehna* (2006, Never Say Good Bye). The association of adultery with murder is replaced here by its equation with love. But in KANK as well, the behavioural vocabulary of the adulterers is acquired in a global milieu, a space from which the nation has been removed though the adultery itself receives only a modest reprimand. It is possible to read KANK as emblematic of the second phase in Bollywood's encounter with globalization, when the global is to be welcomed, though after taking into account the associated hazards to traditional lifestyles.

If Bollywood's discourses are tentatively identified with the nation's responses to different issues, KANK's cautious welcome might be interpreted as the response to globalization today. Still, while Bollywood addresses a constituency distributed across India, it is simplistic to assert that this distribution is equally across all classes or evenly across India because the economic importance of each segment is coming into the reckoning of the market. Films such as Nikhil Advani's *Kal Ho Na Ho* (2003, Oblivious of Tomorrow) and KANK are so exclusively about non-residents and global lifestyles that non-residents appear the targeted segment rather than an undifferentiated pan-Indian audience. This implies an 'asymmetry' in the constitution of the 'imagined nation' facilitated by mainstream Bollywood cinema. The constituency of Hindi cinema appears a more exclusive, a more privileged and a more metropolitan segment than is commonly assumed and the concerns of this cinema, likewise, those of a more privileged and largely urban audience. For the articulation of responses by other segments within the social order, we might look to the minority cinemas, which often contradict it. This chapter is about the response of Kannada language cinema to global Bangalore but interpreting the cinema involves understanding the context, specifically the place of the Kannada language in the city.

Language and Bangalore

Being located on a semi-arid plateau and with no major rivers nearby, Bangalore occupies an unlikely spot for a prosperous metropolis. From its rather humble origins it gained importance in 1807 when the British arranged with the government of Mysore for a regiment of European cavalry and another of infantry to be based in the north-east of the city with administrative offices in the fort south of it. The importance of the cantonment increased when the British intervened to wrest power from the King and his advisors in 1831 on grounds of the prevailing corruption. The relocation of government offices to Bangalore and the presence of the garrison meant that there was an influx of service providers from all over southern India – especially Urdu speaking Muslims and Tamil speakers. The migrant populace concentrated around the Cantonment area while the City area was mostly Kannada-speaking like the majority in Mysore state.[10] A linguistic gulf separated the two since the Cantonment housing the garrison was deliberately kept apart by the British from the City.

With the linguistic reorganization of the states in 1956, Bangalore became the capital of Kannada-speaking Karnataka though it was only a few hours away from Tamil-speaking Tamil Nadu, Telugu-speaking Andhra and Malayalam-speaking Kerala. As the two sections of Bangalore grew into each other, Bangalore exhibited an unusual degree of cosmopolitanism. While in Karnataka as a whole 66 per cent of the population had Kannada as their first language, in urban Bangalore itself only 37 per cent spoke the language as their mother tongue.[11] Another factor of great importance was the growth of education in English. The British administration had supported the establishment of the first English medium school in 1842, and over a period of time private schools mushroomed in the city with over 90 per cent of the secondary schools being privately run in the 1990s. As against the Kannada-medium government schools, the private schools were mostly English medium.

The bungalows of the Cantonment area were built by the British as a refuge from the sweltering heat of Madras and, in contrast with the more cramped City it was natural that the cantonment should acquire glamour. An association was also made between the Cantonment – with its wide boulevards, its bungalows and its upper-class lifestyle – and English-medium education[12] because the first English-medium schools were in the Cantonment. While the older City developed a composite culture dominated by Kannada, a balance between various languages was achieved in the Cantonment under the dominance of English.[13] As may be expected, Bangalore was and still remains deeply divided on the language issue.

Bangalore became a hub of the public sector with the establishment of four large industrial units by the Central government after Independence. There was already a scientific establishment in the Indian Institute of Science and there were several engineering colleges capable of providing the industries with an educated workforce. The more pertinent factor is however that until well into the 1960s these public sector industrial units had predominantly Tamilian and Keralite employees and the mother tongue of the employees was an issue as late as 1981.[14]

The new economy companies in Bangalore became visible slowly. IT and IT-enabled services accounted for only 60,000 jobs in the late 1990s but this has increased several-fold since then with medical transcription, back offices and call centres expanding. Here again, language is the key and the opportunities offered by the new economy to those with English-medium education are only too evident. N. R. Narayana Murthy, a doyen of the IT industry, made a plea for a massive expansion of English education to wrest the opportunities offered by the global market. This was contested by the writer U. R. Ananthamurthy, a spokesman for Kannada, who called for measures to protect the beleaguered Kannada language and culture.[15] There are popular estimates that only 10 per cent of the jobs in the new economy companies are held by Kannada speakers[16] because the companies recruit from all over India. Since the new economy companies pay their employees substantially higher wages, the spending power of the non-Kannada segment in Bangalore makes it very visible.

Crucial developments occurred when the Congress government took office in 1999 under S. M. Krishna. The Chief Minister retained the portfolio for Bangalore city development and, as a move, set up the Bangalore Agenda Task Force (BATF) as an advisory body/think tank. Conceived as a public–private partnership, the BATF was able to get the involvement of the business community, generating confidence within them and showing visible progress in Bangalore's management. But chief minister Krishna was also widely perceived as an agent of new economy/business because his name was closely associated with those of its leaders in the city[17] after these measures. Some of these leaders of industry (such as N. R. Narayana Murthy) are Kannada speakers but that does not prevent them from being perceived as anti-Kannada by the Kannada-speaking populace. The suggestion by Narayana Murthy and others that Bangalore should be centrally administered as a Union Territory also received hostile publicity.[18]

Another reason for the disaffection of Kannada speakers is, perhaps indirectly, Bangalore's expansion. The entry of the private builder into the housing market led to housing sites and layouts gradually making way for apartment blocks/complexes.[19] This has not only resulted in the original families of bungalow owners making over their properties to developers but farmers on the periphery of Bangalore have disposed of their land – only to find land prices skyrocketing. Those now occupying the apartments where the ancestral houses/land of the local people once stood are new entrants to Bangalore with visibly more purchasing power.

Kannada and the film industry

Before we go on to examine the political role of the Kannada film industry, it should be noted that Kannada cinema began before 1947 in the erstwhile state of Mysore nominally ruled by the king but indirectly controlled by the British. With the linguistic reorganization of the states in 1956, parts of the Madras and Bombay Presidencies, a part of the Nizam's Hyderabad and the district of Coorg (or Kodagu) were added to the state (subsequently renamed Karnataka), which is how it is constituted today. Kannada cinema nonetheless continues to be largely an 'Old Mysore' cinema – although it has a market in the rest of Karnataka – and the language it commonly uses is the Kannada spoken around Bangalore and Mysore.

Most southern Indian cinemas have been dominated by one or two male stars and the actor to dominate Kannada cinema ever since the 1950s was the late Rajkumar, who passed away in 2006. Unlike the male stars in Tamil and Telugu cinemas, Rajkumar did not enter politics and his political appeal was never tested in an election. His iconic presence nonetheless has a huge significance for Kannada-speaking people, especially witnessed during the Gokak agitation of 1982. The other side was that the Rajkumar Abhimanigala Sangha (a fan association) resorted to violence, specifically targeting the non-Kannada subaltern classes.[20] Kannada film enthusiasts are also suspected to have played a key role in the Cauvery riots of 1991 and the anti-Urdu agitations, when attacks against those considered a threat to Kannada sons of the soil were orchestrated by Kannada nationalists.[21]

More recently, Kannada organizations associated with the film industry have been concerned largely with film-related issues. The largest disturbance caused by them was perhaps in July–August 2000 when the film actor Rajkumar was kidnapped by the notorious poacher and sandalwood smuggler Veerappan and life in the city came to a standstill for three whole days, disturbances continuing for the entire 108 days of his captivity. That these disturbances are often in support of 'causes' with no remedy is indicated by the widespread violence sparked off by Rajkumar's death (by natural causes) on 12 April 2006 when public transport and police vehicles were torched and a constable murdered. It is convenient to assert that the disturbances were orchestrated but the nature of the violence witnessed on television suggests that the constituency of Kannada film enthusiasts is also united by an impulsive rage. That the violence was confined to Bangalore and did not spill over to the other cities suggests that the object of the anger was specifically Bangalore.

Explanations have not been offered hitherto for the recurrent outbursts of anger by Kannada film fans but no hypothesis can fail to take into account the perceived marginalization of Kannada speakers in the city. Since fan violence and Kannada cinema are articulated responses from the same constituency, the film researcher could understand the one by interpreting the other. The following is an examination of three successful Kannada films of the past two years in which Bangalore has an important presence – to seek out clues through which the causes may be identified. Kannada cinema, it can be argued, is crucial in the construction of the identity of a subcategory of Kannada speakers and this analysis pertains to them. For want of a better term, we shall call them '*Kannadigas*' although the term is mostly used inclusively to denote all people with Kannada as their mother tongue.

Three Kannada films

Jogi *(2005, Hermit)*

Significantly, the past few years have witnessed an increase of violence in Kannada cinema. One dominant category in the Kannada film usually advertises itself through a poster in which the protagonist wields a weapon – a chopper, a razor, a chain or a knife – and signals her/his belligerence. Prem's *Jogi*, which belongs to this category, was apparently the biggest Kannada hit of 2005. In *Jogi*, Madesha (Shivrajkumar) leaves his village after his father's death and comes to the city in search of employment while his mother (Arundhati Nag) stays behind. Madesha is a fighter and becomes involved in the underworld after his killing of a gangland boss and his subsequent imprisonment. Although he is dreaded, he retains his innocence, does not rise materially and continues to work in a tea stall. His mother comes to Bangalore searching for him, finding shelter in the home of a woman reporter who has also been in touch with Madesha, whom she has interviewed as the dreaded 'Jogi'. Mother and son are destined never to meet and Madesha sees his mother only when she is dead and he accidentally joins her funeral procession.

A motif that *Jogi* shares with other films from the mould – for example, *Majestic* (2002), *Durgi* (2004) and *Kitti* (2004) – is that Bangalore figures in all the films as a lawless space and the viewpoint is that of the Kannada-speaking migrant. Second, not only do the films identify with a Kannada migrant but they also regard his/her integration with the city as impossible. Migrants in temporary dwellings constitute a special community to Madesha even when he rules gangland as Jogi. This inability to integrate is given emphasis when the possibility of romance (with a woman from the city) is deliberately underplayed.

A crucial requirement in our analysis is to identify/characterize the community represented in the film and the Hindi gangster film *Satya* (1998, Truth) may be useful here because that film is also about a migrant joining the city underworld and gaining prominence. The difference between the two films lies in the protagonist of *Satya* rising in stature and acquiring power. The protagonists in both *Jogi* and *Satya* come into contact with the police but while the protagonist *Satya* connects with them at the highest level (and plots the killing of the police chief) Madesha deals with underlings who still tower above him. I will argue that in a narrative that charts the rise of a heroic individual from humble origins to stature, the limit placed on the stature he/she attains is broadly indicative of the limits to which his/her community may rise. If Madesha's community is identified as that of 'Kannadigas'[22] the film is placing a small limit on what is achievable by it. The film is set in Bangalore, a city known to be glamorous, but it locates its action in the rundown areas (in the 'City' and never in the 'Cantonment') as if a Kannadiga cannot be equal to the glamour of Bangalore.[23] The film is deliberately carving out an unglamorous city out of Bangalore to fit the image of its protagonist and this is singular because Madesha is presented as heroic.

Duniya *(2006, The world)*

Soori's *Duniya* is in many ways similar to *Jogi*. Its protagonist Shivalingu (Vijay) works in a quarry and comes to Bangalore when his mother is critically ill. When she dies and he has to bury her, he is drawn into a gang by a need for money. Shivalingu also meets Poornima (Rashmi), an orphan and the two take up residence in an abandoned bus with the help of Sathya, a good-hearted drunkard. Particularly important is an assistant commissioner of police Umesh Kumar who liquidates grovelling gangsters in 'encounters' when they gain in importance. The film concludes with Shivalingu and Poornima consuming poison rather than surrender to the Assistant Commissioner and his constables.

Shivalingu, based on his occupation as a quarry worker, can be identified as a dalit (a former untouchable) but the film de-emphasizes caste when Poornima is vegetarian and apparently born into an upper caste. Shivalingu himself cheerfully admits that he has eaten every creature from dog to lizard while working in the quarry. *Duniya* is even more extreme than *Jogi* in as much as Shivalingu's valour is useless to him, money hardly comes his way and he does not rise in stature. The first time he earns anything is when the boss gets him to assault one of the members of his own gang – for fun. The second occasion is when this gang member wants 'revenge' and pays Shivalingu to submit to a thrashing.

The gang itself comprises a handful of layabouts in one of the seedier quarters of the city – Srirampuram – known as the home of Bangalore's 'rowdies'. The gang is not engaged in any lucrative trade and if their leader Prabhi has grown enough to be outside the policeman's reach, it is because of his elder brother Raghupathy, a small-time politician. The drunkard Sathya is their mascot and he spends his time playing the clown in the market, donned in the ceremonial turban associated commonly with Old Mysore gentility.

As if to correspond to the lowliness of the protagonists, the policeman Umesh is not a high-ranking official. We are never certain why he is casually eliminating members of the gang – who appear to pose no threat to anyone except each other – and the only explanation is that he is maintaining 'law and order'. There is perhaps a clue in a brief shot before a minor liquidation when the assistant commissioner is seen talking on a mobile phone from a high rise and we see a more glamorous part of Bangalore sprawling below. This is perhaps interpretable as the machinery of the state is being pressed into ruthless maintenance of 'law and order' for the glory of Bangalore more visible to the outside world. The title of the film is also significant here because 'duniya' is the Hindi and not the Kannada word for 'world'. There is evidently an equation made between Bangalore and the cruel world but, more importantly, the use of the *national* language to denote the world suggests the defeat of local claims upon the Karnataka's capital city.[24]

Another aspect of *Duniya* is its repeated references to the Rajkumar film *Sakshatkara* (1971, Truth). Rajkumar, in films such as *Kasthuri Nivasa* (1970, Name of a House) and *Bangarada Manushya* (1972, Man of Gold) powerfully identified a set of virtues that long defined the self-image of Kannadigas – aristocratic, noble, trusting, generous and tolerant – and one sees the reference to the film as a lament on how such a class of people could be so reduced.[25] Where *Sakshatkara* was not specifically about Kannada speakers – these were the virtues that all humanity should possess – *Duniya* confining its characters to a space inhabited by a subclass suggests that the Kannadiga (as I defined the term) cannot claim to speak for humanity and this can be interpreted as due to the injury done to her/his self-image by Bangalore.

Mungaru Male *(2006, Pre-monsoon Rain)*

Yograj Bhat's *Mungaru Male* is being touted as the biggest grosser ever in Kannada cinema and it is different from the other two films largely because it contains very little violence and has a well-to-do protagonist. It begins with Preetham (Ganesh) catching sight of Nandini (Sanjana Gandhi) outside a Bangalore shopping mall and being so smitten that he accidentally steps into a manhole. Nandini helps him out but she departs and the rest of the film is about Preetham and his mother in Kodagu, where she is visiting a friend – the wife of a decorated Kodava army officer and coffee planter named Subbaiah. Nandini is actually Subbaiah's daughter and Preetham gradually learns many facts. Preetham is in Kodagu with his mother to attend her wedding to a junior army officer who once saved Subbaiah's life. Preetham intends to leave but the girl teases him, coaxing him to remain behind and press his suit. Preetham returns, the girl gradually returns his love and consents to elope with him. Still, events make Preetham eventually realize that Nandini is not for him. After letting the girl understand this and saving the actual bridegroom from the villain, he finally leaves for Bangalore.

At first glance *Mungaru Male* does not appear to have much to do with Bangalore city but the first cause out of which the action emerges is Preetham spotting Nandini outside a Cantonment mall. The 'first cause' is crucial in Indian popular cinema and the meaning in both *Jogi* and *Duniya* materializes out of the protagonists' first encounter with the monstrousness of Bangalore city. But the cultural identities of the protagonists still need to be recognized before we interpret the first cause.

Preetham may be identified as a well-to-do Kannadiga and his domineering father is a businessman – with connections in the government because policemen recognize him respectfully. Preetham is looked upon as a wastrel by his father and Preetham in turn, resents him. Nandini, on the other hand is a Kodava and the daughter of a *national* hero. Kodavas have not generally been identified with Kannada speakers perhaps because they have been highly anglicized, often connecting directly with the nation. Two of India's greatest generals have been Kodava but they are rarely celebrated as 'Kannada' heroes. I will argue that Nandini's identity, despite her speaking Kannada, is pan-Indian just as Preetham's is Kannadiga. The pan-Indian and the Kannadiga identities are not mutually exclusive but intersect, which does not mean that there is no tension between them. If this is conceded, the first cause is interpretable as the Kannadiga's love/desire being awakened by a woman with a pan-Indian identity in a space straddling two worlds – local Karnataka and global India (a shopping mall is the most visible sign of the 'global' in Bangalore).

An aspect of *Mungaru Male* which is intriguing is why the film is a 'tragedy' or why circumstances could not have been arranged so that Preetham marries Nandini – because there is no class barrier separating them. I will argue that the gap between them is 'unbridgeable' because of the social distance it allegorizes, a gap not between individuals but between the identities they represent. It is perhaps because the disparity between the Kannadiga and the pan-Indian identity in Bangalore is perceived to be so large that *Mungaru Male* is conceived as a tragedy.

Preetham has a pet rabbit which he names Devdas (after the icon of unrequited love). At the conclusion he tries to address the rabbit cheerfully on the notion of 'sacrifice' in love but the rodent expires abruptly and Preetham is heartbroken. The insertion of the animal into the story is strange but even stranger is an insipid 'joke' that assumes disproportionate importance. Preetham explains that 'Devdas' is wanted by the police for raping an elephant. The meaning is evidently the unfairness of a creature as mild and inoffensive as a rabbit being accused of an act so horrific. *Mungaru Male* is also implicit that the rabbit is Preetham's alter ego and the death of the rabbit hurts him more than the loss of the heroine. It is significant that being mild and peace-loving is an important component of the Kannadiga's self-image.[26] If the rabbit's qualities are equated with the Kannadiga's, the question is why the issue of 'rape' should be introduced and the rabbit accused of it. I would like to argue that after the recent rape/murder of women employees in new economy companies,[27] there is a perceived threat to them in Bangalore and the threat is from locals.

An aspect of the film that still needs reading is Preetham's oedipal conflict with his father. The father, although a businessman, is connected to the state through the incident of the policeman greeting him respectfully. It can be argued that the proximity between the father and the state and the estrangement between Preetham and his father covertly distances Preetham from the state. This discourse is perhaps comparable to that in *Jogi* and *Duniya* in which the state/state authority is clearly the adversary of the respective protagonists.

Conclusion

The three films examined have aspects in common and the first is that they are all about defeat. The character with whom the spectator is invited to empathize fails to achieve his goals and the phenomenal success of all three films suggests that the discourse touches a deep chord. Second, the films contain no apparent discourse against the outsider in Bangalore. Such a viewpoint might also have been disallowed but there have been 'local' films such as N. Chandra's (Hindi) *Ankush* (1986, The Goad) – which railed against the North-Indian presence in Bombay. There has also been little violence against outsiders in Bangalore,[28] this suggesting that the Kannadiga's 'failure' is not due to the doings of non-locals; it might even be in the nature of a 'tragic flaw', perhaps a virtue in better times.

Overall, it will be astute to interpret the tragic conflict in *Jogi* and *Duniya* by taking note of an absence – the global/glamorous Bangalore that the characters have little access to and excluded from the narrative space. If the Kannadiga has an implacable enemy, that is state authority[29] which functions as the agent of an unseen power, the domain of which is apparently this space.

The three films are also about unfulfilled promises, the promise being of a different sort in *Mungaru Male*. The important thing is that when the promise of Bangalore in *Jogi* and *Duniya* remains unfulfilled, the protagonists have no home territory in which they might seek refuge. In *Duniya* the 'home space' is only a dusty quarry and, with granite and stone suggesting frenzied urban construction, Bangalore is perhaps the monster drawing Shivalingu in by destroying his habitat, but offering little to him in return, not even a livelihood.

Mungaru Male is different from the other films but it still provides us with the means to interpret them. I have tried to demonstrate that the film problematizes the tragic gap between the Kannadiga and the pan-Indian identities in Bangalore. Mainstream Hindi cinema is upbeat today while Kannada cinema is distinctly downbeat, though it is doing well financially. The absent space in *Duniya* and *Jogi* is the space in which the first encounter between Preetham and Nandini takes place and there is adequate reason to propose that this represents upbeat, pan-Indian, global Bangalore. It is perhaps to protect the welfare of this inaccessible space that the state works so ruthlessly in both *Duniya* and *Jogi*.

The strong motif of the mother in the three films can be interpreted by relying on its significance in Hindi cinema. The sacred mother is a recurring presence in Kannada cinema and since the strong mother in Hindi cinema is often interpreted as 'mother-as-nation', the mother in Kannada cinema may be taken to represent the notion that confers her/his identity upon the Kannadiga – the Kannada space, or Karnataka. If this is conceded, the tragedies in *Jogi* and *Duniya* arise because of Bangalore (as seductress) coming between the protagonist and his duty to his mother. *Mungaru Male* is apparently different but it is Preetham's mother who puts the final seal of *disapproval* on his wooing of Nandini.

If the common agencies invoked/represented in the three films are global Bangalore, the Kannada mother and state authority, the consciousness giving coherence to their relationship is that of the Kannadiga. On the evidence of the three films one might say that the mother and Bangalore stand on opposite sides of the protagonist. 'Bangalore' is attractive but it is also either treacherous or inaccessible. Preetham suggests to his mother in *Mungaru Male* that she divorces his father and the sought for separation is perhaps between Bangalore and Kannada.[30] State authority itself, in serving and protecting Bangalore, is prepared to injure or destroy the Kannadigas, themselves fighting each other for paltry rewards. The message is strong but what makes it palatable is perhaps its being delivered so subliminally, as it were. But the message nonetheless reinforces whatever we know about the different forces/interests fighting for control over Bangalore city.

Notes

1 For instance, see Yves Thoraval (2001) *The Cinemas of India*, Chennai: Macmillan India.
2 With the new developments in media studies one is permitted to say that media texts are 'co-authored' by audiences. Also see Sudhir Kakar (1980) The ties that bind: family relationships in the mythology of Hindi cinema. *India International Center, Quarterly* Special Issue, Vol. 8 (1), March, p. 13.
3 Local language cinemas also cater to different international segments. The Tamil film, for instance, is widely seen in countries such as Malaysia by a significant Tamil populace and the Bhojpuri film is seen in Mauritius.
4 Lothar Lutze, Interview with Raj Khosla. In Lothar Lutze and Beatrix Pfleiderer (1985) (eds) *The Hindi Film: Agent and Reagent of Cultural Change*, Delhi: Manohar Publications, p. 39.
5 For instance, see Sumita S. Chakravarty (1998) *National Identity in Indian Popular Cinema*, New Delhi: Oxford University Press, and M. Madhava Prasad (1999) *Ideology of the Hindi Film*, New Delhi: Oxford University Press.
6 According to Jameson 'Third World' texts are most usefully read as national allegories. See Frederic Jameson (1987) World literature in the age of multi-national capitalism. In C. Koelb and V. Lokke (eds) *The Current in Criticism*, West Lafayette, IN: Purdue University Press, p. 141.
7 Ravi Vasudevan (2000) Shifting codes, dissolving identities: the Hindi popular film of the 1950s as popular culture. In Ravi Vasudevan (ed.) *Making Meaning in Indian Cinema*, New Delhi: Oxford University Press, p. 110.

8 For instance, see Ashish Rajadhyaksha and Paul Willemen (1995) *The Encyclopaedia of Indian Cinema*, New Delhi: Oxford University Press, p. 300.
9 Despite the Congress Party slipping from power in 1977, the victorious Janata Party did not abandon Nehru's policies, perhaps because many of its leaders were former Congressmen or Socialists – Morarji Desai, Chandraskekar, Madhu Dandavate.
10 James Heitzman (2004) *Network City: Planning the Information Society in Bangalore*, New Delhi: Oxford University Press, pp. 28–9.
11 Census of India 1971. See also, U Suryanath Kamath (ed.) *Karnataka State Gazeteer*, (2000) Part 1, Bangalore: Govt. of Karnataka, p. 439.
12 James Heitzman, *Network City: Planning the Information Society in Bangalore*, p. 60.
13 Janaki Nair (2005) *The Promise of the Metropolis: Bangalore's Twentieth Century*, New Delhi: Oxford University Press, p. 63. Incidentally, it was only in 1949 that the twin municipalities of Bangalore City and Bangalore Cantonment were brought together under the Bangalore City Corporation.
14 The occasion was a 77-day public sector strike when there was an attempt to divide the workers over the language issue. Janaki Nair, *The Promise of the Metropolis: Bangalore's Twentieth Century*, pp. 255–7.
15 Ibid., pp. 265–6.
16 For instance, see Venkatesh, M. S., *Is it a Sin to be born as a Kannadiga in Karnataka?* http/:news.indiainfo.com, posted on 11 September 2003. The author is a Kannada speaker working in the IT industry. It is not so much knowledge of Kannada as the identity conferred by the mother tongue that is important. See Janaki Nair, *The Promise of the Metropolis: Bangalore's Twentieth Century*, p. 264.
17 The businessmen cited are Narayana Murthy, Azim Premji, Vijay Mallya and Sanjay Khan. See *Is it a Sin to be Born a Kannadiga? – Reactions*. Posted on http/:news.indiainfo.com on 13 September 2003.
18 For instance, see *Karnataka News, The Hindu* online edition, Friday, 7 January 2005.
19 Janaki Nair, *The Promise of the Metropolis: Bangalore's Twentieth Century*, p. 132.
20 Ibid., p. 112. It is false to assert that the non-Kannada speakers as generally better off because much of the low-end work in the city is done by migrant labour from the neighbouring states.
21 The Cauvery riots mainly targeted Tamil speakers while the anti-Urdu agitation targeted Muslims.
22 The other options for the 'community' – 'human beings', 'Indians', 'people from Karnataka', 'Kannada speakers' and 'Bangaloreans' – are evidently ruled out. It must also be remarked that the community is not denoted as Kannadiga and Jogi's gang even includes a Sikh. The community is perhaps simply 'us' with 'us' being connoted as Kannadigas.
23 The impossibility of the hero's romance with the born and bred Bangalorean girl also substantiates this.
24 Of course words make their way from one language to another and 'duniya' is one such word used sometimes in Kannada. But the privileging of a Hindi word in the title of the film should also be given attention.
25 U. R. Ananthamurthy laments the 'mindboggling tolerance of Kannadigas'. See *Do not Sacrifice Karnataka's Interests, The Hindu*, 16 February 2002.
26 For instance, see *Kannadigas are at the Root of Kannada's Problem*, Thursday, 19 April 2007, posted in http/:churumuri.wordpress.com. This is how the writer describes Kannadigas: 'Soft. Mild. Docile. Laidback. … Not aggressive. Not ambitious … Lacking in drive …'. Also see responses on the same site.
27 For instance, see BPO Employee Rape and Murder Causes Furor in Bangalore, *Yahoo Indian News*, Monday, 2 January 2006. That the woman in question was from Karnataka is not significant because call centre employees as a class may not be perceived as locals – because of what was said about the representation of Kannada speakers in the new economy companies.

28 The violence against Tamils has to do with the river water sharing with Tamil Nadu and may not be related to the visibility of Tamil success in Bangalore. A large number of Tamils in Karnataka are engaged in low-end work.
29 *Mungaru Male* places the same discourse within the joke about the rabbit – as the police accusation against it.
30 A frequent complaint voiced against recent governments of Karnataka is that they give disproportionate attention to Bangalore.

References

Ananthamurthy, U. R. (2002) Do not sacrifice Karnataka's interests *The Hindu*, 16 February.
Chakravarty, S. S. (1998) *National Identity in Indian Popular Cinema*, New Delhi: Oxford University Press.
Heitzman, J. (2004) *Network City: Planning the Information Society in Bangalore*, New Delhi: Oxford University Press.
Jameson, F. (1987) Third world literature in the age of multinational capitalism. In Koelbe and Lokke (eds) *The Current in Criticism: Essays on the Present and Future of Literary Theory*, West Lafayette: Purdue University Press.
Kakar, S. (1980) The ties that bind: family relationships in the mythology of Hindi cinema, *India International Centre Quarterly*, Special Issue, Vol. 8 (1), March.
Kamath, U.S. (ed) (2000) Karnataka State Gazeteer, Part 1, Bangalore: Govt. of Karnataka, p. 439.
Nair, J. (2005) *The Promise of the Metropolis: Bangalore's Twentieth Century*, Chennai: Oxford University Press.
Pfleiderer, B. and Lutze, L. (eds) (1985) *The Hindi Film: Agent and Reagent of Cultural Change*, Delhi: Manohar Publications.
Prasad, M. M. (1999) *Ideology of the Hindi Film*, New Delhi: Oxford University Press.
Rajadhyaksha, A. and Willemen, P. (1995) *The Encyclopaedia of Indian Cinema*, New Delhi: Oxford University Press.
Thoraval, Y. (2001) *The Cinemas of India*, Chennai: Macmillan India.
Vasudevan, R. (2000) Shifting codes, dissolving identities: the Hindi popular film of the 1950s as popular culture. In Vasudevan, R. (ed.) *Making Meaning in Indian Cinema*, New Delhi: Oxford University Press.

2 'Breaking news, Indian style'

Politics, democracy and Indian news television

Nalin Mehta

Deepa Mehta's 1999 film *Earth* has a telling scene that characterizes the sharp disconnect between English and vernacular languages in India. Set amidst the horrific violence that characterized Punjab during Partition, it depicts the three protagonists – a Sikh, a Hindu and a Muslim, all friends – sitting and discussing the political situation casually in Hindi when they are suddenly interrupted by Nehru's regal voice delivering his famous 'tryst with destiny' independence day speech on radio. Suddenly, there is pin drop silence. As Nehru intones about the 'soul of a nation' awaking to 'life and freedom' in his aristocratic English, for a brief, poignant moment, the helpless expressions on the faces of the silenced protagonists say it all: they do not understand a word of what is being said but realize it must be important from its tone and gravitas. Yet they do not seem to want to admit their ignorance and the camera lingers on their stupefied expressions with powerful effect for a brief moment until they decide that there is no point in listening further, resuming their banter as Nehru's voice recedes into the background. It is a cinematic scene that captures in its entirety the broad disconnect between the broadcast media and popular cultures in India until the arrival of satellite television well into the early 1990s. It is a disconnect that social scientists have long written about and one that I have personally confronted on numerous occasions as a broadcast journalist, most recently in February 2008 on the day when Maharashtra Navnirman Sena (Maharashtra Reconstruction Army) Chief Raj Thackeray was arrested in Mumbai for threatening to throw non-Maharashtrians out of the city. As I waited in Congress MP Sanjay Nirupam's office to catch his reaction to the arrest, the office filled up with policemen and political workers, all crowding around the lone television set to watch the live coverage of the arrest on a Marathi satellite news channel. Everyone had an opinion on the political implications of the arrest. As I waited, someone politely asked me if I wanted to watch the coverage on Times Now, the English news channel I was then representing. I nodded happily but within minutes of the channel being switched I realized to my own embarrassment that all conversation in the room had stopped. The same men – and they were all men – who had been talking animatedly about the political implications of Raj Thackeray's brinkmanship were now suddenly silent and it was then that I realized that I had seen the same looks before – on the faces of the three protagonists in *Earth*. I immediately switched the television set back to the Marathi private news channel that had been on previously and the mood changed instantly. It was like someone had switched on a light in the dark. The animated political discussions began again and it was difficult to imagine that even five years ago these Marathi men did not have a news channel in their native language to stimulate such debates.

Robin Jeffrey (2003) has shown that India's 'newspaper revolution' truly began in the late-1970s with the expansion of regional language newspapers. Broadcasting, however, had to wait for satellite television for a comparable change. On one level, the disconnect that characterized it accrued from the fact that before the advent of satellite television, the state-controlled All India Radio and Doordarshan[1] largely concentrated on English and Hindi, to the detriment of other languages. There were powerful regional language broadcast centres but the creation of a national television service after 1982 was accompanied with Delhi-centric and North Indian cultures becoming the focal point. This is why the imposition in 1982 of what became known as the daily 'National Programme' on Doordarshan was sharply resisted in many regions. Symbolically launched on Independence Day in 1982, the 'National Programme' was in Hindi and it was the first time that all of India saw the same image at the same time. Between 8:30 p.m. to 11:00 p.m. everyday, all regional language stations had to, per force, link up to the 'National Programme' from Delhi but Hindi programming was seen in many regions as an imposition by New Delhi. Bhaskar Ghose, a former director general of Doordarshan, cites how the Chief Secretary of Tamil Nadu accused him of dividing the country and the Chief Minister of Karnataka sarcastically thanked him for reducing the load-shedding in his state as 'all television sets were switched off after 8:30 p.m. as soon as the National Programme started' (Ghose, 2005: 28–30). At a deeper level, state broadcasting, with its emphasis on puritanical language and 'high brow' statist developmental objectives, reflected a vast gulf between elite and subaltern public spheres (Jeffrey, 2006). There were undoubtedly exceptions to this. Arvind Rajagopal has shown that the unprecedented mass hysteria in North India over Doordarshan's televised version of Ramayana in the 1980s – 'Ramayana fever' (Lutgendorf, 1995: 224) – was characteristic of what he called a 'split public'. By catering to non-elite public spheres, the series played a pivotal role in the refashioning of the politics of religion and ethnicity in North India and facilitated the creation of a new Hindu public that was mobilized for the *Ramajanmabhoomi* agitation (Rajagopal, 2001). The popular mass appeal of Doordarshan's mythological and nationalist programmes apart, through the years of government monopoly, broadcasting was seen by the state as a powerful tool of political and cultural control; a unique portal, in a Foucaultian sense, for entering the homes of its citizens daily with the audio-visual message of its idea of India, conflated often with the idea of the ruling party.[2] Doordarshan remained a state bureaucracy that had not only 'standardized mediocrity but institutionalized it' (Mitra and Kaul, 1982: 17).

The rise of private satellite television in multiple languages, after decades of state monopoly over the medium, has engendered a transformation in India's political and public culture, the nature of the state and expressions of Indian nationhood. Much like India's 'newspaper revolution' (Jeffrey, 2003: xi) that started in the 1970s, and the 'cassette culture' (Manuel, 1993) of the 1980s, the availability of privately produced satellite television has meant that 'people discovered new ways to think about themselves and to participate in politics that would have been unthinkable a generation before' (Jeffrey, 2003: 1). Operating at the junction of public culture, capitalism and globalization, satellite networks are a new factor in the social and cultural matrix of India with profound implications for the state, politics, democracy and identity formation. These are the linkages this chapter sets out to explore and delineate in detail by focusing on one genre of satellite television: news channels.

As late as 1991 – and in legal terms, until as late as 1995[3] – Indian viewers could only watch one television channel, Doordarshan. Between 1995 and 2007, however, India experienced the rise of more than 300 satellite networks. More than 50 of these were 24-hour satellite news channels, broadcasting news in 11 different languages (Table 2.1) – the equivalent of more than 50 Indian CNNs.

The numbers are a stark illustration of how the Indian state lost control over television broadcasting despite its best efforts to the contrary. No other country in the world has such a concentration of private news channels as India.

These upheavals in the nature of Indian television have been accompanied by a simultaneous expansion in its reach and penetration. In 1992, if you divided India's population of 846,388,000 (*Projected and Actual Population of India, States and Union Territories, 1991*) by the total number of television sets in

Table 2.1 Satellite news channels in India[4]

Language	Channels that broadcast news	24-hour news networks
All	106	54
Hindi	25	19
English	15	14
Malayalam	9	4
Tamil	12	2
Telugu	10	4
Bengali	8	4
Punjabi	7	3
Kannada	7	1
Marathi	4	1
Assamese/Manipuri	2	—
Gujarati	3	—
Oriya	2	1
Urdu	1	—
Nepali	1	1

the country,[5] the number of people clustering around a set would have been a little over 26. By 2006, that ratio had come down substantially to just over ten people per television set, despite a substantial increase in the population.[6] In a little over a decade, the total number of Indian television households tripled to reach an estimated 112 million (National Readership Study, 2006: 4). It made India the world's third largest television market, just behind China and the United States (PricewaterhouseCoopers, FICCI, March 2005: 36) and more than 60 per cent of these television sets are estimated to be connected to satellite dishes.[7]

The creation of a television public has significant implications for democracy and this chapter focuses on what 24-hour news means for India. It focuses, in particular, on the meaning of 24-hour television in the vernacular languages and it argues that the emergence of television news networks has greatly enhanced and strengthened deliberative Indian democracy. There is no evidence to show that satellite television has benefited Indian democracy if we understand it in the narrow procedural terms defined by the voting process alone.[8] My claim refers to a broader understanding of democracy as a deliberative process involving larger collaborative processes of decision-making, identity and interest formation with the media acting as a crucial hinge. Democracy is intimately connected with mechanisms of public discussion and interactive reasoning. Indeed, the new disciplines of social choice theory and public choice theory are connected to ideas of individual values and their impact on decision-making (Sen, 2002). In this context, Amartya Sen has famously shown that no substantial famine has ever occurred in a country with a democratic form of government and a relatively free press (Dreze and Sen, 1989). When the audience for news expands, the shape of politics changes.

The meaning of private television in India can only be understood if we understand what came before. In the United States for instance, private industry initiated the medium, and the state later regulated it. In India, it was the reverse. The state brought in broadcasting and private industry broke down the barriers of statist control through a confluence of economic, technological and political factors in the 1990s (Mehta, 2008b). In the interim, in a country, where the print press was always free, except for a brief period during the Emergency, television was run by a 'Kafkaesque bureaucracy' that ensured that Doordarshan was never more than an insipid propaganda machine (Mitra and Kaul, 1982: 17). Since their inception, debates over private satellite channels in India have veered between the extremes of seeing them as agents of foreign culture (Bhatt, 1994: 86) or as agents of 'a kind of liberation' (Page and Crawley, 2001: 268). Yet, most of the scholarship on Indian television predates the rise of 24-hour news channels with scholars struggling to keep pace with the rate of change.[9] This chapter uses separate case studies of regional language news television from West Bengal, Maharashtra, Chhattisgarh and Punjab to illustrate what happens to politics and society when television emerges as an independent factor. It focuses on the specific ways in which the new medium affected the daily spectacle of Indian politics and how political leaders and parties adapted their daily practises of politics to the 24-hour publicity it provided.

'More impact than in Delhi': the meaning of local television

When Network Eighteen launched its Marathi language 24-hour news channel, channel IBN Lokmat in April 2008 it began by setting up 13 bureaux across Maharashtra and hiring more than 100 stringers. The channel began its coverage by devoting a half hour-daily special to the farmer suicides in Maharashtra's Vidarbha region. This is a chronic issue that since 2005 has only been covered sporadically by the national press which, with few honourable exceptions, failed to build sustained coverage around the crisis (Sainath, 2005). Within hours of the first telecast, Lokmat's Managing Editor received an angry phone call from an angry Member of the Legislative Assembly (MLA) on whose constituency the first part of the series had been based. He wanted the story to be pulled off air and threatened to use his clout with the local cable operators to blank off the new channel from the airwaves. The incident revealed both the potential and the limitations of satellite television. On the positive side of the ledger, the MLA's phone call was proof that he was worried about viewers in his constituency watching the story and drawing conclusions about his performance. As Lokmat's Managing Editor explained:

> We have done many similar stories on farmer suicides on our English [CNN-IBN] and Hindi [IBN-7] channels but never have I received a phone call from any minister or elected representative. It is like they did not care. But in this case, in the Marathi channel, for the first time, I got a call. The MLA was angry because he knew the people who would vote for him would be watching. I realized that this was the real impact. If you show something to people in the language that they speak then it percolates down to the grassroots and that is why the MLA was worried. It had much more impact there than in Delhi.[10]

This contention ties in with my own observations while covering Parliament proceedings in Delhi. In the late 1990s when private satellite news networks were still a novelty, members of Parliament would happily give interviews to national networks such as NDTV and Zee. This was partly due to the glamour of the new media but as India's politicians became more savvy with television a new pecking order emerged. Reporters for national networks like myself found that we were no longer the first choice to give interviews to. MPs discovered that it made more political sense to speak in their own language on their own regional language channel. All through 2004–07 for instance, the Teleugu Desam Party's Parliamentary Party Leader Yerran Naidu who began by being the most accessible of politicians for reporters in Delhi gradually became more difficult to get hold of for national channels. Yet, he would make it a special point to step out of Parliament virtually on a daily basis when it was in session to give long interviews on the Telugu ETV network because he knew that his constituents would be watching. He had decided who was important for him. This was about space as well as strategy. According to the Tamil Jaya TV's Vice President KP Sunil:

> For a public figure in a state the most important platform now is the most local cable channel. Earlier they used to come on Jaya TV easily. Now if a murder happens in a district the District Magistrate knows that if he speaks to a national channel he will get 15 seconds of a sound byte, on a regional channel he will get maybe a minute but on a local cable channel he will get half an hour. Localisation translates into power and they have understood this. [11]

Coming back to the Marathi farmer suicides, Network Eighteen also runs two other national news channels – in English and Hindi – and its Managing Editor also felt that market dynamics made it difficult for his network to run such campaigns on social issues on these 'national' language platforms.[12] I have shown elsewhere that in economic terms, the Indian satellite networks are inordinately dependent on weekly ratings, more so than their Western counterparts. This is a direct derivative of the peculiar 'illegal' origins of satellite broadcasting in India and in a market where more than 50 news channels are competing for advertising the structural economy of television forces many channels to focus on content with the lowest common denominator that will register on television rating panels (Mehta, 2008b). Given the narrow base of these ratings, cricket and Bollywood have emerged as an easy option to register on them. Both have a pan-Indian appeal cutting across socio-economic and regional categories. News of a farmer suicide in Vidarbha may not interest anybody in Kerala but news of the Indian cricket team interests people in every region of India. This is why when national news editors want to lift the ratings of any show they look towards cricket and Bollywood and these genres increasingly dominate news space.[13] News, as such, is a commercial product packaged to suit commercial targets.

As Sardesai (2008), however, points out, in a local language channel important stories that are cut out of national networks – due to commercial constraints – do find space. This is not because of any special altruistic reason but because on this platform, local stories make imminent commercial sense. Ratings are as important in Marathi television as in the so-called national languages of Hindi and English: IBN Lokmat is competing with Zee and Star's 24-hour news channels in the language, but here in-depth local coverage is a sure way of registering on the ratings.

The economic imperatives of creating a market and sustaining it drive news channels to create a public sphere. The public sphere is an important normative category and is crucial for democracy but in a way that substantially differs from the ideal sketched by Habermas, and those that base their work on his ideas. Politics now passes through a mediated arena and the media create a new kind of publicness that is de-specialized, non-dialogical and received in settings spatially and temporally remote from the original context of production (Thompson, 1995: 27–49). Reception is often at odds with the intentions of its creators – the recipient's own assumptions and expectations regulate how they are interpreted and appropriated. The meaning of the message is not static and takes different forms for different people (Thompson, 1995: 34–41). The crucial point is that politics, unlike before, has to unfold in an open arena and in the glare of a new visibility that has a life of its own and is often difficult to control. The media's importance lies not in whether anybody is watching or is getting influenced, but in the assumption of it by political leaders and decision-makers, as Schudson (1995: 22–5) has argued persuasively. It is in this context that television assumes an important role and – regardless of its actual impact on the voting public – becomes central to the political process.

When the Bengali news channel STAR Ananda started operations in June 2005, it announced its launch by instituting daily live public debates between candidates contesting the Kolkata municipal election. These debates marked an important signpost in the political campaigning culture of the city. They were conducted in the city's open public spaces and took the form of public meetings where sometimes as many as some of 10,000 people turned up as live audiences in addition to regular television viewers.[14] The tapes of that programming make for riveting viewing. They show large public rallies of the kind that are familiar to observers of Indian politics but differ in one crucial aspect: these were joint political events, organized by a television channel and moderated by a STAR Ananda newsman as rival candidates debated their political views while their followers raised lusty slogans (STAR Ananda, n.d).

This was happening in a city which had been ruled by the same political conglomerate, the Left Front, since 1977. The debates unleashed political passions and for the first two weeks, mini-riots broke out during virtually every one of the daily events. Rival political groups attacked each other with swords and sticks. In one instance, petrol bombs were also used. The news anchors were roughed up for daring to ask tough questions and all this happened on live television. The debates created such a problem that the police commissioner of Kolkata called up the channel and asked it to stop, citing the fear of public rioting. As the founding editor of STAR Ananda, who also anchored these debates, explains:

> It created such a furore and became such an instant hit ... I didn't even know ... that these two warring groups would come with daggers and bombs, and there was one shoot-out incident.... The police commissioner personally requested me 25 times.... He said to please withdraw this programme.... This is creating hell of a lot of jhamela [problem].[15]

STAR Ananda responded to the commissioner's suggestion with a public campaign for the strengthening of democratic traditions and debate. The editor went on air with news that the police commissioner wanted the public debates to stop and argued that this was a dangerous precedent for Bengali democracy. The important point here is that this tradition of public television debates was not a Bengali innovation. Hindi news channels such as Zee TV and STAR News had run numerous such events in various constituencies during national and state elections across north India in the preceding five years. This is what STAR Ananda emphasized, along with the long Bengali tradition of public culture, *adda* and political activism that goes back to the Bengal renaissance of the nineteenth century.[16]

The public appeal to democratic principles and Bengali-ness worked and the political violence ceased within two weeks. Many localities in Kolkata began to invite the channel to hold similar debates between contesting candidates and that single event turned STAR Ananda into a market leader in the Bengali news sphere. Following this success, a year later two more Bengali news channels started from Kolkata in 2006 in the run-up to the West Bengal assembly election. These two, Zee's 24 Ghanta and Kolkata TV, both followed similar programming formats of public debate and developed these even further.

Bengali television shows how news television feeds off, and into, liberal democratic values, which themselves are rooted in a long heritage of argumentation and debate. In this context, I have argued elsewhere (Mehta: 2008b) that news channels tap into strong oral traditions and heterodox structures of social communication that Amartya Sen has labelled 'the argumentative tradition of India' (Sen, 2005: 14). For Sen, these traditions are an important support structure for the sustenance of Indian democracy (Sen, 2005: 12). Indian television thrives on programming genres that marry older argumentative traditions with new technology and notions of liberal democracy to create new hybrid forms that strengthen democratic culture. Argumentative television fits into broader cultural patterns but the very nature of the medium is such that they mutate into newer forms when mediated by television. In a separate analyses of the uses of video technology for religious purposes in India, John T. Little (1995: 254–83) and Philip Lutgendorf (1995: 217–53) suggest that new electronic presentations are not overwhelming traditional religious performance genres. Instead, a new layer of interpretation is being added to what is likely to remain a vibrant and multi-vocal cultural tradition. Precisely the same thing is happening in the arena of politics with news television's focus on politics and civic life.

The advent of 24-hour news necessitates a fresh look at what happened to the politics-television equation after the rise of news channels. Twenty-four-hour news introduces a new dynamic into the political process. It introduces the element of permanent publicity and forces politicians to adapt to new forms of electronic mediation. First, 24-hour news makes politicians visible on a daily basis. The kind of high publicity that politicians desire during election campaigns is now thrust upon them on a daily basis. The daily television camera symbolizes the scrutiny of public opinion. Even if that public is a 'phantom' one, the politician has to behave as if it is always there. The demands of 24-hour news force politicians to be on the campaign trail all the time. Anyone who has followed television reporters on their daily rounds of party offices in Delhi knows that it is often the insatiable drive of news channels to 'take the story forward' that induces party spokespersons to 'react' to the latest political controversy. Twenty-four-hour news leads to 24-hour politics.

Political parties, regional languages and television

Satellite networks have taken different meanings in different regions and in different languages. By the 2006 Tamil Nadu assembly election, for instance, it had become so important that the DMK made the free allotment of colour television sets to every family a key plank of its election manifesto. It is a promise the DMK has begun to fulfil since winning back political power. As Maya Ranganathan writes, 'not only had the DMK catapulted "television" into a premier position in the electoral discourse but also granted the status of an essential commodity on par with subsidised rice and reservation in jobs … for the first time ever, television viewing moved to be part of the political discourse....' (Ranganathan, 2006: 4949).

Similarly, Tamil television is very different from television in, say, Chhattisgarh where broadcast journalists encountered a very peculiar kind of censorship during the run-up to the 2003 state election. Every time any of the news channels broadcast a news item that was even mildly critical of then chief minister Ajt Jogi, it was blanked from the air. Chhattisgarh viewers watching that particular broadcast would suddenly find their television sets going blank and the pictures would return only 15 minutes or so after the offending news story was over. This unannounced censorship would happen only within the territorial boundaries of Chhattisgarh and television viewers in the rest of India did not encounter this problem at all. This was because supporters of the Chief Minister had set up a state-wide private television network – Akash (Sky) TV – that bought over, or took control of, cable distribution networks across Chattisgarh and this provided an easy mechanism for controlling the broadcast of national news channels within the state's borders. The national networks could be turned off each time their product did not suit the ruling establishment. It was an ingenious form of censorship: it wasn't officially announced, it technically did not come from the state and there was nothing any of the channels could do about it.[17] The uses, or misuses, of Akash Television became an important part of the BJP's electoral campaign against Jogi in 2003 and within hours of his losing power on December 4, its television studios were taken over by a triumphant crowd of the party's supporters.[18] Anecdotes like these reveal the complexity and the centrality of television across India's regions and they offer a rich ground for future research.

Like the Congress in Chattisgarh, the ruling Akali Dal has been accused of forcibly capturing cable TV operations in Punjab. In August 2007, the Cable Operators Federation of India complained to the Ministry of Information and Broadcasting of physical threats and arrests of cable operators in the state. Like Jogi in Chattisgarh, Sukhbir Singh Badal [President, Akali Dal] denied the charges but the parallels were undeniable. Many cable operators in the state were forced to replace the popular Punjab Today channel with the new Akali-friendly channel PTC on their prime frequencies soon after the Akali Dal came to power. As one cable operator from Patiala said after being released from prison on charges of violence:

> This is state terror being used against us and the police are being used freely and scores of false cases are being filed.... First they put me behind the bars and then they took over our cables, painting the name of their company on all our amplifiers and other equipment out in the field, and even took our poles.
>
> (Chakraborty: 8 August 2007)

Congress MPs, now on the back foot, even planned to approach the National Human Rights Commission on the issue and whichever side one chooses to believe in this dispute it is undeniable that across India political parties are taking private television seriously.

In 2008, when the Ministry of Information and Broadcasting decided to investigate the ratings system of the television industry, arguing that it was lop-sided, many argued that the move was rooted in the fact that channels supported by the Congress and its allies were not doing well in the existing ratings and therefore not drawing enough advertising (Raman, 2008). As such, the Ministry wanted to change the goalposts. What is interesting is that by 2008 numerous channels were openly owned or aligned with political parties. Doordarshan continued to be a state controlled enterprise. In Tamil Nadu, the DMK has shifted patronage from Sun TV to Kalaignar TV while the AIADMK controls Jaya TV. Makkal TV is considered close to the PMK while ETV has long had close ties with the TDP. In Karnataka, Kasturi TV is identified with JD (S) while the CPI (M) patronizes Kairali TV in Kerala. The Congress has recently backed Jaihind TV in Kerala while Akash Bangla in West Bengal is controlled by the CPI (M) (Raman, 2008).

Yet, independent channels continue to thrive and technology has created new possibilities like the wonderful all-women's local news programme 'Apna Samachar' [Our Samachar] in Bihar's Muzaffarpur district. Run by two women with a handycam and two cycles, the weekly 45-minutes has emerged as a powerful local tool of empowerment and is broadcast weekly at the village *haat* [market]. Funded by local traders, the programme's production is also supported by housewives and local students and it is a powerful example of the intoxicating new possibilities of television in India (Kumar, 2008).

Conclusion

It is not my claim that satellite television's influence on India has always been positive. Television performs many of its transformations 'subliminally'. Simply by being there, available for viewing, for debate and for participation, it has effected changes in the way Indians operate in and interact with society. In a country where the state monopolized television for the first four and a half decades of independence, the eruption of privately controlled satellite television from the mid-1990s inserted a new factor in the societal matrix, with profound consequences. The capitalists who led the move towards private satellite broadcasting in India did not do it for altruistic reasons – their objective was to make money – but their efforts have led to the creation of newer modes of public action and publicness. Television has been adapted by Indian society – by its entrepreneurs, by its producers and by its consumers – to suit its own needs. Looking to create markets for advertisers, Indian producers and entrepreneurs searched for publics and, as purveyors of identity, they tapped in to, but also altered, existing social nodes of identity and communication. This has not always been rational or 'positive', but it is fundamentally different from the past when television was nothing more than a governmental tool. Television has opened up avenues that previously did not exist and brought many more people into the public arena. This is why Rajdeep Sardesai (29 May 2006) has argued that

> The television picture and sound-bite has been one of the most dramatic political developments in the last sixteen years ... mutually competitive 24 hour news networks are almost direct participants in public processes: not only do they amplify the news, they also influence it.

Sardesai goes as far as to argue that had the *Ramjanmabhoomi* movement unfolded in the age of 24-hour television, the Babri Masjid would never have been demolished in 1992. That may or may not be true, but the very fact that such an assertion could be made in 2006 is testament enough of the role that television has come to occupy in Indian public life. Measuring the political effect of television is, however, an inexact science. Television does not explain every social and political change in contemporary India. To make such a claim would be an overstatement. It is my argument, however, that it is impossible to imagine, or explain, modern India without reference to television, that it just would not make sense without it.

Notes

1 Doordarshan ran as an *ad hoc* division of All India Radio until 1976 when it was bifurcated and set up as a separate entity.
2 See for instance, Chatterjee (1991), Awasthy (1965) and Brosius and Butcher (1999).
3 Until 1995, the Indian state retained a monopoly over broadcasting through the colonial Indian Telegraph Act, 1885.
4 The numbers are updated up to January 2008. Mehta (2008b: 3).
5 India had 34,858,000 TV sets in 1992. Joshi and Trivedi (May 1994: 16).
6 The Indian population in 2006 had gone up to 1.12 billion. Population Reference Bureau (2006: 1).
7 In 2006, the National Readership Study (4) estimated 68 million satellite and cable households.
8 Procedural models of democracy focus on the systems and institutions of democracy as symbolized predominantly by the act of voting.
9 For studies of pre-satellite television see for instance, Chatterjee (1991), Mankekar (1999), Ghose (2005) and Rajagopal (2001). For studies of satellite television see Gupta

(1998), Shah (1997), Ninan (1995), Brosius and Butcher (1999), Price and Verhulst (1998), Page and Crawley (2001), Kohli (2003), Mehta (2008a) and Mehta (2008b).

10 Conversation with Rajdeep Sardesai, Managing Editor, CNN-IBN, IBN-7 and IBN-Lokmat (New Delhi: 1 May 2008).

11 Interview with KP Sunil, Vice President, Jaya TV (Chennai: 15 October 2005). Designations are accurate as of time of interview.

12 Conversation with Rajdeep Sardesai, Managing Editor, CNN-IBN, IBN-7 and IBN-Lokmat (New Delhi: 1 May 2008).

13 Interview with Uday Shankar, CEO and Editor STAR News, 2003–07 (Shanghai: 22 August 2005).

14 Interview with Uday Shankar (Shanghai: 22 August 2005), CEO and Editor, STAR News, 2003–07.

15 Interview with Suman Chattopadhyay (Kolkata: 22 December 2005), Founding Editor, STAR Ananda.

16 Ibid.

17 Personal Interview with Sanjeev Singh, Principal Correspondent, STAR News (New Delhi: 25 January 2004).

18 Ibid.

References

Ahmedabad Development and Educational Communication Unit, Indian Space Research Organisation.

Awasthy, G.C. (1965), *Broadcasting in India.* Bombay: Allied.

Bhatt, S.C. (1994), *Satellite Invasion of India.* New Delhi: Gyan Publishing.

Brosius, Christiane and Butcher, Melissa (eds) (1999), *Image Journeys: Audio-Visual Media and Cultural Change in India*. New Delhi: Sage.

Chakraborty, Sujit (2007), 'Akali Dal Accused of "State Terror" on Cable Aug 8 Ops in Punjab', www.indiantelevision.com [Accessed 9 August 2007].

Chatterjee, P.C. (1991), *Broadcasting in India*. New Delhi: Sage.

Dreze, Jean and Sen, Amartya (1989), *Hunger and Public Action*. Oxford: Clarendon Press.

Ghose, Bhaskar (2005), *Doordarshan Days*. New Delhi: Penguin/Viking.

Gupta, Nilanjana (1998), *Switching Channels: Ideologies of Television in India*. New Delhi: Oxford University Press.

Jeffrey, Robin (2003), *India's Newspaper Revolution: Capitalism, Politics and the Indian-Language Press*. New Delhi: Oxford University Press.

Jeffrey, Robin (2006), 'The Mahatma didn't like movies and why it matters: Indian broadcasting policy, 1920s–90s', *Global Media and Communication*, August Vol. 2, No. 2, pp. 204–24.

Joshi, S.R. and Trivedi, B. (May 1994), *Mass Media and Cross-Cultural Communication: A Study of Television in India*, Report No. SRG-94-041.

Kohli, Vanita (2003), *The Indian Media Business*. New Delhi: Response.

Kumar, Ruchir (2008), 'When news is just round the corner', *The Hindustan Times*, May 2 (New Delhi).

Little, John T. (1995), 'Video Vacana: Swadhyaya and Sacred Tapes' in Lawrence A. Babb and Susan S. Wadley (eds.), *Media and Transformation of Religion in South Asia*. Philadelphia: University of Pennsylvania Press.

Lutgendorf, Philip (1995), 'All in the (Raghu) family: a video epic in cultural context'. In Lawrence A. Babb and Susan S. Wadley (eds) *Media and the Transformation of Religion in South Asia*. Philadelphia: University of Pennsylvania Press.

Mankekar, Purnima (1999), *Screening Culture, Viewing Politics: An Ethnography of Television, Womanhood, and Nation in Postcolonial India*. Durham: Duke University Press.

Manuel, Peter (1993), *Cassette Culture: Popular Music and Technology in North India*. Chicago: Chicago University Press.

Mehta, Nalin (ed.) (2008a), *Television in India: Politics, Culture and Globalization*. London: Routledge.

Mehta, Nalin (2008b), *India on Television: How Satellite TV Has Changed the Way We Think and Act*. New Delhi: Harper Collins.

Mitra, Sumit and Kaul, Anita (1982), 'Doordarshan: the tedium is the message', *India Today*, May 31.

National Readership Studies Council (2006), *NRS 2006 – Key Findings*, August 29 Press Release. Mumbai: NRS.

Ninan, Sevanti (1995), *Through the Magic Window: Television and Change in India*. New Delhi: Penguin.

Page, David and Crawley, William (2001), *Satellites Over South Asia: Broadcasting, Culture and the Public Interest*. New Delhi: Sage.

Population Reference Bureau (2006), *2006 World Population Data Sheet*. Washington: PRB.

Price, Monroe E. and Verhulst, Stefaan G. (eds) (1998), *Broadcasting Reform in India: Media Law from a Global Perspective*. New Delhi: Oxford University Press.

PricewaterhouseCoopers, FICCI (March 2005), *The Indian Entertainment Industry: An Unfolding Opportunity*. New Delhi: FICCI.

Projected and Actual Population of India, States and Union Territories, 1991 (4 April 2001). New Delhi: Office of the Registrar General, India.

Rajagopal, Arvind (2001), *Politics After Television: Religious Nationalism and the Reshaping of the Indian Public*. Cambridge: Cambridge University Press.

Raman, Anuradha (2008), 'Down for the count', *Outlook*, May 12, New Delhi.

Ranganathan, Maya (2006), 'Television in Tamil Nadu Politics,' *Economic and Political Weekly*, December 2, Vol. 41, No. 48.

Sainath P. (2005), 'When farmers die: India's agrarian crisis, farmers, suicides and the media', Melbourne South Asian Studies Group Seminar, Australian Volunteers International (Melbourne: 13 July 2005).

Sardesai, Rajdeep (2006), 'Prime Time Reservation,' URL May 29 (accessed: 30 May 2006): http://www.ibnlive.com/blogs/rajdeepsardesai/1/11708/prime-time-reservation.html

Schudson, Michael (1995), *The Power of News*. Cambridge, MA: Harvard University Press.

Schudson, Michael (2003), *The Sociology of News*. New York: Norton.

Sen, Amartya (2002), *Rationality and Freedom*. Cambridge, MA: Belknap Press.

Sen, Amartya (2005), *The Argumentative Indian*. London: Penguin.

Shah, Amrita (1997), *Hype, Hypocrisy, and Television in Urban India*. New Delhi: Vikas.

STAR Ananda (n.d.), *Kolkata Municipal Election* tapes, STAR Archives.

Thompson, John B. (1994) 'Social Theory and the Media'. In David Crowley and David Mitchell (eds) *Communication Theory Today*. Cambridge: Polity, 1998, first pub. 1994.

Thompson, John B. (1995), *The Media and Modernity: A Social Theory of the Media*. Cambridge: Polity Press.

3 Emancipation or anchored individualism?

Women and TV soaps in India

Shehina Fazal

Introduction

Earlier soap operas on Indian television such as *Hum Log* (We People) tackled the issues of emancipation of women with some success. Research has shown that such pro-social soap operas were immensely powerful in disseminating messages, particularly those concerning gender issues (Singhal *et al.* 1993). However, since the deregulation of television in India in the early 1990s and the resultant proliferation of private television channels, it is essential to understand the modifications in representations of women in soap operas in the era of post-economic liberalization. This chapter states that although there is greater representation of women on television, these are bounded by national as well as patriarchal considerations. Further, the chapter argues that contemporary images have erased the earlier gains made in television representations of women in India. The popular drama serials have disposed the emancipated role models and replaced them with those that focus on the traditional cultural values as well as participation in global consumerism.

Feminist analysis of soap operas in the West has been widely documented but not revisited in this chapter (Ang, 1985; Geraghty, 1991; Hobson, 1982; Modleski, 1982). Most of these studies claim the genre as a site of resistance for women, particularly from the demands of daily life. In the post-feminist era, McRobbie provides an analysis on the 'new gender regime' where in the channels of communication, 'feminism is routinely disparaged' (2006: 63). A question that McRobbie poses is 'Why is feminism so hated?' She then goes on to state that we need to go beyond the simplistic overview of the change in perceptions of feminism to its unpopularity in the twenty-first century rather than explain it as a 'backlash' to feminism. McRobbie writes:

> We would certainly need to signal the full enfranchisement of women in the West, of all ages, as audiences, active consumers of the media and the many products they promote, and, by virtue of education, earning power and consumer identity a sizeable block of target market. (2006: 63)

McRobbie also states that there is an undoing of feminism within popular culture, where feminist perspectives are dismissed and deemed as unnecessary within the framework of postmodern irony. Depictions of women in popular culture consist of representations that are contrary to feminist sensibilities. In order to understand these changes on the Western feminist terrain, McRobbie claims:

> We would also need to be able to theorize female achievement predicated not on feminism, but on 'female individualism', on success that seems to be based on the invitation to young women by various governments that they might now consider themselves free to compete in education and in work as privileged subjects of the 'new meritocracy'. Is this then the New Deal for New Labour's 'modern' young women: female individualization and the new meritocracy at the expense of feminist politics? (2006: 63)

Within the context of India, Maityaree Chaudhuri (2000) offers extensive analysis of feminism basing her work on the coverage of women in the print media. She says that there is widespread dissemination of feminist ideas than ever before; however, it is 'both complex and mediated' (p. 3). Chaudhuri goes on to state that in order to demonstrate a meaningful relationship between feminism and the media, there are two important social processes that must be taken into consideration: the coalition of women's organizations into the very successful women's movement and the course of economic liberalization that began in the late 1980s. Chaudhuri writes that in the context of the print media

> Increasingly visible now are the more upmarket magazines' projection of a post-liberalised post-feminism, where the individual corporate woman is the icon. And more middle-class magazines' enunciation of an authentic and traditional 'feminism' criticises 'so-called feminism' on the grounds that it portends ill for the family and the Indian woman, apart from being a Western luxury that a poor country like India can ill afford. (2000: 3)

Mary John points to the problems that Western feminism poses within the Indian context. She argues that the colonial legacy together with the incorporation of women in the national culture, have made discussions on the 'westernness of feminism appear dated, a problem that we well have to put behind us' (John, 1998: 197). She also proposes that, given the long and rich history of the women's movement in India, the time has come for renewed interrogation on the issues of gender and empowerment. For John, this interrogation is particularly important due to the alarming developments that include the rise of the Hindu right and the empowerment of women within this frame. John (1998) states that the time has come for the women's movement to reclaim the feminist project.

Rao (2001) in her essay entitled 'Facets of Media and Gender studies in India', proposes that we need to further understand the reception of media content by women. Rao suggests that a greater understanding of the reception of texts is equally important as is the ideology and cultural politics within the critical analysis frame. However, these issues tend to be appropriated by organizations that are so keen to establish a relationship between receiver and the text, as international agency McCann Eriksson did when conducting focus groups with urban middle-class Indian women. Results from these focus groups enabled the agency to produce a profile of the urban Indian woman co-existing between traditional values and a somewhat modern outlook. Rao says that it is then not surprising that

> One therefore, sees a large number of serials on television that are woman-centric, where the protagonist goes through the harrowing saga of transition from tradition to modernity, often with a lot of uncertainty in her choice. (2001: 3)

Such perceptions are widespread in other Asian countries as attested by the survey on 'Gender Reflections in Asian Television' conducted by the Asian Network of Women in Communication (Siriyuvasak *et al.* 2000).

These trends also point to the complexities surrounding representations of women in India in the post-liberalized era. Kumar (2006) writes about the nationalism emergent with the rise of electronic capitalism in the Miss World contest held in Bangalore in 1996. The protests held at the event consisted of an unholy alliance of feminists, the left- and the right-wing Hindu politicians. However, these protests where somewhat muted when young women from India became Miss Universe (Sushmita Sen in 1994) and Miss World (Aishwarya Rai in 1994) who were hailed as India's representatives on the global (beauty) stage. Usha Zacharias states that the politics of gender within the postcolonial framework has taken an incongruous form, 'where the linkages between the partriarchal community, the market, and the state create the ground for conservative alliances' (2003: 404). Parameswaran, when writing about the same Miss World contest as a 'spectacle of gender and globalization', says that the textual analysis of the coverage of Miss World contest in 1996 in the *Times of India* newspaper showed that the event received better coverage in the paper thereby legitimizing the organizers as well as the sponsors and the participants through the revival of 'hegemonic cultural politics of consumer modernity while the visual imaging of activist groups inscribed protesters within paradigms of delinquency and disorder' (2004: 371).

It is within the above framework that this chapter intends to understand the representations of women within contemporary soap operas in India. The argument here is that in an increasingly transnational world of television, we need to understand representations of women within the transnational feminist frame. As Sreberny (2001) states that in the twenty-first century feminist media studies should be 'thinking transnationally'.

The issues raised by McRobbie above, relating to postmodern irony and individualization may not seem directly relevant to the analysis of representations of women in TV soap operas in India. Leaving aside postmodern irony, issues concerning individualization have direct relevance towards understanding media representations of women both, in India and the United Kingdom. In order to theorize changes exacerbated by the transnational media corporations we need to move into the terrain of decolonization of theory and recognize the commonalities. To borrow Chandra Mohanty's (2003) book title, *Feminism Without Borders*, where she makes a strong case for transnational feminist analysis which could provide a better understanding of the representations of women as well as their impact on female audiences throughout the world. This chapter therefore, proposes that the analysis of soap operas in the post-feminist era and the increasing individualization of women, will be strengthened by the incorporation of the transnational and may provide somewhat different dimensions to notions of the 'New Indian woman' in the postcolonial, globalized India.

Below is an overview of some of the key studies concerning women and their changing relationship with Indian soap operas. It will begin by providing an evaluation of the studies connected with soap operas on Indian television. In the following section, it will assess how the idea of individualism, anchored or not, has permeated within Indian popular culture and portrayed in contemporary soap operas. Some of these studies argue that representations of women in soap operas are inextricably linked with the economic repositioning of India within the global marketplace (Fernandes, 2000; McMillin, 2002; Mankekar, 1999; Parameswaran, 2004; Rajagopal, 2001).

Women and Indian soap operas

There is a significant amount of literature on the commonalities and differences between television soap operas in India and the United States (Gokulsing, 2004; Mitra, 1993; Singhal and Rogers, 1988). Additionally there is a substantial body of literature on the conventional and non-conventional designs of Indian soap operas (Gokulsing, 2004). Indeed in most parts of the world soap operas provide entertainment, whereas in India before liberalization in the early 1990s, soap operas on state television deployed the education-entertainment model in the context of development and nation building. One of the early serials made by the Space Applications Centre in Ahmedabad as part of the pro-development initiative was *Nari tu Narayani* (Women You Are Powerful, broadcast in 1983–84). This 40-part television serial was broadcast to Gujarat's Kheda district in the early 1980s with the specific intention of raising the socio-economic status of women. Evaluation on the impact of the serial indicated that women in the district set up cooperatives in order to gain economic independence (Bhatia and Karnik, 1985).

In 1984–85, the popular serial *Hum Log* addressed issues of gender equality by embedding the educational content within the overall entertainment component using the well-known actor Ashok Kumar. The actor who, although not part of the soap opera, revisited the key issues at the end of each episode. The serial was broadcast for a year-and-a-half in the mid-1980s and consisted of 156 episodes in total. The pro-development stance of the soap opera addressed somewhat difficult social issues that were portrayed through positive rela-tionships. *Hum Log* was also the first commercially sponsored serial on the state television broadcaster Doordarshan. The sponsor Maggi 2-minute noodles (a subsidiary of Nestlé) saw major increases in sales during the broadcast of the serial. *Hum Log* sponsorship raised Rs.363,63 lakhs for Doordarshan, almost double its yearly revenue (Krishnan and Dighe, 1990: 114).

Singhal *et al.* (1993) also found that many female viewers identified with the two women protagonists in *Hum Log*. The younger women in the audience identified with the character Badki, who rejected the traditional domestic role for Indian women to those which included seeking professional work outside the home and choosing her own husband. This depiction of the character was a positive role model in terms of gender equality. Likewise, the older women in the audience identified with the character Bhagwanti, who represented the role of the wife and the mother.

Despite these positive identifications, Krishnan and Dighe's study, which decoded women's images on television, found that the expansion of commercialism on television did not improve the representations of women. On the contrary they note that the earlier primary definer, the state, was being replaced with growing commercialization of the medium with the result that 'it consistently devalues women; on the other, it holds up as desirable the values of bourgeois liberalism, individual gain and subsequent consumerism' (1990: 113). Serials such as *Hum Log* as well as *Khandaan, Karamchand* and *Buniyaad* had major followings in the urban areas in India, as well as overseas where these programmes were available to viewers via video cassettes.

Deploying the ethnographic approach on the analysis of *Hum Log*, Mankekar states that the serial was the first of its kind that was concerned with improving the status of women. However, at the heart of the serial lay the 'ambivalence towards women's struggles' (1999: 154). Although the serial's narrative was clearly raising issues of women's rights within the liberal frame, however, when women did fight to improve their status both in the family as well as the community, such endeavours resulted in more 'suffering and loneliness' for the characters within the serial (Mankekar 1999: 154).

Literature on the overall analysis of the reception of the Hindu epic serials *Mahabharata* and *Ramayana* has provided narratives on the emotional appeal and ambiguities that utilized modern conventions of television discourses (Kumar, 2006; Mankekar,1999; Mitra,1993; Rajagopal, 2001). Mitra (1993) states that in televising *Mahabharata*, Doordarshan has circulated the set of practices that they perceived to be 'good' and that these were represented in the epic via the daily activities of the Pandava family. Additionally, in the packaging of *Mahabharata* the signature section, the language, the music and the north Indian costumes, the state broadcaster was able to privilege such representations as typical of Indian rural life.

Mitra (1993) rightly points out that *Mahabharata* should not be viewed in isolation, but that we should attempt to connect the 'television text and the ongoing struggles and contradictions in India'. Such contradictions have become the pillars around which the struggle continues to take place in the country. The four key sites of these struggles are language, regionality, religion and gender and which have also been the focus of discussions and debate in the post-liberalized India. Mitra explains,

> [T]he struggles around language are closely articulated with the strife between regions in India, as well as with the question of religion. Religion, on the other hand, is articulated with the struggles around age (particularly in the practices that distinguish between the young and the old) and gender ultimately describing the specific gender roles in India. At the same time, each of these axes divide India in its own specific way, illustrating the relative autonomy of its effects. (1993: 122–3)

Continuing on the theme of gender representations in Indian media, Purnima Mankekar (1999) provides us with quite a detailed analysis of how television in the post-economic liberalization era focuses on the upscale middle-class consumers who in the decade before watched Doordarshan religiously as citizens. This transformation from citizens to consumers explains Mankekar, has come from the state television re-engaging with the middle-class viewers within the frame of the 'New Indian Woman'. The recasting of *Bharatya Nari* (Indian woman) to *Nai Bharatya Nari* (New Indian Woman) is that she is modern, educated, Hindu and aspiring to be, if not already, part of the middle-class socio-economic group. These revised representations are woven into nationalist serials to engage the middle-class audiences and consumers.

On the role of the state broadcaster Doordarshan, 'in the ideological construction of nation, womanhood, identity and citizenship', Mankekar (1999: 4) provides quite a valuable and detailed analysis. She lucidly explains the influence of television in turning local and gendered relationships into metaphors of national identity. The ethnographic perspective that Mankekar bases her analysis on, extends beyond the familiar and well-rehearsed 'Euro-American' lens of cultural studies. Mankekar proposes that the ethnographic approach can provide valuable perspectives in understanding media in 'non-Western' countries and that the methodological approach could influence revisions in the 'fundamental assumptions about mass media, cultural politics and subjectivity' (1999: 7).

Post-liberalization and images of women on television

Leela Fernandes in her research raises issues on the impact of India's economic liberalization and whereby there is a re-articulation of the 'national' and how it connects with the 'global'. In this re-articulation, the media's role is to 'produce a vision of the Indian nation based on an idealized depiction of the urban middle classes and new patterns of commodity consumption' (2000: 3). In this frame, Fernandes argues that there is a redefinition of gender roles that focuses on the middle-class women where the concerns are of 're-territorialization' and linked to the 'preservation of gendered social codes' (2000: 3).

This hegemony of the Indian middle classes was echoed in a recent report by the McKinsey Global Institute entitled 'Tracking the Indian Middle Class', which states that consumer spending in India is expected to grow from Rs.17 trillion in 2005 to Rs.70 trillion in 2025. All this is due to the growth of the middle classes from 50 million to 583 million in the same period (Beinhocker, Farrell and Zainulbhai, 2007). The report advises the 'attackers' to focus on the spending power and the evolving consumer tastes of this lucrative middle class.

The increasing size and spending power of the middle class have attracted many players both from within the country as well as overseas to the Indian media landscape. The arrival of Zee TV and Satellite Television for the Asian Region (STAR television) as well as many others in the post-liberalized era of television has resulted in the realist elements of earlier state broadcast soap operas being replaced by middle and upper-class characters and settings with beautiful living rooms and urban lifestyles. The state broadcaster Doordarshan devised its soap operas on the premise of the national project, whereas the new cable and satellite television channels base their programming content and strategies on the viewers' disposable incomes. As Gokulsing states, 'Liberalization and globalisation became the new mantra, private enterprise was being openly welcomed by the government and Zee TV was a symbol of this enterprise culture for the middle and upper classes' (2004: 20).

This change in the Indian television landscape, state Malhotra and Rogers (2000), who evaluated representations of women in the top ten programmes broadcast by these private channels in 1997, showed that women are more visible on Indian television. However, this visibility is couched in representations that are constructed around interests of nationalism as well as patriarchy. The findings of this study indicate that the earlier gains made on the positive representation of women in Indian television were overturned in the post-liberalization phase.

According to McMillin who wrote about programmes on Doordarshan before the onslaught of liberalization,

> As scholars of Indian television note, programmes on Doordarshan were part of a political strategy to propagate the idea of a unified Hindu nation, which placed Hindu men at the centre of power as implementers of capitalist and development policies, and relegated women and backward classes and tribes to positions on the periphery as recipients and objects of development initiatives. (2002: 2)

Continuing her analysis on the transnational, national and regional TV channels in the post-economic liberalization frame, McMillin examined representations of women as well as the narratives of women's status at the end of the twentieth century. She found that representations of women in her chosen sample of programmes had not changed much from the 1980s. In general, the findings of the study show the,

> [C]ultural continuity in the construction of woman as chaste, passive and vulnerable. The woman's weakness, vulnerability and sexuality become a site

of viewing pleasure for male and female audiences who subscribe to the same ideological realism that television draws its codes from. (2002: 20)

However, McMillin ends her article on an optimistic note stating that the increased presence of female viewers as well as talk show hosts on transnational television channels in India marks a departure from the earlier representations and opens up the possibilities of 'realistic' and 'empowering' portrayals of women.

Sujata Moorti (2007) provides an analysis of the reception of soap operas in the Indian diaspora communities in the United States. In particular, Moorti's analysis focuses on one diasporic serial melodrama *Mausum* (Weather) made by an Indian producer living in the United States. The 13-part serial depicts everyday life of an Indian family in New Jersey and portrays the struggles that immigrant families go through in order to be accepted into the host society yet at the same time are assertive about their Indian identity and, therefore, their distinctiveness. Moorti states that in Indian diaspora communities in the United States, the preservation of cultural identity and the surrounding anxieties are bound to the women whose behaviour is observed and scrutinized. Moorti says, 'Although Indian masculinity is depicted as vulnerable to the predations of the West, it is woman, not man, whose behaviour comes under scrutiny and regulation' (2007: 8).

Parallels in the above enquiry are from the anti-colonial movement in India in the nineteenth century where the domestic sphere was 'sealed off' from the influences of colonialism. In the colonial context, the woman became the carrier of Indian culture as well as the symbol for freedom from the past and in the construction of nationhood in the future. Likewise, in the twenty-first century women have once again become sites of resistance as well as cushions for the daily struggles in Indian diaspora communities where, 'external threats to the stability of the family are countered by recuperating the "traditional" Indian woman, one who will help sustain and maintain *a cultural imaginary*' (Moorti, 2007: 10).

On the depictions of women in soap operas on Indian television, Moorti says,

> Contemporary prime-time narratives have reverted to formulaic depictions, which some commentators have characterized as constituting a 'backlash'. Independent women are presented as those requiring regulation and by the narrative's end revert to being doormats or shadows. The 'traditional' Indian woman whose activities center on and are limited to the domestic realm is celebrated in these narratives. (2007: 13)

Emancipation or anchored individualism?

In attempting to understand the evolving representations of women in Indian soap operas, the serial *Kyunki Saas Bhi Kabhi Bahu Thi* (Because Mother-in-law was Once Daughter-in-law) broadcast on STAR Plus, the most popular cable channel will be used to illustrate some of the arguments. STAR television was one of the first private satellite system whose footprint covered the Asian countries and beyond. STAR was originally a Hutchison Whampoa corporation. Now it is subsidiary of News Corporation, owned by Rupert Murdoch and has its headquarters in Hong Kong. STAR television was launched in 1991, beginning with five television channels and it now broadcasts to over 300 million viewers in 53 Asian countries, where well over 100 million viewers watch STAR channels.

STAR Plus is rated as the top cable channel in India and was in that position between 2000 and 2006. STAR has teamed up or created partnerships with many companies to develop and provide content in countries where it has a strong presence. In India, it owns nearly 26 per cent of Balaji Telefilms, which is one of the largest content providers in India. Balaji Telefilms provides Hindi serials such as *Kahaani Ghar Ghar Kii* (The Story of Every Home), *Kyunki Saas Bhi Kabhi Bahu Thih, Kesar, Kahin to Hoga, Kasauti Zindagi Kay* to Star Plus.

The post-liberalized framework also attracted other satellite players into India. In addition to satellite actors from the West, Sony Entertainment Television (SET) local entrepreneurs such as Zee TV competed with STAR. The latter has been immensely successful in its strategic approach of introducing reality and entertainment programmes such as *Kaun Banega Crorepati* (Who Wants to be a Millionaire). The collaboration between STAR and its India-based partner Balaji Telefilms, who 'localised' the company's programming strategy with serials such as *Kyunki Saas Bhi Kabhi Bahu Thih* and *Kahaani Ghar Ghar Ki* which have been so successful that they have become flagship programmes in India for the transnational media corporation.

The serial *Kyunki Saas Bhi Kabhi Bahu Thih* captures the changing representations of women on Indian television. The soap opera is cited as an example of India's 'soft power', whereby the programme is dubbed and shown at prime time in many countries of South Asia, including more recently in Afghanistan. The serial *Kyunki Saas Bhi Kabhi Bahu Thih* has achieved television ratings of ten; however, more recently it seems that it has lost some of its sparkle as in April 2008 it achieved television rating of four. Jilmil Motihar describes the growth of the soap operas in India as a 'sari spectacle' in an article in the December 2007 issue of *India Today.* Motihar writes about *Kyunki Saas Bhi Kabhi Bahu Thih:*

> Over 1,600 episodes later, the show, which gave birth to the term saas-bahu sagas, is still on air and has spawned an entire industry that feeds on glycerine, pancake and women who sleep in their Kanjeevarams. (http://indiatoday. digitaltoday.in/sari-spectacle-5.html)

In April 2008, just over 1700 episodes of the serial had been broadcast. The producers of the serial are both women: Ekta Kapoor (Creative Director) and Shobha Kapoor (Director) of Balaji Telefilms have become well-known and wealthy from the success of television drama that the company provides to various broadcasters. The story concerns an upper-class family – the Viranis from Gujarat – whose eldest son marries Tulsi (initially played by Smriti Irani) who is from a middle-class family, in fact the daughter of the family priest. The series focuses on the battles between Tulsi and the family's other three daughters-in-law and depicts the trials and tribulations in the household. Balaji Telelfilms gave the serial an 'age lift' in 2006 when a younger cast was brought in by introducing seven new characters including Krishna Tulsi, the heir apparent of Tulsi.

The *saas-bahu* sagas and others in the genre are made and broadcast in the twenty-first century within the transnational and post-liberalization frame. A country perceived to have one of the largest middle-class population and therefore, a major consuming market has led to large numbers of companies including the transnational media companies to tap into the bonanza. Within this scenario, representations of women, particularly in the soap opera genre are being recast into multiple frames. Women are expected to be modern, continue to unify the family and preserve the cultural heritage whilst the globalization process re-positions India's ranking in the global market place. In the *saas-bahu* soap operas, the mother-in-law is often depicted as out of date with the times, who finds it difficult to reconcile the competing demands of Indian values and the modern consumer lifestyle, whereas the daughter-in-law is often represented as well-educated and becomes the celebratory figure who is portrayed as dynamic and constantly adjusting to the changing conditions arising from globalization and the influx of the consumer culture. Such representations mark the family as the site where issues of Indian identity and values are articulated. Moorti says that such narratives,

> [E]xpand the horizons of domesticity, adding politicized dimensions to femininity, but a dimension that specifically erases concerns with social and gender justice to foreground the interests of a unitary family. These narratives contest modern secularism; they offer 'traditional' notions of community obligations and mutuality as liberatory. (2007: 15)

These constructions of national identities, where the symbols of identity and heritage are deployed quite deliberately in the 'localization' of programming by the global media companies to attract viewers in the locale, are issues that need to be included in the revisiting of feminist theorizing. This revisiting would include representations of women in Indian soap operas where foregrounding of the family has replaced the earlier representations of emancipation of women as well as their contributions to national development. This undoing of feminism in Indian popular culture echoes the concerns raised by McRobbie on the undoing of feminisn in the Western popular culture. However, further theorizing of this process needs to take place within the transnational context. As Chandra Mohanty (2003) discusses in revisting her essay entitled 'Under Western Eyes' we need to bring women to the fore in the 'nongendered' and 'nonracialized' discourses that are so prominent in the context of globalization. In Indian soap operas, the emancipation project has been abandoned in favour of individualization that is regulated, where the preferred narrative is one where women protect and nurture the interests of the family rather than issues of equality and social justice. In order to untangle such issues Mary John then poses the question,

> Why should questions about the West be brought in to discuss entangled clusters such as personal law, religion, communalism, secularism and

diversity, or middle class, caste, Dalit, OBC (Other Backward Classes), and minority (categories which have emerged in relation to debates on the uniform civil code and on reservations respectively), problems that are so identifiably 'ours'? Shouldn't the West be kept in its place, its power tackled around issues of, say, liberalization and globalization, the new imperialism? My answer, quite simply, is that the West is an intrinsic part of our current entanglements. Indeed, and this is what needs to be explored, the unique role of the West in our lives may turn especially on contemporary dilemmas in naming and describing ourselves.

(John, 1998: 3)

Conclusion

The explosion of television in India has resulted in a major change in the soap operas' that are shown on Indian television. This proliferation has resulted from the liberalization and privatization of television since the early 1990s. This chapter has attempted to provide an overview of the development of soap operas in India that were initially a tool for development messages. The success of this approach followed the broadcast of the mythic epics *Mahabharata* and *Ramayana* on state television. In the post-liberalization era, there are many more soap operas as well as increasing number of television channels available to Indian viewers. Within this post-liberalized context, representations of women need to be analyzed within the transnational frame. In order to unpack the changes of representations of women in popular culture both in the West and in India, feminist discourse needs to encompass transnational issues and perspectives.

Bibliography

Ang, I. (1985) *Watching Dallas: Soap Opera and the Melodramatic Imagination*. London: Methuen.

Beinhocker, E. D., Farrell, D. and Zainulbhai, A. S. (2007) 'Tracking the growth of India's middle class'. *McKinsey Quarterly*, No. 3, available at: http://www.mckinseyquarterly. com/Tracking_the_growth_of_Indias_middle_class_2032 (accessed: December 2007).

Bhatia, B. S. and Karnik, K. (1985) *'The Kheda Communication Project'*. Report by the Space Applications Centre, Ahmedabad, India.

Brown, W. J., Singhal, A. and Roger, E. M. (1989) Pro-development soap operas: a novel approach to development communication. *Media Development* 36(4): 43–8.

Chaudhuri, M. (2000) ' "Feminism" in print media'. *Indian Journal of Gender Studies* 7(2): 273–88. New Delhi: Sage Publications.

Fernandes, L. (2000) Nationalising the global: media images, cultural politics and the middle class in India. *Media, Culture and Society*, 22(5): 611–28.

Geraghty, C. (1991) *Women and Soap Opera*. Cambridge: Polity Press.

Gokulsing, M. K. (2004) *Soft-soaping India: The World Of Indian Televised Soap Operas*. Stoke-on-Trent: Trentham Books.

Hobson, D. (1982) *Crossroads: The Drama of a Soap Opera.* London: Methuen.

John, M. E. (1998) Feminism in India and the West: recasting a relationship. *Cultural Dynamics* 10: 197–209.

Krishnan, P. and Dighe, A. (1990) *Affirmation and Denial: Construction of Femininity on Indian Television.* New Delhi: Sage.

Kumar, S. (2006) *Gandhi Meets Primetime: Globalisation and Nationalism in Indian Television.* Urbana Champaign, IL: University of Illinois Press.

McMillin, Divya, C. (2002) Ideologies of gender on television in India. *Indian Journal of Gender Studies* 9(1): 273–88.

McRobbie, A. (2006) 'Post-feminism and popular culture: Bridget Jones and the new gender regime', in James Curran and David Morley (eds) *Media and Cultural Theory.* London: Routledge.

Malhotra, S. and Rogers, E. M. (2000) Satellite television and the new Indian woman. *International Communication Gazette* 10(62): 407–29.

Mankekar, P. (1999) *Screening Culture, Viewing Politics: Television, Womanhood and Nation in Modern India.* New Delhi: Oxford University Press.

Mitra, A. (1993) *Television and Popular Culture in India: A Study of the Mahabharata.* New Delhi: Sage Publications.

Modleski, T. (1982) *Loving with a Vengence.* London: Methuen.

Mohanty, C. T. (2003) *Feminism Without Borders: Decolonising Theory, Practising Solidarity.* Durham and London: Duke University Press.

Moorti, S. (2007) Imaginary homes, transplanted traditions: the transnational optic and the production of tradition in Indian television. *Journal of Creative Communications,* 2(1–2):1–21.

Parameswaran, R. E. (2004) Spectacles of gender and globalisation: mapping Miss World's media event space in the news. *The Communication Review,* No. 7: 371–406. Taylor Francis Inc.

Rajagopal, A. (2001) *Politics after Television: Religious Nationalism and the Reshaping of the Indian Public.* Cambridge: Cambridge University Press.

Rao, L. (2001) Facets of media and gender studies in India. In *Feminist Media Studies,* 1(1): p. 45–8.

Singhal, A. and Rogers, E. M. (1988) Television soap operas for development in India. *International Communication Gazette* 41: 109–26.

Singhal, A., Rogers, E. M. and Brown, W. J. (1993) Harnessing the potential of entertainment-education telenovelas. *International Communication Gazette* 51: 1–18.

Siriyuvasak, U., Leela R. and Wang Lay Kim (eds) (2000) *Gender Reflections in Asian Television.* New Delhi, India: Asian Network of Women in Communication.

Sood, S. (2002) Audience involvement and entertainment – education. *Communication Theory* 12(2): 153–72.

Sreberny, A. (2001). Gender, globalization and communications: women and the transnational. *Feminist Media Studies* 1(1): 61–5.

Zacharias, U. (2003) The smile of Mona Lisa: postcolonial desires, nationalist families, and the birth of consumer television in India. *Critical Studies in Media Communication,* 20(4): 388–406.

4 Indian feminisms

Issues of sexuality and representation

Geetanjali Gangoli

Indian feminism is characterised above all by its passionate allegiance to polyvocality, and respect for difference and differences. This chapter will explore the diverse responses of Indian feminisms to shifting patriarchal challenges in the context of consolidation of globalisation and right-wing politics, and the role of law within these discourses. This will be done through a study of feminist campaigns against sexual harassment and in favour of sexual freedoms, the former through an assessment of sexual harassment cases and law and the latter through feminist discourses around lesbianism relating to the film *Fire* (1996). It will thereby assess the diversities within feminist responses to these issues, including the use of law within the campaigns, and whether legal feminisms relating to law and women's legal rights can be effective in the Indian context.

Context

India experienced a transition to globalisation, initiated through what has been called 'market reforms' in 1991. These changes included increased reliance on the market mechanism manifested through state policies including deregulation of the Indian economy, reduction of governmental controls, increased autonomy for private investment, reduced state investment in the public sector and foreign capital given greater access to the Indian market (Sen, 1998). There have been intense debates on whether these 'reforms' have improved the lives of women and men in the country. On the one hand it has been suggested that these changes have led to an efficient system of economic governance, decreasing governmental control and regulation. India is currently the second fastest growing economy in the world with the growth rate in 2006 at the all-time high of 8.1 per cent. However, critics have suggested that the main beneficiaries of liberalisation of the economy have been the middle classes, and that globalisation has increased social and economic stratification (Sen, 1998). Opponents include left-wing parties in India who see in deregulation an erosion of labour rights for the urban working class, a decline in agricultural profits for the rural poor, and environmental movements such as the

Narmada Bachao Andolan, who analyse 'development' as contributing to increased marginalisation of tribal communities.

The impact of globalisation on women has been the focus of feminist debate, with some arguing that economic changes have led to increased hardships for working class and lower caste women. The changes to the environment, for example, have had serious repercussions for tribal women, due to loss of livelihoods and traditional resource bases, forced displacement and increased impoverishment (Baviskar, 1995). Feminists have also noted the ways in which multinational companies in India, as in other parts of the world, exploit the labour of 'young, underpaid and disadvantaged women' in free trade zones and sweat shops; and call centres use 'young lower middle class, educated women' (FAOW, 2005: 2) with few labour rights, or limited ability for collective action.

In addition, it is suggested that global capital through multinational corporations attempt to homogenise a universal image of the body of the ideal women (FAOW, 2005). This is manifested, for instance, in nationalist pride vested in the bodies of Indian women winning international beauty pageants. While some feminists feel that these developments have led to women enjoying greater sexual autonomy, and increased control over their own bodies (Ghosh, 1996), others fear that these contribute to increased commodification of the female body that serves male fantasies (Kishwar, 1995). Similarly, debates on representation of women's bodies are divided on an understanding of whether the global influences of satellite television in the 1990s have contributed to women's liberation, or its reverse, enslavement by consumerist ethos.

Globalisation in India has been accompanied by the strengthening of right-wing Hindu fundamentalism. The rise of Hindu fundamentalism in postcolonial India has been analysed as having its origins in the 'divide and rule' policy successfully implemented under colonial rule, contributing to the partition of India and Pakistan in 1947, that accompanied independence from colonial rule (Sarkar, 1995). Prior to independence, Hindu fundamentalism was represented by the Rashtriya Seva Sangh (henceforth RSS) founded in 1925, and the RSS continues to see itself as 'the antidote to ... the dangerous tendencies of modern-day tendencies' (Narula, 2003: 44) including secularism. Post-independence, India adopted a secular constitution, but the newly created Indian state simultaneously witnessed communal riots, that took the form of widespread carnage against Muslims; leading to loss of life, and a sense of insecurity for the Muslim community, and the emergence and electoral success of Hindu fundamentalist political parties, including the Bhartiya Janata Party (henceforth BJP) and the Shiv Sena.

In the 1980s, Hindu fundamentalism was manifested in the Ram Janambhoomi movement, which agitated for the construction of a temple to commemorate what they believed (with little archaeological or historical evidence) was the birthplace of Rama, the protagonist of the Hindu epic Ramayana. The birthplace was 'located' at what was at the time a mosque, called the Babari Masjid, constructed by Babar, the first Mughal emperor in India. The mosque was demolished by Hindu fundamentalists in 1992, resulting in a symbolic defeat of secularism, and followed by anti-Muslim pogroms in different parts of India.

The Ram Janambhoomi movement was accompanied by debates on the Shah Bano case in the 1980s, which followed from a Supreme Court judgment regarding a divorced Muslim woman's right under Section 125 of the Criminal Procedure Code to claim maintenance (Mohommed Ahmed Khan vs Shah Bano Begum and Others, 1985: 945).[1] The details of the case are as follows: Shah Bano filed for maintenance in the Court of Judicial Magistrate after she was abandoned by her husband and thrown out of the matrimonial home after 30 years of marriage. Following this, she was divorced by her husband who maintained that he had fulfilled his obligations under Muslim Personal Law by paying her *mehr*[2] and as a Muslim was not liable to pay her any more maintenance. The Supreme Court judgment upheld the lower court rulings on this case, stating that as Section 125 was a part of the criminal law of the country, it was applicable to all Indians. However, the judge made a number of contentious remarks about Islamic law, citing a statement made by Sir William in 1843 that the fatal point in Islam was its degradation of women and calling for '…a common civil code [to] help the cause of national integration' (Mohommed Ahmed Khan vs Shah Bano Begum and Others, 1985: 945). The Hindu right responded to this judgment by criticising the insularity of the Muslim community in India; Muslim fundamentalist groups by asserting that Shah Bano's claim for maintenance post-divorce was 'un-Islamic', Muslim intellectuals and liberals disagreed with this interpretation of Muslim law and left-wing parties and feminists addressed the issue in terms of women's rights (Das, 1995).

Feminists have argued that religious fundamentalism in India reflects the crisis of both modernisation and democracy, and has serious implications for women's rights, and women's movements, arguing that 'fundamentalism … refashions patriarchies to legitimise participation of women in the nationalist project' (FAOW, 2005: 3). The following sections examine how this political context situated feminist debates around sexuality in the 1990s and the twenty-first century.

Sexual harassment

> Eve teasing lives in post-colonial India as a cognitive category that refers largely to sexual harassment of women in public spaces, thereby constituting women as 'eves', temptresses who provoke men into states of sexual titillation.
>
> (Baxi, 2001)

> Do we want the heavy weight of the law to block the lurid stare? Silence the embarrassing joke? Modulate one's sexual tones?
>
> (Kapur, 2001)

Sexual harassment of women in the public sphere has been an endemic part of public life in India (Baxi, 2001), and is as an expression of masculine sexual control over women who have stepped out of the normative private sphere. A study conducted by the Gender Study Group in Delhi University (1996) revealed that 91.7 per cent of women students living in hostels had faced sexual harassment on the campus almost every day, from men outside the university, male students and faculty members. Up to 45 per cent said that they were adversely affected by the harassment, and that their mobility and choices were restricted as a result.

Sexual harassment of women in public places is named and culturally constructed in India as 'eve teasing', a specifically 'Indian-English' term. While there are specific laws that can be used in cases of sexual harassment, most of them are based on outdated notions of women's propriety. For instance, Section 509 IPC criminalises any 'word, gesture or act intended to insult the modesty of a woman' and Section 354 IPC criminalises 'assault or criminal force to a woman with the intention to outrage her modesty'. In addition, Section 209, IPC criminalises 'obscene acts and songs'. These provisions date back to the nineteenth century and are based on Victorian notions of sexual propriety, and feminists have argued that they are wholly inadequate in defining the experiences of women in the contemporary context (Agnes, 1992).

The Indian women's movement campaigned on sexual harassment of women in the workplace through the 1980s and 1990s (Chakravarti and Wahi, 1995), but the first feminist challenge to the paucity of legal provisions on sexual harassment was made in 1997, when a Public Interest Litigation (PIL) was filed by women's organisations in the Supreme Court of India, following the gang rape of Bhanwari Devi, an employee of the Rajasthan state sponsored Women's Development Programme as a reprisal for her efforts to stop child marriage primarily among upper-caste Gujjars and Brahmins in 1992. She was raped by Gyarsa and Badri Gujjar, members of the locally influential Gujjar community, while she belonged to the 'lower' Kumbhar caste. Unlike most incidents of rape, this one was witnessed by her husband, who was restrained by Ram Karan Gujjar and Shravan Panda. Gyarsa, Badri and Ram Karan were all members of the same family. The local police proceeded on the assumption that Bhanwari Devi was lying. Her case, however, was supported by women's groups in different parts of the country. One important issue raised by the campaign was the role of the state and its failure as an employer to provide a safe working environment for Bhanwari (Srivastava and Ghosh, 1996).

The campaign, however, made no impact on the judgment by the Sessions Court, Jaipur passed on 5 November 1995. The five men implicated in the case were acquitted. The judgment based its acquittal on two planks. One, a romanticisation of Indian culture, the second the technical grounds of lack of evidence. Justice Jaspal Singh stated that since the five accused were of different castes – four were Gujjars, and one a Brahmin – the rape was impossible, since according to the judge, rural gangs are not multi-caste. He stated that Indian rural society would not degenerate to the extent that they would lose 'all sense of caste and class, and pounce upon a woman like a wolf'. Finally, he believed that no Indian man would stand and watch his wife being raped when 'only two men twice his age are holding him' (cited in Gangoli and Solanki, 1996). The sessions court judgment was based on patriarchal assumptions of the normative protective role of the husband in the public sphere, the role of women in the family and a protection of caste interests. While some feminists saw in the judgment a vindication of their position that the legal system, given its inherently patriarchal nature, could not give justice to women, others decided to use the Bhanwari Devi case to get rights for all women in cases of sexual harassment and assault taking place within the workplace situation, thus resulting in the PIL.

The Supreme Court judgment responding to the PIL addressed sexual harassment in the workplace as violation of Fundamental Rights in the Indian constitution, and international conventions on gender equality, suggesting that absence of adequate civil and penal laws made it necessary for the court to create guidelines to ensure prevention of sexual harassment of women (Vishakha and Anrs vs Union of India, 2007). The judgment was a part of a general trend of judicial activism in the 1990s, and reflected the growing influence of social movements on the judiciary. The guidelines placed the responsibility of preventing and addressing cases of sexual harassment in the workplace on employers, including setting up complaint mechanisms and complaint committees. The Supreme Court judgment was followed by a national law on sexual harassment, passed in 2003 (Sexual Harassment Bill, 2003).

The judgment and the law shift the 'responsibility' of the incidents of sexual harassment from the individuals involved to the employer. Proscribed behaviours include 'physical contact and advances; demand or request for sexual favours; sexually coloured remarks; showing pornography; any other unwelcome physical verbal or non-verbal conduct of sexual nature', especially where such behaviour can create 'a hostile work environment' (Vishakha and Anrs vs Union of India, 2007). The judgment however provided a wider definition of sexual harassment than the law does; the former defining it as 'unwelcome sexually determined behaviour', and the latter as 'including avoidable sexual advances'. The judgment therefore takes women's experiences as the defining factor.

Feminist responses

Many feminists welcomed the law as recognising, for the first time in Indian legal history, the importance and role of sexual harassment in shaping the public experience of Indian women. Women's movement activists have participated in the establishment of sexual harassment committees in a range of workplace situations. To some extent, the committees and the campaign follow the logic of the Western radical feminist theories of Catherine MacKinnon who argued that sexual harassment was a form of discrimination against women in employment, and the liberal feminist agenda of changing the law. In India, the radical and liberal agendas have often coalesced and the appeal to legal solutions is seen in such instances as a legitimate response to feminist concerns (Gangoli, 2007).

However, even within the radical and liberal agenda on sexual harassment, there have been some reservations about the sexual harassment law. Some feminists have focused on the lacunae within the judgment and the law, suggesting that it is not comprehensive enough to meet the diverse needs of contemporary Indian women. The law is not widely applicable, leaves out of its scope, several workplace locations, including 'free trade zones, special economic zones, multinational companies, offices/firms of professionals such as lawyers, doctors, chartered accountants, teachers, and many others such as religious bodies and institutes' (Raymond, 2003). Within the context of globalisation and newer forms of employment the sexual harassment laws therefore leave out a range of experiences. These limitations point to the complexities or perhaps the impossibility of creating a law that is entirely comprehensive, or inclusive of all potential experiences that women have in the workplace especially in the nebulous and shifting world of globalisation.

Other feminists have a more fundamental opposition to the sexual harassment laws and policies. One view is that sexual harassment laws cast women as victims needing protection from male attention, and could feed into employers' reluctance to employ women (Kapur, 2001). Therefore, the laws could restrict rather than enable women. This can be compared with trade unions employers' response to other legally enforceable provisions such as maternity benefits and provision of crèches which are used as excuses to not employ women employees of childbearing ages, or to remove from employment young women who are seen as most likely to use these provisions (Gangoli, 1992). Feminists have therefore the difficult task of convincing trade unions and employers that women employers are not an employment liability, while arguing that they have rights as employees.

In addition, Kapur suggests that sexual harassment laws create and feed into right-wing conservatism about women's sexuality and appropriate sexual behaviour. She cites the example of a judgment made in 1999, following a case where the Apparel Export Promotion Council (AEPC) terminated the services of an employee after a departmental enquiry found substance in the sexual harassment complaint filed by a woman colleague. The employee, however, appealed in the Delhi High Court, which ordered his reinstatement on grounds that he had only tried to molest the lady, and did not actually molest her. The AEPC appealed to the Supreme Court, which held that actual assault was not the question, and stated that 'objectionable overtures with sexual overtones are enough' striking down the Delhi High Court order. The judgment drew on the 'pristine conduct' of the complainant, including her unmarried (and presumably virginal) state (cited in Kapur, 2001).

In this regard, the AEPC judgment followed the logic of rape case law in India, where the testimony of the victim is judged according to the sexual 'purity' and class status of the woman (Gangoli, 2007). In a case of custodial rape in 1990, the judges held that to disbelieve a woman, especially a 'young girl' was to insult womanhood, as Indian women do not lie about rape. The judges A. M. Ahmedi and F. Fatima Beevi stated:

> Ours is a conservative society where it concerns sexual behaviour....Courts must also realise that ordinarily a woman, more so a young girl, will not stake her reputation by levying a false charge concerning her chastity.
> (State of Maharasthra vs Chandraprakash Kewalchand Jain, 1990)

The following section will examine some of the debates around women's sexuality in the context of debates around representation of women.

Sexuality, lesbianism and representing women

Right-wing concerns of creating the ideal Hindu woman are also based on a partial acceptance of the rights of middle-class women to assert their physical beauty – as in the case of Hindutva support for Hindu women such as Sushmita Sen and Aishwarya Rai winning international beauty contests, somewhat contradicted by discomfort with the sexual freedom that this could imply for women. To be acceptable, women are allowed to look 'Westernised', but demonstrate that they have not lost 'Hindu' values of chastity and modesty.

While feminists have not entered in debates around women's sexuality on the grounds of morality or chastity, it has been suggested nevertheless that there is an element of Hindu middle-class morality within some of the responses to the assertion of women's sexuality. This is evident in early feminist campaigns around sexualised representation of women. Women's groups in the 1980s had mainly agitated against films and advertisements that showed women in sexually suggestive poses, therefore reinforcing 'the notion that anything sexual is obscene, and that respect for women is equivalent to treating them as asexual' (Agnes, 1995: 137–8). In addition, the campaign involved the defacing of 'obscene' posters, where to their horror, feminists were supported by right-wing Hindutva groups.[3]

On the issue of lesbianism, between the 1970s and the 1990s, there have been two strands within Indian feminism; one that ignored the issue of lesbianism, and the other that raised it in strategic, and initially in informal ways (Bacchetta, 2002). Some of these issues came to the fore in the debates around the representation of the assertion of women's sexuality, where it poses a frontal challenge to the heteronormative family, in the film *Fire* by Deepa Mehta, a Canadian director of Indian origin.

Fire

The plot of the film is as follows: Sita (Nandita Das) and Radha (Shabana Azmi) are two sisters-in-law who are both unhappily married in a Hindu middle-class Delhi household. They are married to two brothers, and look after their old and disabled mother-in-law. Jatin (Javed Jaffery) is newly married to Sita, but is in love with Julie, a Chinese-Indian, who refuses to marry him. Ashok (Kulbhushan Kharbanda) the elder brother is married to Radha, but has taken a vow of celibacy, as he is the disciple of a Hindu religious sect. Mundu (Ranjit Chowdhry) is the man-servant/housekeeper, secretly in love with Radha. Sita and Radha fall in love, and are discovered by Mundu. When he is caught masturbating while watching a pornographic movie in front of the mute mother-in-law, Mundu reveals the affair between Sita and Radha to Ashok. Sita and Radha decide to leave the marital home; Radha is confronted by Ashok, and her sari accidentally catches fire. She escapes, and the film ends with Radha and Sita embracing in a Sufi shrine in Delhi.

Communal responses

The film was the focus of intense controversy in India. It was released for screening in India in late 1998 after having been subjected to scrutiny by the Indian censor board – a normal procedure for all films released in India, both Indian and foreign – and was passed without any cuts. It initially ran to full houses in several cities in India, but after a few weeks Hindu right-wing groups, Shiv Sena and Bajrang Dal attacked some of the cinema theatres screening the film. Members of the Shiv Sena also protested by stripping down to their underwear in front of the house of actor Dilip Kumar, who had filed a petition against the attacks on the cinema theatres. In an interview the Shiv Sena leader, Bal Thackeray stated that lesbianism did not exist in Hindu families. He further objected to the projection of the family as a Hindu family, references to the epic Ramayana, and the trial by fire and calling the two main women characters Sita and Radha, names of Hindu goddesses (AFP, 1998).

Sita's story is a part of the Hindu epic, Ramayana. She was the consort of Lord Rama, and she underwent a number of trials and tribulations, including following her husband in a nomadic and penurious life when he was unjustly exiled for 14 years; being abducted by Ravana, King of Sri Lanka; being rescued by Rama, but then forced to go through a 'trial by fire' to prove her chastity; and then abandoned by him when she was pregnant, and being asked to prove her faithfulness by Rama several years later, at which point, she asked for Mother Earth to swallow her as a sign of her virtue. Radha in the Hindu tradition was a married lover of Lord Krishna, and her adulterous relationship with the boy god places her at a less 'respectable' status within the Hindu pantheon, however she was still appropriated as a goddess in this debate.

Thackeray believed that the image of Sita as the symbol of Hindu wifely devotion was defiled by her projection as a lesbian. This has resonances of earlier Lok Sabha debates on prostitution in 1986, when the law governing prostitution and trafficking was amended, leading to a change in the name of the law from Suppression of Immoral Traffic in Women to Immoral Traffic abbreviated to SITA to the proposed Immoral Traffic in Women and Children (Prevention) Act abbreviated to PITA. This change was met with relief by some MPs, because they believed that it was inappropriate to try prostitutes under a law sharing its name with a respected Hindu goddess:

> Another feature of the bill is that the nomenclature … which was very ridiculous has been changed. The Suppression of Immoral Traffic Act, which was popularly known as SITA has been changed. I remember in courts of law so many hundreds of Sitas used to stand and we used to refer to them as Sita No. 1, Sita No. 2 and Sita No. 3. It is very rightful that this name has been changed.
> (Shri Shantaram Naik, Lok Sabha Debates, 1986: 158)

There is clearly an elision between Sita, the ideal Hindu wife and Indian womanhood, contrasted with, in these debates with the image of the prostitute, and to call the latter Sita causes anguish and discomfort. Within this context, Thackeray's objections were clearly communal, alluding to the fact that the actors playing Radha and Jatin were Muslims, he called for the two leading characters be called 'Muslim' names such as, 'Shabana, Saira or Najma' (AFP 1998: 1), and the aforementioned protest outside Dilip Kumar's house, who happens to be a Muslim.

Feminist responses

Prior to the *Fire* controversy, debates around homosexuality in India were around the existence of the law criminalising the practice of male homosexuality through Section 377, Indian Penal Code. Section 377 IPC criminalises sodomy, not homosexuality per se. The law therefore applies only in cases of male homosexual activity, not for lesbian sexual activity. While the law seems to work to women's advantage, it does not encourage or even condone lesbianism either, rather it ignores it as irrelevant (Aids Bhed Bhav Virodhi Andolan, 1991). Protests against Section 377 have been led by gay rights groups and supported by lesbian women from feminist organisations, who are not directly affected by the law. This is partly due to Indian feminists' links with other social movements and, but also due to a recognition that lesbianism in India is only tolerated when it is invisible.

There was no single feminist response to the controversy around *Fire*. While most feminists believed that the screening of the film should be allowed on the grounds of freedom of expression and an opposition to Hindu right-wing appropriation of women's sexuality (Bose, 2000; John and Niranjana, 2000; Kapur, 2000; Kishwar, 1998; Upadhyaya, 2000), there were nevertheless variations within this theme. It was also argued however that lesbian and feminism opposition of Hindu right moves to ban the film in some ways contradicted their earlier positions on free speech, that is, feminist protests against sexually explicit film posters alluded to earlier, and against Miss World competitions in India (Kapur, 2000).

While some believed that the right-wing response was a hysterical counter to the feminist challenge to Hindu patriarchy posed by the film (Bose, 2000; Upadhyaya, 2000); others argued that the film was problematic in portraying control over and denial of women's sexuality as the *sole* plank on which Hindu patriarchy rested. It was argued that this reified sexuality as the single-most important feminist struggle (John and Niranjana,1999), denying the ways in which sexual control is linked to other forms of oppression within the family.

It was also suggested that the film denied the spaces available to Hindu and Indian women and men in same sex relationships; therefore was a 'crude caricature' of India from a 'self hating Indian' (Kishwar, 1998: 4), who portrayed India as a homophobic country. Some self-identified lesbians critiqued the director for her hasty denial of the film as being on lesbianism, and the film's depiction of lesbianism caused by a denial of conjugal sex and not out of choice (VS, 2000). It was argued that the film both exposed lesbian women in India to increased scrutiny and argued eventually for the possible for women's sexuality to be contained within marriage, if their sexual needs were met within marriage. On the other hand, some lesbian feminists believed that the film allowed them to break the silence on Indian sexuality, and argued that despite Mehta's disavowal of the theme of lesbianism in the film, it portrayed the possibility of a lesbian relationship within a Hindu middle-class family (SL, 2000). There were indeed protests against the Hindu right outside some cinema theatres in Delhi, where some lesbian feminists carried placards stating 'lesbian and Indian', therefore asserting publicly for perhaps the first time in Indian history the existence of lesbian sexuality in India.

Conclusions

The feminist debates on sexual harassment and representation of women reveal several, often contradictory patterns. Sexual harassment is seen as a form of patriarchal control over women, and a way to reduce the mobility of women in the context of increasing economic opportunities following globalisation. On the other hand, it is also argued that excessive feminist focus on reducing sexual harassment can lead to increased surveillance of sexual behaviour with possible consequences of reducing women's mobility even further. To a large extent this has resonances with other debates on whether feminist justice is indeed impossible within law (Menon, 1995). I suggest that feminist preoccupation with gender as the sole or primary category of activism, and indeed of oppression, is responsible for leading some feminists to ignore other categories of oppression, including caste, class and community. It is the feminist understanding of Indian women as universally oppressed and needing protection (Pathak and Sunder Rajan, 1989) that forms the basis of appeals to the state to create new laws, or amend existing ones that work in favour of 'women's interests'; while they have also acknowledged that 'women are not a collectivity' (Sen, 2000: 54). Some feminists have argued that there is an inherent contradiction in approaching the Indian state for redressal of rights, since it legitimises the powers of an inherently exploitative and misogynist state and allows the co-option of feminist language (Gothoskar *et al.* 1994).

On the question of representation of women's bodies and sexuality, concerns about excessive commodification of women are challenged by fears that free speech would be threatened by feminist censorship. While the women's movements campaigns have in the main redefined sexuality in various significant ways, rejecting patriarchal and normative conceptualisations of female sexuality, they are nevertheless divided in the ways they conceptualise their understanding of sexual difference. Therefore, streams within feminism have sometimes ignored aspects of female sexuality that they have felt uncomfortable with, therefore there has been a feminist rejection of the overtly sexualised images of women or an acceptance of heterosexual and marital monogamy as being beneficial to women, and therefore desirable (Sanlaap, 1998). However, others have questioned the normative nature of Indian heterosexuality and its impact on feminisms, based on a celebration of sex within marriage, and a rejection of non-marital sex (FAOW, 1998). Similarly, appropriation from communal right-wing forces of the campaign against pornography pushed some Indian feminists to reconsider their positions on the campaigns on sexuality, moving them towards an opposition of non-sexual, discriminatory representations of women. Others continued to focus on degrading sexualised images of women, as ways to understand how patriarchy constructs women's bodies, while not advocating censorship (Gandhi and Shah, 1989).

Therefore feminists have displayed an immense capacity for self-reflection and for change, and the ability therein to focus on the 'unconscious' and unstated assumptions of feminist politics and rhetoric. The lack of resolution of these debates is not a weakness of Indian feminisms. It reflects, on the contrary, the strengths and ability to challenge and respond to these challenges within the women's movements, and to work together on issues, even while disagreeing with individual perspectives.

Notes

1 Section 125 Cr. PC is a part of criminal law, the purpose of the section being to prevent destitution. Under this section, the 'destitute' person was entitled to relief to the maximum amount of Rs.500.
2 Mehr refers to the provision under Islamic law that requires a husband to make a gift, or settle money upon the bride at the time of marriage, which may also be divided into portions, one to be given the bride at marriage, the other to be given to the wife if she is widowed or divorced. The details of the mehr are stipulated in the nikaah, or marriage contract.
3 Interview with Sandhya Gokhale.

References

AFP (1998) Hindu leader says lesbian film should be about Moslem family. *Pioneer*, 14 December 1998.

Agnes, F. (1992) Protecting women against violence: review of a decade of legislation, 1980–89. *Economic and Political Weekly* 27(17), ws 19–33.

Agnes, F. (1995) *State, Gender and the Rhetoric of State Reform. Gender and Law: Book 2*. Bombay: RCWS, SNDT.

Aids Bhed Bhav Virodhi Andolan (1991) *Less Than Gay. A Citizens' Report on the Status of Homosexuality in India*. New Delhi: ABVA.

Bacchetta, P. (2002) Rescaling transnational 'Queerdom': lesbian and 'Lesbian' identitary-positionalities in Delhi in the 1980s. *Antipode* 34(5), 947–73.

Baviskar, A. (1995) *In the Belly of the River. Tribal Conflicts over Development in the Narmada Valley*. New Delhi: Oxford University Press.

Baxi, P. (2001) Sexual harassment. *Seminar*, 505, http://www.india-seminar.com/ 2001/ 505/505%20pratiksha%20baxi.htm

Bose, B. (2000) The desiring subject: female pleasures and feminist resistance in Deepa Mehta's *Fire. Indian Journal of Gender Studies* 7(2), 249.

Chakravarti, U. and Wahi, T. (1995) Recent gender crimes in the University of Delhi: two case studies. *Revolutionary Democracy* 1(2), available online at: http://www.revolutionarydemocracy.org /rdv1n2/gender.htm

Das, V. (1995) *Critical Events*. New Delhi: Oxford University Press.

FAOW (1998) *Visions of Gender Just Realities*. Bombay: Forum Against Oppression of Women.

FAOW (2005) *Concept Note for the Feminist Dialogues at Porto Alegre*. Mumbai: Forum Against Oppression of Women.

Gandhi, N. and Shah, N. (1989) *The Issues at Stake: Theory and Practice in the Contemporary Women's Movement in India*. New Delhi: Kali for Women.

Gangoli, G. (1992) *Gender Relations in the Cotton Mill Industry in Bombay, 1900–1993*. M.Phil. Thesis, Delhi: Department of History, University of Delhi.

Gangoli, G. (2007) *Indian Feminisms. Campaigns against Violence and Multiple Patriarchies*. Aldershot: Ashgate Publishers.

Gangoli, G. and Solanki, G. (1996) Misplaced myths. *Humanscape* 3(4), 22–6.

Gender Study Group (1996) A Report on Sexual Harassment in Delhi University. Delhi: *Gender Study Group*.

Ghosh, S. (1996) 'Deviant pleasures and disorderly women. The representation of the female outlaw in Bandit Queen and Anjaam' in Ratna Kapur (ed.) *Feminist Terrains in Legal Domains. Interdisciplinary Essays in Women and Law in India*. New Delhi: Kali for Women, 150–83.

Gothoskar, S. *et al.* (1994) Maharashtra's policy for women. *Economic and Political Weekly* 29, 3019–22.

John, M. E. and Niranjana, T. (2000) Mirror politics: fire, Hindutva and Indian culture. *Inter-Asia Cultural Studies* 1(2), 374–9.

Kapur, R. (ed.) (1996) *Feminist Terrains in Legal Domains. Interdisciplinary Essays in Women and Law in India*. New Delhi: Kali for Women, 150–83.

Kapur, R. (2000) Too hot to handle: the cultural politics of Fire. *Feminist Review* 64, 53–64.

Kapur, R. (2001) Sexcapades and the Law. *Seminar*, 505, http://www.india-seminar.com/2001/505/505%20pratiksha%20baxi.htm

Kishwar, M. (1995) When India 'Missed' the Universe. *Manushi*, 88, 26–31.

Lok Sabha Debates (1986) Volume LXX, 22 August 1986, 158–200.

Kishwar, M. (1998) Naïve outpourings of a self-hating Indian. Deepa Mehta's *Fire*. *Manushi* 109, 3–14.

Menon, N. (1995) The impossibility of 'Justice': female feoticide and feminist discourse on abortion. *Contributions to Indian Sociology* 29(1–2), 369–92.

Mohommed Ahmed Khan vs Shah Bano Begum and Others. AIR 1985. SC 945.

Narula, S. (2003) Overlooked danger: the security and rights implications of Hindu nationalism in India. *Harvard Human Rights Journal* 16, 41–68.

Pathak, Z. and Sunder Rajan, R. (1989) ShahBano. *Signs: Journal of Women in Culture and Society* 14(3), 558–82.

Raymond, N. (2003) Analysis of the bill to prevent sexual harassment of women in workplace. *Combat Law*, available online at: http://www.pucl.org/Topics/ Gender/2005/harassment.htm

Sanlaap, (1998) *Yet Another Right. A Report on a Seminar to Discus Different Views on Legalisation of Prostitution*. Kolkata: Sanlaap.

Sarkar, S. (1995) *Modern India*. New Delhi: Macmillan.

Sen, A. (1998) Radical needs and moderate reforms. In Jean Dréze and Amartya Sen (eds) *Indian Development. Selected Regional Perspectives.* New Delhi: Oxford University Press, 1–28.

Sen, S. (2000) *Towards a Feminist Politics? The Indian Women's Movement in Historical Perspective* (The World Bank: Development Research Group/Poverty Reduction and Economic Management Network, Policy Research Report on Gender and Development, Working Paper Series No. 9).

Sexual harassment of women in their Workplace (Prevention) Bill, 2003.

SL (2000) Fire! Fire! It's the lesbians! *Inter-Asia Cultural Studies* 1(3), 524–6.

Srivastava, K. and Ghosh, S. (1996) Against our will. *Humanscape* 3(4), 20–1.

State of Maharasthra vs Chandraprakash Kewalchand Jain with Stree Atyachar vs Chandraprakash Kewalchand Jain. January 1990. Cri L J 889.

Upadhyaya, C. (2000) Set this house on fire. *Inter-Asia Cultural Studies* 1(2), 374–9.

Vishakha and Anrs vs Union of India. AIR 2007 SC 3011.

VS (2000) A lesbian critique of *Fire. Inter-Asia Cultural Studies* 1(3), 519–20.

Part II

Folk Theatre–Myths Mahabharatha–Ramayana– Religious Nationalism

5 The Tragada Bhavaiya contribution to the making of Hindu identity in Saurastra

Jayasinhji Jhala

Traditional performance in contemporary Saurastra

The Bhavai tradition is a fascinating subject, a vital subject that should engage all persons concerned with India and its complex, hierarchical and democratic society. The issue of Muslim contribution to the performing arts as well as to the culture of the Saurastra peninsula has become more urgent in light of the deplorable events of the past few years in Gujarat, where Muslims have been victimized by Hindu segregationist forces. Happily, this has not happened in Saurastra, but it could.

My focus will be on the Muslim Tragada Bhavaiya role in the making of Hindu identity. The caste of Bhavaiyas claim to be both Hindu and Muslim and use both rites for their marriages, but as they bury their dead, most locals consider them Muslim despite their use of Hindu names. Bhavaiyas are performers of rural theatre for the landless community of the Kolis (Enthoven, 1920). Demographically, Kolis form a majority population in many local villages but hierarchically they represent the bottom of the social order and form the constituency of the poor, the landless peasants (Pocock, 1972; Srinivas, 1987). Yet they have been and are patrons of this ancient form of theatre. This is but one example of a Muslim community that is the custodian of Hindu values. The Mir and Langha – a caste of Muslim singers – have long been the custodians of song and dance in the royal Rajput courts of the peninsula. The Muslim salat stone carvers are, with the Hindu Sompuras, makers of Hindu temples and also of the very icons of the deities that Hindus worship. In the eighteenth, nineteenth and twentieth centuries many of the divans of Hindu kingdoms were Muslim and many Muslim kingdoms had Hindu Divans (Amarji, 1882; Tambs-Lyche, 1997, 1989). There are many additional examples that point to a long and enduring tradition of Hindu–Muslim interdependence.

The question will immediately be asked that if local society is in fact a woven fabric of Hindu and Muslim interdependence, then why has there been this terrible singling out of Muslim communities for discrimination and violence in recent years in Gujarat? Before I go on to demonstrate the degree to which Muslim Bhavaiyas contributed to the identity of Hindu patron castes, it is important to provide some historical context, which may throw some light on this matter.

Some 60 years ago, the political map of Saurastra and Gujarat was very different (Acharya, 1977; Bayley, 1970; Mayne, 1921; Rushbrook-Williams, 1958;

Walker, 1893; Wilberforce-Bell, 1916). Some 15 Muslim kingdoms lived alongside many Hindu kingdoms. There was a religious balance provided by the existence of these small principalities of Muslim and Hindu kingdoms as they demonstrated local power and culture and above all a multi-religious presence of tradition in long durée. These local Hindu and Muslim aristocracies were patrons of the performing arts and participated in the festivals of the other faiths. With the coming of Indian independence, there was the break up of the subcontinent into two nation states, one predominantly Hindu and the other Muslim. With their birth came the simultaneous erasure of the traditional multi-caste and multi-religious kingdoms. In the case of Saurastra some of the Muslim ruling families chose to migrate to the new Islamic state of Pakistan and with them went many Muslims of high standing and accomplishment. The Bhutto family of Pakistan is one such example. This made for a power vacuum. Emerging democracy further exacerbated the condition of Muslims as they are now the demographic minority in the province, unlike their centrality in former Muslim kingdoms. Over time, there has been an increasing perception amongst Muslims that they are second-class citizens in perpetuity, dwarfed by the overwhelming Hindu majority. This sense of vulnerability has been further heightened in the years following the flows of funds from the Middle East, from the states of Saudi Arabia and others. This incoming financial resource used to make madrasa has contributed towards crude and negative depictions of Muslims. They are seen as recipients from foreign powers and in consequence, as being unpatriotic.

This is the circumstance and perception in many parts of Gujarat today and it is with this backdrop that I present ethnographic evidence to suggest a close bond that Hindu and Muslim communities have had and continue to retain in the present time, as witnessed by the Bhavaiya–Koli relationship. This tradition can be further strengthened by the state support of traditional performance traditions such as the Bhavai.

Within the Bhavaiya texts, Bhavaiya performances and Bhavaiya social relationships there is a pre-nationalistic constitution for communal harmony that predates the arrival and adoption of Western democracy and its organizational principles. The Indian nation state as emerging from the idea of the nation that comprises a people who spoke a single language, lived in a particular geography, had a common religion and a common history may have limited application in Saurastra where a continual procession of people, ideas, religions and professions has taken place. Arrivals from Africa, the Arabian Peninsula, the Middle East and other parts of India suggest a dynamic procession of people and ideas. Anderson's ideas of an imagined community and Appadurai's notion of ethnoscapes and mediascapes also suggest a common inheritance that inevitably emerges and consolidates existing social communities and suggest an inevitability that seems a somewhat forced proposition (Anderson, 1991; Appadurai, 1991). The unwritten, non-Western, traditional way of coexistence seems well articulated in practice and in the Bhavaiya performance tradition. It illustrates Sally Falk Moore's ideas of accommodation, réglementation and adjustment that local society engages in (Moore, 2000) to retain the confidence of minority populations as well as those communities that were poor and without power. In looking at this earlier model it is easy to trace various types of prejudice and so it was far from perfect but the central point of this chapter is to underscore that it had room for the diversity of peoples and ideas and that these were not simply promised in a written constitutional guarantee but rather that it was lived and enforced by public acclaim and practice.

Emergence of Bhavai and its practice

The Bhavai claim to be descended from Gugali Brahmins and they were priests at Shiva and Krishna temples until the fourteenth century when the Muslim Emperor Alla-ud-din 'the bloody' converted them to Islam. Since that time they have been Bhavai performers of rural theatre in Saurastra and have been clients to their patrons Koli because it was the Koli who provided them shelter after they had been excommunicated from their former Brahmin community. Like patron peasant societies elsewhere, the players are beholden to the Kolis and they must perform in villages where there are Koli populations (Desai, 1972). They are a curious caste in their traditions and customs, retaining both Hindu and Muslim rituals with regard to marriage. They have both Muslim and Hindu names. Their homes have both Muslim and Hindu symbols such as the swastika and pictures of Hindu Gods and Goddesses and places of pilgrimage as well as Muslim symbols such as the star and crescent, pictures of the holy Kaba at Mecca and of sacred shrines such as the tombs of saints. Only the men folk are involved in the performance tradition. The Bhavaiya women are not even allowed to watch the plays or see their men perform.

Bhavai performance, like similar traditions in the Middle East and Indonesia, is a theatre and spectacle (Beeman, 1993; Peabody, 1997; Peacock, 1968). The Bhavai stage is a simple affair (Jhala and Sandall, 1981). Approximately an area 12 feet by 12 feet square is marked off by setting up bamboo poles. There is a simple cloth backdrop normally of some simple commercial flower design. This stage normally is set in the village square and behind the cloth screen is the green room, which in turn is a room of the village temple or school or some public building. There is no furniture on the set. Along one side there is an orchestra comprising tablas, drums, cymbals and reed trumpets. There are seldom more than three characters on the stage when there is extended dialogue or war scenes. For dance scenes there can be as many as six persons. Occasionally an animal such as a horse can be walked onto the stage (Jhala, 2006). Today most of the conversation is relayed through a broadcast microphone so that the protagonists rotate around the microphone that is set up at the head of the stage (Jhala, 1997).

Acting is very stylized with exaggerated and often repetitive expressions. Kings strut, ministers fawn, servants clown, ghosts and elephants sway and women flirt and dance most suggestively with an astonishing dexterity and fluidity. Gods and Goddesses are always solemn and often stiff like the stone icons of the deities in temples. Combining poetry, song and recitation of prayers and soliloquy makes up the dialogue conventions. The actors are all men and the men who play women's roles cultivate a high-pitched female accent. Gestures are exaggerated and the best dancers are very skilled in cabaret style provocations as well as in the traditional communal dances called garbas[1] and rasadas[2]. Sword play is quite unique and the sword is largely used as a flashing twirling instrument. The bamboo staff is the weapon of contact and this fighting too is highly ritualized and skilled, more akin to dance coordination and choreography than a fight.

The costumes range from the drab to the elaborate and fantastical, drawing upon urban theatre and popular cinema for their rendition of traditional and historical costumes. Bright colours and white powders are used to prepare the actors' complexion for their roles. Most carry their own make-up kits and apply their own make-up. Some own their costumes while the manager sometimes retains a stock of standard costumes. Goddesses are almost always depicted with a mukuta or coronet. They wear red or green or gold. Demons are in black and white with bloodstained faces and when wearing masks they have long hair and claw-like hands. Muslim kings and warriors always wear beards while their Hindu counterparts wear moustaches.

In early days, oil lamps and torches lit the after-dark event but today electric lighting illuminates the stage. The audience sits on all three sides of the stage and in most villages women sit together on one side. Young boys sit immediately near the stage while men sit further back. At all times members in the audience get up and go out to do various errands, sometimes they walk through the stage while the actors are performing upon it. There is a lot of interaction between the players and the audience and the players are always inserting the idea of audience orderliness as a prerequisite for a successful performance.

Content of Bhavai plays and performance gaze

Bhavai plays are about the affairs of Hindu Gods and Goddesses, legendary and historical heroes and skits about present-day caste population. Muslims feature most prominently in every performance that the Bhavai undertake but it is a restricted role. There are no traditional plays in which Muslims make up the central characters. This is probably because their clients, the Kolis, are Hindu and because these patrons wish to know about their past from the caste perspective and in which their religious traditions are celebrated which makes them comfortable in a performance where their contemporary society is depicted.

I now recount the number of times that the Muslim Bhavaiyas invoke the Hindu Gods, especially the Goddess in the course of one package of theatrical presentation, by way of ritual, dance, theatre and announcements. A performance package is normally a two-day event.

On the first day there is a negotiation about the performance and that is followed by the recitation of a story the whole duration of which could be two hours. The second and main performance occurs the following day, and is an all night affair, starting around nine in the evening and continuing until the early dawn. The evening performance has a number of elements, which when combined together, could be called a variety show. Important events include the purification of the green room, the sanctification of the village and the directions, the sanctification of the theatrical space, collection of dues, a mandatory miracle play, comic skits drawing their inspiration from everyday events and anecdotes from the lives of the villagers, folk dances, juggling, a main play that is either a play from the heroic tradition or a religious play that is based on the mythology of local Goddesses and Gods.

In studying several performances between 1979 and 2004, in the Jhalavadi villages of Gajanvav, Bavari, Baisabgadh, Kankavati, Jessada, Rajpar and Vrajpur, I found the invoking of Hindu deities on an average of eight times in the course of this two-day event.

The first time the Hindu Gods are brought to public recognition occurs immediately after the negotiation has been satisfactorily concluded. To cement and broadcast this, the manager of the troupe requests a member to announce the agreement. The announcement in fact is a declaration and a warning. It warns that if any person were to upset the performances they will be struck by the wrath of various Goddesses, village deities and Hanuman especially. The village should also know that the Bhavai performances are akin to public health initiatives and they drive disease and sickness away. This announcement is conveyed by the crier who stands above the seated audience so that he can be heard by all.

The next time the Gods are propitiated is in the green room. Here the singing of hymns and the sounding of drums supported by special long reed trumpets invoke the Goddesses and the Goddess as Maya or illusion. She is represented by an oil lamp flame, and requested to empower and enable the Muslim players to play out their roles faithfully and with conviction.

From the empowering of the players in the green room, the Goddess's presence is next actualized in the empty stage where the performances are to take place. A torch lit from the flame of the oil lamp is sprinkled with red powder that represents the Goddess. The flaming torch is brought onto the stage by a senior member of the troupe. It is waved ritually in the four directions of the universe and again serves to purify the stage, as well as the seated audience and the village and its lands that radiate out from this sanctified central spot. This ritual permeated with religious elements serves as a policing mechanism because by proclaiming the attendance and oversight of the event, by witness-bearing Gods, this poor caste can expect the cooperation necessary from the village audience to cooperate with the players and contribute towards their effort. There are no policemen in these villages, no tickets, no doors, and because the performance occurs in the open the divine presence serves to keep decorum and civility. This personal restraint allows for the excessive buffoonery that occurs in comic skits alongside other features of the traditional crowd-pleasing performance.

The next appearance of the Goddess is in the person of an actor. This occurs in the mandatory miracle play that is required by the Bhavai caste. No Bhavai performance can take place until and after the performance of the miracle play called Patai Raja. This short play suggests it is the time of navratri – the nine-day festival celebrating the Goddess – that occurs each year in Saurastra and Gujarat during which the people of this province dance. At this time Patai, the Hindu King of Gujarat, misbehaves. His bad conduct is seen in three ways. One he is drinking excessively, next he is teasing women and lastly he propositions a Brahmin woman who has come as the Goddess's messenger. This personal failure is recognized as an institutional failure and the Goddess summons the good king Mohamad Begda to destroy Patadi, the Hindu Rajput ruler.

Begda appears on stage as a typical Muslim king with a full beard and he and the beardless Patai fight. At the end of the fight scene the Goddess herself appears and kills the bad king Patai. This is done to underscore the fact that it is the Goddess herself who is replacing the bad Hindu king with the good Muslim king. The last scene in this play shows the Goddess taking her sword and drawing a circle on the stage.

Immediately thereafter the manager of the troupe enters the stage and cries out.

ACTOR: 'Hail Mahakali'
AUDIENCE ANSWERS: 'Hail'
THE ACTOR CRIES OUT: 'Hail Deities of the village'
AUDIENCE ANSWERS: 'Hail'
Actors inform 'Brothers and sisters, this short play is required by our caste. Now MahaKali will be with us throughout the night.'

Several points can be immediately extracted from this presentation. First, the most important one concerns the conduct of the Hindu Goddess. The Goddess has an agenda in meting out her verdict. She is not supportive of the bad Hindu king and transfers the custodianship of Gujarat to the good Muslim king. The Goddess wants a king who will uphold justice, protect her worshippers from kingly oppression; it matters little to her in this instance that he is Muslim rather than Patai who as a Hindu worships her.

Second, when the Goddess first appears she is presented frontally as if she were a living deity or as a worshipful icon in any Hindu temple (Eck, 1998; Tambs-Lyche, 1989). She appears in a 'stop action' freeze. Then she turns perpendicular to the audience and performs as a living avatar who is more human-like. This is when she is fighting with the king. Lastly she, as the protector, draws the circle on the stage transforming the simple village courtyard as a sanctified location fit for the Gods and other heroes.

These five occasions when the Hindu Gods are invoked are always part of any Bhavai performance. Their presence helps anchor the event and transform secular space to a performance space that is framed in a religious context. Sanctifying and purifying various spaces is vital for the performance. The fact that Muslims or Muslim/Hindus are the communicants of Hindu religiosity, sensibility and sentiment is a testimony to the Bhavaiyas dedication to be active students of the culture of their patrons. This immersion into Hindu culture is deep. To convey the sentiments of their characters to their predominantly Hindu audience requires an investment of time and knowledge of hierarchical relationships that obtain in general and in each distinctive village because each village has different caste populations that make its community.

The ShaktiMa play

The ShatktiMa play is part of the larger bardic and poetic tradition of Saurastra and conveyed in the oral storytelling performances that extend well beyond the boundaries of India and conveyed by many communities of custodians (Hitchcock, 1959). The ShaktiMa play, the main play of the evening is divided into 15 scenes. These are interspersed with comic stand-alone skits that deal with a variety of issues the material for which comes from contemporary village and town life as well as from historical past. As a consequence, the performance that begins at nine o'clock in the evening ends well after midnight. I present it in some detail because it will then enable me to demonstrate how the Bhavaiyas as custodians of Hindu religious traditions associated with the Goddess go about the business of serving this tradition to their Hindu patrons. The play also reveals the traditions of the Rajputs and from the skits we can learn about the values and aspirations and practices of various other castes. From the ShaktiMa play we are first presented with Hindu religious ideas in the main and second about some aspects of Rajput ethos and the values of other castes (Jhala, 1991; McGrath, 2004; Shah and Shroff, 1972).

1. The first scene is one where the Goddess appears as a worshipful figure standing frontally before the audience. She announces that 'From time to time when evil forces rise in the world I return to defeat them and restore order and happiness.' She stands immobile, like an icon with eyes blazing, while actors worship her with prayers and protestations. In this appearance she inhabits a location in cosmic time.

2. The second scene places the play in historical times. King Kesar Dev Makhwana, the father of Harpal Dev the Rajput hero of the play, is conversing with his astrologer and his bard. The astrologer predicts that the King has a short time to live. The bard asks the king to seek glory in keeping with the Rajput code of honour called Rajputai. After listening to this conversation, Kesar Dev announces that it is better to die in battle fighting the Muslim invader Hamir Sumra than to be found in bed by Yama, the God of Death.

3. He battles the Muslim forces in the next scene and repulses them at first. Hamir Sumra claims that Kesar Dev has an unfair advantage over him as his troops have no food and hence are not strong enough to fight properly. Kesar Devi, by an act of danvirta or generosity, tells the Muslim king to return next year as he will have a 1,000 acre planted with wheat for his army.

4. This happens and in the next encounter. Kesar Dev is defeated and killed, his country is overrun and his son the Prince Harpal Dev has to flee Sindh, the land of his forefathers and seek shelter with his sister's husband, King Karan of Gujarat. Harpal Dev decides to ride his horse south to Patan the capital of Gujarat.

5. The next scene shows King Karan of Gujarat misbehaving with the wife of his Brahman minister. The wife complains to her husband who seeks to reform the king. Angered by the minister, the King demands that the minister defends himself.

They fight and the king kills the minister. Now something strange and supernatural happens. The minister becomes the demon Barbara Bhut and he prevents the king from being able to approach his wife the queen. All attempts by the king to fight the demon and his associates are in vain. The ensuing sterility spreads to all living creatures, so there is despair in the court and in the land.

6. It is this sorrowful state that Harpal Dev the hero finds when he comes to Patan. He seeks an explanation and when told by the King of the unfortunate condition, he vows: 'To defeat the Demon and restore the kingdom to normalcy, for was he not the son of a lion and this is his dharma or duty and the reason Rajput heroes are born in this world.' King Karan agrees that Harpal Dev should undertake this task.

7. The next scene is at night and Harpal is passing by a cremation ground in search of the demon as demons frequent such places, when he hears an akashvani or celestial announcement. The cry is from a female voice and repeats the message: 'I want meat' Give.' He sees a huge arm appear from a fire on the ground. Harpal Dev in soliloquy says this is a test of my virta or bravery or my ability to make a sacrifice or 'balidan'. So he begins to cut portions of his thigh and place the meat in the giant hand. He continues until there is hardly any more that he can cut from his body and so he prepares to cut his head off and give it to this force. When he is about to decapitate himself the voice cries out, 'Stop'. The Goddess now appears as a resplendent warrior.

The restored hero and the Goddess fight with swords, the drums build up to a crescendo. At the height of the crescendo the Goddess shouts out again 'Stop, Ask' I am pleased with you.' Harpal Dev asks the Goddess for help with subduing Barbara Bhut and for 'Deviputra' or children born from the womb of the Goddess. The Goddess replies that she will agree to be his wife and the mother of his children on two conditions. The first is that he asks her advice when taking any important decision and the second that when her divinity is revealed to society she will depart to her celestial abode. Harpal agrees. The Goddess also tells him to go to the home of a Rajput nobleman by the name of Pratapsinh Solanki. Pratapsinh has a daughter called ShaktiBa. The Goddess says that she will present herself in the person of ShaktiBa. Harpal Dev should wed her. The proof that he is marrying the Goddess and not a human being will be revealed when Harpal sees red power fall from the bride's hands during the marriage ceremony. No one else will know the true identity of the bride but the bridegroom.

8. The next scene shows Harpal fighting and scattering the various demons that are part of Barbara Bhut's following. Finally, the demon in white with a bloody face comes onto the stage. The two fight. Eventually the demon is overpowered and he begs for mercy. Harpal demands that he no longer torments king Karan and in fact liberates the forces of creativity from his grasp. The demon agrees to do so. Harpal also demands from the demon the promise that whenever and wherever he needs the demon, the demon is to appear with his supporters and do his bidding.

9. The next scene shows Harpal with the reunited king and queen who are delighted with the restoration of their normal life. The king asks Harpal what he would like as a reward for this tremendous service. Harpal asks that he be given as many villages and towns as he can tie torans or festoons made of asopalav tree leaves, in the course of one night. The king agrees.

10. During the next scene we see Harpal and Barbara and ShaktiMa the Goddess traversing the night to the accompaniment of a religious song recounting this very event. The scene ends at the last village called henceforth the 'The hour of daybreak' where the hero and the Goddess tie the last festoon. Two thousand three hundred villages have the festoon of Harpal and Shakti tied within the span of one night.

11. During the next scene Harpal reports to King Karan the accomplishments of the night and departs. The king is astonished at the feat and regrets the loss of 2300 hundred villages. While in this state his wife appears. She calms him and tells him that as Harpal is her brother he will give her a gift shortly on the festive day of RakshaBandhan.

12. During the next scene of Rakshabandhan, Harpal Dev promises to give 500 villages to the queen in gift. No sooner has he made the gift, there is another 'akashvani' or celestial announcement: 'You have broken your solemn promise. You have given 500 villages without consulting me. For this your descendants will grow in number but they will continually to lose territory.' Only Harpal Dev hears the rebuke and he departs lamenting from the scene.

13. The next scene takes place in the town of Patadi, which is now the capital of the new kingdom. Outside the palace the three sons of the hero and the Goddess are playing in the courtyard with their friend, the son of the bard. Suddenly a maddened elephant in a state of '*must*' comes charging down scattering all in its path. There is great fear that the boys will be trampled to death. The Goddess appears as a mother Goddess with trident in hand and rescues the sons by lifting them out of harm's way. The orchestra and the singers proclaim that by this 'act of lifting up' or '*jhalvun*', which in Gujarati means to raise up, is how the Jhalas got their names. The three boys and their descendants thereafter were called Jhalas or those 'raised up' to life and kingship.

14. In the next scene the queen Goddess whose divine identity is now known to all appears as the great Goddess with trident in hand and prepares to leave human society and enter the ground. There is a general lamentation, the king Harpal rushes in to see the departure of his divine wife. In a last speech the Goddess stands facing the audience and grants rule of the land to her progeny and also promises the farming Kanbi population that make up a large fraction of the audience, that they too will in time get land and secure power.

15. During this speech she appears as a divine force that is acting in the present as the idol does in the temple. The audience is not only seeing a play but also the divine force in their midst. With the conclusion of the speech she descends into the ground as the avatar of the earth Goddess. This concludes the Bhavai performance

of the evening but for the final song performed by the entire cast. This song is their traditional song sung at the end of each Bhavai performance. The song speaks of them being Jhalavadis, the salutation to the land, the ruling Rajput clan of the Jhalas and the Jhala king, describes the sacred geography of the region of Jhalavad and in the final verses asks the audiences forgiveness for any mistakes that may have been made by the players during the performance.

Describing in some detail the scenes and events of agency that the Goddess demonstrates in this two-day event will now allow me to reveal the many aspects of the Hindu divine and the composition of society and its obligation that these scenes present to the largely Hindu audience. This presentation is of course being portrayed by the Muslim Bhavaiyas, who are both the custodians of the Hindu stories of the good and the great and also are the keepers of the forms and modes of representation that make this presentation both acceptable and edifying to the Hindu audience. It is the Bhavaiyas who refine and adapt these Hindu values over the centuries for the benefit of the Hindu believer and worshipper. They must cultivate a sensibility that knows the pulse and mindset of recipients and to do so they may need to develop an attitude that respects this tradition.

The Goddess appears as the champion of the following values. As Bhavani she is witness and guarantor to the verbal agreement to enact the play between the rural peasants and the Muslim Bhavaiya. In the green room she as Maya is invoked to protect the players and the performance so that it goes through without any mishap. As MahaKali she protects the stage, the audience, village and the village lands. In the miracle play called Patai she is the giver of justice and the selector of the good king over the bad, and religious affiliation is not an important criteria for consideration. In this play she also encircles the stage and in doing so sanctifies it. In the legendary epic of ShaktiMa, she first appears as Durga the great Goddess who must visit the earth periodically to bring balance to the world by subduing evil. As Kali she presents herself as the tester of male prowess, bravery and capacity when she challenges the hero to first sacrifice himself to her and later tests to see if he is brave and able to fight with her. As ShaktiMa she is the maker of polity when she assists Harpal in acquiring a kingdom. It is significant that it is imagined as an ideal kingdom won without bloodshed. Later she appears as the saviour of children when she protects the children of Harpal. Thereafter she appears as the King maker, when she grants the divine right to rule to Harpal's sons by revealing in public that they are the sons of the living Goddess and co-maker of the polity. Finally she shows herself to be the giver of fertility and fecundity, by appearing as Dharti Mata or mother earth, when she descends into the earth, the same earth that shall nurture the population that resides upon it for all time in the future. This idea of her being both Dharti Mata and Laxshmi is better seen in the popular poster which shows two white elephants, saluting her with their upraised trunks. This is reminiscent of poster images of Gaja Laxshmi who is seated on a lotus and two elephants holding gold vessels held high above her head from which flowers cascade onto the Goddess.

To convey all these aspects of the Hindu Goddesses, the Bhavai use a number of presentation devices. She appears as a Great Goddess, erect, immobile with a trident in her left hand and with her hand held open and outward in the mudra or gesture of abhaya or fearlessness. She appears as a God granting darshan as does the deity's image in a Hindu temple. She appears as an avatar where she acts like a great woman who shows proper or desirable conduct. As an avatar she slays or subdues demons and bad kings. A third device used for the Goddess is the 'akashvani' or 'sky voice' an announcement from off stage that represents the invisible Goddess. She also appears as the magical and the supernatural when she is portrayed by a prop. In this case the prop is an enormous arm that emerges from the ground accompanied by the 'akashvani'. The Goddess speaks sometimes directly to the audience, sometimes to worshippers who are actors, sometimes to other characters, human, demonic or animal, in the play. The audience receives communications in the traditionally appropriate way. Entertainment may be the primary objective of the performance but instruction, education, reverence and reflection are also attitudes that the Muslim troupe is attempting to inculcate in the audience.

This examination of theatrical performance, of its address of Hindu values and respect and recognition of the diversity of castes by the Muslim Bhavaiyas is significant. By the presentation of Hindu Gods, Muslim and Hindu kings, poets, saints, ghosts, animals and personalities and persons of all castes, the performance presents the underpinning structures and values of a tolerant and stable local society as it emerged gradually over a period of millennia. The glue of nationalization suggested by a common region, common history, common language that makes for a polity and should be the foundation for the construction of a modern society is manifestly inadequate in the context of the polity of Saurastra. Many communities came in many guises, with different skills and beliefs from different parts of India, from the Middle East and from Africa. The imagined worlds of Anderson and the ethnoscapes of Appadurai premise also a blending and merging where new forces and social formations must emerge and where the original constellation of societal players eventually disappears by morphing into new forms. This projection of societal process and evolution is inadequate in the Saurastrian historical reality. It would appear from the evidence presented in these performances, that Sally Falk Moore's suggestion that what occurs is a process of accommodation that makes space for emergent forms and entities and that a parallel 'réglementation' and adjustment gives them space to coexist in the existent and emerging hierarchy. This understanding explains the collaboration between caste groups even as they resist cohabitation and possible extinction by cohabitation.

Thus in conclusion, I repeat my earlier assertion that the Muslim Tragada Bhavaiyas of Kankavati village are exemplary champions of the Hindu ethos in the towns and villages of Saurastra and that they and their performances make vital contribution in the forging and maintaining of a tradition that welcomes difference and which in turn makes for a rich mosaic of beliefs in a hierarchical, multi-caste, multi-religious society that has historically been tolerant with regard to religion. This pre-Western, pre-democratic and indigenous model that acts as an unwritten constitution of social organization may continue to have potency and relevance in India today. In the tyranny of the majority that can result from blind democratic practice based on demographic constituencies that make for perpetual minorities, that in turn foster separatist tendencies, and a hopelessness that gives birth to unacceptable violence, there is a need for a mechanism to curb such a tendency. In this indigenous model that can be seen in Bhavaiya performance and the text of their plays, we have vital evidence and a remnant instrument of the old social contract that beckons for a re-examination. It hides in plain sight and in the vibrant repository of popular culture and its adherent entertainment industry. It is a resource that needs to be deployed again to make for a more harmonious polity.

Notes

1 Garbas are songs that are also sung when a group of people dance in a circle. These dances can be exclusively male or female or ones where both men and women take part.
2 Rasadas are 'praise songs' sung to honor gods, kings and queens and saints. They are also sung while dancing in a circle by men or women. At cartain times both men and women make up the circle of dancers. A variation of the danced rasada is called dandiyaras. Dandiya means stick and daniyaras means the 'stick dance'.

References

Acharya, I. N. (1977) 'History' in Gujarat state gazeteers: Surendranagar district Ahmedabad. In Patel G. D. (ed.) *Gujarat, India.* Gujarat State Director Government Printing Stationery Publications.
Amarji, R. (1882) *Tarikh-I-Sorath.* Translated by J. Burgess. London: Trubner and Co.
Anderson, B. (1991) *Imagined Communities: Reflections on the Origin and Spread of Nationalism.* London and New York: Verso.
Appadurai, A. (1991) Global ethnoscapes: Notes and queries for a transnational anthropology. In Fox, R. G. (ed.) *Recapturing Anthropology: Working in the Present.* 191–210. Santa Fe, NM: School of American Research Press.
Bayley, Sir Edward Clive. (1970) *The History of India as Told by its Own Historians: The Local Muhammadan Dynasties.* New Delhi: S. Chand & Co.
Beeman, W. (1993) The anthropology of theater and spectacle. *Annual Review of Anthropology* 22: 369–93.
Desai, S. R. (1972) *Bhavai: Ahmedabad.* Gujarat University: Thesis Publication Series 10.
Eck, D. (1998) *Darsan: Seeing the Divine Image in India.* New York: Columbia University Press.
Enthoven, R. E. (1920) *Tribes and Castes of Bombay.* Bombay: The Government Central Press.
Hitchcock, J. T. (1959) The Idea of the Martial Rajput. In Singer, M (ed.) *Traditional India: Structure and Change* 10–17. Philadelphia: Publications of the American Folklore Society 10.
Jhala, J. (1991) Marriage, Hierarchy and Identity in Ideology and Practice: An Anthropological Study of Rajput Society in Western India, Against a Historical Background. AD 1090–1990. Harvard University Ph.D. Thesis.

Jhala, J. (1997) Some speculations on the concept of indic frontality prompted by questions on portraiture. *Visual Anthropology* 10: 49–66.

Jhala, J. (2006) *ShaktiMa Noh Veh: The Drama of ShaktiMa.* Watertown MA: Documentary Education Resources.

Jhala, J. and Sandall, R. (1981) *Tragada Bhavai: Rural Theatre of Gujarat.* Watertown M.A: Documentary Education Resources.

McGrath, K. (2004) The Sanskrit Hero: Karna in Epic Mahabharata. In Brill's *Indological Library 20*: Brill Academic Pub.

Mayne, C. (1921) *History of the Dhrangadhra State. Calcutta and Simla.* Thacker, Spink and Co.

Moore, S. F. (2000) *Law as Process: An Anthropological Approach.* Berlin-Hamburg-Münster: LIT Verlag.

Peabody, N. (1997) Inchoate in Kota? Contesting authority through a North Indian Pageant-Play. *American Ethnologist* 24: 559–84.

Peacock, James L. (1968) *Rites of Modernization: Symbolic and Social Aspects* of *Indonesian Proletarian Drama.* Chicago: University of Chicago Press.

Pocock, D. F. (1972) *Kanbi and Patidar: A Study of the Patidar Community of Gujarat.* Oxford: Clarendon Press.

Rushbrook-Williams, L. F. (1958) *The Black Hills.* London: Weidenfeld and Nicolson.

Shah, A. M. and Shroff, R. G. (1972) The Vahivancha Barots of Gujarat. In Singer, M. (ed.) *Traditional India: Structure and Change,* 40–70. Philadelphia: Publications of the American Folklore Society 10.

Srinivas, M. N. (1987) *The Dominant Caste and Other Essays.* Oxford: Oxford University Press.

Tambs-Lyche, H. (1989) *Power and Devotion*: *Religion and Society in Saurastra.* PhD Thesis.

Tambs-Lyche, H. (1997) *Power, Profit and Poetry: Traditional Society in Kathiawar.* Western India Delhi: Manohar Press.

Walker, A. (1893) *Selections from the Records of the Bombay Government*: *Memoirs on the District of Jhalavad.* Bombay: Government Central Press.

Wilberforce-Bell, H. Capt. (1916) *History of Kathiawar.* London: William Heinemann.

6 The Mahabharata's imprint on contemporary literature and film

Pamela Lothspeich

In English-speaking metropoles, Shashi Tharoor's *The Great Indian Novel* (1989), with its serendipitous blending of epic and modern history, has been warmly received by many postcolonial critics. They typically laud Tharoor for his whimsical history, and that too in the language of India's former colonial masters. Anita Mannur relates, 'Tharoor uses "English" to subvert "English" because he is finding the strength to overcome the hegemony within the language itself' (Mannur, 1998: 82). Similarly, Kanishka Chowdhury says that 'Through his innovative use of the English language and in his effort to recover an indigenous epic "tradition," *Tharoor* effectively recovers a version of India for a portion of its people' (Chowdhury, 1995: 47).[1]

Other critics, Harish Trivedi among them, are not so impressed. Trivedi writes, 'Altogether, Indian writing in English is to Indian literature rather like the creamy layer on top of a large jug of milk … or like a crust of thin ice on the surface of a long and deep lake' (Trivedi, 1996: 239). The implication? Writers such as Tharoor and Rushdie are hardly representative of the vast number of writers from the subcontinent; what's more, they are overvalued by Western critics enamoured of the simple fact of English and the diasporic postcolonial. Both in terms of its content (Indian history through an epic lens) and its style (magical realism), *The Great Indian Novel* speaks to an elite, Western or Westernized, English-speaking audience. Tharoor, justifiably unapologetic about his use of English, says he wrote the novel primarily for Indians like himself who speak English (Tharoor, 2003: 247).

My intention is not to discredit Tharoor or to argue uncritically for the 'indigenous', but to point out that, although well known in the West, Tharoor's novel, though masterful, is hardly representative of the body of cultural production in India engaging with epic themes.[2] There Indian authors and filmmakers working in regional languages have incorporated elements of the Mahabharata to not only 'write' the nation, but also to rectify and recast it. That is, the orientation of their works is often not so much descriptive, as it is proactively political, at times in the spirit of *pragatiśīl* (progressive) literature of the 1930s and 1940s.[3] Some works are also very much invested in *local* problems and struggles ancillary to those on the national stage. And this especially separates vernacular works within India from English, diasporic works. Literature and films on epic themes were very popular in the period from the early 1970s to the early 1990s, with works such as Sunil Gangopadhyay's novel *Arjun* (1971) and Mahasweta Devi's short story 'Bhishma's Thirst' (1979), in Bengali, and Lakshminarayan Lal's play *Mr. Abhimanyu* (1971), and Shyam Benegal's film *Kalyug* (1981), in Hindi. These are stories about exile, corruption, bureaucracy and social injustice. And it is to them I turn now.

Arjun: the plight of landless East Bengali refugees

Gangopadhyay's *Arjun* gives 'epic colour' to a specific local event: the mass migration of East Bengalis into West Bengal and their resettlement on the fringes of West Bengali society. The Arjun of this novel is a Hindu refugee who makes a harrowing journey from East Bengal to Kolkata at the time of Partition.[4] Much of the narration – which shifts between first and third person – is set in the present, 1962, in a refugee colony in Dum Dum on the outskirts of Kolkata. Arjun tells his story through a series of flashbacks, mostly stream-of-consciousness ramblings. Arjun's family falls victim to the violence which broke out in East Bengal in response to the 'Great Calcutta Killings', rioting in August 1946, in which thousands perished. In its wake, Muslim peasants in East Bengal turned on Hindu landlords and traders. Meanwhile, Muslims in Bihar, Uttar Pradesh and Punjab were the victims of Hindu reprisals. When East Bengal fell to Pakistan on 15 August 1947, upwards of three million people (mostly Hindu) fled to India, the majority settling in West Bengal. Hindus continued to migrate out of East Bengal throughout the 1950s and 1960s, but especially around the time of the Bangladesh Liberation War in 1971.

Like the Pandavas, Gangopadhyay's Arjun is displaced from his ancestral land, a mere five *bighas*. Suggestive of the lac house in the Mahabharata, Arjun's home is burned to the ground by his Muslim neighbours just when his family is mourning the death of his father. A young Hindu widow is also gang raped, hacked to death, and left to die in a jute field, evocative of the rape of Draupadi. The escalating violence causes Arjun, his mother, and his mentally disturbed brother to flee to India, along the way staving off starvation and rape. Even so, Arjun does not harbour any animosity towards Muslims. Speaking of a Muslim boy from a Kolkata slum, Arjun notes that he had the 'oily look of fear. In my childhood in East Bengal, I had seen this self-same look on the faces of all my relatives and neighbours. I am sure I had had it too. The humiliation of being a minority. The mortification of not being part of things' (Gangopadhyay, 1971: 109–110). The boy reminds Arjun of himself, a boy too afraid to report the theft of his favourite pencil by a Muslim classmate.

Arjun's family and a band of refugees ultimately take possession of an unoccupied country estate. Like Krishna instructing Arjun to fulfil his dharma in the *Bhagavad Gita*, a local firebrand tells them, ' "Isn't this your own country? It was not your fault that the country was partitioned. ... You just can't afford to sit back and wait, you must fight for your rights" ' (Gangopadhyay, 1971: 62). Although reluctant at first, Arjun's family and their co-refugees ultimately settle on the property, and as a young man, Arjun becomes embroiled in their struggle to gain official rights to the land.

While one might expect that Arjun would undertake to reclaim his family's ancestral land in East Bengal in keeping with the Mahabharata, instead he remains 'in exile' in India, ironically finding his own Kurukshetra in Kolkata, and Kauravas in his Indian countrymen: Mr Dutta, the original owner of the land, Kewal Singh, a businessman whose plywood factory is adjacent to the colony, and disinterested (if not dishonest) politicians, police officers, and lawyers. The local inhabitants of West Bengal are even culpable in their almost complete disregard for the plight of the refugees, as are some of the refugees themselves who defect to the 'Kaurava' camp.

Early on in the novel, Arjun is mysteriously bludgeoned while his mother is off, uncoincidentally, listening to a recitation from the Mahabharata! The implication is that Singh orchestrated the attack since Arjun has been emboldening the refugees to press for their land rights. Mr Dutta is desperate to sell his land to Singh, since the government will only pay him a fraction of what it is worth. Singh especially covets the land of the five families closest to his factory, even offering them Rs.1,000 each to relocate – an allusion to Krishna's failed peace mission in which he asked the Kauravas for a mere five villages in order to avert war.

Singh plays the role of evil Shakuni, while local toughs Dibya and Sukhen play Duryodhan/Duhshasan and Karn, respectively. Perpetually unemployed or underemployed, they also act as cronies for Singh. There is even a Draupadi figure in Labonya, a co-refugee who aspires to be Arjun's intellectual equal, and possibly wife. Of course Sukhen is enamoured of Labonya and jealous of Arjun. And in the manner of Duhshasan, Dibya grabs her by the hair and brutally rapes her when she refuses to marry Sukhen. But unlike many folk accounts of the Mahabharata, she is not miraculously spared by Lord Krishna.

There is also a Krishna figure in the novel, Arjun's cultured college professor and mentor, Abanish Mukherjee. Fittingly, he uses his connections to assist Arjun, but does not become directly involved in the refugees' struggle. Even more central to the novel is Abanish's sympathetic sister, Shukla, who acts as a beautiful and headstrong Subhadra. Arjun is clearly drawn to her, but senses that, given his status as a refugee, she is out of his league. In Shukla's room there is a rather gratuitous allusion to the epic when Arjun strikes a bird on her calendar squarely in the eye (Gangopadhyay, 1971: 145). This, of course, references Arjun's successful piercing of a bird's eye while in training under Dronacharya.

The role of Dhritarashtra is played by Labonya's grandfather Nishi. A great patriot, Nishi lost his sight while being tortured in the days of the British. He relies on his grandson Naru to act as Sanjay, relating to him events he can't see. He ultimately sides with the 'Kauravas', advising Arjun to give in to Singh's demands: ' "The scriptures tell us that in times of danger the wise man is happy to give up half what he has. If we are to save this colony, we must give up something" ' (Gangopadhyay, 1971: 156). Naturally, Arjun is resolute, and urges the refugees not to give up an inch of their land.

Finally, Singh takes the provocative step of burning down the five homes adjacent to his property and annexing the land by constructing a wall. Arjun initially hesitates to strike back, especially given that some of his co-refugees are backing

Singh, lured by the promise of jobs. The bow metaphorically slips from his hand as he sees his friends arrayed against him. After getting nowhere with the police and a lawyer, Arjun instructs the colony to tear down the wall and rebuild the five homes. Even Arjun's loyal dog Becharam is not spared, struck dead by a hurled brick. The novel ends with Arjun seriously injured, lying in a hospital bed. The fate of the colony is uncertain.

Several points are worth mentioning in terms of the epic quality of Gangopadhyay's novel. First, whereas there is never any question as to the Pandava's right to reclaim their ancestral land in the Mahabharata, here Arjun and the refugees, particularly in the beginning, are very conflicted about the legitimacy of their claim to land they have appropriated. This is clear in an angry confrontation between Singh and the refugees. One says to Singh, ' "Why should we move our houses? This is sheer anarchy. Do you think this is your land, that you are ordering us around?" ' To which, Singh responds, ' "No, of course not. This is your land, and your forefathers' too. Why should I try to order you around?" ' (1971: 73). The reference to their 'forefathers' back in East Bengal especially stings the refugees, for they know they are uninvited guests.

There is also Arjun's nagging shame and humiliation at his refugee status, despite his academic success. In his dialect and manners, he feels he can never quite pass as a West Bengali. His fears and insecurity come to the fore one day when passing by Sealdah station with his west Bengali friends. Abanish's wife Maya exclaims, ' "Oh God, look, more refugees!" ' Arjun's thoughts: 'I felt as if somebody had hit me straight in my chest, I could feel the blood draining away from my face. I looked around. Hundreds of refugees were lying all over the platform – most of them were from the peasant class' (Gangopadhyay, 1971: 112–113). One of the girls even reminds him of the raped 'Draupadi' from his village. It is not for nothing that Maya's name means 'illusion' for she is insensitive and deluded about the predicament of the refugees.

What does Arjun blame for the tragedy in Bengal? Religious distinctions among the people of India. He says that if he were involved in politics, he would have as his highest priority 'the abolition of religious distinctions among the people of India'. And not only that, the people of East and West Bengal should 'stop thinking of themselves as Hindus or Muslims, but as Bengalis'. It is not religion but 'cohesion of culture' that he says binds them together (Gangopadhyay, 1971: 110). This may strike some as an odd comment in light of the 'Hindu-ness' of the Mahabharata, but it only shows the secular and progressive outlook of Gangopadhyay's novel.

Kalyug: internecine conflict in Mumbai's industrial world

In the context of post-Independence cinema, Geeta Kapur has argued that it is a hybrid form that brings in the archetypal and iconoclastic, and simultaneously works to 'excavate mythic material; even more to exorcise mythologized realty' (Kapur, 1987: 80). Like *Arjun*, Shyam Benegal's film *Kalyug* 'excavates mythic material' not to debunk it, but to strategically place reality and myth in playful apposition. The screenplay was co-written by Benegal and the Kannada playwright Girish Karnad, known for his plays inspired by myth and history. Although *Kalyug* wasn't an immediate commercial success, it did garner critical acclaim. Stripped bare of melodramatic flourishes and the ubiquitous *nāc-gānā* (song and dance) of commercial films, *Kalyug* is a suspenseful drama that can captivate even an ambitious audience unfamiliar with the Mahabharata. Like *Arjun*, *Kalyug* attempts to capture the full analogy of the epic war, while scaling it down with fewer characters (some of them composites) and a compressed time frame.

When the film was released, Indira Gandhi had recently swept back into office as prime minister, inheriting the India of her father Nehru who had adhered to a strict protectionist economic policy. Nehru's goal had been to quickly modernize India on a socialist model using Soviet-style five-year plans. Building the industrial and agricultural sectors was paramount. Moreover, in 1981 India was still reeling from Indira Gandhi's Emergency of 1975–77, when she shut down state governments to stifle opposition, and in the process, severely curtailed civil liberties.

The central conflict in *Kalyug* is between the three sons of the deceased Puranchand (Pandu) – Dharmraj (Yudhishthir), Balraj (Bhim) and Bharatraj (Arjun) – and the two sons of wheelchair-bound Khubchand (Dhritarashtra) – Dhanraj (Duryodhan) and Sandeepraj (Duhshasan). Both sets of brothers are wealthy steel industrialists in Mumbai, vying for lucrative government contracts. Khubchand and Sons benefits from the sage advice of one of their top executives, Karan, played masterfully by Shashi Kapoor. Meanwhile, Puranchand, Dharmraj and brothers receive sporadic counsel from 'Grandfather Bhishamchand' and moral support from Kishanchand (Amrish Puri), a detached Krishna-like figure. Bharat marries the latter's daughter, appropriately named Subhadra. While courting, Bharat and Subhadra actually go to see a *kathakali* dance drama which enacts Bhim's slaying of Dushasan! Draupadi is evoked by Dharmraj's wife, Supriya (Rekha); Karan once dated her and now secretly pines for her, evidenced by the photo of her next to his bed.

Kalyug is by no means a rousing mythological. The characters standing in for the Pandavas are seemingly as culpable and morally tainted as those representing the Kauravas. The Arjun-inspired character, Bharat, is not a noble warrior and pious devotee; rather he is as greedy, driven, and calculating as his cousin Dhanraj (king of wealth), played by a brooding Victor Banerjee. When he learns that his cousins have been awarded their fourth large contract from the government by secretly acquiring special machinery, allowing them to underbid them, Bharat engages in an all-out battle to steal the contract away from them – or at least ruin them in the process.

Puranchand's sons appeal and manage to steal the contract away from their cousins. Meanwhile, Grandfather Bhisham tries in vain to avert a calamity by assuaging Dhanraj. But Dhanraj merely repeats his constant refrain throughout the film 'What's done is done', and presses forward, conspiring with Karan. They humiliate Savitri (Kunti) by inviting the biological father of her sons, Swami Premanand, to her home. Unable to conceive with Puranchand, she bore four illegitimate sons with him. Bhisham is abashed and withdraws from Khubchand

Figure 6.1 Dhanraj to Karan: 'You're number one now.'

and Sons. Dhanraj then appoints Karan 'general' saying 'You are number one now' (Figure 6.1). *Duryodhan appoints Karn general.*

Karan's next strategy is to engage a labour leader, Bhavani Pandey, played with great aplomb by Om Puri, to incite the factory workers of Puranchand, Dharmraj and brothers to strike. *Krishna preaches that one should fulfil his dharma and act.* Balraj strikes back by bringing in his own strong man, Mhatre, who tries to placate the workers. But violence escalates when Mhatre's 'goondas' kill one of the strikers in Pandey's camp. However, Pandey is successful in pressing for a lockout.

Meanwhile, Bharat is called back from his honeymoon to help deal with the crisis. He negotiates directly with Pandey, brokering a deal to end the strike. Having miscalculated in his gamble on Pandey, Karan then hatches a new 'action plan' to frame the 'Pandavas'. In a pregnant *film-noir* moment, he calls his henchmen, his voice sombre and his face dramatically framed by darkness, and tells them to hijack a shipment of imported steel bound for his rivals' factory. After the 'Pandavas' have alerted the authorities over the 'theft', he has the hijackers deposit the steel at the same factory, leaving the impression that the 'Pandavas' have committed fraud. At the same time, Sandeepraj meets his tragic end, presumably by a heart attack. Lurking outside the factory gates in a blood-red shirt, Balraj unexpectedly stumbles upon Sandeep, whom he follows in a high-speed chase. When Balraj finally confronts him, Sandeep is so shaken that he crumples at his feet unconscious (Figure 6.2). *Bhim slays Duhshasan, rips open his chest, and drinks his blood!*

Karan then fittingly consoles a distraught Dhanraj who considers Sandeep's death cold-blooded murder. Bharat and his brothers, meanwhile, are faced with a major setback when their first samples are rejected, thanks to a manager who has defected. They are also hounded by tax inspectors who are literally at their door. They humiliate Supriya/Draupadi by rifling through her 'unmentionables'

Figure 6.2 Sandeep crumples in Balraj's arms; the first 'Kaurava' perishes.

Figure 6.3 Karan learns of his parentage.

in a mock 'disrobing'. Desperate, Savitri takes counsel from Bhisham who convinces her to tell Karan the truth about his parentage. Savitri does do so, urging Karan to broker peace with his brothers. Karan maintains his steely exterior, dressed in black against a dark terrace (Figure 6.3). Later, alone in his room, he curls into in the foetus position, tormented. *Karan agonizes over Kunt's revelation about his birth.*

Now Khubchand and Sons' three other contracts are stalled and Bharat is making a bid to gain a significant number of shares on his rivals' board. The stakes become higher as Bharat vows to slit his nemesis Karan's throat, and Dhanraj sends his cronies to murder Bharat in a staged car accident. But Dhanraj's plan is

Figure 6.4 Bharat is spared from the '*cakravyuha*'. (Bharat, Sunil, Savitri and Supriya.)

foiled as a guilt-ridden Karan has anonymously tipped off Savitri (Figure 6.4) . Still, he is unable to save Balraj's son Sunil, an idealistic executive-in-training, sent in Bharat's stead. *Abhimanyu becomes ensnared in a* cakravyuha *(circular battle formation) from which he cannot escape!* In an angry tirade to Karan, Bharat, Arjun-like, vows to avenge Sunil's death.

Dhanraj discovers Karan's betrayal, and Karan hastily resigns as Dhanraj's creditors are closing in. Karan then appeals to Bhisham for guidance, anguishing over his illegitimacy and blaming him for his present quagmire. Bhisham advocates truth as the remedy, but Karan fires back, 'You've made my life miserable by uncovering the truth!' Bhisham urges him to take responsibility for his life, and his part in the striker's death. Karan then hastily departs and, in a master stroke by Benegal and Karnad, is struck dead while changing a flat tyre on the side of the road! *Karan is unethically slain by Arjun as he tries to extract his chariot wheel from the mud.* Next, Savitri, in a pathos-filled scene, confesses to her three sons that they have a brother – and unbeknownst to her – a brother whose death Bharat engineered.

Overwrought and demoralized, Dhanraj finally commits suicide alone in his home. *Duryodhan emerges from the lake in which he is hiding; Bhim crushes his thighs and decimates him!* The three elders decamp to an ashram in the Himalayas, while Bharat despairs in a drunken stupor, caressed by Supriya. And in the final scene, young Parikshit, son of Dharmraj and Supriya, dramatically returns from boarding school, taking his rightful place as heir to the family, like his namesake, the lone Pandava survivor (Figure 6.4).

The film thus cynically exposes the greed, materialism and corruption of the corporate elite in Mumbai. It evokes the dark pessimism of Indira Gandhi's post-Emergency India. And it suggests a breakdown in family cohesion in modern, urban India, as cousins ruthlessly compete and even kill to attain their ends.

Mr. Abhimanyu: the *cakravyuha* of corruption and bureacracy

Whereas *Arjun* and *Kalyug* obliquely reference the main events of the Bharata war, other modern works allude to fragments of epic material, typically emotionally potent scenes, themes, or characters. This is the case with Lakshmi Narain Lal's play *Mr. Abhimanyu* which, as its title signals, uses the *cakravyuha* as a metaphor for modern society, its political system and corporate world fully immersed in the *kaliyuga*. The play is very much in the experimental mode of other literary works from that period, its realism overlaid with strange coincidences and symbolic meanings. The action of the play is dream-like, the dialogue cryptic and the tone dark and foreboding.

The protagonist of the play caught in the *cakravyuha* is Mr Rajan. Like Abhimanyu in the Mahabharata, his father has groomed him to enter the field of government bureaucracy, but has not taught him how to extricate himself from a web of corruption and resist the temptation for bribes. Unlike Abhimanyu's father, however, Mr Rajan's father, a lawyer, is thoroughly venal and materialistic. He urges his son to accept a promotion from Collector to Commissioner in exchange for ignoring the tax fraud committed by the owner of Kajariwal Sugar Mills. His father even represents the fraudulent Mr Kajariwal, though Rajan fears he may blackmail his father. Rajan's wife, Vimal, is equally money-grabbing and concerned about station.

To the extent that there are 'Kaurava' and 'Pandava' factions in the play, they are characters who represent aspects of Mr Rajan himself who is embroiled in internal conflict. In this regard, *Mr. Abhimanyu* has much in common with another play with epic undertones, Surendra Verma's *Draupadi* (1970), which I have discussed elsewhere (Lothspeich: 2007). The 'Kauravas' in Lal's play are represented by the corrupt politician, Gaya Dutt, who has recently won a seat in the state parliament through illicit means. Dutt is pressuring Rajan to unseal Kajariwal's godown and drop his case against Kajariwal for not paying his taxes in 13 years – the same number of years as the Pandavas' exile. Dutt even threatens to bring a trumped-up corruption case against him.

The 'Pandavas' are represented by Mr Atman, an upstanding labour organizer, who has been defeated by Dutt in the recent election. He pushes Rajan to persevere in his case against Kajariwal. Especially given that Atman's name means soul or self, it is clear that both characters are essentially aspects of Rajan's psyche. This is dramatically shown in Act 2 when first Atman and then Dutt emerge from darkness on either side of Rajan. The protagonist's conflict is essentially internal as he debates whether to acquiesce to a corrupt system or to fight that very system. The British are the ones blamed for India's endemic corruption and burdensome bureaucracy. Mr Atman: 'Red-tapism is all we have learnt from the British. Bureaucracy has vitiated politics too' (Lal, 1971: 22). It is not for nothing that Vimal's friend, the catty Mrs Rathor, swoons over Atman's excellent English!

Rajan recognizes that his profession is 'slavery', and the system a 'quagmire' (Lal, 1971: 27). When he asks Atman how he can escape the system, the latter responds that he has to create his own path, though he later calls man 'a blind fungus … a cosmic waste of matter' (Lal, 1971: 49). Escape from the *cakravyuha* is elusive as Atman eventually begs for Rajan to kill him. He does not.

Ultimately, Rajan caves in to Dutt's blackmail and has Kajariwal's mill unsealed, but then types his resignation letter. Just then Atman returns with damning evidence, a letter from Kajariwal offering him a bribe, and a letter from Gaya Dutt ordering his assassination. Shortly thereafter Atman departs, a gunshot outside announcing his death. Dutt and Rajan's father declare it a suicide, but Rajan calls it murder, naming Dutt and then himself as the triggerman. 'I can go out of this system now' (Lal, 1971: 55), he concludes, but in the end he seems as trapped as ever. He gives a monologue in which he rails at Atman, his weakened moral self. In the end Rajan is left all alone though surrounded by those celebrating his promotion.

Like *Kalyug*, *Mr. Abhimanyu* gives a bleak assessment of governmental bureaucracy in postcolonial India. Here it is the political system itself that is tainted, while in the *Kalyug*, it is India's powerful industrialists. The play encourages one to have the moral fortitude to rise above the system, all the while hinting that such efforts may well be in vain.

'Bhishma's Thirst': the struggle for social justice among the rural poor

Mahasweta Devi has been one of the most innovative and successful of contemporary writers taking inspiration from the epic. In the manner of Buddadev Bose in his verse plays on the Mahabharata from the late 1960s and early 1970s, she has also written several short stories about the epic ('Panchakanya', 'Kunti o Nishadi' and 'Souvali') in which she improvizes and invents new scenes and characters: ordinary widows of the Kurukshetra war, the daughter-in-law of the tribal woman who burned in the lac house, and the bastard Yuyutsu's mother. Devi thus straddles two trends in epic appropriation – realistic retellings of the epic and thematically inspired original tales.

Devi takes up the plight of the dispossessed rural poor in two Mahabharata-tinged short stories, 'Bhishma's Thirst' and 'Draupadi'. The latter is about a Naxalite tribal woman, Dopdi, interrogated by an Indian army officer. Western readers were introduced to this story largely through Gayatri Spivak's translation and analysis of it. In her reading of it, Spivak links the heinous army officer with a 'First-World scholar in search of the Third World' (Spivak, 1988: 179).

'Bhishma's Thirst' alludes to the scene in the Mahabharata in which Arjun first fells Bhishma in battle through morally questionable means, then later lovingly offers water to his parched granduncle as he lies reclining on a bed of arrows. He does this by shooting an arrow into the ground which causes a stream of water, *gangajal* in fact, to spring up to quench his thirst. Like his namesake, Devi's Bhishma has never married, foregoing a sweetheart so that he could raise his adoptive son Arjun. He is not a royal, but a poor farmer who rents the skies with his pleas for water – both for himself and for his scorched fields. 'The tips of the withered *urid* and *kalai* pulses trembled fearfully like beggar children' (Devi, 1979: 86).[6] He must pawn his fields to survive.

While Bhishma's winter crops utterly fail, his wealthy neighbours' fields are bright green, thanks to their large tube wells. Childlike despite his years, 'Bhishma, with his white head of hair, stood there and cried all of the time' (Devi, 1979: 87–8). Pitcher in hand, he strains to remember the rain-granting mantras. From January until April, 'the sky's eyes have been dry' (Devi, 1979: 88). Bhishma too has withered, sick with worry and anxiety. Now the spring paddy has been planted, but Bhishma's fields are still dry. Dismissive of Bhishma's mantras, Arjun thrusts his hoe into the soil and lashes out at Bhishma. But life-giving water does not spring from the ground. He merely rails about how their attempt to get their own tube well has been frustrated. In spite of their best efforts – an application and endless trips to a governmental office – a new well was sunk on another neighbour's property. Bhishma's prayers are finally answered and the rains come, but they flood the fields. Then Bhishma dies after Arjun, in a fit of rage over the spoiled crops, strikes him in the leg with his hoe, accidentally killing him. With his head in Arjun's lap, Bhishma dies still thirsty, though not for water – for paddy.

As in the other three works described above, the protagonists of this story are ironically and effectively juxtaposed to their epic counterparts. In this case, the effect is to expose the perpetuation of class-based social inequities in rural India as well as inefficacy of government bureaucracy.

In Sanskrit poetic theory, the Mahabharata has traditionally been hailed as a prime example of poetry imbued with *sāntarasa*, the aesthetic mood of peace, or equanimity. The idea is that one should remain resolute and detached even in the face of the breakdown of *dharma* in the depraved, corrupt *kaliyuga*. None of the works treated here invite such a positive interpretation, nor do they display the kind of disinterested, selfless action Krishna advocates in the *Bhagavad Gita*. The villains of these works are closer to Tagore's anti-hero Sandip in *Ghare baire* (Home and the World) who announces, ' "Who wants fruit? … We go by the Author of the *Gita* who says that we are concerned only with the doing, not with the fruit of our deeds" ' (Tagore, 1915: 59). Thorns, and not fruit, are what Sandip claims to want. However, Sandip is disingenuous for there are many a fruit he craves – glory, power, wealth, women and of course political freedom.

The four vernacular works discussed above share certain assumptions about epic content: the past is illustrative; it can be used to make sense of and improve upon the present – in terms of the nation and sometimes, just as importantly, in terms of specific, local contexts. The themes, problems, conflicts and personalities of the epic are timeless and can find expression in ever new forms, relevant to the present. And yet, if these works are any indication, the logic of *dharmic* morality in the epic seemingly does not hold sway in contemporary globalized India.

Notes

1 Some, Western critics, however, are not especially fond of epic-inflected works. John W. Hood gives short shrift to *Kalyug* whose intrigues he calls 'singularly dull'

(Hood, 2000: 209), and a critic for *The New York Times Review of Books* says of *The Great Indian Novel* that while parts of it are ingenious and even inspired, 'much of it, frankly, is simply dull' (Gorra, 1991: 16).

2 Tharoor once explained why he was drawn to the Mahabharata: '[It] struck me as a work of such contemporary resonance, it helped crystallize my own inchoate ideas about issues. I wanted a vehicle to transmit some of my political and historical interests in the evolution of modern India' (Tharoor and Sen, 1990: 18).

3 It is beyond the scope of this chapter to deal with realist reworkings of the epic in modern languages, of which there are many. I discuss this in my forthcoming monograph, *Epic Nation: Reimagining the Mahabharata in the Age of Empire*.

4 Another Partition novel *Epar Gangā opar Gangā* by Jyotirmoyee Devi, was originally titled *Itihāse strīparv* (The Book of Women in History), about a young Hindu girl raped in East Bengal. Its chapter headings are inspired by the Mahabharata: 'Ādi Parv', 'Anuśāsan Parv' and 'Strī Parv'. For Devi, the title 'Strīparv' in disingenuous, for the book relates the history of men by men (Jyotirmoyee Devi xxviii).

5 I have, for the most part, used the translations as given in the film's subtitles. But I have made some slight revisions to them.

6 I would like to thank Meenakshi Dutt for helping me with the translations from this story.

References

Benegal, Shyam (director and writer) (1981) *Kalyug*, DVD, Eros, 1981.

Bose, Sugata and Ayesha Jalal (1998) *Modern South Asia: History, Culture, Political Economy*, Lahore: Sang-e-Meel Publications.

Chowdhury, Kanishka (1995) 'Revisioning history: Shashi Tharoor's *Great Indian Novel*', *World Literature Today*, Winter, 69(1): 41–8.

Devi, Jyotirmoyee (1967, 1995) *The River Churning* [*Epar Gangā opar gangā*], trans. Enakshi Chatterjee, Delhi: Kali for Women.

Devi, Mahasweta (1979) 'Bhishmer pipasa', in *Stanodayini o anyanya galpo*, Kolkata: Nath Publishing House.

Gangopadhyay, Sunil (1971, 1987) *Arjun*, trans. Chitrita Banerji-Abdullah, Delhi: Penguin.

Gorra, Michael (1991) [Review of *The Great Indian Novel*], *The New York Times Book Review*, March 24: 16, col. 1.

Hood, John W. (2000) *The Essential Mystery: The Major Filmmakers of Indian Art Cinema*, London: Sangam Books.

Kapur, Geeta (1987) 'Mythic material in Indian cinema', *Journal of Arts and Ideas* 14–15 (July–December): 79–108.

Lal, Lakshminarayan (1971) *Mister Abhimanyu*, trans. Suresh Kohli, Delhi: Motilal Banarsidass.

Lothspeich, Pamela (2007) 'The *Kaliyug* of modernity in Surendra Verma's *Draupadi*', in Malashri Lal and Sukrita Paul (eds) *Interpreting Homes: South Asian Literature*, Delhi: Pearson Education.

Mannur, Anita (1998) ' "Back" translation in a postcolonial Indian context: language construction in the works of Shashi Tharoor and Salman Rushdie', *World Literature Written in English*, 37(1–2): 80–92.

Pandey, Gyanendra (2001) *Remembering Partition: Violence, Nationalism and History in India*, Contemporary South Asia Series 7, Cambridge: University of Cambridge Press.

Spivak, Gayatri Chakravorty (1988) 'Draupadi', in *Other Worlds: Essays in Cultural Politics*, New York: Routledge.

Tagore, Rabindranath (1915, 2005) *Home and the World*, trans. Surendranath Tagore, London: Penguin.

Tharoor, Shashi (1989) *The Great Indian Novel*, London: Viking.

—— (2003) 'A bedeviling question in the cadence of English', in *Writers on Writing, Volume II: More Collected Essays from The New York Times*, New York: Times Books.

—— and Sudeep Sen (1990) 'Interview [with Shashi Tharoor]', *India Currents*, 4(8): 18–19, 25, 41.

Trivedi, Harish (1996) 'India and post-colonial discourse', in Harish Trivedi and Meenakshi Mukherjee (eds), *Interrogating Post-colonialism: Theory, Text and Context*, Shimla: Indian Institute of Advanced Study.

7   India

Religious nationalism and changing profile of popular culture

Ram Puniyani

Introduction

During the last two and a half decades, the political scenario in India has undergone a sharp transformation. This has been running parallel to the process of globalization at the economic level and the emergence of a uni-polar world at the political level. At the political horizon in India, while on the one hand we witnessed the rise of job losses and industrial closures, a rise in unemployment, a change in labour practices for the worse and a decline in the labour movement, on the other hand there was a greater hegemony of newer types of production processes, the rise of information technology industry and the affluence of a small section of the population. Sections of society started being affluent, a section of the middle class benefited from this trickle down affluence while a larger section started getting trapped in the pangs of destitution. This deprived section formed the major chunk of the foot soldiers of the pogroms, unleashed by religious nationalism. The dominance of religious nationalism ran parallel with the change in different facets of popular culture. The dominant politics during this phase 'manipulated the social mechanisms, used public platform for percolation of its cultural nationalism, through the "saffronization" of text books... The conservatism in society went up by leaps and bounds. Even earlier the relay of the serials Ramayan and Mahabharat had created a fertile ground for the rise of religiosity and blind faith, which was to see its furtherance in the coming up of innumerable babas, Acharyas and Sri Sri's who ruled the roost at cultural level' (Puniyani, 2008: 11).

Change in political paradigm

The major political outfit which spearheaded this social phenomenon for obliterating the democratic space and repressing the weaker sections of society is the vehicle of Hindutva politics, the RSS combine. At the core of this politics is Rashtriya Swayamsevak Sangh (RSS) (National Volunteers Organization), an organization, with the agenda of building a Hindu nation by abolishing the secular democracy. This organization has a plethora of subordinate organizations, each devoted to one section of the people and one aspect of social, economic and political life. It dictates the agenda at the cultural and political levels. It has Bharatiya Jan Sangh (BJP) (political), Vishwa Hindu Parishad (VHP) (World Hindu Council) for the propagation of a Brahminical version of Hinduism, Vanavasi Kalyan Ashram (for Hindutvasing Adivasis [tribals]) and Bajarang Dal (storm troopers) amongst others. It has infiltrated the bureaucracy, police, judiciary, media and education to slowly put its version of right-wing politics.

The main politics which was seen during this period began with some dalits converting to Islam in the temple town of Meenakshipuram in the south, when Hindutva organizations raised hue and cry against conversion and started the process of crystallization around religious identity. Around the same time the anti-dalit (literally broken people, used for India's ex- and current untouchables) violence was initiated in Gujarat against the affirmative action for them. Later, the Shah Bano movement by groups of orthodox Maulanas and of the Muslim population contributed grist to the mill of rising communalization. The RSS combine strongly attacked this movement and at the same time began its mobilization work amongst the upper caste, elite sections of society. Its mobilization around religious symbols, through Rath Yatras (chariot processions) paid substantial dividends.

This raised the issue of the Babri Masjid, with the claim that there was a Ram Temple there, which was demolished by the Muslim aggressor, Babar. This myth, without any historical basis, was widely propagated and it became part of a social common sense and helped the RSS combine to reach larger sections of society. With the promise of the implementation of the Mandal Commission[1] another affirmative reservation for the other backward classes, the Hindu right wings' Ram Temple movement became stronger and on 6 December 1992, the Babri Masjid was demolished in a well-planned manner. This led to a massive anti-minority violence in different parts of the country.

To co-opt the tribal, Adivasis, the RSS combine intensified its activities in the remote areas, spreading hate against Christian missionaries, on the grounds that they were doing forcible conversion. On the same pretext, the Australian Pastor, Graham Steward Stains, working amongst the leprosy patients of Keonjhar, Orissa, was burnt alive and scattered acts of violence against Christian missionaries and attacks on Christians became a regular feature of political life of the country. This simultaneously resulted in the polarization in the society and the BJP became politically stronger. It governed the country from 1996 and was in power in an interrupted way for six years. In 2004, it was defeated in elections. Meanwhile during its rule, in Gujarat, the massive anti-Muslim pogrom was launched by the RSS combine leading to the death of over 2000 Muslims. Today this right-wing politics has 'successfully' been able to raise various emotive issues, around the national anthem, cow slaughter and the propaganda about 'threat posed to Hindus' by Muslim terrorists.

These political processes were preceded and accompanied by the change in different aspects of popular culture: social common sense, religiosity, films, television serials, intercommunity relations and more particularly the increasing ghettoization of minorities.

Politics manipulating popular culture

Culture is a phenomenon which mainly evolves with different social, economic changes and interaction with diverse sections of people, far and near. There is another instance also which affects culture and that is the political dominance of external or internal forces, which deliberately concoct aspects of culture, which can help them either to come to power or sustain the power. One recalls that British rule in India did bring forward a change in culture by various mechanisms. While some of these were due to the economic and educational changes, some of them were consciously planted to ensure the sustenance of their rule here. Similarly Hitler's ascendance was preceded and accompanied by a set of cultural manipulations in the field of painting, music and education, in particular which prepared the ground for the rise of fascist ideology and then the fascist onslaught on democracy leading to genocide.

In India apart from other socio-economic changes, the rise of RSS combine has been spearheading the cultural manipulation of the society. RSS as such calls itself a cultural organization. Its infiltrating influence in most of the aspects of social life has had a tremendous boost with the Ram Temple movement, which led to the demolition of Babri Masjid. The popular culture has been influenced by different mechanisms, TV serials, books, media, the movement for demolition of Babri Masjid – all these have been the building blocks of the cultural manipulation of right-wing Hindutva movement.

This chapter takes up with the backdrop of the impact on politics of the RSS combine and goes on to analyse different aspects of popular culture, the way they have changed gradually and how there has been a qualitative transformation in the paradigms of this culture. The essay takes up the social thinking process, the process through which the minorities, particularly Muslims and also Christians have been targeted by the communal onslaught. It then goes on to elaborate the rising religiosity of the people over these decades and the phenomenon of God men who are the major cult figures ruling the popular psyche. Education has contributed to the formation of ideas and this curriculum has been saffronized overtly and covertly over a period of years. Today while technology has high acceptability the rational thinking is being pushed to the backyards, giving way to faith-based knowledge and ascendance of blind faith in various arenas of social life and culture.

The social thinking process, social common sense has also been taken up for treatment here because this social common sense has ensured a silent sanction to communal violence, leading to post-violence ghettoization and its consequent impact on the syncretic traditions, which are being attacked and being pushed back and the identity of the people is changing drastically under the influence of this cultural manipulation. The aim of this has been to deconstruct the aspects which today in India are having the impact on popular culture. The Indian identity which was the dominant identity in the decades of 1950s to 1970 is being challenged on the ground by religious identity.

Social common sense

The aspect of culture which affects people's relationship with 'other' communities, is greatly affected by the prevalent notions about the "others". 'Hate other' has been at the root of communal violence. The communal violence generally gets a social sanction because of the prevalence of biases and misconceptions about the 'other' community. This set of understandings, prevalent and uncritically accepted, will be called as 'social common sense' by us. The social atmosphere was dominated by the rising hate and suspicion for the 'other' community. This is the basis of communal violence and later leads to the ghettoization of communities. Most of the facets of social and political life are permeated by the social common sense, targeted especially against minorities.

The commonly held perceptions amongst both the religious communities of Hindus and Muslims started building up from late nineteenth century, after the landlord elements felt threatened by the incipient rise of Indian Nationalism. The processes were more or less similar but with opposite effect amongst the communities.

The Hindu communalists adopted the view propagated by the colonial masters about the nature of medieval rule and the Muslims, 'that medieval rulers in India were anti-Hindu, tyrannized Hindus, and converted them forcibly' (Chandra, 1989: 412). This feeling developed, building more intensely over a period of time and the 'sins' of Muslim rulers were transferred on to the Muslim community of the day. With its formation in 1925, the RSS developed its indoctrination module in which Muslims were projected as the central enemies. RSS *shakhas* (branches) taught the young cadres that the Hindu nation has been repeatedly conquered by aliens, particularly the Muslims and then by the British (interestingly British are not presented as Christians in this historiography). And that India is being ruled by pseudo-secularists like Nehru who are appeasing Muslims, 'The threats remain because the present state is ruled by traitors to Hindu nation, "pseudo secularists" who "appeased" Muslims in their pursuit for a political vote bank' (Basu *et al.*, 1993: 36).

All through the freedom movement and more so after the assembly elections of 1937 when the Muslim League and the Hindu Mahasabha lost elections, both these started spreading the venom of propaganda against the 'other' community. After Independence it had a relatively 'quiet' period lasting from the 1950s to 1960s. During this period also the communal polarization kept taking place through the RSS shakhas, through molecular permeation, and also through sections of the media and other means of communication. In the decade of the 1980s on the one hand we saw the rise in the intensity of communal violence, and on the other hand the worsening of this demonization of Muslim minorities.

Bharatiya Jansangh (BJS), previous incarnation of BJP, had taken up communalization at the political level. Its demands at one level did get propagated amongst a section of people to begin with. 'Almost all the issues he [Advani] raised such as, "minorityism," "pseudo secularism," "cow-protection," "article 370" ... were very dear to BJS' (Puri, 2005: 2). These were adopted by the BJP and were converted into a mass consciousness through political agitations and campaigns. In a way the ongoing process through RSS shakhas received a boost through these programmes of BJP.

History was the core around which the social common sense was built. Savarkar modified the communal historiography started by the British and presented a glorious picture of ancient India, 'Every village has its temples, in all districts are sacrifices performed; every family has plenty of wealth; and people are devoted to religion' (Savarkar, 1969: 41–2). This was counterpoised to 'suddenly, rudely, unprovoked invading Muslims put an end to all that. The early Muslim period saw brief incursions by Muslims bent on the destruction of Hindu temples' (Nussbaum, 2007: 212). This was the base around which the history of medieval India was constructed. To this was added forcible conversion by sword, atrocities on Hindu women by Muslim kings and the imposition of *Jazia*.

This projected history was propagated and its reflections in present day Muslim community were intensified through various means. The full spectrum of the communal common sense includes many more perceptions which related to large Muslim families, their orthodox nature and their eating habits, like eating beef, some of them being butchers by profession, slaughtering cows and lately being terrorists. The last one has been projected and implanted in the social psyche, more so after 9/11, 2001.

> That pertains to the Babri Masjid as the British Gazetteer A.F. Beveridge put the unfounded question mark that there might have been a temple at the site where the mosque is located. There are infinite examples of Hindu kings destroying Hindu Temples. There are also instances where Muslim Kings destroyed mosques, like Aurangzeb destroying the Golconda mosque when tribute was not paid by the ruler of Golconda, Tana Shah for a few consecutive years. Hindu kings had the initial mosques made on the Malabar Coast. Tipu Sultan went on to repair the temple Shrirangpatanam, which was destroyed by the retreating Maratha armies.
>
> (Puniyani, 2007: 61)

Similarly, conversion to Islam in this country is seen as the act of the kings while in reality Islam spread in India because of the humane teachings of Sufi saints. Surely some individuals and landlords did convert to Islam out of fear or expectation of reward but those are few compared to the Shudras[2] who embraced Islam in large numbers. Many Islamic/ Hindu communities imbibed the traditions from both the religious communities, Navayat[3] Muslims of Kerala, Mevs[4] of Rajasthan are examples of that. Today the source of the origin of many of our traditions, food and customs cannot be attributed to any one particular religious source. We have syncretic traditions in all streams of our life. Celebrating diversity is one way of looking at it. As such communities do live with each other, constantly interacting and transforming their norms of life. It cannot be related just to religion.

The freedom movement too saw the rise of Hindu and Muslim communalism. Elite landlord sections were the ones to begin these communal streams which were later joined in by some middle-class intellectuals, who provided the ideological elaboration for the communal politics. It was the British goal to have a foothold in South Asia due to which they were keen on partitioning the country and the Muslim and Hindu communal streams played into their hands.

These perceptions went unchallenged for many decades and have been unshakably planted in the social thinking. It is the base around which communal violence takes place and the post-violence insecurity amongst the minorities, the exclusionism of dominant communal thinking leads to the formation of Muslim ghettoes in the cities which have suffered the violence and in a more subtle form in other cities.

Religiosity

Religiosity is probably the basic ground of popular culture in many societies. And this determines many political issues in society. The changing profile of religiosity to which we now turn is probably the most obvious impact during the rise of religious nationalism. There was a constant harp on religiosity in the social space from the decade of the mid-1970s; this was also reflected in the films in particular. 'The widespread success of the religious mythological films of Bombay had to an unprecedented extent removed the cultural products of religion from religious institutions themselves, and reassembled in cinema halls the congregations that would normally gather in temples' (Basu *et al.* 1993: 107). The release of the film *Jai Santoshi Maa* created a huge religious fervour, it was a super hit on the screen and one saw the people visiting cinema halls with all the piousness in their hearts. One of the norms followed by Hindus is to remove their footwear while visiting temples. Many people removed their footwear before entering cinema halls and threw the coins as offering on the screen. At the same time popular culture came in handy to boost the religiosity. The Jagrans, Jagratas, (whole night song and dance in praise of Mother Goddess) became very popular. Most of these were financed by the traders, the base of the RSS combine.

To make matters more fertile for the rise of the Hindu right-wing politics, the nationwide broadcast of the serials Ramayana and Mahabharata, took religiosity to the higher level. Ramayana in particular reduced Hinduism to its mythology which was then presented as the essence of nationhood. The image of national pride could be served more effectively by the mass popularity of devotional traditions revolving around Ram. Since television was the monopoly of the state, this religiosity beamed into every household and the nation used to come to a grinding halt to watch these syrupy mythologies constructed for the glorification of the Lord, and around him the Babri demolition campaign was also built up. It also was prevalent in South India where earlier Ram was not so popular. The *jagrata* (whole night singing of devotional songs of mother goddess) functions were the supplements to the media-invented Goddesses such as Santoshi Maa. Devotional pop music was a great hit in different parts of the country. The pilgrimage to Viashno Devi became more popular particularly amongst the high-tech middle classes. This also saw a plethora of God men rising and preaching their own version of Hinduism, the common bond of these new breeds of God men was their harping on tradition, their eulogy for the values of caste and gender hierarchy. 'Certain tentative connections may also be suggested between the growth of Hindutva and the specific patterns of the north India city and small town development in recent years' (Basu *et al.* 1993: 112).

Religion has gradually made serious intrusions into the public space. Hindu religious symbols and some festivals have been popularized as national festivals. At the same time the message of patriarchy has also been given by popularizing festivals such as Rakhsha bandhan. Rakhi is now 'invoked as a common tradition as part of the larger agenda of cultural homogenization as well as the reassertion of patriarchal values, which are integral to the Hindu fundamentalist project of cultural nationalism' (Panikkar, 2002: x). Similarly, the Ganesh Festival has become one of the major festivals in most parts of the country. It was earlier restricted to only parts of the country, especially Maharashtra. This festival was started by Tilak and was invoked for political mobilization. Now dalits and lower castes have become more interested in this festival. It is an accompaniment of religious nationalism, 'The tendency of religious homogenization and internal consolidation is shared by all religious events. They also tend to reinforce religious division and widen the inter-religious distance' (Panikkar, 2002: xii).

Many festivals which were in the background are now becoming important. The rise in the observance of Karva Chauth (a fast undertaken by a wife for the long life of her husband) is becoming a big craze. This not only runs *pari passu* with the conservatism in the social life but also with the increase of patriarchal values overall. No doubt it is also being exploited by the market gimmicks of many business enterprises.

New rituals devised during that period became part of popular culture, Rath Yatras, Shila Pujans (worshipping bricks meant for construction of temples), collective worship rituals such as maha artis, conceptualized as the new mechanism of mobilizing the community, also came into being.

God men to the fore

The new set of Gurus and Acharyas, Sri Sri Ravishankar, Asaram Bapu, Pandurang Shastri Athwale, Sudhanshu Mahraj, Aniruddh Bapu, Maa Amritanand mai, among others, have been stalking on the social scene influencing the cultural expressions of society. They are the nerve soothers for the existential tensions of the middle class. These Gurus are pushing the Manusmsiriti and the feudal values of caste and gender hierarchies to a new discourse, one laced with modernity. Similarly, one notices the presence of Muslim Ulamas, Mullahs and followers of Shahi Imam who have been promoting obscurantism in the Muslim community. Starting from their role in putting pressure to reverse the Shah Bano judgment, to their opposition to the abolition of triple talaq and polygamy amongst Muslims, their retrograde role is a bane of the Muslim community in India. Temple visits and temple functions have become the major events of communities. The media is devoting more and more space to the discourses of swamis and saints and to religious values and religious functions. Television serials depict the 'guiding role' of the clergy and there are special television channels such as Astha and Sanskar to propagate particular versions of religiosity. The struggling middle-class hero of the previous decades is replaced by the rich patriarch constantly in touch with the priest for guidance in his regular affairs.

The Hindutva movement has engineered a particular type of religiosity amongst the Adivasis in particular. From the mid-1980s, a series of VHP propagators have been working in the Adivasi areas of Dangs (Gujarat), Jhabua (MadhyaPradesh) and Kandhmal (Orissa) and others. They have been trying to indoctrinate the Adivasis into the norms of Brahminical Hinduism. Proclaiming that the Adivasis are Hindus who left for the forests to avoid conversions into Islam after the invasion of the Muslim kings, they fell low in the caste structure and so have forgotten their religious moorings and base. It is necessary to bring them back. And this is being done by different, newly invented baptism techniques like giving them a bath in hot spring water and washing their feet with holy water. 'Along with these, Hindu Congregations involving thousands of Adivasis are being held in these areas. Also the preachers from some ashrams of God men work to wean them to Hindutva politics through religious mechanisms. One such Hindu Sangam was held in Jhabua in Madhya Pradesh in 2002' (Kumar in Tiwari, 2004: 27).

At the same time Hanuman, the monkey god, was popularized as the God in this area and lately Shabri, the destitute woman who had the privilege of offering wild berries to Lord Ram is being projected as the Goddess of Adivasis. The cultural symbolism cannot be missed in the selection of these deities. Hanuman was the unquestioning devotee of Lord Ram, with muscular power as his main virtue. He is capable of flying while carrying a huge mountain. But he carries the mountain because he could not identify the herb needed for the treatment of Laxman, Lord Ram's younger brother. This is the signal to Adivasis unquestioning loyalty to Lord Ram, there is no need for education. So what are the Christian missionaries doing here? Why should they be trying to educate you? They are foreigners. So Pastor Stains is picked up for the treatment which they want to mete out to the white-robed priests and nuns.

Shabri, the embodiment of poverty, is being glorified on purpose. Your great ancestress had the privilege to offer wild berries to the Lord. She is your role model, poor, powerless and with blind reverence and devotion to the upper caste. In the festival held in Subir, the Dangs district of Gujarat, in 2005, Shabri was celebrated and many Adivasis were brought from the neighbouring areas for the event. The local people were scared that Sangh's festival may create trouble and they may try to forcibly convert to Hinduism. It was declared that Christians and Muslims are foreigners and are a threat to the Hindu religion. This Kumbh is meant to protect the Hindus from the foreigners. In the beginning it was announced that conversions are the aim of Kumbh and that silence was kept on this point once various groups questioned their motives. This was boldly stated in the CD produced by the Shabri Kumbh organizers. By the time the court ruling came to ban the CD, many of its copies were already circulated and had the desired effect of threatening the Christianity community.

Films: media

On the one hand, the cultural scene is well reflected in the films and on the other, the films influence popular culture. This period saw the rise of super hit films such as *Hum Aapke Hain Kaun* (HAHK 1994, Who am I to You?) and *Dilwale Dulhaniya Le Jayenge* (1995, The Brave-hearted will Take the Bride), two typical examples of the values these reflected and then strengthened in turn.

In HAHK, in particular, the honey-coated script flows to present the happy world of an affluent family bereft of problems and contradictions. 'Claustrophobic, homogenized and totalizing are some of the words to describe the master narrative of our times, which reasserts not just possibility, but the visceral immediate presence of utopia in contemporary India' (Bharucha, 1998: 170).

Reflection on culture in the television serials is very revealing. Amongst the most popular is one *Saas bhi Kabhi Bahu Thi* (Mother-in-law was Daughter-in-law once). The theme revolves around the hierarchical position of women in the family, upholding the gender hierarchy and propagating the view to how 'good' women are those who act as the vehicles of these values. The current breed of soaps revolves around the affluent and their 'problems', while the issues of common people are swept under the carpet. Most of the channels are competing with one another to project this image of women. The family priest has become the wisest counsel for the major decision of the family, astrology is glorified and blind faith is being promoted.

The expression of religious nationalism has much to do with the way the media carries the news. Apart from commercialization, there is a great deal of the communalization of the media. Sensationalization and communal biases are an important part of the media fare. While the media in the English language is relatively less communal, the language press is much more communal in its approach. Most of the newspapers carry divine columns; the language press gives huge publicity to the priests and their sermons. Much space is devoted to the religious aspects of the festivals.

The visual media is growing in its clout and here again there are many channels and many TV personalities thrive in the communalization of their programmes. The news is tilted, more often in the communal direction. The commercialization of the media has gone hand in hand with the rise and increase of the impact of Hindutva: 'in as much as Hindutva has a market and communal stereotypes and religious tension make for easily saleable news, media outlets revert to feeding stereotypes and "popular" discourses back to 'buying' public, … ninety percent of Hindi papers have grown into Hindu papers' (Matthew, 2006: 15).

Education

Aspects of education are directly shaping the understanding of other communities. This in turn shapes the attitude to other communities and thereby is the major input of culture. Education is one terrain on which the Hindu right wing has been trying to spread its influence Even before BJP-led NDA changed the NCERT books during its regime, the books in the non-CBSE schools, managed by state governments, had many communal biases. Currently, the major observations in the field of education can be summed up as,

> Secular values and secular culture continue to be seriously undermined in both higher education and school education sectors even after the direct interference and manipulation by BJP-led NDA government has come to an end after May 2004 elections… Excessive political interference in academic institutions was most clearly noted in states that have BJP governments, though there were several examples of such interference and manipulation in other states as well. The communal campaign is more systematically carried out in BJP ruled states but also evident in institutions of higher learning in other states.
>
> (Kamat and Puniyani, 2006: 19)

Aspects of culture in educational institutions are deeply influenced by the Hindu right wing, with an increase in the culture of pujas (worship, rituals) going up in the academic institutions. Many Hindu religious festivals are becoming a matter of major focus in these places. RSS has started multiple Shishu Mandirs, Sarswati Vidyalayas, which had deep influence in the villages in particular. In addition EKAL Vidyalay, single-teacher schools, were also initiated which gave communal education and promoted sectarian norms in cultural areas. It is in the impact of these that the Adivasi areas were to see the rise in violence, especially after 1996.

Various Peoples' tribunals and inquiry reports have studied this phenomenon. In a tribunal led by Justice Usha, Angana Chatterjee and Mihir Desai point out, 'Communal organizations have instituted an extensive educational network for conducting rural and disenfranchised peoples in Orissa into Sangh Parivar … the curriculum taught in these educational institutions, such as Ekal Vidyalayas, one-teacher schools, and Vanvasi Kalyan Ashrams often denigrates minorities' (Chatterji and Desai, 2006: 79).

Cultural spaces: intolerance to the fore

Over a period of time intolerance is increasing in the cultural spaces. The fundamentalists of both factions are breaking the programmes, destroying paintings, and exhibitions. The creative expressions of different artists and film makers are prevented from being screened or exhibited; the list goes on. The book by Salman Rushdie *Moore's Last Sigh* was banned. Taslima Nasreen's books commenting on Islam and Muslim women were boycotted by a section of Muslims.

Similarly, M. F. Hussein has been on the receiving end of Hindu fundamentalists. His painting exhibition, Gufa in Ahmadabad, was destroyed. His paintings Sarswati, Bharat Mata were practically banned and he himself has been forced into exile from India. The concerts of the famous Pakistani singer, Gulam Ali, were rampaged in Mumbai. Deepa Mehta's film *Water*, depicting the plight of Hindu widows was not allowed to be shot in India.

Documentary film maker, Anand Patwadhan's film on Babri demolition, *In the Name of Lord*, was not given censor certificate for a long time and it was prevented from being screened on the national channel. Aamir Khan who happened to comment on Narmada issue was boycotted and his film *Fanaa* (2006, Destroyed in Love) was not permitted to be screened in Gujarat by the RSS combine volunteers.

Many documentary films are not given the censor certificate, some are being asked for cuts, and others are not permitted to be screened by the 'hooligans'.

> Censor board Chief Anupam Kher personally calls the police commissioner, urging him to arrest film makers daring to show their films in a film festival, traditionally a censorship free space. The censor board drags its feet to clear Parzania and forces Govind Nihalani to cut words from Dev dialogues ... while Praveen Togadia of VHP freely distributes a million of copies of CD 'Ramsevak Amar Raho', a VHP propaganda film exploiting the Godhra tragedy.
>
> (Sharma, 2006: 33)

University campuses are the worst sufferers. The progressive events are banned; undermined and religious festivities are encouraged. The case of the arrest of a student of Arts Faculty of MS University Baroda, for the painting which he made for his course work is too shocking to believe.

Rational spaces

The decade of the 1980s saw a great deal of the spread of rationalism, a struggle against blind faith. Now from every social forum blind faith is being glorified. The borderline between myth and history is being eroded as seen in the case of the Setusamudram issue, which was brought to a halt on the ground that Lord Ram had built an engineering marvel called Ram Setu and this project will involve the destruction of that Setu (bridge) built by our Lord. Similar issues are also happening in archaeology where, breaking all the rules of archaeological sciences, the Babri Masjid is demolished and then when the work of destruction is done, an analysis is made that there was a Ram temple. Similar trends are coming into architecture and other social spheres of life.

Conclusion

The multiple global changes which have taken place have also had an adverse impact on the Indian society. The ascendance of religious nationalism in the form of Hindutva, the politics of Hindu nationalism of the RSS combine have influenced the cultural spaces severely, there is a growing intolerance towards the ways and ideas of others. This is reflected in the prevalent social common sense, which is very obvious and holds the minorities as culprits, reminding one of German Nazism which blamed Jews for Germany's plight. The major issues of people have been bypassed and the mass hysteria is being created intermittently, which further deepens the Hate Other ideology. At the same time there is a rise in the religiosity all around, the increased presence of God men. The media is heavily communalized and the Indian identity is under severe threat from the narrow sectarian identities. The audio visual media is not only becoming increasingly commercialized it is also becoming increasingly communalized. This has influenced the educational system, where the curricula have moved in the communal direction. The result is multiple partitions amongst the communities along religious lines. Popular culture is turning towards conservatism and retrograde values are being promoted.

Note

1 Mandal Commission: This commission was appointed by the Government of India for making provisions of affirmative action, reservations in jobs for other backward castes. The Commission had recommended a reservation of 26 per cent of jobs for these castes. The report was lying in the cold storage till V.P. Singh, for his political benefit, to counter the politics of Devilal, implemented it. BJPs' electoral constituency was totally opposed to it. Still for electoral purpose BJP could not dare to oppose it. So it turned the tide and focused more on the Ram Temple. Advani's Rath Yatra, which was planned already before the Mandal Commission implementation got more response due to this implementation as now the upper caste saw this as a political response to OBC reservation.
2 Shudras: Low caste, untouchables
3 Navayat: A sect of Islam which developed on Malabar Coast, Kerala, having any traditions from Hinduism.
4 Mev: A sect of Muslims, in Rajasthan area, who were converts and carried lt of traditions from Hinduism

References

Basu, T., Datta P., Sarkar, S., Sarkar, T. and Sen S. (1993) *Khaki Shorts Saffron Flags*. Hyderabad: Orient Longman.
Bharucha, R. (1998) In the name of Secular. In Chandra, B. (ed.) *India's Struggle for Freedom*. Delhi: Penguin.
Chandra, B. (1989) *India's Struggle for Independence*. Penguin: New Delhi.
Chatterji, A. and Desai, M. (2006) *Communalism in Orissa, India Peoples Tribunal on Environment and Human Rights*, IPT Mumbai.
Kamat, S. and Puniyani, R. (2006) Education. In R. Sharma (ed.) *Breaking Silence*. Anhad: Delhi.

Kumar, R. (2004) In Tiwari *The Names Of The Others Mazhab ke Naam Par. Bharat Gyan Vigyan Samiti*: Bhopal.

Matthew, B. (2006) Media. In R. Sharma (ed.) *Breaking Silence*. Anhad: Delhi.

Nussbaum, M. (2007) *The Clash Within*. Permanent Black: Delhi.

Panikkar, K. N. (2002) *An Agenda for Cultural Action*. Three Essays: Delhi.

Puniyani, R. (2007) *Fundamentalism: Threat to Democracy*. Maithri: Tiruananthpuram.

Puniyani, R. (2008) *Contemporary India: Overcoming Sectarianism and Terrorism*. Hope: Gurgaon.

Puri, G. (2005) *Hindutva Politics in India*. UBSP: Delhi.

Savarkar, V. D. (1969) (5th edition) *Hindutva: Who is a Hindu?* Bombay: Veer Svarkar Prakashan.

Sharma, R. (2006) *Breaking Silence*. Anhad: Delhi.

Part III
Music – Dance – Fashions

8 Private music

Individualism, authenticity and genre boundaries in the Bombay music industry

Peter Kvetko

For half a century, mass-mediated popular music in India has been dominated by the sounds of cinema. While regional diversity and considerable class differences prohibit a single, national popular music to supersede all other local and subcultural styles, the Hindi/Urdu songs of Bombay's commercial film industry (known around the world as 'Bollywood') hold an indisputable position as the musical mainstream in North India and beyond. During the 1990s, however, a new type of national popular music emerged in tandem with the liberalization of India's economy, the expansion of the consuming middle class and the growth of satellite television. Though known by several names, such as Hindi Pop and private album music, there is growing consensus among artists and executives in Bombay to call this non-film music 'Indipop'.

This chapter explores the relationship between Indipop and Bollywood music, between an emergent niche music and the established, mainstream music from the Hindi film industry. Using materials drawn from my interviews with artists and executives in Bombay's music industry, I will focus on the tension surrounding the manner in which these individuals define the concepts of musical performance and musical authenticity. Bollywood films feature the simulation and representation of performance styles ranging from rock to Hindustani classical music. While Indipop, in reality, is similarly produced by privileged members of a pop culture industry, it purports to offer the vision of an authentic self and an alternative to the perceived escapist fantasy of Bollywood. After outlining some of the attempts by those in the non-film pop music industry to distinguish their work from the Bollywood norm, I present a comparative analysis of the musical, ideological and visual differences between Indipop and *filmi* music at the turn of the millennium. One must bear in mind, however, that distinctions prominent at the discursive level may be less evident in practice. Thus, while the boundaries between Indipop and Bollywood may appear rigid and impermeable, in reality the two share a complexly intertwined relationship. Exploring the tensions within that relationship allows me to approach culture as a contested, dynamic and symbolic network of words and actions.

The late 1990s set the backdrop for an intensified evaluation of national culture and identity in India, and the rise of Indipop must be viewed in this historical context. The media landscape changed radically with satellite television allowing an explosion of private channels to overrun the state-managed Doordarshan network throughout urban India. The country celebrated 50 years of independence in 1997 with the print media devoting much coverage to national identity past, present and future. A new level of international recognition came a year later when India declared itself a nuclear power by conducting a series of weapons tests near the border with Pakistan. Finally, the economic boom of the 1990s and the growing visibility and power of the non-resident Indian (NRI) community fuelled the optimism of those backing neo-liberalism and business privatization in India. In all of these contexts, Indipop seemed to play a role: as programming for the new media, as a symbol of a new national identity, as a force to be reckoned with on the international stage, as a soundtrack for the transnational identities of NRIs and cosmopolitan Indians, and as a slick, legitimate business for the new economy. Meanwhile, of course, the massive film industries in Mumbai and elsewhere, with their playback singers and celebrity icons, continued to dominate the popular music landscape across the subcontinent. With the largest shares of the domestic and international markets, Bollywood film soundtracks are firmly embedded in Indian public culture, and any act of popular music making invariably will be measured in relation to the norms, trends and expectations of film music. In scholarly literature, Bollywood is particularly associated with concepts of the collective, of the masses, and its songs are often seen as the epitome of public experience in Northern India.[1] Popular film songs 'permeate the aural environment of India's public spaces, from markets and festivals to long-distance buses and trains' (Majumdar, 2001: 161).

In urban areas such as Mumbai's large suburbs of Bandra and Andheri, the sonic environment in many public spaces can be a dense cacophony of sounds in which film music blasted from speakers competes with the sounds of rickshaw engines, taxi horns, passing trains and the sounds of construction from ever-present 'digging' projects. In contrast, the sonic environment of many middle-class, private spaces in the same suburbs is just the opposite – cool, quiet and sheltered. I argue that the differences in sonic texture and iconography between Indipop and film songs often correspond to these two lived environments, that while *filmi* music and imagery evokes collective experiences and sensibilities, Indipop articulates an individualist sensibility more in line with the era of neo-liberalism and global capitalism.[2]

Many of Indipop's promoters and fans argue that contemporary Bollywood films offer little more than escapist fantasies that cannot respond to individual experiences or local realities. While Hindi cinema once focused on populist messages of development (both moral and economic), by the end of the century an increasing number of commercial films focused on Hindu nationalist sentiments, *masala* entertainment and global capitalist aspirations couched in fairy-tale family values melodrama. Like many critics, Indipop artists and producers complain that Bollywood films rely on formulae and mass production, with actors, directors and singers commonly working on several films simultaneously. Drawing on an ideology of artistic self-expression as commodity, Indipop's promoters and artists attempt to define their work in opposition to Bollywood by emphasizing the creative mind of the individual. It is the persona of the singer, not the narrative context of the song that is for sale. If Bollywood's collective, oral tradition of production is the established norm, the efforts of Indipop's promoters and artists to establish a star system[3] modelled after global music markets can be read as an act of defiance, or at least a statement of an alternative cultural orientation. In an attempt to carve out a share of the popular music market, Indipop stars position themselves as the creativity-driven antithesis to the market-dictated sounds of commercial cinema.

In his study of global popular music, Peter Manuel writes,

> Indian film music producers, to cite an extreme example, prefer to employ a handful of well-known playback singers rather than hazard an unfamiliar voice or style; this extreme homogeneity of vocalist selection is all the more notable given the extraordinary linguistic, class, and ethnic diversity of the North Indian audience.
>
> (Manuel, 1988: 11)

Concern over the dangerous and exploitative nature of Bollywood music as critical theory's dreaded 'mass culture' is evident in Manuel's use of the term 'extreme'. Yet while Manuel assumes that this homogeneity is a reflection of the filmmaker's preference for the familiar, economic and time constraints certainly dictate their choices as well. Film music directors compose under constraints, often working on several films simultaneously and having little time to rehearse new experiments.[4] Even in the heyday of 'evergreen hits', rehearsals were limited to immediately prior to the recording – which 'encouraged music directors to rely upon the experience of established singers' (Arnold, 1991: 225) at the expense of new voices.

Other scholars express a sense of disbelief that the audience could even take Bollywood's standardized sounds seriously. Das Gupta, for example, writes,

> Invariably, the voice of the same playback singers emanate from all the characters in film after film. Instead of appearing absurd, the sameness of the voice in different characters seems to provide a comforting sense of security. Whenever a song is played, the projectionist immediately pushes the volume to the loudest. The only concession to verisimilitude is in the difference of singing voices for different characters within the same film.
>
> (Das Gupta, 1991: 62)

Das Gupta's annoyance at the predictability of sounds (and the volume at which they are publicly consumed) is tempered by his belief that this sameness 'seems to provide' a sense of comfort to the masses. Like members of Bombay's Indipop community, critics writing for an academic audience often see film culture as both an exemplar of typical Indian consumption and the result of a cultural orientation that they do not claim to share.

Describing the identity of the playback singer as a mere voice, these critics evoke concepts of musical performance and musical authenticity that have much in common with the views of Indipop artists and producers who emphasize the creative, personal nature of their music. While some may discredit the playback singer as an unseen cog in the machine of mass production, Neepa Majumdar provides an important response to this assertion by arguing that the playback singer and film actor are mutually dependent:

> Hindi cinema's song sequences function as a unique star vehicle, simultaneously drawing upon two different star texts, those of the singer and of the actor ... The two intersecting star texts of the singer and the actor exist in a symbiotic relationship, appealing simultaneously to two sets of pleasures, the aural and the visual. While the disembodied voice of the playback singer attaches itself to the body of the actor and thereby acquires visual presence, the actor's figural gestures also similarly acquire an aural dimension through the borrowed voice of the singer.
>
> (Majumdar, 2001: 164)

The most familiar 'disembodied voice' in Bollywood belongs to playback singer Lata Mangeshkar. For nearly five decades, her voice brought piety, longing and nostalgia to Bollywood song. Indeed, one could hardly speculate at the number of films that may have flopped or disappeared from memory were it not for the emotive power of voices belonging to Lata, Asha Bhosle, Kishore Kumar, Mohammad Rafi and a handful of other playback singers. Yet for some critics, Lata and her contemporaries ushered in an era of musical conservatism and predictability.[5] With the rise of music videos and the entrance of multinational record companies into the Indian market, new artists and executives positioned themselves by emphasizing the fractured nature of the Bollywood song sequence. In contrast, they offered pop stars who unified the voice and body. Each would have a different personality, a unique look and a distinctive sound. In the following section, I will explore the measures taken by the producers and promoters of Indipop music to redefine the parameters of musical performance and musical authenticity for the new millennium.

In my interviews with Indipop singers, producers and marketers, it was clear that most people wanted to draw a clear line of distinction between Indipop and film music. The terms 'us' and 'them' came up in almost every conversation, creating the impression that Bollywood and Indipop exist separately on both professional and social levels. This is somewhat surprising given that two of Indipop's biggest stars, Lucky Ali and Lezz Lewis, are sons of major figures in the film world,[6] and that practically all of the major Indipop artists have contributed to film soundtracks.

Yet even with a substantial amount of social interaction evident, the vast majority of the singers, songwriters and executives I interviewed saw themselves in a different social category than the *filmi* crowd. One Indipop producer distinguished himself and his non-film peers from what he called 'the Hindi film cats', and when I asked Biddu, perhaps the most influential Indipop songwriter, about the relationship between Indipop and Bollywood, he said:

> What Indipop offered was a bridge between the east and west. But Bollywood is wonderful; it's like a sponge, because it's taken that. It's also created a bit of that bridge. Not as much as Indipop, because Bollywood works with the masses. A lot of the people involved in Bollywood are very what I call 'desi' people. They're not very westernized, not very educated. Because sometimes you have to please your distributor who comes from some small B town or C town. Because most of the people involved in Indipop are Bombay or Delhi based. More forward thinking, or western thinking, or whatever terminology … more advanced.

Biddu and many of his peers interact with the film music world as outsiders, and like many elites in Bombay, they habitually associate education with Westernization and assume that Bollywood is produced by and for the less educated masses. Even though Biddu achieved great success with the song 'Aap Jaisa Koi' in the film *Quarbani* (1980), he exhibits a degree of animosity towards the nepotism in the film world. When I asked if 'Aap Jaisa Koi' led to more offers from music directors, he replied:

> No, I just did that one song, because Feroz Khan [the film's director] did it against the will of the film community. He was using an outside…. The thing is this, in this country … Film directors, film music writers, music directors, singers; they're working on 20–30 films a year. You'd think they'd be happy. But they want more. They don't want anybody coming in.

On a business level, the executives of the new non-film market sometimes evoke Bollywood's alleged relationship with organized crime and under-the-table financing. When asked what his single biggest business success was, the pop music executive Shashi Gopal answered: 'The decision to not go with films. To create an alternative independent genre of music in a scene which was controlled by films. We broadened the legitimacy of the business. We enhanced its respectability' (Nandy, 1999).

The makers of Indipop express certain fundamental differences between themselves and film music makers in regards to their very understanding of music and its social meaning. For example, the singer Hariharan said to me, 'I basically feel film music is for the screen, for people to lip-synch. Non-film music is *music*. Their parameters are totally different.' To Hariharan and others, the difference lies at the level of musical authenticity. For many in the Indipop world, music is the veritable window to the soul, an expression of an individual's mood and experiences, whereas film songs are written to fit the specific characters and narrative contexts of the film.

The connection between popular music and individual personality is by no means unique to Indipop, but rather is a sign of Indipop's ideological connection to rock music.[7] In *Performing Rites*, Simon Frith claims that 'as listeners we assume that we can hear someone's life in their voice' (Frith, 1996: 185–6). Indipop artists consistently evoke this idea in interviews and view playback singing as a denial of true self-expression. According to singer Hema Sardesai, this has encouraged more and more playback singers to venture into pop: 'That's simply because they don't have an identity as playback singers. Every singer always feels the need for his talent to be recognized more deeply. To be a playback singer means standing behind the curtains.' Similarly, Alisha Chinai states, 'Most often playback singers are relegated to the background. Even if they try to sell their own music, people don't accept that. It won't sell. It's not easy to be a pop star. You have to have that distinctive sound that people relate to.' For Sardesai, Chinai and others, the film format is first and foremost a commercial venture, and singers who do playback forfeit their individual identity for the sake of the film's needs. Non-film, 'private' albums, on the other hand, are represented as the proper venue for an artist who intends to express himself or herself.

Yet Indipop artists struggle with their own position as popular artists who are not often commercially viable. Kalyan Baruah, guitarist for Lucky Ali and KK, reveals the frustration that he and his colleagues feel regarding the wide commercial gulf between Indipop and Bollywood music:

> [KK] came out with his solo album, and after about 15 days or so, he sang one song for a Hindi movie which became huge. That was amazing. And by that time I was pretty convinced with, you know, non-film music, and that it was good music. People listened to it, you know? It's very happening. But I was a little doubtful about that when, after about 15–20 days when the 'Tarap Tarap' [from the film Hum Dil De Chuke Sanam] came out in the market, overnight it became a hit. And we were just talking like, 'Man you've been working on your solo album for the past one year and now the album is out. You just sang one Hindi film song, and overnight it worked like magic.' You know, you start getting a little. ... You know, you try so hard to do an album, and you try to do your best and ... it takes a long time to really happen. But with film music one song can make you an instant success.

The debate about 'going *filmi*' is not unlike the dilemma of moving from an independent to a major record label in the West. KK, Shaan, Lucky Ali, Adnan Sami and others have faced difficult decisions when choosing to focus on the reliable income from playback singing over their independent projects. These artists and many others emphasize that their solo recordings are authentic expressions of their personal identities, that they pour their heart and soul into their own music, and that film music is at best an enjoyable and profitable distraction from their true artistic endeavours.

The executives who try to sell Indipop albums share similar explanations of their struggles. Anand Prasad, former head of A&R for Sony Music India, expresses his frustration at the Indian consumer's failure to appreciate what he sees as the value of 'real' music over the artificial yet seductive songs from Bollywood:

> Unlike in the west, people here are used to playback singing. They're used to not seeing the actual artist on the video. They don't care. They are very happy to see models lip-synching. So I have to build an artist image or whatever. For most people here, the artist is incidental. It is the song that becomes more important than the artist.

Prasad, who lists Led Zeppelin, The Rolling Stones, and Deep Purple as his greatest musical influences, feels he must struggle to educate the Indian consumer to appreciate the value of an 'actual artist' over the *filmi* fantasy of playback singing.

Given the well-established role of Hindi films in Indian popular culture, many pop singers feel they need to fight even to be recognized. According to Hariharan, this is a fight that cannot be won: 'The film media is a permanent thing. It's like a monster. You cannot surpass it. You cannot become more than that. It is there to stay.' His characterization of Bollywood as 'a monster' reflects some of the antagonism towards the *filmi* world is not uncommon in Indipop circles. In a competitive struggle over the consumer, film music plays the role of the well-established Goliath, while the underdog Indipop artist must struggle to validate his or her very existence.

In this section, I present a comparison of the prevailing musical and visual characteristics of mainstream Hindi film music and contrast them with what I see to be the most typical traits of Indipop music. Given its ties to Western rock and pop ideologies of individualism and self-expression, I argue that Indipop music provides a challenge to and subversion of the dominant film song aesthetic and images of the collective. Through musical and visual articulations, Indipop style resonates with the global imagination and embodied experience of urban, cosmopolitan classes in a way that Bollywood music, until recently, did not.[8]

While many film music directors employ the modal *raga* system of traditional Indian music and craft melodies around a catch phrase, or *mukhra*, most Indipop songwriters base their compositions on chord changes. Harmony (in the Western sense of composition) is very much on the minds of most Indipop songwriters such as Biddu, Lezz Lewis, and Lucky Ali, all of whom start by working out riffs and chord changes on a guitar or keyboard when composing. By laying claim to the Western tradition of functional harmony, jazz changes, secondary dominants, and other terminology, Indipop song writers align themselves with the West and characterize film music as staid, bound by tradition, and functional but not musically inventive.

Given the emphasis on melody over harmony in Bollywood, the structure of a typical film song is designed to enhance the affective power of the melody. For example, many songs contain slow, unmetred introductions that, much like *alap* sections of classical performances, outline the melodic and scalar materials used in the piece.[9]

While the Indian public now views classic film music (and figures such as Naushad and Lata Mangeshkar) nearly as an extension of the Hindustani art music tradition, Indipop songwriters rarely if ever claim that their songs are based on *ragas*. While many pop vocalists have been trained in classical or light classical music, the forms of their songs rarely reflect traditional concepts such as *mukhra*, *antara*[10] or *tala*-based rhythmic patterns. Biddu, whose early compositions laid the basis for Indipop style, claims: 'I know nothing about Indian music. Zilch.' Many of Biddu's hit songs, such as 'Disco Deewane'[11] and 'Johnny Joker',[12] demonstrate a clear disco-pop style in both form and instrumentation. Other compositions, such as 'Tu'[13] and 'Mehendhi ki Raat',[14] make use of Indian percussion instruments but continue to follow a 'riff-based' rather than 'raga-based' form. The differences are even more distinct in Indipop artists whose sound is based on a guitar-bass-drum format, such as Lucky Ali, Strings and Silk Route.

Furthermore, the overall structures of many Indipop songs often are formed around moments of harmonic tension and release. In songs such as Alisha's 'Made in India' and Lucky Ali's 'Tere Mere Saath', the chorus is deferred by a sequence of chords to create the effect of a build-up. After building the listener's anticipation, we reach a moment of musical release through a resolution of the harmonic tension.[15] This fetishization of the act of listening itself stands in direct opposition to the functional role of film songs whose length and arrangement must meet the demands of the accompanying film scene, and whose melodies must be appealing enough to immediately catch the ears of a diverse public.

Beyond harmonic and melodic influences on form, Bollywood and Indipop composers often use rhythm in remarkably different ways. For many film songs, particularly for the cathartic group dance numbers, the tempo of the piece increases in stages until the final section reaches a climax of speed and energy. Again, this practice derives from traditional practices, as both folk and classical music in North India feature dramatic tempo increases. With very few exceptions, Indipop songs follow the conventions of Western pop where the tempo established at the start of the piece is maintained throughout the song. Thus, one might even argue that studio produced Indipop songs that are recorded to a steady 'click track' draw more on the emotive power of harmony to create feelings of tension and release, while film songs emphasize the manipulation of melodic expectations and the anticipation of accelerating tempos in creating their own feelings of tension and release.

Even the manner in which songs are named reveals key differences. The verse-chorus-bridge form of many Indipop songs leads some songwriters to use the memorable and harmonically significant chorus as the song's title. The more typical pattern in Indian film song derives the song title from the first line of the lyrics sung to the opening melodic phrase. Practically all film songs and some Indipop songs use the first line to be sung as the title. However, a sufficient number of Indipop hits are titled after the chorus that the practice merits attention as an example of the differences in musical (and indeed cultural) orientation between Indipop and *filmi* composers.

One of the clearest ways that Indipop distinguishes itself from 'the *filmi* sound' is through studio production. When I asked Alisha Chinai to talk about the production of a recent album, she replied:

> I told [Sandeep Chowta] that I want really nice melodies, because that's what the Indian ear likes. I think with most of the songs the melody is very catchy, and the grooves are kind of western … essentially dance grooves. He hasn't given me that squeaking, you know, sound. Sandeep would never do that, because he listens to a lot of western music. His ear is tuned into the pop production sound.

Alisha's language illuminates the ways in which Indipop and *filmi* music are being constructed as dichotomous and unrelated. Her preference for a producer who does not create a 'squeaking sound' implies that the *filmi* sound (particularly the violins and high-pitched voices) is both undesirable and unrelated to Western popular musical aesthetics.[16]

Indipop albums typically lack the heavy reverb that characterizes the vocal tracks of many Bollywood songs, particularly those of the 1980s and 1990s.[17] Indipop producers prefer a clear tone that will sound good on headphones, personal stereos, and in other modes of individual consumption. This is in direct opposition to the echoing sounds sought by film music producers who, I would argue, create a sonic space compatible with the modes of public consumption associated with films – such as movie theatres, rickshaws and taxis, and open-air bazaars where film music is blasted from loudspeakers.

In another difference of production aesthetics, Indipop producers reduce the treble and boost the mid-range and bass in their mixes, while those familiar with the Bollywood music of recent decades recognize screechingly high strings and stratospheric women's voices as typical.[18] According to one author: 'The high pitched three-octave range of Lata Mangeshkar or Asha Bhonsle's voice is thrown at the audience in the same way as an itinerant folk singer's in the open spaces of the countryside. It is always on a high enough scale to be heard across streets and buildings and over the noises of the city' (Das Gupta, 1991: 63). These sounds are more useful in outdoor, crowded spaces and open-air rickshaws, while the bass sound and deeper, softer voices of Indipop music come through better on personal stereos and inside air-conditioned cars with the windows rolled up. Thus, I argue that there is sufficient evidence to claim a relationship between physical space and sonic space, that Indipop music can be an iconic reference to the private, more individualized physical environments inhabited by middle-class urban Indians, while *filmi* music – the music of the masses, according to Indian public discourse – corresponds more immediately to public spaces and a dense, crowded sonic environment.

A review of the Colonial Cousins's album *Atma* encapsulates this distinction by emphasizing the autonomous, bourgeois mode of consumption associated with Indipop music: 'Wait for the song to take on your every nerve, and soak you in the warmth that you experience when you are in a Jacuzzi.'[19] While few consumers are likely to take up this offer, I find this reference significant. The world of Indipop would seem to be a world of quiet, soothing and solitary existence.

As I have argued above, the sounds of Indipop conjure up private spaces and personal intimacy, but videos and album covers go further to enhance this atmosphere of neoliberal individualism. Video after video shows the pop star alone in a finely furnished room, alone on the open road, or exploring a deserted beach or waterway. Bollywood, while it does have its share of romantic escapes to Swiss mountaintops, maintains a more direct connection to imagery of the collective via images of large family gatherings and choreographed dances featuring dozens of people filling the screen in perfectly synchronized movement. Furthermore, while album covers for Hindi films feature loud graphics and star actors (often in a memorable scene from the film), album covers for Indipop records reinforce an ideology of autonomous self-expression by presenting artists in simple, personal portraits devoid of sensationalism or theatrics.

I have argued that Indipop purports to offer the sonic experience of an intensely personal revelation of an authentic self, something that Bollywood music by its very nature cannot deliver. I conclude this chapter by presenting a selection of images from Indipop album covers, demonstrating that the visual associations used to market Indipop also signify an individualistic, uncrowded and quietly domestic existence most relevant to elite consumers in urban India and abroad.

The best-selling Indipop album to date is Alisha Chinai's *Made in India*. Released in 1995 on the Bombay-based Magnasound label, the record sold a reported three million copies, and the album's title song was a hit not only in India but across a wide international market. Having evolved from a bubble-gum pop singer and Indian version of Madonna, Alisha became a central figure in the emergence of Indipop just as the country prepared to mark its 50th anniversary of independence from British colonial rule. The theme of 'Made in India', therefore, marks both the pride in a new domestic popular music ready for export (made more possible after India's 'economic liberalization' reforms in 1991) and a patriotic anthem encouraging citizens to stay true to the homeland even in an era of free trade and burgeoning labour migration.

The cover of Alisha's album presents the artist in a simple, yet personal fashion. Dressed in pure white clothes and clasping her hands together on her cheek, the primary appeal of the image is Alisha herself. She looks directly into the camera, allowing the consumer a direct link to her personality. The consumer of this album does not buy the drama of Bollywood, nor the captured memories from a filmic scene. Rather, it is Alisha herself that is for sale.

Another founding act in the Indipop movement, the Colonial Cousins brought a mature, thoughtful identity as songwriters. Singing about the turmoil of Hindu–Muslim communal tension and the need to maintain ties to tradition in the face of rapid modernization, the duo of Lezz Lewis and Hariharan struck a chord with consumers both at home and abroad among the NRI community. They began recording their debut album in 1994 but did not release it until 1996, largely because their label, Magnasound, was unsure of how they could market it. Once released, it proved to be a remarkable success, and the Colonial Cousins quickly became the standard of quality against which other pop acts with global aspirations would be judged.

Like the cover of *Made in India*, this album cover emphasizes honesty and authenticity. Set against a white background, Lezz and Hari wear matching Indian suits and strike a playful pose, as if caught in the midst of a joke. The same marketing strategy continues. As they look directly into the camera, the artists invite us to share in their intimate, honest experience of human music making.

The Delhi-based group, Silk Route, goes even further in emphasizing a direct connection between artist and consumer by eliminating all images other than their faces. The group's debut video in 1998, 'Dooba Dooba', was filmed at an empty lake where the band performed most of the song submerged underwater. The crooning vocals of the lead singer, Mohit, also evoke a feeling of intimate honesty and are the aural antithesis to the *masti* and *dhoom* of many a Bollywood song.

While they may not be able to compete with the massive sales numbers of film music, Indipop groups such as Silk Route vie for a piece of the market by evoking the sense of an unmediated, intimately personal musical expression. Emerging from an all black background, their faces call us to view them, to engage directly with them, and to trust them to deliver to the listener a musical experience true to their identities as artists.

While the Indian label Magnasound suffered the loss of many of its major stars in the late 1990s to the newly formed multinational record company branches such as Sony Music India and Universal India, the company was briefly revived by the popular crooner, Adnan Sami. Sami's popularity among the masses can be partly attributed to his use of *filmi* musical style as well as his collaboration with Bollywood stars in his videos. While others artists who have released private albums make a concerted effort to avoid being associated with Bollywood, Sami has embraced Bollywood conventions and has therefore been rewarded with greater sales. His most successful album, *Kabhi to Nazar Milao*, features a duet with the playback singing legend Asha Bhosle and his videos have featured Bollywood actors such as Amitabh Bachchan, Govinda and Rani Mukherjee.

This album cover reveals a new adaptive strategy for Indipop promoters. Sami's name and image come as subordinates to the more familiar Bollywood diva. Asha Bhosle's presence and trustworthy gaze offer validation that the album is worth the consumer's time. Furthermore, the cover features a still shot from a music video, evoking a fragment of theatrical drama to go with the earnest personalities of the two singers. While this approach places Sami the artist as only one part of the image, it does seem to represent an important step toward the increasing fusion between the Indipop and *filmi* styles. At the same time, Asha Bhosle's face (like Sami's a bit less glamorous than the typical Bollywood supermodel turned actor or actress) graces the cover, thus demonstrating the possibility of overcoming the 'disembodied voice' of the playback singer.

While some critics dismiss Indipop as an example of Western cultural imperialism, and while 'the masses' prefer the familiar faces and voices of Bollywood, I am fascinated by the struggles of artists and executives to establish a mainstream pop music market outside the realm of cinema and apart from regional or religious affiliations. As I have argued, Indipop has its own affiliations, primarily to the culture and ideologies of the highly individualistic, neoliberal formations of the global economy. Yet Indipop is decidedly local, and it both contributes to the artistic vitality of cities such as Mumbai and reveals the ways in which popular culture is contested terrain.

The existence of Indipop calls into question radical differences in the way people across the subcontinent understand the very nature of music. Bollywood songs are recorded by professional playback singers but 'picturized' on screen by lip-synching actors, thus creating a disjuncture between the face one sees and the voice one hears. To borrow from Michael Taussig's 1999 book, *Defacement*, this disjuncture becomes a 'public secret' that Indian consumers can choose to embrace, reject or ignore. But since the playback singing system has been naturalized as a form of doxa in Indian popular culture, the 'defacement' of that system then can be read as an act of symbolic resistance. By emphasizing concepts of musical authenticity that define Bollywood as the other, as a fractured and manufactured system of escapist fantasy, Indipop music offers the appearance of a true artist expressing himself or herself through song.

Through musical and visual cues, Indipop articulates an ideology of self-expression and an individualistic experience that is becoming more and more apparent in India's urban centres. ATM machines, personal computers, iPods, and air-conditioned shopping malls all contribute to the growing manner of ways in which private, middle-class experience can be insulated from the demands of public interaction. Popular music often does more than simply reflect the social environment. By studying the tensions and transformations within the Bombay music industry, I argue that the emergence of Indipop, in fact, anticipated the broad social transformations pervading urban India today.

Notes

1 See Pinney (2001) and Appadurai (1996) for further analysis of the concepts of popular and public in South Asia.
2 Again, these two categories should not be viewed as entirely exclusive. Indipop music and videos are sometimes clearly derived from *filmi* models, and many Indipop artists, such as Alisha Chinai, Shaan, Lucky Ali, Daler Mehndi, Vasundhara Das, KayKay Menon and Hariharan, have sung for (or acted in) Bollywood films. Likewise, the sound and style of current Bollywood hits has changed due to the involvement of artists and songwriters (such as Shankar, Ehsaan and Loy) from the non-film scene.
3 See Buxton (1990) for an insight into the relationship between rock music, consumerism and the star system.
4 In contrast, the Bombay productions of staged musicals such as *Tommy, Jesus Christ Superstar, The Man of la Mancha*, and *Evita* were well-rehearsed and experimental productions and featured performers such as Sharon Prabhakar, Suneeta Rao and Alisha Chinai, all of whom went on to become pop divas in Bombay's Indipop music scene.
5 According to Vijay Mishra, Lata's emergence on the scene in the 1952 film *Baiju Bawra* signalled the end of the era of rich diversity of Hindi film singers such as Noor Jehan, Suraiya, Wahidan Bai and Mehtab. 'In displacing these varied voices', Mishra writes, 'Lata prized out the female voice from its great, heterogeneous tradition' (Mishra, 2002: 166).

6 Lewis's father, P. L. Raj, was the biggest choreographer in Bollywood during the 1960s and 1970s, while Lucky Ali's father was the great comic actor Mehmood.

7 The relationship with rock music is no coincidence. Several key executives were in bands during the thriving English-language rock scene in Bombay and elsewhere during the 1960s and 1970s. And not only do Indipop artists frequently name Western artists as their inspirations, but they are often marketed as local versions of rock stars as well ('The Indian Madonna', 'India's Bryan Adams' and so on).

8 During the 1990s, the musical differences between Bollywood and Indipop were more readily apparent. While Indipop recordings have begun to sound 'more *filmi*', the opposite is much more apparent. Bollywood soundtracks since 2000 are clearly moving towards the sound I describe here as the Indipop sound. One obvious reason is that more and more film songs are written by and recorded by individuals coming out of the non-film pop scene.

9 In Hindi film songs, the playback singer often outlines such melodic phrases using vocables such as 'La', 'Hey', or 'Ooh', a practice that is much less common in Indipop songs.

10 In classical music, *antara* refers to the section of the composed piece that moves to the upper tonic. Film music directors often use *antara* when referring to the verse section of a song.

11 Recorded by Nazia Hassan in 1981 and by Sagarika in 1995.

12 Recorded by Shweta Shetty in 1994.

13 Recorded by Sonu Nigam in 1998.

14 Recorded by Models in 1996.

15 'Made in India' and 'Tere Mere Saath' both achieve this by minor key riff-based verses sung in a mid register, staccato style leading to catchy choruses in major keys sung with an open throat and in a higher range.

16 Interestingly, Sandeep Chowta is best known as a film music director, but his music (like that of A. R. Rehman and Shankar-Ehsaan-Loy) can be seen as a part of the new Bollywood sound that has emerged because of the influence of non-film pop.

17 In a footnote to her dissertation, Alison Arnold notes that some playback singers even complain if their voice sounds too natural (Arnold, 1991: 244). In contrast, the vocal qualities of Adnan Sami, Lucky Ali and others are considered to be highly personal, natural and without artifice.

18 In an interesting historical connection, T. C. Satyanath notes that the use of extremely high pitches in public spaces has been around for a long time: 'Decades ago, before the modern amplifiers increased noise pollution, tea shops played old horn-type gramophones faster than 78 r.p.m., in almost super-human speed, and women in "drama-records" often sounded like a cackle of Donald Duck. The motive was to increase the volume of sound to attract the unwary passer-by' (Satyanath, 1981: 15).

19 See http://music.indya.com/reviews/nonfilm/aatma.html

References

Appadurai, Arjun (1996) *Modernity at Large: Cultural Dimensions of Globalization.* Minneapolis: University of Minnesota Press.

Arnold, Alison (1991) *Hindi Filmi Git: On the History of Commercial Indian Popular Music.* Ph.D. Dissertation. University of Illinois at Urbana-Champaign.

Buxton, David (1990) 'Rock Music, The Star System, and the Rise of Consumerism.' In Simon Frith and Andrew Goodwin (eds), *On Record: Rock, Pop and the Written Word*, New York: Pantheon Books, pp. 427–41.

Das Gupta, Chidananda (1991) *The Painted Face: Studies in India's Popular Cinema.* New Delhi: Roli Books.

Frith, Simon (1996) *Performing Rites: On the Value of Popular Music*. Cambridge, MA: Harvard University Press.

Majumdar, Neepa (2001) The Embodied Voice: Song Sequences and Stardom in Popular Hindi Cinema. *Soundtrack Available: Essays on Film and Popular Music*. Durham, NC: Duke University Press.

Manuel, Peter (1988) *Popular Music in the Non-Western World*. New York: Oxford University Press.

Mishra, V (2002) *Bollywood Cinema: Temples of Desire*. London: Routledge.

Nandy, Pritish (1999) Rediff Business-Interview with Shashi Gopal http://rediff.com/business/1999/sep/08nandy.htm

Pinney, Christopher (2001) Introduction: Public, Popular, and Other Cultures. In Rachel Dwyer and Christopher Pinney (eds), *Pleasure and the Nation: The History, Politics and Consumption of Public Culture in India*. Oxford: Oxford University Press.

Taussig, Michael (1999) *Defacement: Public Secrecy and the Labor of the Negative*. Stanford, CA: Stanford University Press.

Satyanath, T. C. (1981) The Harmonium Comes Back, *Shanmukha* 7/1: 12–16.

Bollywood dance and anti-*nautch* in
twenty-first-century global India[1]

Anna Morcom

Towards the end of the first decade of the new millennium 'Bollywood' can be
seen as having gained unprecedented cultural legitimacy in India and worldwide.[2]
This is even apparent on the level of official representations of India, with stars
dancing to film songs at the closing ceremony of the 2006 Commonwealth Games
in Australia. With the new extension of legitimate culture beyond the boundaries
of classical or folk into the realm of the popular, there is a sense that the culture of
'the people', 'the masses', is embraced, validated, approved. However, that 75,000
'bar girls' who danced to Bollywood numbers in beer bars in Mumbai were made
redundant in August 2005 following a virulent moral campaign indicates that areas
of Bollywood culture exist that are by no means legitimised. Beginning with an
examination of the Bollywood dance craze that has become one of the trendiest
parts of globalised India and then moving onto 'other' arenas of Bollywood dance
starting with the bar girls, this chapter seeks to problematise the question of
'the people' in Indian popular culture through an examination of hierarchies and
processes of inclusion and exclusion at work *within* the popular sphere.[3]

The new legitimacy of Bollywood dance in globalised India

Traditionally, given the taboo on women appearing in the public realm, professional
female performers have generally existed outside of the bounds of marriage,
enabling them to perform not just in public, at festivals or weddings, but for
specifically male audiences, for whom they are available (in theory) for sexual
liaisons (Brown, 2003: 118–76; Qureshi, 2006; Srinivasan, 1984). The association
of professional dance with disrepute was broken by the mid-twentieth century
in the field of classical performing arts through a process of nationalist 'reform
and revival' where female hereditary performers were excluded and 'respectable'
middle-class women began to perform (Post, 1987; Srinivasan, 1985). Bollywood
dance, however, un-legitimised by nationalism and also overtly sexy, was not
a respectable career for women.

The situation is very different now. As one Anglo-Indian dancer in the film
industry said, whereas ten years ago, people assumed that she danced as some
kind of 'last resort', now they easily understand that she dances because she likes
it (interview, Justine, 21 April 2006, Mumbai). Although many families still do not

approve of dance as a profession, a great many now do, and at least at the level of a hobby or occasional/temporary occupation, countless Indian children and young adults are now studying Bollywood dance in classes and performing in live shows with the kind of star-struck dedication and frenzy for fitness of *Fame* or *Break-dance*. Shiamak Davar's Institute for the Performing Arts (SDIPA), the first popular dance institute in India apart from dance schools catering just for the film industry, began in 1985 as a class for jazz dance with seven students. SDIPA now has 25,000 members in major cities across India, and teaches dance that draws off (and feeds into) Bollywood, as well as 'Indo-Jazz' and other modern styles (Shiamak Davar interview, 30 April 2006, Mumbai). Countless other enterprising dancers have also started setting up their own dance schools. The ethos of such dance classes is fitness, feeling good, looking good (in the sense of fit, toned bodies), performing in shows and getting the experience of 'being on stage' to build self-confidence and gain a taste of fame. Dancers trained in these classes feed into extensive networks of live shows and competitions that span the full gamut of small, local, amateur, fun-oriented events to big televised shows and competitions that pick dancers for the big league, such as *Nach Baliye*. While big star shows involving dance have been going on since the 1990s, shows that draw from members of the general middle classes who are passionate about dance and talented is a far more recent phenomenon, though with much the same ethos, an 'everyman' version of the big shows. Dancing in the industry and the star shows, or in shows outside the film industry with a successful dance troupe such as those from SDIPA, can offer an extremely good salary, in the region of Rs.30,000–50,000 per month or more. For those able to set up successful dance schools and/or enter into choreography, the salary can be in lakhs or, in the case of Shiamak Davar himself, presumably in crores.

While there are hosts of ultra-keen and competitive youngsters wanting to go far with Bollywood dance, there are also many classes full of (affluent) middle-class housewives aiming more at losing weight, fighting boredom and having fun. This is happening even outside the big metros. In a class in Jalandhar I visited, Punjabi housewives, many of whom were attending classes daily, enthusiastically told me how the class had changed their lives, that they had lost ten kilograms, recovered from 'bored housewife syndrome', or even had given up anti-depressants. While previously dance had been a taboo, some women were joining because not being able to dance at weddings and such ocassions was embarrassing. (Interviews with director Gaggan Bedi, and various students of Sparkling Pearlz Institute of Fine Dances and Grooming, 26 April 2007, Jalandhar.)

The Bollywood dance craze, as may be surmisable from its *Fame* and *break-dance* air and its enthusiasm for keep fit, weight loss, personal happiness and the pursuit of a sexy, toned body, is very much an East–West hybrid cultural phenomenon. Apart from pioneers in India such as Shiamak Davar (himself from a highly elite and Westernised Parsee background in Mumbai), the craze appears to have begun with NRI communities in the United Kingdom and United States, almost certainly following on from the *Bhangra* craze.[4] The staging of a lavish and often professionally choreographed performance at weddings where the bride, groom and potentially whole extended family and friends dance apparently also originated amongst NRI communities, in the United States, and has become one of the most important parts of the Bollywood craze in India and worldwide. As with the new, glossy Bollywood films of the 1990s (Dwyer, 2000: 96–167), Bollywood dance can be seen as flourishing from practical, ideological and aesthetic links between NRIs in the United Kingdom, United States and Australia in particular, and the new middle classes in India. The growing importance of dance in films has also both fed into and fed off these trends, as have the big, live, star shows. In particular, it was Yash Chopra's 1997 Hindi film *Dil To Pagal Hai* with choreography by Shiamak Davar telling the story of a love triangle of *Fame* type Jazz dancers that can be seen as the point of critical mass which saw Bollywood dance become 'a rage' in India, (interview Shiamak Davar 30 April 2006, Mumbai).

This new, extremely prominent dance culture represents nothing short of revolutionary change in the traditional relations of dance, public performance, sexuality, gender and patriarchy amongst the middle classes. The impression from the entertainment media and the 'all walks of life' dance classes is that now, in India, 'everyone dances', that it is great to perform, to look good, look sexy, feel good, and to celebrate the energy of India's increasingly acclaimed modern dance form, Bollywood. It seems that Indian popular culture has truly arrived nationally and internationally. However, when we push beyond the middle-class, trendy, international, media world of Bollywood, it becomes clear that this is only half the picture.

'Other' worlds of Bollywood dance

In August 2005, a ban came into force that made as many as 75,000 girls who danced to Bollywood songs in approximately 1,250 beer bars in Mumbai redundant.[5] This was the result of a fierce campaign led by the Deputy Chief Minister of Maharashtra, R. R. Patil, and a range of NGOs and women's groups. The campaign to ban dancing in bars essentially focused on two moral arguments:[6]

- The girls were prostitutes, ruining the fabric of society, breaking homes and so on, *and* making easy money out of it; dance bars were a nexus of trafficking.
- The girls were helpless victims, 'trafficked', or forced to sell themselves through poverty and lack of education, and were exploited by the bar owners and drunken, lascivious men.

The ban was strongly protested by the bar girls union, which had 12,000 signed up members at the time of the ban (when they stopped taking new membership), as well as other NGOs and women's groups (Figure 9.1).

Here I concentrate in particular on the role of the press, which in addition to covering the main developments of the affair, included strongly pro-ban and anti-ban factions. While the pro-ban factions repeated the above arguments, the anti-ban factions, strongest in the English language press, gave a different slant on the presentation of the girls as victims: the girls were poor, uneducated,

Figure 9.1 Poster advertising bar girls rally © Indian Bargirls Union.

unfortunate, and were dancing because they had no choice; they were working hard in pitiful circumstances, *not* earning easy money. By losing their jobs they would be driven to prostitution. Anti-ban factions also argued for liberalism against moral policing.

The moral arguments went round in circles, like a dog chasing its tale, going over and over standard 'issues' of gender, sexuality, morality, poverty and victimhood. Nowhere in the pro-ban lobby or the general press coverage was there anything like a proper engagement with the actual historical and social context of these girls.[7] This, I argue, is what would have given the dog something productive to follow, as opposed to its tale. While it would seem initially that this Bollywood dance arena was denied a place in mainstream culture simply because it was immoral or exploitative, the situation is far more complex.

From the late nineteenth century, an anti-*nautch* (literally 'anti-dance') campaign had seen the hereditary female performers of the North and South Indian classical arenas, the courtesans and devadasis, excluded from the modern world of classical music. The basic arguments were the same as those being made in twenty-first- century Mumbai against the bar girls:

- These women were basically prostitutes, leading lives of immorality.
- This is a form of exploitation, an insult to Indian womanhood.[8]

The similarities of anti-*nautch* and Mumbai bar girls, however, go far deeper than the core moral arguments. First, both movements were affecting basically the same communities of women: hereditary female performers. While the bar girls certainly included some helpless, destitute girls 'driven to dance', the vast majority (80/90 per cent by insider accounts) are in fact hereditary professional performers from a range of tribes across India: Deredar, Gandharva, Nat, Rajnat, Bedia, Kanjar, to name a few. These constitute the ranks of the old classical courtesans as well as other dancing girls. Second, both anti-*nautch* and the dance ban have led to the socio-economic impoverishment of these communities through loss of livelihood and increased and increasing stigmatisation and involvement in sex work.

The bar girls' débâcle was in fact a rare glimpse in India's public sphere of what is a very extensive 'other' world of performing arts. While the courtesan tradition in classical music was brought to a demise (Post, 1987), what is less known is that the women themselves, the *lineages*, lived on, and many continued performing, though, excluded from classical music (except for a few exceptions), they slipped down the cultural hierarchy and lost status (Maciszewski, 2001, 2006; Saeed, 2002). It is not possible to tell how far wider communities of dancing girls were affected by anti-*nautch*, but they were certainly hit by the loss of patronage following the abolishment of the princely courts, and more recently, by alternative entertainment such as sound systems and DJs. Police harassment has also become a big problem in the last 10–15 years.

As discussed earlier, historical and contemporary communities of traditional hereditary female entertainers have necessarily been 'other' to the women of mainstream society. Unmarried and performing in public, these women were/are 'open' or 'available' in theory, and that was part of the appeal of their performance. For such performers, their cultural capital, that is their skill in music and dance performance, is fundamentally linked to the capital of an erotic and (at least theoretically) available body. Through a logic of deduction, if they are unable to use their cultural capital (due to moral campaigns from mainstream society or other reasons), they would tend to increasingly capitalise on the erotic body. In other words, they would dance less and focus more on selling sex only, becoming more sex workers than courtesan-type performers. This is exactly what has happened in the history of the twentieth century to these communities (Maciszewski, 2001, 2006, 2007; O'Neil *et al.* 2004; Saeed, 2002). Some are involved since the 1980s in highly organised community forms of sex work, as well as being trained in dance, performing in *mujras* – the gathering where a courtesan performs to a male audience – and other traditional contexts such as marriages, or dancing in bars.

The ex-classical courtesans of North India, excluded from mainstream classical music, perform *mujras* with Bollywood songs sung to the accompaniment of harmonium and tabla and with a *kathak* basis in dance, as well as traditional repertoire including *ghazal*, seasonal songs and *qawwali*. In some contexts they also perform to recorded Bollywood music.[9] While *mujras* properly involve traditionally-based sensual dancing by very decently clad girls, some forms now involve more overtly sexual gestures and less or even no clothes and/or exposing of breasts or less commonly, pubis, bringing *mujra* into the modern Indian and Pakistani sex industry. This side of *mujra* is also found on DVDs and very extensively on the Internet.[10] Dancing in bars, in contrast, always involves girls clothed fully in traditional dress.

Like India's official popular Bollywood culture, this 'other' world is also global, with Indian dance bars across the Gulf, and also in Singapore, with mostly hereditary dancers performing.[11] *Mujra*, including the explicitly erotic end, is also global, found in the Gulf and also in the United Kingdom,[12] and quite likely in other countries with large Indian or Pakistani diaspora communities.

This invisible (to mainstream society) 'other' world of Indian performing arts is vast. According to the 1991 census, the population of Nat, just one of the hereditary female entertainer communities, in Rajasthan alone was over 23,000 (O'Neil *et al.* 2004: 856). That such communities across India had generated some 80 per cent of the 75,000 bar girls in Mumbai points to the numbers involved.

This 'other' world of Indian popular culture also extends beyond such female hereditary performers into the domain of unauthorised/unofficial gender and sexuality. A parallel world to that of the female hereditary performers is that of feminised men, performing in female or effeminate dress, known in many parts of India as *kothis* (Figure 9.2).[13] *Kothis* perform traditionally in a range of folk genres across South Asia as professionals and are also commonly very keen amateur dancers. In many (but not all) cases, they have an erotic role, and like the female hereditary performers they are perceived as, and are to a certain extent, available for sex (as the passive, 'feminine' partner) with men in the audience.[14] This is an extensive world in contemporary India. In one district of Uttar Pradesh alone, 1,000–1,500 *kothis* come during the wedding season to dance, largely to Bollywood songs. That local men get in relationships with *kothis* is well known, with people keeping *kothis* proudly, like feudal landowners may keep a courtesan/mistress. There is also an extensive network of underground *kothi* shows and *mujras*, again, largely of Bollywood songs. Also in exact parallel to the female hereditary dancers is the fact that such *kothis* are increasingly unable to survive as courtesan-style performers and are seen more as sex workers, with customers more interested in sex than dance.[15] Even more than the hereditary female dancers, this very extensive Bollywood dance world is unknown to and excluded from 'Indian popular culture', despite the fact that it has a clearly traditional and historical basis, and includes many passionately talented performers.[16]

Figure 9.2 Divya Sagar, staff member at Bharosa Trust, performing informally to a film *mujra* in Naz Foundation International office, Lucknow, March 2007.

Social exclusion

Historically, the dancing girls, courtesans and devadasis of India had a legitimate and important role in mainstream society in terms of culture and entertainment,[17] as well as direct relationships with elite or men of high status. As Maciszewski puts it, they had a 'liminal place' in society, but it was nevertheless a place (2007: 121); a stigmatised place but in many ways a powerful place. This liminal place first began to be undermined with anti-*nautch*, which denied female hereditary performers the status of artistes, labelling them as ultimately 'just prostitutes' (Maciszewski, 2006: 334; Srinivasan, 1984: 9–16 and 1985). Anti-*nautch* completely misunderstood the fact that the lifestyle of these women was fundamental to their ability to perform in public, that such 'immorality' has in fact been crucial to the existence of large swathes of Indian Culture.

In contemporary Mumbai, the legacy of anti-*nautch* meant that although journalists were told again and again that the girls were from traditional dancing communities by the bar girls' union leader in interviews,[18] these details of social organisation and history were never entered into by the press. This kind of dancer is simply understood to be a prostitute, who at best uses dance as a cover, or a desperate woman who, if truly good at heart, does not want to dance, that is, be a prostitute.[19] Similarly, a dancing girl has become an iconic representation of a prostitute in India, even, as Figure 9.3 shows, for modern commercial sex workers with no relation to dance.

It is hard for most people from mainstream society to believe a girl would dance *in this way* through choice, for it to be 'just a job', a norm, and moreover,

SEX WORKERS' OFFER

Taxes to keep police at bay

Rakeeb Hossain
Kolkata, March 1

SEX WORKERS in Bengal want to talk business with the state government. We are willing to pay if you promise to keep the police away, they have said in a proposal they intend to present to the finance ministry next week.

The sex workers have worked out the arithmetic. The state exchequer will gain at least Rs 5.4 lakh a day or Rs 1.62 crore a month from the 60,000 sex workers who were willing to pay.

The payment will be recovered from the clients. "If their proposal is accepted, they will charge each of their clients Rs 5 extra," said Dr Smarajit Jana, chief adviser to the Durbar Mahila Samanwaya Committee (DMSC), which has over 60,000 of the state's nearly 80,000 sex workers as its members.

Dr Jana said that Rs 3 of the extra charge would go to the exchequer, while Re 1 would be "condom charge". The remaining Re 1 would go to the Self Regulatory Board which looks after their health and other problems. On an average, a sex worker gets three clients a day.

"We are ready to pay to the government and in return we want the police atrocities on us to stop," said Gauri Das, president of the DMSC. "We want to be given the right to live and carry on with our trade peacefully."

Government officials said the proposal would fail as the sex 'industry' was illegal. Finance ministry officials said the Social Welfare Department will look into the proposal if it is sent to them. The department's principal secretary Sheikh Nurul Haque said: "It is not possible for the government to accept money from sex workers."

Illustration : JAYANTO

Figure 9.3 Motif of a dancing girl used to illustrate an article about Calcutta sex workers with no traditional performing background.

not shameful.[20] The bar girls themselves also reel out clichéd stories of helplessness, which can translate effectively into enhanced generosity from men, or sympathy from journalists and mainstream society. They are well aware of the moral laws of mainstream society and know that telling the truth would get them nowhere.[21]

However, beyond the monolithic morality of anti-*nautch*, it is also possible to see the bar girls trapped in forms of alienation and marginalisation deriving from the social and cultural politics of contemporary India. As is now well known, disparities of wealth in India have risen dramatically since economic liberalisation began in 1991 and the middle classes of India are living in a world that is increasingly distant from the India of nearly half the population that survives on less than a dollar a day. This massive gulf means that even when there is a will to make things fairer and better for the 'have-nots', this may be impaired by a total unawareness of some basic realities. An English language journalist of elite background based in Mumbai, for example, who did some reports on the bar girls and was extremely sympathetic to their plight, told me they suffered from 'addictions': they chewed tobacco to help counter exhaustion as they had to dance all night. Chewing *paan* is a part of lower-class Uttar Pradesh and Bihar life; yet this too was interpreted in terms of the omnipresent victim story. There is not infrequently a sense in the English language press in particular that the only known India is that of shopping malls, multiplexes, credit cards, nightclubs and luxury consumer goods. The enlarged middle classes, who grow up on *The Bold and the Beautiful* and are eager to see India on the level of first world countries, have little sense of or interest in the 'other' India, except, at best, as a problem or in certain circumstances, a tourist attraction. In a strong critique of the new middle classes in India, Pavan Varma asserts that the poor have lost their place in India's collective identity post-economic reforms (1998: 130–7). He quotes an 'ideologue of the new school of thought from the editorial page of a national newspaper' (Gautam Mukherjee, in *The Pioneer*, 26 February 1996):

> We should all get this clear, that a country of the size and importance of India has no choice but to clamber to its new tryst with destiny inside shiny buildings of chrome and glass at the free market. There is no mileage in looking wistfully at quaint mud huts rushing by the car windows because they, and their ilk, cannot meet our burgeoning needs, and if truth be told, never have (ibid.: 176–7).

The lack of engagement with the social and historical facts of the bar girls by the press, *even when informed of them*, is a symptom of the growing marginalisation of such groups from dominant society due to economic and social disparity. However, it is itself part of the *cause* of marginalisation, since understanding the history of these communities and their role in Indian cultural heritage would necessitate seeing them as a part of India, of including them, and even of questioning their previous treatment by society. This has been further intensified by the universal and absolute nature of the discourses of development and morality that the bar girls were framed in, which became a highly authoritative and emotive vortex that (conveniently) rejected social specificity and history, seizing instead on the 'problems' and 'issues'. In addition to the contradictory moral arguments outlined earlier, the girls were described as 'backward', 'uneducated', 'illiterate' and 'impoverished', but with no *specific* historical or social context given. The most potent term used, however, was 'trafficking'; it was said that the bar girls were trafficked and the bars a nexus of trafficking. This term, encompassing some of the most extreme human suffering and injustice of the subcontinent, carries with it an immense emotional and moral force. Furthermore, with India dangerously near to being declared by the United States a Tier 3 country with regards to trafficking and being subjected to sanctions, the term also carried a very heavy financial clout, and was crucial to the money, time and energy available to governmental and non-governmental organisations for the campaign against the bar girls. The ban managed to make redundant 75,000 girls who were earning decent wages and sending their children to school and so on, and was heralded as a victory against trafficking. However, when the ban was challenged in the High Court, no evidence of trafficking in connection to the bar girls was found (Agnes, 2006).

Hegemonic culture and questions of development and social justice

Some of the biggest paradoxes of the bar girls' débâcle lie in the fact that to really treat them fairly would involve facing extremely difficult questions concerning the core construct of contemporary India. It is not just that communities like hereditary performers and bar girls, and *kothis* and *hijras* also, are not wanted in middle-class India, but that this part of India reveals a still existing threat to the social, economic and cultural hegemonic integrity of the middle classes. This is particularly so now legitimate culture has spread outside the circumscribed arena of 'classical' arts from which hereditary performers have long been safely excluded, into popular culture. To see the bar girls in historical context would have shown them to be a part of Indian cultural heritage, and to acknowledge their actual social organisation would have shown them to be part of the diversity of India. Hence, these matters were (conveniently) elided, *even by those who were sympathetic to them*. Perhaps most dangerously, however, the bar girls in historical context would have presented an India that was plural in the domain of sexual morality (and in the case of *kothis* and *hijras*, gender and sexuality). Hence, while the society of the upper-middle classes grows increasingly sexually permissive and culturally liberal (the acceptance of Bollywood being a part of this), and it is acceptable for girls to dance to sexy Bollywood numbers or go to discos in mixed groups wearing mini skirts and halter-neck tops, it is not acceptable for bar girls clothed in a way conforming to traditional standards of modesty to dance for (largely) male audiences, seducing them into showering them with money, and ultimately, having sex with them only if they wish to.[22] While the historical and social context of the bar girls was not discussed in the general press, the High Court nevertheless touched on some of these issues when it declared the ban on dancing in beer bars discriminatory and therefore unconstitutional because dancing in three star and above restaurants was made exception for.[23] The case is now with the Supreme Court where it is endlessly adjourned. The ban is still in force.

The world of female hereditary performers and the specific relationship of music and dance with seduction and sex it embodies was excluded from the new 'Indian culture' of the middle classes. However, although rendered invisible from mainstream India, this world has remained, in fact becoming more shocking and debauched than ever before. It is in many ways a monster made by the middle-class reforms, an 'other' created through exclusion rather than a part contained and perhaps tamed through inclusion, albeit liminally, in the whole. It reminds me of the story of Sleeping Beauty, where the wicked godmother, excluded from the christening, curses the princess. Everything would have probably been fine if they had just invited her in the first place. To use Jerry Pinto's language from his book on the famous Hindi film vamp *Helen*, we can see it as the lurid 'underbelly' of global India's (popular) culture (2006).[24] The virulence of feeling against the bar girls can be seen in this context of threat to middle-class hegemony by its own shadow. The bar girls became *prominent*, Mumbai's colourful dance bars started to become part of the *face* of Mumbai, its *identity*, and the most liberal members of society were accepting this culture as a part of their city (without delving into history).

While issues of social and economic exclusion are at the centre of development work, *cultural* exclusion is generally seen at the most only as the broad context for such work. With female sex workers one of the target groups in India's fight against HIV/AIDS, the wider communities of hereditary performers that the bar girls come from are receiving increasing attention from sociologists, development people, journalists and so on, who, however, tend to focus only on the 'problems' and 'issues'.[25] Conversely, musicologists, for reasons of taste and social milieu tend not to focus on worlds of performing arts that are so stigmatised they barely count as 'culture' at all.[26] Either way, the marrying of social and development 'problems' to performing arts is largely missed. The case of the female hereditary performers, however, shows clearly how exclusion from the national culture in the early twentieth century has led to their impoverishment and marginalisation. That cultural exclusion is central to the loss of status and marginalisation of these communities as well as some of India's biggest problems – HIV/AIDS and a massive economy of sex work (including underage girls) – is clear when the *kolhati* female hereditary performers of *lavni* and *tamasha* are considered. *Lavni* has made the transition to a stage 'folk' art in Maharashtra and the female performers have largely retained their traditional liminal status and are not involved in wholesale commercial sex work like some other communities.[27] The fact that dancing in bars *was* rehabilitation from the industrial style sex work found in some villages of hereditary performers for many bar girls has apparently been considered only by the bar girls union (see Agnes, 2005).

Popular culture and 'The People'

Anti-*nautch* and the exclusion of hereditary female performers paved the way for the birth of Indian national performing arts. The bar girls débâcle needs to be seen in the context of a parallel though more diffuse phase of national construction, with processes of inclusion and exclusion, concealment and falsification at work in the 'invention' of a new culture and identity of high GDP, globalised India. More dangerously, it is this new identity of India that gives the impression, consciously or unconsciously, that it is not just a national culture, but a *popular* national culture, a culture of 'the people'. In the world of the middle classes, 'everyone' can dance, and there is an eagerness to include more and more people, in the case of SDIPA, extending to underprivileged, handicapped and HIV/AIDS infected/affected children (interview, Shiamak Davar, 30 April 2006, Mumbai). However, to make an albeit crude comparison, while Shiamak Davar has an astounding 25,000 students, there were twice that number or more hereditary performers dancing in Mumbai's beer bars alone. The populist image and rhetoric of the current celebration of Bollywood dance implies an *all*-inclusiveness in contemporary Indian Culture which does not exist.

The term 'popular' has been criticised as implying hierarchies of culture irrelevant to the Indian, postcolonial case (Appadurai and Breckenridge, 1988; Pinney, 2000). I would go further and say that in the cultural arena of the twenty-first century, 'popular' culture, in the sense of opposed to 'elite' culture, actually masks fundamental hierarchies and processes of exclusion. The new, celebrated, middle-class Bollywood culture can be identified as popular, but only in the sense of a popular whose 'other' is the hidden, denied, repressed, excluded world of hereditary female performers (including *kothis*). Even the term 'public' culture, aiming 'to capture ... the mainstream authorized quality of much Indian public culture, and still leave room for the subaltern' (Pinney, 2000: 5) does not encompass the reality of what is more like two parallel worlds of dance, where the subaltern one is as extensive as the 'official' world, and moreover, occupies realms that are private or not talked about. At least in the world of dance, there is a need to re-conceptualise the topography of Indian culture in ways that adequately describe the new levels of socio-economic inequality.

Notes

1 This chapter is based on a year's fieldwork on global Bollywood dance carried out between 2005 and 2006 in India, Nepal, Tibet, Singapore and the United Kingdom, funded by a British Academy Larger Research Grant. In India, I met a range of film industry and other middle-class dancers and choreographers, as well as hereditary and *kothi* transgender dancers. I would like to thank all those who gave me time for formal and informal meetings, in particular Varsha Kale, Ankush Deshpande and Divya Sagar.
2 While Dwyer in 2000 discusses the contested nature of cultural legitimacy of Hindi films, writing eight years on, it can be seen as well established.
3 The focus is particularly on female performers. The case for male performers is different.
4 See Ann David (2007) for a study of Bollywood dance in the United Kingdom.
5 See Forum Against Oppression of Women (2005) for statistical information on the bar girls.
6 The breakdown of consensus on the bribes paid by bar owners to police and government officials and the license fees of the bars, as well as US pressure on India regarding trafficking were also significant to the campaign. See Agnes for analysis of these matters and the moral arguments (2005).
7 These details were raised by the Bar Girls Union. See Agnes (2005).
8 See Reddy (1930: 108–32 in particular), responsible for the devadasi legislation in Madras.
9 This requires a different license.
10 A search for *mujra* on You Tube rapidly reaches links for 'triple X' material and porn. These *mujra* videos on DVD and the Internet seem to derive from Pakistan.
11 There are also dance bars in Nepal, Malaysia, Korea, Tibet and Dallas in the United States, though not apparently a part of the Indian hereditary dancer circuit.
12 This briefly made the mainstream UK press. See for example, Thompson writing in *The Observer* 27 July 2003 'Revealed: Bollywood craze that is fuelling London's vice rackets'.
13 See Seabrook (1999) and Shah and Bondyopadhyay (2007) for information on *kothis*.
14 See Brown (2003: 146–53) for historical material relating to such performers during Aurangzeb's reign. There are men who perform as women in India in a variety of traditional folk genres as well as urban theatre who are not necessarily *kothi*, that is,

feminine in gender identity and sexual role. See Hansen (1998), who discusses female impersonators in Parsi theatre.

15 Personal communication, Shivananda Khan, NFI, Lucknow, 8 April 2007.

16 The passion for dancing female dance is clearly linked to being and feeling feminine, with dance a highly gendered form of behaviour.

17 In the case of the devadasis, this was also a ritual role.

18 Various personal communications with Varsha Kale, Indian Bargirls Union leader, 2006–07.

19 See Kasbekar (2000: 301–3) on this cliché in Hindi films.

20 Existing outside of the patriarchal structure that constrains women through the concept of honour, these hereditary performers are generally not ashamed to be dancing in bars and have the full support of their family. Their attitudes to doing sex work, which they usually refer to as *galat kaam*, 'wrong doing', may be more complex, but would need careful ethnographic research to understand.

21 Also, mentioning details of the bar girls' background would lead into the explosive issue of caste, which is something that understandably needs to be approached with caution.

22 Similar arguments can be made for the greater acceptance of elite men adopting the global 'gay' identity versus *kothis*.

23 The ban was also deemed unconstitutional as it was contrary to the 'right to livelihood', which the girls were seen as pursuing through dancing (Agnes 2006).

24 This also echoes Nandy's well-known 1998 analysis of Hindi films. However, here, the 'underbelly' is live culture and communities.

25 An example of this is Agrawal (2008), which includes only brief references that implicitly refer to the Bedia's artistic role and identity historically and in contemporary society. The front cover of the book, however, shows a Bedia woman dancing.

26 Publications by Maciszewski (2001, 2006, 2007) and Saeed (2002) are exceptions, the latter belonging more to sociology than musicology.

27 Personal communication Varsha Kale. The inclusion of *lavni* and *tamasha* and its traditional performers is in many ways surprising, and perhaps reflects the fact that it is presented as a 'folk' art, and is a state-level rather than national phenomenon.

References

Agnes, F. (2005) 'Hypocritical morality', *Manushi*, 149, October. Available online at http://www.indiatogether.org/manushi/issue149/index.htm (accessed 5 May 2008).

Agnes, F. (2006) 'The right to dance', *Manushi* July. Available online at: http://www.indiatogether.org/2006/jul/soc-dancebar.htm (accessed 5 May 2008).

Agrawal, A. (2008) *Chaste Wives and Prostitute Sisters: Patriarchy and Prostitution Among the Bedias of India*. New Delhi: Routledge.

Appadurai, A. and Breckenridge, C. (1988) 'Why public culture?' *Public Culture* 1(1): 5–10.

Brown, K. (2003) 'Hindustani music in the time of Aurangzeb', Upublished PhD Thesis, School of Oriental and African Studies.

David, A. R. (2007) 'Beyond the silver screen: Bollywood and *filmi* dance in the UK', *South Asia Research* Vol. 27(1): 5–24.

Dwyer, R. (2000) *All You Want Is Money, All You Need Is Love. Sex and Romance in Modern India*. London and New York: Cassell.

Forum Against Oppression of Women (2005) Working women in Mumbai bars, truths behind controversy – Results from survey among 500 women dancers across 50 bars. Research Centre for Women's Studies, SNDT Women's University, Juhu Campus, Mumbai 49.

Hansen, K. (1998) '*Stri bhumika*: Female impersonators and actresses on the Parsi stage', *Economic and Political Weekly*, 29 August, 2291–300.

Kasbekar, A. (2000) 'Hidden pleasures: Negotiating the myth of the female ideal in popular Hindi cinema', in Pinney and Dwyer (eds) *Pleasure and the Nation: The History, Politics and Consumption of Public Culture in India*. New Delhi: Oxford University Press: 286–308.

Maciszewski, A. (2001) 'Stories about selves: Selected North Indian women's musical (auto)biographies', *The World of Music* 43(1): 139–72.

Maciszewski, A. (2006) 'Tawa'if, tourism, and tales: The problematics of twenty-first-century musical patronage for North India's courtesans', in Feldman, M. and Gordon, B. (eds) *The Courtesan's Arts: Cross-Cultural Perspectives*. New York: Oxford University Press: 332–51.

Maciszewski, A. (2007) 'Texts, tunes, and talking heads: Discourses about socially marginal North Indian musicians', *Twentieth Century Music* 3(1): 121–44.

Nandy, A. (1998) 'Indian popular cinema as a slum's eye view of politics', in Nandy, A. (ed.) *The Secret Politics of Our Desires: Innocence, Culpability and Indian Popular Cinema*. London: Zed Books: 1–18.

O'Neil, J., Orchard, T., Swarankar, R. C., Blanchard, J. F., Gurav, K. and Moses, F. (2004) 'Dhandha, dharma and disease: Traditional sex work and HIV/AIDS in rural India', *Social Science and Medicine* (59): 851–60.

Pinney, C. (2000) 'Introduction: Public, popular, and other cultures', in Pinney and Dwyer (eds) *Pleasure and the Nation: The History, Politics and Consumption of Public Culture in India*. New Delhi: Oxford University Press: 1–34.

Pinto, J. (2006) *Helen: The Life and Times of an H-Bomb*. New Delhi: Penguin.

Post, J. (1987) 'Professional women in Indian music: The Death of the Courtesan Tradition', in Ellen Koskoff (ed.) *Women and Music in Cross-Cultural Perspective*. New York: Greenwood Press: 97–109.

Reddy, M. (1930) *My Experience As A Legislator*. Madras: Current Thought Press.

Qureshi, R. (2006) 'Female agency and patrilineal constraints: Situating courtesans in twentieth-century India' in Feldman, M. and Gordon, B. (eds) *The Courtesan's Arts: Cross-Cultural Perspectives*. New York: Oxford University Press: 312–31.

Saeed, F. (2002) *TABOO! The Hidden Culture of a Red Light Area*. Karachi: Oxford University Press.

Seabrook, J. (1999) *Love in a Different Climate: Men Who Have Sex with Men in India*. London: Verso.

Shah, V. and Bondyopadhyay, A. (2007) *My Body Is Not Mine: Stories of Violence and Tales of Hope. Voices from the Kothi Community in India*. India: Naz Foundation International (NFI) and Centre for Media and Alternative Communication (CMAC).

Srinivasan, A. (1984) 'Temple "prostitution" and community reform: An examination of the ethnographic, historical and textual context of the devadasi of Tamil Nadu, South India', Unpublished PhD thesis, Wolfson College, Cambridge University.

Srinivasan, A. (1985) 'Reform and revival: The devadasi and her dance', *Economic and Political Weekly* 20(44):1869–76.

Thompson, T. (2003) 'Revealed: Bollywood craze that is fuelling London's vice rackets', *The Observer* 27 July. Available online at: http://www.guardian.co.uk/crime/article/0,,1006717,00.html (accessed 11 May 2008).

Varma, P. (1998) *The Great Indian Middle Classes*. New Delhi: Penguin.

10 From *zenana* to cinema

The impact of royal aesthetics on Bollywood film

Angma Dey Jhala

When Aishwarya Rai lights up the screen as the Rajput princess Jodhbai in Ashustosh Gowarikar's historical drama, *Jodhaa Akbar* (2008), it is her jewellery and ornate dress which captivate as much as this former Miss World's beauty. Countless early reviews of the film and blogs by avid moviegoers, whether in India, the United States or Britain, highlight the pageantry of costume and sets in this film. Jodhaa blazes onto the screen in a kaleidoscopic palette of colours. She wears heavy ornate red, orange, green, vermilion and yellow silk and chiffon *gaghras* and *odhanis*, while flashing strings of pearl and diamond necklaces, gold *naths* and jewelled toe rings and amulets. The opulence of royal India, whether that of the imperial Mughal court or the festively decorated palaces of the Rajasthani kingdoms, is as much a leading character in this film as the life stories of the pseudo-historical figures it chronicles.

Even though the princely states officially lapsed with India's Independence in 1947, they remain prominent in the public sphere and cultural life of the postcolonial republic. Indeed, Bollywood film has reflected from its origins the pageantry and theatre of royal visual splendour in ornate textiles, glittering jewels and palatial settings. From the glamour of Sadhana Bose in *Raj Nartaki* (1941), Meena Kumari in *Pakeezah* (1972), Rekha in *Umrao Jaan* (1981) and Sharmila Tagore in *Eklavya* (2007), the courtly Indian aesthetics of the women's world, or zenana, have transformed Indian fashion and the definition of the ideal cinematic heroine. The early Bombay film houses were influenced by regional cinematic traditions, which themselves had adapted the courtly culture of *nautch* dance and music from local princely states. In large part, these films have depicted the women of the zenana in two ways: as courtesans and royal wives. The courtesan films ordinarily reflect the lost glory of an earlier Indo-Islamic musical tradition, whether performed in the Mughal imperial harem or its successor, regional princely states of various religious ancestries, Hindu, Muslim and Sikh. Arguably, the most famous courtesan films were those made in the 1960s, 1970s and 1980s: *Mughal-e-Azam*, (dir. K Asif, 1960) which chronicles the love between Emperor Akbar's son Salim and the dancing girl Arnakali in sixteenth-century Lahore; *Pakeezah* (dir. Kamal Amrohi, 1972), which was shot in the former princely state of Patiala and narrates the story of an early twentieth-century Muslim courtesan; and *Umrao Jaan* (dir. Muzaffar Ali, 1981), which charts the romantic trials of a Muslim *tawaif* in nineteenth-century princely Lucknow and was directed by a descendent of the Lucknow aristocracy. The genre has had an updated rendition in Shyam Benegal's *Zubeida* (2001), which tells the tale of a Muslim courtesan and her relationship with the former Hindu Rajput Maharaja of Jodhpur in twentieth-century Rajasthan.

Royal princesses, Maharanis and dowager queens figure large in recent historical epics, such as *Ashoka* (dir. Santosh Sivan, 2001), *Eklavya* (dir. Vidhu Vinod Chopra, 2007) and *Jodhaa Akbar* (dir. Ashustosh Gowarikar, 2008). These films are invariably shot in princely locations, such as the former palaces, forts or temple grounds of erstwhile ruling families. *Ashoka*, an epic film about the life of the famous Mauryan emperor, was filmed on the *ghats* of Maheshwar fort, built by the Maratha regent queen, Ahilyabai Holkar of Indore, and still owned by her descendant. *Eklavya*, which chronicles a fictionalized story of internecine rivalry in a former Rajput royal family, was shot in Rajasthan at Devigrah, a former Jhala Rajput fort in Udaipur and Jaipur's City Palace. Not only did it have a royal setting, but its main lead was performed by the princely film actor, Saif Ali Khan, heir apparent to the erstwhile Muslim state of Pataudi, and the costumes were created by the fashion designer Raghuvendra Rathore, himself a member of the Jodhpur royal family. *Jodhaa Akbar*, which lavishly portrays a largely fictionalized relationship between Emperor Akbar and one of his Rajput wives from Rajasthan, was filmed in parts of Jaipur and received the support of the current Maharani and Maharaja of Jaipur, who have validated the film's credibility in wake of widespread criticism by Rajputs in Rajasthan and medieval historians on the film's factual inaccuracies.

Some scholars have argued that this fascination for courtly aesthetics and royal drama, particularly the courtesan genre, expresses a popular nostalgia for the past, whether a lost Indo-Islamic aesthetic in the *gazal* and recitation of Urdu poetry or the majesty of pre-Independent royal India.[1] I argue that these films, particularly those produced in the 1990s and first decade of the twenty-first century, not only reflect a yearning for past grandeur, but also a late twentieth-century reinvigorated nationalist sentiment, which mirrors India's growing economic prosperity and political stability on the international stage.

By way of introduction, this chapter will first provide a brief discussion on the history of princely India and the women's courtly world of the zenana. It will then investigate the two major genres through which zenana aesthetics have been depicted in Hindi cinema: courtesan narrative and royal dramas, particularly those that take place in a Rajasthani context. Due to the limitations of space, some films will receive greater discussion than others. It will conclude with a larger critique of the zenana and its general influence on Indian popular culture.

A brief history of the princely states

Until 1947, India was divided into two distinct regions: the territories of British India and approximately 600 semi-autonomous kingdoms. These 'native' or 'princely' states, as they were termed, formed a diverse, cosmopolitan and powerful polity. Some states were as large as European countries and as wealthy, such as Kashmir and Hyderabad.[2] Indian kingship itself was not static or homogenous, and each princely state had its own history, culture, religion, language and kinship groupings, which differentiated it from other 'little kingdoms' as did the zenanas within them. They ranged from the Hindu Rajput and Maratha states of western India, the Sikh kingdoms of the Punjab in the north, the Muslims states of Bhopal and Hyderabad which had Mughal, Persian and Afghan antecedents, the Buddhist tribal kingdoms of eastern Bengal such as the Chakma Raj which had ties with Burma and the powerful southern states of Travancore and Mysore. Some upheld primogeniture; others were matrilineal in succession, such as the South Indian kingdoms of Travancore and Cochin.[3]

The conquest of Bengal in the mid-eighteenth century by the British East India Company augured the subsequent spread of British imperial power within the subcontinent. With the treaties of 1818 and the defeat of the Marathas and the Pindaris during the decline of the Mughal Empire, the East India Company emerged as the single paramount power in the subcontinent. The aim of British paramountcy, however, was not to directly rule the whole of India, but rather only those areas, which were financially profitable and politically expedient, such as Bengal and the presidencies of Bombay and Madras. For the remaining 'terra incognita', the British implemented a policy of 'indirect rule,' which provided 'a cheap means of pacifying and subordinating regions not under their own direct control' by forming subsidiary alliances and treaties with the native rulers.[4]

Under the umbrella of the Pax Britannica, the princes held full authority in internal matters of state governance such as taxation, state revenue collection, criminal and judicial law and the development of educational and cultural institutions.[5] However, they could not conduct foreign policy and were obliged to maintain a body of Company troops, which would be stationed in their kingdoms under the control of a British political officer.[6]

By the mid-nineteenth century, the crisis of the 1857 Mutiny highlighted the vital role of the Indian princes in Britain's policy of 'indirect rule'.[7] While it can be argued that Dalhousie's earlier strategy of annexing Indian princely states was one of the many grievances leading to the mutiny, some princes also served as important allies for the British. During the revolt, certain 'patches' of the native states, such as Gwalior, Hyderabad, Patiala, Rampur and Rewa, proved to be 'breakwaters in the storm' which would have otherwise 'swept away' the British, in the words of the first Viceroy Lord Canning.[8]

Henceforth, the princes were 'accorded a permanent position as part of the British Empire'.[9] The Queen's 1858 Proclamation which was announced shortly after the events of the Mutiny, sought to '"respect the rights, dignity and honour of native princes as our own," because they were the quintessential "natural leaders" of South Asian society'.[10] In shifting from Company to Crown rule, the statement aimed to establish a new social order with the British monarchy as the focus of sovereignty, capable of structuring into a single hierarchy all its subjects,

Indian and British.[11] It encouraged and embellished a 'language of feudal loyalty' among the Indian princes.[12]

In the subsequent period, a system of 'personal' relationships between the Indian rulers and their British sovereigns, as romantically portrayed in the literature of the late nineteenth and early twentieth century began to emerge. The adoption and gifting of imperial 'honours', such as medals, gun salutes, seating placement at durbars, orders and knighthoods further tied the Indian princes to their colonial masters. Royal Indian women, such as wives and other female relatives of Indian rulers, were included in this process of 'ornamentation' and were awarded The Order of the Crown of India for meritorious acts of service.[13]

In 1921, the princes founded their own body, The Chamber of Princes, which provided a forum of dialogue and cultivated 'an environment in which good government became more fashionable'.[14] As 'modern' statesmen, they attempted to combine indigenous forms of *rajadharma* (kingly duty) with British models of good governance. Some exercised vital powers in local, regional and all-Indian imperial politics during this period.[15]

However, the differences between the princes proved to be too great. Rajput kshatriya kings in Jaipur and Jodhpur looked down upon the Sudra-descended Maratha kings of Gwalior and Indore, as well as the Jat-Sikh kings of Punjab (such as Patiala, Nabha and Kapurthala). In equal measure, the Maratha kings, such as Gwalior, retained aged resentment against the Rajputs for siding with the East India Company, which lead to their own demise. Even closely related dynasties 'were not immune from vendettas'.[16] Morvi and Cutch in Kathiawar were locked in a dispute over a piece of the Rann; Patiala with his Sikh kinsman Nabha over the rulership of the *Khalsa*.[17] The ruler of Indore, Tukoji Rao, noted that 'on account of the differences in the education, training, methods of thought, status and position of the Indian Princes, it would be impossible to secure ... unanimity ... on any subject placed before the council'.[18]

This inability to maintain cohesiveness arguably led to the wane of the princely order and its weakened place in Indian politics by the mid-twentieth century. The period of rapid metamorphosis, which brought modernization, independence and democracy to the new nation, can be interpreted as the twilight years for princely India. The princes were generally characterized as the losers in the battle for power between the British Empire and the Indian nationalists with the resolution of Partition in 1947.[19] In the 30-year period from 1919 to 1947, the lives of the Indian princes were forever altered. At the end of World War I, the princely states were still relatively secure. Indian rulers were admired by their subjects and even by nationalists. In the 1920s, Mahatma Gandhi, whose father and grandfather had served as chief ministers under Indian princes, was himself 'positive' towards the states, which were close to his ideals of Ram Rajya, the 'acme of swaraj'.[20] Yet, a few years later they were virtually extinct and non-existent players in the construction of the Indian republic.[21]

While the nation won Independence from foreign rule, the princely states lost their autonomous identities. Rulers were stripped of their executive rights and their territories merged with the new democratic republic. In 1971, under

Prime Minister Indira Gandhi, the erstwhile princes lost their last major entitlement, their constitutionally granted incomes, the 'Privy Purse', which was based on an annual percentage of the revenue from their former kingdoms. With the absorption of the princely states, their systems of administration and land tenure were gradually abolished. During Indira Gandhi's 1975 Emergency, when leaders of the Congress Opposition were jailed without habeas corpus during a period that has largely been described as 'dictatorial', princely politicians, such as Swatantra MP Maharani Gayatri Devi of Jaipur and Bharatiya Janata MP Rajmata Vijaya Raje Scindia of Gwalior, were inmates at the infamous Tihar Jail outside Delhi. Nonetheless, many of these erstwhile sovereigns remained active in the public life of the nation, engaging in electoral politics, religious and cultural patronage, business, law and education. They have served as diplomats, governors, patrons of educational and charitable institutions, local magnates, company directors, cabinet ministers and, particularly, as elected politicians.[22] Rather than bygone remnants of an antiquated age, they are very much part of the new nation. Perhaps the most significant way royal heritage has remained in the public imagination during the postcolonial period is through the guise of film.

Princely women: the world of the zenana

Princely courts had in addition to male arenas of power, female segregated spaces where women resided. The zenana, the 'women's quarters of the palace' or 'female courts', housed women from several kingdoms, regions and religions, serving as what can be described as a microcosmic 'united nations' within the kingdom. Originally a Persian institution, which entered India with Muslim invasions in the thirteenth century, the zenana altered local customs as Hindu dynasties emulated the mannerisms of the Muslim court. Although the concept of gender-segregated living spaces was ancient to India, finding reference in the Sanskrit epics and the *Kamasutra* as well as classical Hindu architecture, such as the Rajput fort of Chittor in Rajasthan, it was not rigidly enforced until the arrival of Islam.[23] During Mughal Emperor Akbar's reign in the latter half of the sixteenth century, there was a marked move towards the confinement of women and the creation of a harem structure.[24] As he and a number of his descendents married Hindu Rajput princesses, Mughal courtly life and architecture was in turn imitated by non-Muslim royal elites.[25]

As the exclusively female quarters in the ruler's palace, each Zenana had its own unique history and socio-political identity. During the colonial period, it brought together women with different religious, caste, regional, linguistic, aesthetic and clan affiliations, creating a heterogeneous, cosmopolitan world within the already cosmopolitan universe of princely India. Hierarchical and polygamous institutions, Hindu Rajput zenanas, for example, were presided over by predominantly Kshatriya women who were supported by females from Brahmin, Sudra and Vaisya castes as well as Muslims and Jains. The royal household could hold as many as 30 or more wives as well as female relations, serving women and attendants.[26] In 1940, when Maharani Gayatri Devi of Jaipur

first arrived in the Jaipur Zenana as a young bride she was amazed by the sheer
number of women:

> In the year of my marriage, there were still 400 women living in the
> Zenana. Among them were widowed relatives and their daughters as well
> as their servants and attendants; the Dowager Maharani and her retinue of
> ladies-in-waiting, maids, cooks, and other servants; comparable retinues for
> each of [my husband's] three wives and all the retainers of the late Maharaja's
> other wives. Presiding over them was the only one of the late Maharaja's wives
> who were still alive. She was known to us as Maji Sahiba and we treated her
> with the utmost deference. As one of Jai's wives, I could almost never uncover
> my face in her presence and always had to be seated a few places to her left.[27]

In addition to the wives, mothers and sisters, the female relations of the dynastic
family and the aristocracy, the zenana also included courtesans (which often
exceeded the number of royal wives), women in service capabilities, such as
maids, cooks, dyers, weavers, astrologers, musicians, singers as well as eunuchs.
In the twentieth century, Christian women also entered the Zenana as wives and
mistresses of Indian rulers and the courtly aristocracy, and as governesses, nurses
and teachers for the children of the household. Until the 1950s, many royal Indian
women still continued to live within the bounds of the palace Zenana.

Bollywood cinema and the aesthetics of the zenana

The first film ever shown in India was by the Lumiere brothers, who had
earlier introduced cinematography in Paris, on 7 July 1896. The event was
marked as the 'miracle of the century' and Indians were soon entranced by
this new format for theatrical storytelling. Three years later, the Indian director
Harischandra S. Bhatvadekhar began making the first Indian films and soon after,
Dhundiraj Govind Phalke, would produce the first full length Indian feature film,
the historical epic, *Raja Harischandra* which was released in 1913.[28] By 1931,
Indian film-making had entered the age of sound with its first Bombay talkie,
Alam Ara.[29]

   From the beginning princely settings and locations were used by the Bombay
film houses. With the advent of sound, dance and music became a staple of
Indian cinema, and one of the key resources for talent were the male and female
descendents of courtesans from royal households. In particular, the courtesans
became 'exponents of the high culture in the courts, performing classical music
and dance in salons for royal patrons' which was reproduced for a larger, popular
audience. Thus the courtly aesthetics of song, musical accompaniment, dress
and jewellery of regional zenanas became an integral part of Indian cinema.[30]
In addition, early Bombay pictures were also shot in local princely states and
produced by directors who had grown up in a zenana culture. Dhiren Ganguly's
Lotus Film Company was founded with the patronage of the Nizam of Hyderabad in
the 1920s. Ganguly shot his historical A *Razia,* a film about the only Muslim queen

of Delhi, against palace backgrounds and gardens in Hyderabad.[31] After the Nizam expressed displeasure with the film, Ganguly subsequently gained the support of the Maharaja of Jaipur, where he continued to shoot movies using local princely settings and architecture.[32] The director P. C. Barua, son of the Raja of Gauripur, made the first sound adaptation of Sarat Chandra Chattopadhyay's novel *Devdas* in 1935, which was a huge success, and has been described as revolutionizing the future of Indian social pictures.[33]

Women who had themselves lived in princely zenanas also became film actresses or brought their stories to the big screen. The notorious Malabar Hill Murder, which came to trial in the Bombay High Court in 1925, involved a Muslim courtesan, Mumtaz Begum, and her princely lover, Maharaja Tukoji Rao Holkar of Indore. Mumtaz had lived since her adolescence as a dancing girl in the Indore zenana as the Maharaja's lover. By 1925, she had escaped to Bombay, where she found a wealthy new protector, a Muslim businessman by the name of Bawla. While on an evening drive with Bawla in Malabar Hill, her car was attacked and her lover murdered by emissaries of the Indore household. Through the intervention of three British army officers, who were returning from an afternoon round of golf, she managed to survive the incident and lived to give damning oral evidence, which eventually forced the Maharaja to abdicate in 1926.[34] This tale had all the ingredients – love, sex, murder, 'debauched' royalty and colonial repression – for *filmi* melodrama. Mumtaz took her story to Bombay where it was transformed into the film *Kulin Kanta* (dir. Homi Master, 1925), an early form of the courtesan genre in Hindi cinema. Later, it was rumoured she left for the even greener pastures of Hollywood.[35] Similarly, Sitara Devi, a performer at the court of the Nawab of Rampur, became a prominent film actress in the 1930s.[36]

Thus traditions of the courtly life, especially the musical forms of courtesan dance and music and the ornate display of costumes and jewellery, were used in filming tales about royal women – those who were princely courtesans or wives and mothers.

The tawaif: the courtesan film

The stories of the courtesan, which filtered in from regional princely states and courtesan *kothas* in zamindari and urban locations, from the beginning constituted its own genre in Hindi cinema. With the success of early films, such as *Kulinkanta* and *Raj Nartaki*, the opulent settings and romanticism of the *tawaif* would magically come to life with the partial colour and colour films of the 1960s through the 1980s, and more recently in remakes of earlier classics since the 1990s. Invariably the part of the courtesan was given to the most beautiful film actress of her generation, such as Meena Kumari in *Pakeezah*, Rekha in Muzaffar Ali's *Umrao Jaan* and Aishwarya Rai in its recent 2006 remake.[37]

Mughal-e-Azam was considered the classic of the golden era of Bollywood. While historically 'dubious', the film chronicles the sixteenth-century Mughal harem of Akbar. Although Akbar had Hindu Rajput wives, he had none named Jodhbai as the film proclaimed. Prince Salim's mother, who was the daughter of the Rajput ruler Raja Bahagara Mal was not named Jodhbai. This would be the same controversy that *Jodhaa Akbar* would inherit by retaining Jodhbai as the name of one of Akbar's wives. Additionally, there was no Anarkali, the courtesan who Salim fell in love with, according to historical chronicles. Nonetheless, K. Asif recreated an idea of courtly life and culture in the film, knowing that there was an audience for such period piece films, with lavish sets. It became, and has remained, a huge hit.[38] In *Pakeezah,* again the loves of a courtesan – this time set in the nineteenth century and filmed in the erstwhile princely state of Patiala in the Punjab – associated with a Nawab's household, took centre stage.

The princely courtesan was often skilled in the performance of music, fluent in the lyrical language of courtly Persian and Urdu poetry and graceful in dance. As film historian Rachel Dwyer notes, the courtesan as subject in film particularly enabled the viewer to enjoy 'the spectacle of the body, the elaboration of scenery and in particular of clothing'.[39] The viewer is overwhelmed by the sensual environment: 'Persian carpets, crystal candelabra, courtyards with fountains, pools, "Islamic arches," and elaborate [traditional] clothes'.[40] Muzaffar Ali, the film's director was himself from a Lucknow aristocratic family and a fashion designer. He was careful in the details for the costumes and film sets as well as the music. Silver *paan dans*, *hookah*s, hand spun rich brocades and Jadau jewellery incorporated the craftsmanship of local Lucknow artisans in the making of the 1981 movie.[41] He personally selected the costumes for Rekha as Umrao Jaan and elements from dress to jewellery relied on nineteenth-century historical data of the Awadhi court.[42]

The richness of these artefacts and the physical surroundings when coupled with the highly ornate, 'flowery' use of Urdu as the language of 'courtly culture', Dwyer associates with a nostalgia for the 'decline and disappearance of courtesan culture' of Indo-Islamic heritage by both Hindu and Muslim moviegoers.[43] I would argue that the recent remakes of these mid-twentieth century courtesan films especially in the 1990s and since reflect not only a nostalgic nod to the past, but also a celebration of India's present and future position through its 'heritage' culture. J. P. Dutta's *Umrao Jaan* (2006) while eulogizing the memory of the *tawaif*, also represents India's current glamour. The costumes, jewels and the architecture (*Umrao Jaan* is shot in Jaipur) are an ideal setting to showcase India's palaces, fashion designers, jewellers and craftsmen as illustrative of the past, but accessible for the viewer (as filmgoer, tourist or property buyer) of a present reality. While earlier zamindari *havelis* or princely palaces were not accessible as places to visit or live in, they are now available to see and inhabit, some can even be bought and lived in by non-aristocratic owners.

In addition, not only are these movies make locations, lifestyles and narratives of the past accessible for contemporary viewers, but unlike the transnational Hindi films which portray a global, modern urban Indian, these films highlight a historic past that can be marketed as uniquely 'Indian', shot in the subcontinent. Where films that feature modern narratives are as likely to take place in London and New York as Bombay, and may often be interspersed with scenes filmed in Singapore, Geneva or Paris, these movies are situated in subcontinental locations and often in rural sites or the city capitals of former princely states, such as Jaipur and Jodhpur, which do not reflect the urban sprawl and high rises of British India's postcolonial metropolises.

The Rajput zenana: the pageantry of colour

The immediate impact of these dramas about princely India, which are increasingly being shot in erstwhile Rajput kingdoms in Rajasthan, is the display of colour. In *Jodhaa Akbar*, which narrates the fictional story of the Mughal Emperor Akbar and one of his Hindu Rajput wives, colour identifies the Rajput locations in the film: in the form of bright, billowing curtains, embroidered vermillion bolsters and cushions and gaily painted walls covered in murals and floral patterns. These interiors are used for the fictional Rajput court of Amer where the heroine originates from, her suites within Akbar's harem and the households of other neighbouring Rajput states. Jodhaa herself dresses in the warm, characteristically bright palette that is considered auspicious for young Rajput women to wear.[44]

Not only are the architectural settings, both internal and external, brightly hued in vibrant paintings and the figures clothed in brocades and silks, but the very sensual environment is saturated by colour. When Akbar arrives in Amer for the first time, he is greeted by a shower of marigolds, which fall before the screen in a curtain of gold. When Jodhaa arrives at the imperial Mughal court, she performs a 'Rajput' tradition, entering the palace with Sindhur-coated feet, leaving a trail of red footprints.

In *Eklavya,* the story of a postcolonial, contemporary Rajput royal family, colour again is used in the clothing of the male and female figures. The fashion designer, Raghuvendra Rathore, himself keenly familiar with Rajput royal costume, has stated that it was growing up with the influence of his mother and the environment of the Jodhpur zenanas that shaped his aesthetics. As he noted in a 2007 interview, 'living in the zenana put me in touch with how women lived in a space that was truly their own'.[45] For *Eklavya*, he designed the costumes, incorporating traditional styles and patterns and local, indigenous fabrics from Jodhpur, Bikaner and Udaipur.[46]

In addition, these films use a uniquely Rajasthani form of dress and jewellery. Rather than the *salwar kameez* or stitched *achkan*s of the *tawaif* courtesan films, Rathore clothed his characters in the *gaghra,* a long gathered skirt, and *oodhani*, a light weight scarf worn around the torso, for the female characters and *chudidars* for the men.[47] Similarly, Neeta Lulla did extensive research for *Jodhaa Akbar*, dressing Jodhaa in *gaghras*. As she noted, she went specifically to Jaipur 'to source the fabrics and the colour schemes to suit that time period' including speaking with the current Jaipur royal family.[48] Relying on contemporary practices in Rajasthan as well as historical miniature painting traditions, she wanted to strike a 'warm colour palette'. She used yellows, saffrons and emerald greens for the Rajputs in the film (epitomized by Jodhaa) and golds, browns and beiges for the Mughals, represented by Akbar.[49] In addition, all the jewellery in the film was made of real gold, diamonds and precious gems.[50]

As Rathore noted in an interview with the *Times of India*, *Eklavya* was 'an opportunity to recreate the authenticity of Rajasthani life as it existed in history books of the past.' His ultimate hope was that the fashion in the film would 'herald the return of traditionalism with a dash of modernity' on the runway.[51] Described as the designer who both embodies 'royal Jodhpuri tradition and the contemporary global aesthetic', Rathore dresses his characters both with attention to the past but also in the current discourse of a dynamic and hopeful present and future.[52]

Furthermore, the costumes of these royal dramas have gone from the screen to *prêt a porter*. Eighteen outfits that Aishwarya Rai wore for *Jodhaa Akbar* will be sold for prices from between Rs.7,000 to Rs.2 lakhs.[53] The jewellery designer Tanishq, who outfitted the caste of Jodhaa Akbar with fine jewellery, has also received several new orders. *Indic Culture* reported that the jewellery in the film was already influencing consumer fashion trends.[54] The 'royal' clothes from J. P. Dutta's rendition of *Umrao Jaan* were also sold in an auction for a notable charity.[55] Not only has a zenana culture influenced ideas of history, nostalgia, gender and romance through these films, but also the contemporary fashion world, catering to an Indian middle-class consumer market, keen for a redefined conception of finery and elegance.

Living like royalty: the influence of zenana films on Indian popular culture

Although princely India ceased to exist some 60 years ago, the courtly culture of royal households still figures large in contemporary Hindi cinema as this chapter has argued. While these films may express a longing for the past, I argue that an emphasis on zenana aesthetics and fashion reflects India's present-day prosperity. Just as sweeping historical epics have come to symbolize China's new confidence in a global marketplace such as *Crouching Tiger, Hidden Dragon* (dir. Ang Lee, 2000), *Hero* (dir. Zhang Yimou, 2002) and *Curse of the Golden Flower* (dir. Zhang Yimou, 2006), these big-budget, opulent courtly dramas highlight both the institutions of India's past as well as her current buoyancy and dynamic fiscal growth as a potential leader in a post-Cold War economic and geopolitical climate.

Alongside fashion, these films have had a huge impact on the tourism industry, serving as indirect tourist brochures for princely locations. Several of the palaces of former Indian princes, whether that of Maheshwar in Indore, the City Palace in Jaipur or the Lake Palace at Udaipur (where John Glen's 1983 James Bond movie *Octopussy* was shot) are now partial hotels, open for the general public, even as some remain private residences for the erstwhile ruling families. While the former princely states merged with the new nation in 1947, the political agency many of these sovereigns lost has now in part been replaced by the spirit of entrepreneurship and business enterprise in the tourism trade. Rajasthan in particular, home to several erstwhile Rajput kingdoms and *thikanas*, has become something of a tourist Mecca, with former palaces, forts, *havelis*, *chattris*, palace trains and tent cities made into tourist destinations, which attract not only an international clientele but an up-and-coming prosperous Indian consumer market.[56]

Since the economic reforms of the early 1990s, domestic tourism has boomed in India.[57] In many ways, Rajasthan has epitomized this new era of historically oriented tourism, as the Tuscany of India. It is a state dotted with idyllic palaces in various romantic, semi-desert locations, that span the styles of the Indo-Persian to the Art Deco, and are equipped with luxury spas, equestrian holidays, British colonial styled safaris in game reserves, local dance and musical entertainments and (invariably) meals or social functions with the royal families who own these properties. Such locations interface history and entertainment, modernity and tradition and give the visitor access to a wide spectrum of experiences – Mughal *mehfils* to *shikars* reminiscent of the high noon of the Raj– to satisfy the curiosity and taste of any kind of tourist. Such holiday locations boast the latest in modern amenities while branding themselves as the 'real' India in their reference to an 'authentic' princely heritage, colonial and pre-colonial.

Palace hotels are increasingly catering to wealthy Indians and expatriate non-resident Indians (NRIs), who are keen to splurge newly found affluence in settings, which are still reminiscent of 'home'. These destinations serve to express a proud, nationalist sentiment while simultaneously satisfying escapist desires. Where earlier, affluent Indians might have honeymooned or married in Europe, there is a growing movement to celebrate such major life events in locations, such as these palace hotels, which have all the modern technology of an international-level experience while simultaneously embodying India's indigenous traditions of luxury. Thus the groom and bride live briefly the life of an 'Indian' Maharaja and Maharani, embodying both the fantasy of celluloid Bollywood and the bygone days of royal India. The much publicized marriage celebrations of Indian businessman Arun Nayar to the British film actress Elizabeth Hurley in Jodhpur is one of many such examples.[58] As anthropologist Carol Henderson notes, 'Rajasthan is a place where one will encounter royalty, will live like royalty, and can enter a royal past.'[59]

In this manner, films on the zenana continue to recreate a 'royal world' for a popular consumer market. Princely India has gained a place in the living history of the nation, even if its own history has become the mythologized, fantastic construct of a Bollywood imagination. The courtly aesthetics – of music, dance, costume and jewellery – have influenced the development of *tawaif* narratives and dramas on royal Indian women, just as the cinema has served to promote 'royal' fashion for ready-to-wear and haute couture runways and palace hotels are serving a growing tourism economy.

Notes

1 Rachel Dwyer, 'Representing the Muslim: The "courtesan film" in Indian Popular Cinema,' in Tudor Parfitt and Yulia Egorova eds *Jews, Muslims, and Mass Media: Mediating the 'other'*, (London: Routledge, 2004), p. 88.

2 Ian Copland, *The Princes of India in the Endgame of Empire, 1917–1947* (Cambridge: Cambridge University Press, 1997), 8.

3 Barbara Ramusack, *The Indian Princes and Their States* (Cambridge: Cambridge University Press, 2004), 34.

4 S. R. Ashton, *British Policy Towards the Indian States, 1905–1909* (London: Curzon Press, 1982), 7.

5 Ramusack, *The Indian Princes*, 2.

6 Ashton, 7.

7 Ramusack, 87. She suggests that the Indian rulers are thus 'an excellent prism' to view the complex hierarchies of the British Raj in India. It was a system of indirect rule, which served as a model in other areas of the Empire, including Malaya and Africa.

8 GOI, Foreign Department, Despatch No. 43A to S/S, 30 April 1860, PCI, 1792–1874, Vol. 85.

9 Ashton, 17.

10 David Cannadine, *Ornamentalism: How the British Saw Their Empire* (Oxford: Oxford University Press, 2001), 44.

11 Bernard Cohn, 'Representing Authority in Victorian India' in *An Anthropologist Among the Historians and Other Essays* (Delhi: Oxford University Press, 1987), 648.

12 C. A. Bayly, *Indian Society and the Making of the British Empire* (Cambridge: Cambridge University Press, 1988), 197.

13 Cannadine, *Ornamentalism*, 90. There are several movies, which 'fictionalize' colonial princely India, notably the Merchant/Ivory films, *Autobiography of a Princess* (1975), *Hullaballoo over Georgie and Bonnies's Pictures* (1978) and *Heat and Dust* (1983).

14 Lloyd Rudolph and Susanne Rudolph, *Essays on Rajputana* (New Delhi: Concept Publishing Company, 1984), 6–7.

15 Ramusack, *Indian Princes*, 8.

16 Copland, *The Princes of India*, 10.

17 Ibid.

18 Note enclosed in Indore to Baroda 21 October 1916, GSAB, Baroda, Pol. Dept. 341, 3.

19 Barbara Ramusack, *The Princes of India in the Twilight of Empire: Dissolution of a Patron–Client System, 1914–1939,* (Columbus: University of Cincinnati Press, 1978), xv.

20 Rudolphs, *Essays on Rajputana*, 18.

21 Copland, *The Princes of India*, 2.

22 Copland, *The Princes of India*, 267–8; Barbara Ramusack, *The Princes of India at the Twilight of Empire: Dissolution of a Patron–Client System, 1914–1939* (Columbus: 1978), 244–6; Cannadine, *Ornamentalism*, 174.

23 Varsha Joshi, *Polygamy and Pardah* (Jaipur: Rawat Publications, 1995), 87–8.

24 Ruby Lal, 'The "Domestic World" of the Mughals in the Reigns of Babur, Humayan and Akbar, *c*. 1500–1605' (unpublished Ph.D. Thesis, University of Oxford, 2000), 179.

25 Ibid., 123–7.

26 Joshi, 24.

27 Gayatri Devi, *A Princess Remembers* (Calcutta: Rupa & Co., 1995), 167–70.

28 K. Moti Gokulsing and Wimal Dissanayake, *Indian Popular Cinema: A Narrative Of Cultural Change* (Stoke-on-Trent: Trentham Books, 2004), 13–14.

29 Ibid.,15.

30 Tejaswini Ganti, *Bollywood: A Guidebook to Popular Hindu Cinema* (New York: Routledge, 2004), 13.

31 Mihir Bose, *Bollywood: A History* (Stroud: Tempus Publishing Ltd, 2006), 68–9.

32 Ibid., 70.

33 Ibid., 89–90.

34 For a more fuller history of the Malabar Hill Murder case, please refer to chapter five of my forthcoming book, *Courtly Indian Women in Late Imperial India*. London: Pickering and Chatto Press, 2008.

35 Kaushik Bhaumik, 'The emergence of the Bombay film industry, 1913–1936,' (D.Phil. dissertation, University of Oxford, 2001), 88.

36 Ibid., 169.

37 Dwyer, 'Representing the Muslim', 85.

38 Bose, 213.

39 Dwyer, 'Representing the Muslim', 85.

40 Ibid., 89.

41 Sheenu Jahan, 'Umrao Jaan – The magic of "ada"', 3 March 2005. http://movies. indiainfo.com/tales/rekha-0303.html.

42 Faridoon Shahryar, 'Ash or Rekha: The Better "Umrao Jaan"?'. *IndiaGlitz*, 23 October 2006.

43 Dwyer, 85.

44 Colour has also become an iconic representative of Rajasthan in India's tourist trade. Since 2002, the state tourism board has launched a campaign, marketing Rajasthan as 'Simply Colorful'. Carol E. Henderson, 'Virtual Rajasthan: Making Heritage, Marketing Cyberorientalism?' in Carol Henderson and Maxine Weisgrau eds *Raj Rhapsodies: Tourism, Heritage and the Seduction of History*, (Aldershot: Ashgate Publishing Limited, 2007), 67.

45 'Prince of Style: Raghavendra Rathore is going to get a lot more serious about fashion', *The Hindu*, 19 September 2007. http://www.hinduonnet.com/thehindu/mp/2007/09/19/ stories/2007091950550100.htm.

46 Rohini Bhandari, 'Raghuvendra Rathore dresses up Eklavya!', 3 February 2007. http://eklavyatheroyalguard.blogspot.com/2007/02/raghuvendra-rathore-dresses-up-eklavya.html.

47 Ibid.

48 'Jodha Akbar was too good an offer', *Khaleej Times Online*, 26 January 2008.

49 Ibid.

50 'The grandeur of Akbar-Jodha', *Times of India*, 3 September 2007. http://timesofindia. indiatimes.com/articleshow/2331190.cms

51 Sreemoyee Piu Kundu, 'Celluloid Couture', *Times of India*. 24 August 2005. http:// timesofindia.indiatimes.com/articleshow/1209995.cms.

52 'Prince of Style: Raghavendra Rathore is going to get a lot more serious about fashion', 19 September 2007, *The Hindu*. http://www.hinduonnet.com/thehindu/mp/2007/09/19/ stories/2007091950550100.htm.

53 'Get the Jodha-Akbar look', *MSN India*, 26 February 2008. http://lifestyle.in.msn.com/ fashion/article.aspx?cp-documentid=1233496

54 'Jodha Akbar – A Trend Setter', *Indic Culture,* 28 February 2008. http://www. indiculture.com/fashion/2008/02/28/jodha-akbar-a-trend-setter/

55 ApunKaChoice, 'Umrao Jaan' apparels to be auctioned, 21 September 2006. http:// www.apunkachoice.com/scoop/bollywood/20060921-2.html.

56 Barbara Ramusack, 'Tourism and Icons: The Packaging of the Princely States of Rajasthan', *Perceptions of South Asia's Visual Past*, eds Catherine B. Asher and Thomas R. Metcalf. New Delhi: Oxford & IBH Publishing Co., 1994, pp. 235–55; Ramuask, *Indian Princes and Their States* (Cambridge: Cambridge University Press, 2004), 279–80.

57 Carol Henderson and Maxine Weisgrau, 'Introduction', *Raj Rhapsodies: Tourism, Heritage and the Seduction of History*, eds Henderson and Weisgrau (Aldershot: Ashgate Publishing Limited, 2007), p. xxx.

58 Stephen M. Silverman, 'Newlyweds Liz Hurley, Arun Nayar Arrive in India', *People Magazine*, 5 March 2007.

59 Carol Henderson, 'Virtual Rajasthan: Making Heritage, Marketing Cyberorientalism?'
    Raj Rhapsodies, 72.

References

Primary sources

Note enclosed in Indore to Baroda, 21 October 1916, GSAB, Baroda, Pol. Dept. 341, 3.
Devi, Gayatri, *A Princess Remembers*. Calcutta: Rupa & Co., 1995.

Newapaper articles

'Get the Jodha-Akbar look', *MSN India,* 26 February 2008. http://lifestyle.in.msn.com/
    fashion/article.aspx?cp-documentid=1233496
'The grandeur of Akbar-Jodha', *Times of India,* 3 September 2007. http://timesofindia.
    indiatimes.com/articleshow/2331190.cms
'Jodha Akbar – A Trend Setter', *Indic Culture,* 28 February 2008. http://www.indiculture.
    com/fashion/2008/02/28/jodha-akbar-a-trend-setter/
'Jodha Akbar was too good an offer', *Khaleej Times Online*, 26 January 2008.
'Prince of Style: Raghavendra Rathore is going to get a lot more serious about fashion',
    The Hindu, 19 September 2007. http://www.hinduonnet.com/thehindu/mp/2007/09/19/
    stories/2007091950550100.htm
ApunKaChoice, ' "Umrao Jaan" apparels to be auctioned', 21 September 2006. http://www.
    apunkachoice.com/scoop/bollywood/20060921-2.html.
Bhandari, Rohini, 'Raghuvendra Rathore dresses up Eklavya!', 3 February 2007.
    http://eklavyatheroyalguard.blogspot.com/2007/02/raghuvendra-rathore-dresses-up-
    eklavya.html.
Jahan, Sheenu, 'Umrao Jaan – The magic of "ada" ', 3 March 2005. http://movies.indiainfo.
    com/tales/rekha-0303.html.
Kundu, Sreemoyee Piu, 'Celluloid Couture', *Times of India,* 24 August 2005. http://
    timesofindia.indiatimes.com/articleshow/1209995.cms.
Shahryar, Faridoon, 'Ash or Rekha: The Better "Umrao Jaan"?', *IndiaGlitz*,
    23 October 2006.
Silverman, Stephen M, 'Newlyweds Liz Hurley, Arun Nayar Arrive in India', *People
    Magazine*, 5 March 2007.

Secondary sources

Ashton, S. R. (1982) *British Policy Towards the Indian States, 1905–1909*. London: Curzon
    Press.
Bayly, C. A. (1988) *Indian Society and the Making of the British Empire*. Cambridge:
    Cambridge University Press.
Bose, Mihir (2006) *Bollywood: A History*. Stroud: Tempus Publishing Ltd.
Cannadine, David (2001) *Ornamentalism: How the British Saw Their Empire*. Oxford:
    Oxford University Press.
Cohn, Bernard (1987) 'Representing Authority in Victorian India', in *An Anthropologist
    among the Historians and Other Essays*. Delhi: Oxford University Press.
Copland, Ian (1997) *The Princes of India in the Endgame of Empire, 1917–1947*.
    Cambridge: Cambridge University Press.

Dwyer, Rachel (2004) 'Representing the Muslim: The "courtesan film" in Indian Popular Cinema' in Tudor Parfitt and Yulia Egorova eds *Jews, Muslims, and Mass Media: Mediating the 'other'*, London: Routledge, pp. 78–92.

Ganti, Tejaswini (2004) *Bollywood: A Guidebook to Popular Hindu Cinema*. New York: Routledge.

Gokulsing, K. Moti and Wimal Dissanayake (2004) *Indian Popular Cinema: A Narrative of Cultural Change*. Stoke-on-Trent: Trentham Books.

Henderson, Carol (2007) 'Virtual Rajasthan: Making Heritage, Marketing Cyberorientalism?' in Henderson and Weisgrau eds *Raj Rhapsodies: Tourism, Heritage and the Seduction of History*, Aldershot: Ashgate Publishing Limited, pp. 61–81.

Henderson, Carol and Maxine Weisgrau (2007) in Henderson and Weisgrau eds *Raj Rhapsodies: Tourism, Heritage and the Seduction of History*, Aldershot: Ashgate Publishing Limited.

Jhala, Angma (2008) *Courtly Indian Women in Late Imperial India*. London: Pickering and Chatto Press.

Joshi, Varsha (1995) *Polygamy and Pardah*. Jaipur: Rawat Publications.

Ramusack, Barbara (1978) *The Princes of India in the Twilight of Empire: Dissolution of a Patron-Client System, 1914–1939*. Columbus: University of Cincinnati Press.

Ramusack, Barbara (1994) 'Tourism and the Icons: The Packaging of the Princely States of Rajasthan', in Catherine B. Asher and Thomas R. Metcalf eds *Perceptions of South Asia's Visual Past*, New Delhi: Oxford & IBH Publishing Co., pp. 235–255.

Ramusack, Barbara (2004) *The Indian Princes and Their States*. Cambridge: Cambridge University Press.

Rudolph, Lloyd and Susanne Rudolph (1984) *Essays on Rajputana*. New Delhi: Concept Publishing Company.

Unpublished works

Bhaumik, Kaushik. 'The emergence of the Bombay film industry, 1913–1936'. D.Phil. dissertation, University of Oxford, 2001.

Lal, Ruby. 'The "Domestic World" of the Mughals in the Reigns of Babur, Humayan and Akbar, *c.* 1500–1605'. Unpublished Ph.D. Thesis, University of Oxford, 2000.

Part IV

Comics/Cartoons–
Photographs/Posters–
Advertising

11 Gods, kings and local Telugu guys

Competing visions of the heroic in Indian comic books

Karline McLain

Introduction: comic books in a globalised India

When Anant Pai founded the first Indian comic book series in 1967, *Amar Chitra Katha*, he did so with a patriotic motive: he wanted to educate Indian children throughout the nation about their own culture and history. During the early months of that year, as India was gearing up to celebrate its twentieth year of independence from British colonial rule, Pai travelled from the western coastal city of Bombay (now Mumbai) to the northern capital city of New Delhi, where he encountered a new visual medium: television. He recalled the impact of that experience in these words:

> In February of 1967, my wife and I were visiting Delhi, and we stopped at Maharaja Lal & Sons Bookstore. The TV was on in the bookstore – Bombay did not have TV yet, only Delhi, and only black and white – and the program was a quiz contest featuring five students from St. Stephen's College. When they were asked, the students could not name the mother of Lord Ram [Rama]. I was disappointed, but I thought, well, that is from a long time ago. But then a question came about Greek gods on Mt. Olympus, and the children could answer that question! This is the trouble with our education system: children are getting alienated from their own culture.[1]

For several years Pai had been concerned that the generation of children born in independent India was learning Western culture and history at the expense of their own. This quiz show – in which Indian college students handily answered question after question about Greek mythology but could not answer the simplest of questions about the God-king Rama (in Hindi: Ram), hero of the ancient Indian *Ramayana* epic – seemed further proof of this phenomenon. Although Pai recognized the need to encourage English language education and knowledge of Western civilization in order for Indians to participate in an increasingly globalised world, he was convinced that Indian children must simultaneously retain a uniquely Indian sensibility and identity. Without this, he feared, newly independent India's national unity could too easily be sundered along its diverse religious, regional, linguistic, economic and other lines. Upon Pai's return to Bombay, he encountered a second popular visual medium that had also recently arrived in India: comic books. While watching his nephews read imported American superhero comics such as *Superman*, *Tarzan*, and *The Phantom*, Pai grew convinced that the comic book medium could be a fun and appealing means of teaching Indian themes and values to children. He immediately began writing a comic book script featuring an Indian superhero – the Hindu God Krishna – and set about finding a publisher and an artist to work with. The first Indian comic book, *Krishna* (no. 11, 1969), was published two years later.[2]

Indian comic strips had previously appeared in Indian publications – such as *Chandamama*, a monthly children's magazine founded in 1947 and featuring a mix of prose stories, games, and short comic strips – but *Amar Chitra Katha* was the first Indian comic book series. *Amar Chitra Katha* means 'Immortal Picture Stories', and these comics seek to indigenize the comic book medium by immortalizing India's own divine and historic figures as heroes. The comics in this series were created as an English language product to target the middle-class Indian children who were attending English-medium schools and receiving 'Westernized' educations – and according to Pai were therefore most vulnerable to losing touch with their Indian identity. Following *Krishna*, other titles retold classical Sanskrit stories of the Hindu gods, including *Rama* (no. 15, 1970), so that every Indian reader could learn the story of this epic god-king, whom Hindus believe to be the human incarnation of God Vishnu, and would be able to name his mother: Kaushalya. In 1971, *Amar Chitra Katha* (hereafter *ACK*) began featuring historical leaders from various regions of India, beginning with *Shivaji* (no. 23, 1971), a seventeenth-century Hindu king from western Maharashtra. Alongside these medieval kings and queens, colonial-era freedom fighters from the various regions of India were also added, including *Subhas Chandra Bose* (no. 77, 1975) and *Lokamanya Tilak* (no. 219, 1980). Pai stressed that these historical titles were added to promote national integration, so that Indians in one region of the country would learn about the people and history of other regions.

Thus although modelled upon American superhero comic books from the Golden Age (1930s–1950s) in their heroic storylines and their standard 32-page layout with panel divisions, narrative text boxes, and dialogue balloons, these Indian comic books stand apart from comics in America and elsewhere in their cast of heroes drawn exclusively from national epics and history books: modern patriots, medieval kings and queens, Hindu gods and goddesses. In February of 1978, *ACK* received a huge boost when a seminar on the role of comic books in education was held in Bombay. Many school principals attended, and the Union Minister of Education, Dr Pratap Chandra Chunder, was the chief guest. Dr Chunder lauded the series, stating that these comics should be used in schools because 'there are biographies of great men from different parts of the country; there are tales from Sanskrit; classics and folktales of various regions – all of which could help in promoting national integration' (*Role of Chitra Katha in School Education*, 1978: 2). Following the seminar, sales soared as schools ordered *ACK* for their libraries and classrooms.

Today, *ACK* remains the leading Indian comic book series. Advertised as 'the only comics welcomed in schools', 'the route to your roots', and 'the glorious heritage of India', the publishers consistently highlight the Indianness of these comics to appeal to the nationalist sentiments of consumers. This marketing strategy has worked well: several generations of Indians living in India and throughout the global diaspora have now been reared on these comics, and sales of issues have surpassed the 90 million mark. Yet *ACK* has also been challenged over the years by those who see its vision of Indianness as a limited, even exclusive vision of national integration in that its selection of heroes entails the marginalization of Muslims and other non-Hindus from the national past, the recasting of women in 'traditional' roles, and the privileging of middle-class, upper-caste Hindu culture.[3]

As Hindu nationalism came to dominate Indian politics and culture in the 1990s, some Indians turned to popular media as a vehicle for rethinking the concepts of national integration and Indianness that they had been raised with. Visual media including film, television, and poster art have begun to receive substantial scholarly attention for their contributions both in support of and in opposition to the idea of a Hindu nation. The comic book medium, however, remains largely overlooked by scholars.[4] Yet in the past decade, a new generation of comic book creators has arisen, with a new vision of the Indian hero. One of these new creators is the Viveka Foundation, which began publishing *Vivalok Comics* in 2001. Viveka is a Delhi-based alternative publisher whose mission is to provide a counterbalance to dominant publishers by upholding 'democratic values, pluralistic traditions, gender equality and cultural, ecological and spiritual heritage'. To date the foundation has produced a handful of comic books that retell Indian myths, legends and folktales. Rukmini Sekhar, the foundation director and editor of *Vivalok Comics*, states that her series stands apart from other Indian comics, including *ACK*, in its depiction of 'the smallest geographical unit, societal unit, and community' in an effort to celebrate 'the smallest suggestion of diversity, showing that only a pluralistic society is sustainable'.[5] This chapter examines several examples from *ACK* and *Vivalok* in an effort to understand how the dominant vision of the Indian comic book hero as found in *ACK* is being rethought, and how the dominant definition of Indianness is being challenged in the process.

Visions of God Rama

The oldest version of the *Ramayana* was composed in Sanskrit by the poet Valmiki around 500 BC, but the epic has been retold in multiple languages, diverse narrative formats, and many media over the past two millennia. As Paula Richman notes in her discussion of these many *Ramayana*s, 'the elements of the *Ramayana* tradition can be seen as a source on which poets can draw to produce a potentially infinite series of varied and sometimes contradictory tellings' (Richman, 1991: 8). Anant Pai, like many Hindus, views the *Ramayana* as a prehistoric story that entails at its core a lesson about ideal *dharmic* (moral and social) behaviour. As the Hindu God Vishnu incarnate in human form, Rama exemplifies the ideal that humans can aspire to; in Pai's words, 'Ram, he is the ideal man: he never lies, he is a filial son, a loving brother.' In embodying these ideal qualities, Pai insists that Rama is a role model not only for Hindus, but for all Indians, and therefore the *Ramayana* is not just a Hindu epic, but an Indian epic. Thus the introduction to the *Rama* issue (no. 15, 1970) by *ACK* acknowledges the diversity of the *Ramayana* tradition, stating that it is 'so much an integral part of our heritage that even our apparent diversities are reflected in the slightly differing versions to be found in the different languages'. But, it continues, these differing versions are but variations on the same lofty theme: 'The idea that God fulfils Himself in the best of men [which] is conveyed by the life of Rama' (introduction).

On the cover of the *Rama* comic, Rama is envisioned as the ideal Indian hero: a muscular, bare-chested, blue-tinged god-king, seated in an active pose with bow and arrow drawn. Behind him sits his wife Sita, a beautiful, fair-skinned woman with dark tresses, watching in admiration. Within the pages of this comic book, Rama demonstrates his heroism by battling the demoness Tataka as a young prince; winning Sita's hand in marriage through an athletic contest; surviving 14 years of exile in the wilderness to fulfil a vow made by his father, King Dasaratha; defeating the ten-headed demon-king Ravana, who had kidnapped Sita, in an epic battle; and returning victoriously with his wife to Ayodhya, where they are crowned king and queen. In the final panel, Rama and Sita sit together on a grand throne, surrounded by their loyal subjects, while the narrative text proclaims: 'Rama was crowned king in Ayodhya and he ruled for many years' (p. 32).

In this *ACK* version of the *Ramayana*, Rama is so perfectly heroic that there is no room for moral ambiguity. Incidents in the epic that are at first glance ambiguous, but ultimately allow Rama to deliver a discourse about *dharma* (proper moral and social duties), are eliminated in the comic book to present Rama as an ideal hero who is beyond reproach. In the 'Kiskindhakanda' book of Valmiki's *Ramayana*, for instance, while gathering an army together to rescue his kidnapped wife Sita, Rama allies with the monkey-king-in-exile, Sugreeva, and helps him slay his brother, the monkey-king Vali. As Vali lies dying, struck by an arrow that Rama shot from behind tree cover, he accuses Rama of acting cowardly and failing to adhere to proper battlefield etiquette. In response, Rama explains that he has adhered to dharma by meting out the necessary punishment to Vali for failing to treat his brother Sugreeva in the proper manner and for forcibly taking Sugreeva's wife as his own. In the *Rama* comic, however, after Vali is shot his lengthy death scene is omitted, so that he does not question the morality or bravery of Rama's action, nor does Rama have to defend his act of taking sides, perhaps for selfish reasons, in the dispute between the two brothers.

A similar omission occurs at the end of the *Rama* comic, when Rama returns to Ayodhya to be crowned king after defeating the demon-king Ravana and rescuing Sita. Here the final book of Valmiki's *Ramayana*, the 'Uttarakanda', is excluded. In Valmiki's conclusion, Rama learns that the citizens of Ayodhya are gossiping about Sita's loyalty, alleging that her pregnancy is the result of her time with Ravana. In response to these rumours of infidelity, Rama decides to banish Sita, sending her into the wilderness where she eventually finds refuge at the forest hermitage of sage Valmiki and there raises her twin sons. In another discourse on the complexity of dharma, Rama explains to his brother that although he knows Sita is innocent, as king he has a higher duty to his citizens that overrides any personal obligations to his beloved wife. By foregoing this incident in the *ACK* comic book through its act of happily-ever-after narrative closure, Rama remains unquestionably the heroic 'best of men'.

In 1992, when Pai and the other creators of *ACK* released a 100-page extended comic book version of the *Ramayana*, titled *Valmiki's Ramayana* (no. 10,001), they preserved their vision of Rama as an ideal hero by again eliminating incidents that allow for moral ambiguity or debate, and again concluding with a happily-ever-after final panel of Rama and Sita's coronation. But as the Hindu God-king Rama was increasingly co-opted by Hindu nationalist groups throughout the 1990s to symbolize the ideal Hindu hero who would martially defend his homeland against all 'invaders', be they demons like Ravana or Muslims or others, and as Rama was depicted in increasingly exercised stances with ever more muscles and weapons, alternative publishers like the Viveka Foundation felt the need to remind their readers of the diversity of heroes available in Indian culture, and of the necessity of questioning hegemonic heroes and narratives.[6]

Vivalok Comics therefore presents a very different version of the *Ramayana* in their comic book *Godavari Tales* (2003), an issue containing short stories told in the Godavari River region of the southern state of Andhra Pradesh. The title of its *Ramayana*-themed story is 'Sita Banished', and the introduction in the first panel reads: 'The pan-Indian epic of *Ramayana* lends itself to many local versions. Here is the well-known episode of Sita's expulsion to the forest. This version is particularly popular among the women of the Godavari region' (p. 37). 'Sita Banished' begins with a frame story, featuring village women from the Godavari region who ask an elderly woman to tell them a story while they take a break from working in the rice paddies. As they speak, another woman walks by, and the young women gossip about how her husband beat her last night and accused her of infidelity, calling her a 'Kulata' (unchaste woman) and other names. This incident inspires the elderly woman to tell the story of Sita's banishment.

This *Vivalok* version of the *Ramayana* then begins where the *ACK* versions ended: Rama and Sita have returned to Ayodhya, and Rama has already been crowned king. But here there is no happily-ever-after ending, for the demoness Surpanakha, Ravana's sister, who lusts after handsome Rama, schemes to eliminate Sita so that she may have Rama for herself. She creates a drawing of the demon Ravana that magically follows Sita everywhere, despite Sita's attempts to be rid of the image by burning and drowning it. In a panel on page 41, the drawing reappears as Rama and Sita sit together (Figure 11.1). In the bottom left panel Rama's anger and jealousy explode as he looks at the image (note the steam jetting from his ears!) and assumes that Sita drew it herself out of longing for Ravana. In the bottom middle panel we return to the frame story, as the Godavari women ask the elderly narrator what Rama did next. She replies, 'Rama's response has disturbed generations of women!!' In the final panel Sita wanders alone in the forest, as the storyteller concludes, 'Since he was king, he banished Sita to the forest.

Figure 11.1 'Sita Banished' in *Godavari Tales.*
Source: *Godavari Tales.* New Delhi: The Viveka Foundation, 2003, 41. From *Vivalok Comics*, with the permission of the publisher Viveka Foundation, New Delhi, India.

That too when she was carrying her first child! So… what do you make of Rama's decision?' (p. 41).

In *Vivalok*'s telling, Rama is clearly not an ideal hero whose every act is beyond reproach. Instead, the hero – albeit a tragic one – is Sita, and the focus of this story is her devotion to her husband and her travails. For instance, when Surpanakha, disguised as a female mendicant, tries to trick Sita into drawing the picture of Ravana, Sita protests: 'What are you saying? Rama Rama! I never set eyes on Ravana. I only saw his toes' (p. 39). Here Sita stresses her loyalty to her husband by explaining that when she was held captive by Ravana she did not even look at this other man, keeping her eyes downcast the whole while. She is the ideal *pativrata* heroine – the loyal and long-suffering Hindu wife who takes a vow (*vrata*) to constantly worship and serve her husband (*pati*) as she would a god.[7] The tragedy is that Sita's loyalty does not save her, and in the end she is banished.

Thus whereas the *ACK* versions end with a happily-ever-after-scenario, the *Vivalok Comic* ends with this disturbing image of innocent Sita's banishment and the didactic insert asking us to evaluate Rama's action. This is a very different approach to storytelling in the comic book medium. When asked about this narrative strategy, Sekhar commented that she tries to 'draw out the undercurrents and subtleties of mythology, and to use comic books for rigorous inquiry'. This version of the *Ramayana* dwells upon the moral ambiguities of the epic, and in so doing calls into question not only the justness of Rama's behaviour towards Sita, but also the now-dominant presentation of Rama as a flawless hero. In so doing, this comic book story preserves the episode from the final book of the Sanskrit *Ramayana* in which Rama banishes Sita, an episode that has been central to women's retellings of this epic for it allows women to think through the injustices they face in a patriarchal society. *Vivalok*'s story also preserves the oral nature of women's retellings of the epic in its insertion of the drawing of Ravana, an item unique to local oral culture and not found in Valmiki's *Ramayana*, and in its frame story featuring the Godavari women.[8]

In *Vivalok*'s 'Sita Banished', the dominant version of the *Ramayana* is called into question visually, as well as narratively, in its depiction of both Rama and Sita. This is not the fair-skinned Sita and blue-tinged Rama (blue being a mark of divinity on earth) that has come to be the iconographic standard in modern images like god posters and calendar art, and is also found in *ACK*. As seen in Figure 11.1, *Vivalok*'s Rama and Sita are imbued with a more ethnic appearance, marked with the darker skin tone and other features common to the Dravidian peoples of southern India, including Telugus, the people who inhabit the Godavari region of Andhra Pradesh. Discussing this visual decision, Sekhar stated:

> We try to consciously deconstruct physiognomy in all of our stories. Here, look at Rama in 'Sita Banished' – he is a local Telugu guy. Look at his hair, his skin tone. He does not wear a sacred thread. He has a subaltern appearance. You see, image is very important in representing diversity – I can't stress this enough.

Whereas the creators of *ACK* sought to reduce the diversity of the many *Ramayanas* to the single and accessible theme of Rama's ideal heroism, the creators of *Vivalok Comics* have presented Rama as a fallible Telugu guy in their effort to preserve not only localized versions of mythology and folktales, but also the local context and imagery associated with such tellings – for this richness, this narrative and cultural diversity, is key to their vision of Indianness; as they write in the introductory insert to each of their comics, 'The ultimate challenge is not about making folklore accessible but it is about making "folklore in context" accessible to audiences' (p. 6).

Visions of Hindus and Muslims

A second way that *Vivalok* challenges the dominant vision of the Indian comic book hero as presented in *ACK* is in the depiction of religious identity, specifically the portrayal of Hindu–Muslim communal relations. In the *ACK* series the heroes are manly Hindu gods such as Rama, who fought demons, and manly Hindu kings such as Shivaji and Rana Pratap, who fought the Muslim rulers of the Mughal Empire in the sixteenth and seventeenth centuries. The introduction to *Rana Pratap* (no. 24, 1971), for instance, lauds the sixteenth century Hindu Rajput king of Mewar in northwestern India as the lone figure who was brave enough to contest the might of Mughal Emperor Akbar:

> With Akbar coming to the throne of the Mughal Empire in early 1556, the Mughals had become a part of India. As a conqueror Akbar triumphed all over North India. … In his efforts to consolidate his empire Akbar appointed Rajput nobles to the highest posts in his empire. Thus he succeeded in winning the goodwill of the Hindus. The Rajputs flocked to serve him and do him honour. During this period when almost everyone in Northern India had bowed down before Akbar, only the lone, unbending figure of Rana Pratap stood against him. He refused to accept Akbar's supremacy (introduction).

The first pages of *Rana Pratap* depict the king's homeland falling increasingly to the suzerainty of the Mughal Empire. Rana Pratap finally decides that he must take the offensive against the 'invading' troops, and in the top half-page panel on page 14, the Hindu king is depicted frozen in heroic equestrian battle posture: Poised above all other figures atop his rearing horse, wearing full battle armour, Rana Pratap holds his spear aloft, ready to strike. Below him, dozens of Mughal forces fearfully scramble about, their Muslim identity made apparent by their beards. The narrative text at the top of this panel explains, 'Rana Pratap attacked a camp of Mughal forces and killed many of them' (p. 14). In the bottom half-page panel, Mughal Emperor Akbar agrees with his general that there is no alternative but war. In this comic book, as in the majority of others by *ACK*, the formula is simple: hero faces off against villain in a grand battle, and then either returns home victorious or dies bravely.

However, Pai maintains that his *ACK* comic books can help foster inter-religious understanding and national integration because in addition to featuring historical Hindu leaders, he has also created a handful of titles featuring Muslim leaders, including *Akbar* (no. 200, 1979). He commented:

> Rana Pratap and Akbar fought one another, but both are heroes. Rana Pratap is a hero in his issue, and Akbar is a hero in his issue. Rana Pratap was right, he was fighting for his country, for the land of his fathers. But Akbar's father's father also claimed India as his homeland.

Yet even when a Muslim such as Akbar is placed in the role of the Indian comic book hero, the same formula remains in place, albeit with the religious identity of the hero and villain reversed: A historical hero is pitted against a historical villain, divided along religious lines. This is a communal understanding of history, an understanding that views Hindus and Muslims as two separate communities that have always been distinct religio-social groups, without any synthesis of philosophy or customs, and with a history of perpetual conflict. Such an understanding does not easily accommodate a composite identity or culture.

In *Vivalok Comics*, on the other hand, the heroes are frequently historical or legendary figures who demonstrate a synthesis of Hindu–Muslim world-views and living habits. One example is the story 'Kinu Ghosh and Manik Pir' in *The Sunderbans* (2002), an issue featuring stories from the forest belt region of Bengal in eastern India. Manik Pir is a Muslim boy who grows up in very difficult circumstances in his Muslim-dominated village, and thus takes to the wandering, mendicant life of a *fakir* (holy man) along with his brother. One day, Manik and his brother arrive at the doorstep of the wealthy Hindu matriarch Hire Ghosh, who states that she is sick and tired of beggars. She insults Manik by refusing to serve him any milk, even after he miraculously draws seven pots of pure milk from her cow. But Hire's daughter-in-law takes pity on Manik and gives him some milk. In thanks, Manik places his hand on her forehead and blesses her, saying, 'Kind lady, may you never become a widow and have a broken heart. Never fear, we will appear before you if you ever need us.' Hire, however, runs and tells her son Kinu that his 'devoted Hindu wife' has been sullied, 'touched by a Muslim' (p. 13).

Angered, Kinu runs after Manik Pir and attacks him. But Manik stops Kinu, saying, 'Young man, a blessing has no religion or community. And it is not male or female' (p. 14). Suddenly, Kinu's body breaks out in pustules, and a snake bites him, killing him. On the next page Kinu's wife grieves over the death of her husband, but then recalls Manik's blessing that she would never become a widow. She calls out, bemoaning her fate as a widow, when Manik suddenly appears, dressed as a Hindu *brahmin* (priest) with a shaved head and wearing a sacred thread (Figure 11.2). Manik miraculously brings Kinu back to life, who begs forgiveness in the bottom left panel, pleading, 'You are none other than Manik Pir. I'm your devotee forever. Bless me!' (p. 15). The final panel depicts Manik resuming his mendicant lifestyle,

Figure 11.2 'Kinu Ghosh and Manik Pir' in *The Sunderbans.*
Source: *The Sunderbans.* New Delhi: The Viveka Foundation, 2002, 15. From *Vivalok Comics*, with
the permission of the publisher Viveka Foundation, New Delhi, India.

wandering on to the next village, while the narrative text states, 'Thus Manik Pir became well known in Biratnagar' (p. 15).

This illustrates how the *Vivalok* stories differ from the dominant *ACK* formula: The hero, Manik Pir, is a holy man who bridges communal divides by appearing at times as a Muslim fakir and at others as a Hindu brahmin, and in the end is recognized as a holy man by both Hindus and Muslims. The villain of this story, Kinu, is equally complex, for he transforms from a raging Hindu chauvinist into a devotee of Manik Pir. Finally, the plot goes beyond the dominant formula by beginning with the standard template of pitting a hero against a villain, who are divided along religious lines and come to blows, but ultimately transcends this template by restoring the villain Kinu to life after his violent encounter with the hero and by redeeming him, so that he is no longer a villain but instead a role model for the transformative power of religious devotion. Sekhar commented on her goals in creating this and other stories on Manik Pir in *The Sunderbans*:

> Manik Pir, he is a Sufi pir, but in this story Hindu–Muslim boundaries don't exist. He crosses boundaries between the communities. In this issue we expose bigotry on both the Hindu and the Muslim sides. We show Hindu religious bigotry, and Muslim religious bigotry. But Manik Pir is not like this. The BJP protested the depiction of Hindus in this issue, they said that we showed Hindus in a negative light. But it is true – there are Hindu bigots, there are Muslim bigots, there are bigots in all religions.

Contrary to the Bharatiya Janata Party (BJP) and other Hindu nationalist groups that envision a Hindu nation and insist that Hindus are the 'good guys' and Muslims the 'bad guys' in Indian history, Sekhar's comments further demonstrate that in her opinion, bigotry is the true villain, not any particular individual or community, and the true heroes are those who embrace a religiously plural society.

Visions of sky gods and earth mothers

A third way that *Vivalok* challenges the dominant *ACK* vision of the Indian comic book hero is in the presentation of non-brahminical, non-Sanskritic Hindu culture and religion. For Sekhar and the other creators of *Vivalok Comics*, true Indianness entails not only the recognition of local diversity throughout the nation and the recognition of the syncretic nature of historical Hindu–Muslim relations, but also the recognition of peoples, cultures, and stories beyond those of the urban middle-class, upper-caste Hindu fold – specifically the cultures and stories of the *dalit* (untouchable) and *adivasi* (tribal) peoples of India. As an orthodox upper-caste Hindu, Pai has focused the devotional issues in his series around the religious figures he knows best: the gods and goddesses presented in Sanskrit scripture, including Rama, Krishna (his personal god of choice, or *ishta-deva*), and Shiva, as well as the gods' devoted pativrata wives. In his effort to keep Hinduism free from 'degradation', Pai has explicitly rejected tales of deities that do not appear in Sanskrit texts or that feature unorthodox practices, such as offerings of alcohol or blood sacrifice. For instance, in the *Tales of Durga* issue (no. 176, 1978) about the many forms of Goddess Durga, classic Sanskrit mythology is altered to omit Goddess Kali's miraculous defeat of the demon Raktabeeja by drinking all of his blood (for he had the power to create a new clone out of every drop of his blood that hit the ground). When asked about this, Pai recited a Sanskrit maxim: 'One must tell the truth, one must tell what is pleasant; but don't tell what is unpleasant just because it is true. In Sanskrit this is "satyam bruyaat priyam bruyaat maa bruyaat satyam apriyam".[9]

When asked to characterize the presentation of Hinduism in *Vivalok*, Sekhar contrasted her series with *ACK*:

> There is a spectrum from Sky Gods to Earth Mother. *ACK* falls at one end of the spectrum, with stories of the male Sky Gods: gods of the Vedic pantheon like Vishnu, Brahma, and Shiva, the male Sanskrit gods that are up there, in the heavens or mountains somewhere, looking down on everything, overseeing things. We fall on the other end of the spectrum. We are about the Earth Mother: the local goddesses that are here, on the ground, that people in each area pray to.

The Santhals (2002), a *Vivalok* issue about the adivasi community in the Jharkhand region of eastern India, introduces the Santhals as a 'non-vedic people' who 'have a distinct tradition and cultural identity' (p. iv), and it features their unique creation myths and gods. In the story 'Jom-Som-Binti', the gods travel to the earth in search of adventure, where they create the oceans, swans and the first pair of humans. When the Gods realize they must teach the human pair to procreate, God Lita does so by getting them drunk on rice beer, figuring that if it works for the gods, why not for humans too? The trick works: that night they become a couple, and thus the Santhal family begins.

Other *Vivalok* stories are equally independent of Sanskrit-based orthodox Hinduism. *Godavari Tales* features the local Goddess Nukalamma, who is worshipped by both Hindu and Muslim low-caste fishermen in the Godavari region (Figure 11.3). Sekhar described Nukalamma as 'a mischievous goddess' who tests her devotees, commenting: 'She is not like the goddesses in *ACK*, not the pativrata type, and does not look like them either.' Here the goddess is presented as an active, even jealous force, who regularly tests the generosity of her devotees, punishing them when they fail to propitiate her properly and rewarding them when they do. At the end of the story, the villagers have been reminded of the material rewards that can result from their devotion, and they pledge to dedicate a new temple to Nukalamma and keep her supplied with offerings. In this final image Nukalamma holds an offering in each arm: a bowl of chicken in one hand and an earthen cup of toddy in the other. Whereas an orthodox, teetotaling, vegetarian goddess would be insulted and defiled by such offerings, Nukalamma embraces them, recognizing that chicken and toddy are favoured savouries among the fishermen, and therefore represent the best offerings the villagers can make. Iconographically, Nukalamma stands apart from orthodox Hindu goddesses in these unconventional emblems;

Figure 11.3 'Goddess Nukalamma' in *Godavari Tales.*
Source: *Godavari Tales.* New Delhi: The Viveka Foundation, 2003, 23. From *Vivalok Comics*, with the permission of the publisher Viveka Foundation, New Delhi, India.

she also stands apart visually from the goddesses of *ACK* and other popular visual media in the way that her sari is tied up in the manner of local fisherwomen, marking her as a lower caste, working-class goddess, and in the way that, like *Vivalok*'s Rama, she too is imbued with an ethnic appearance.

Similarly, *The Sunderbans* features 'Bishalakshmi', the story of another local goddess who is worshipped by lower-caste fishermen. In this story the orthodox Hindu brahmins of the region object to the fishermen worshipping Bishalakshmi with offerings of fish and liquor, claiming it is 'an insult to all of the shastras [scriptures]' and that goddesses should only be worshipped with flowers and fruits (p. 57). When a dispute ensues, the brahmins take the image of the goddess away to enshrine it within their 'pure' temple, and close the doors to the lower-castes. But in the end, as in the end of 'Kinu Ghosh and Manik Pir', bigotry is shown to be the true villain: The upper-castes realize the error of their ways in excluding the lower-castes from temple worship, and open the Bishalakshmi temple to all castes and communities.

Conclusion: comic books and composite culture

What does it mean to be Indian? Fearing that children would be unable to answer this question in a rapidly globalising India, Anant Pai turned to the comic book medium to provide a patriotic answer that would appeal to children in its short, colourful, visual format. Indigenizing the Golden Age superhero formula, *Amar Chitra Katha* comics present a vision of the Indian hero as a virile, martial 'good guy' who bravely fights for his nation, fending off 'bad guys' in the form of invading demons and Muslims. Although the titles in this series are predominantly Hindu-centric, *ACK* does include a handful of titles showcasing heroes from various minority groups in India, including Muslims. In such titles, however, the superhero formula is maintained, so that the Muslim hero fights a Hindu opponent. Thus while Hindus, Muslims, and others are each presented in turn as heroic citizens of India, Hindus and Muslims are shown to be separate communities, divided along religious lines and often at war with one another.

In the wake of rising Hindu nationalism and increasingly vocal and at times violent calls for independent India to become a Hindu nation in the 1990s, many Indians worked to publicly rethink communal understandings of Hindu–Muslim relations by calling for a recognition of India's composite culture. The term 'composite culture' most commonly refers to the argument that Hindus and Muslims are not two completely separate communities, but that 'the unique genius of India worked to evolve, over the centuries since the coming of Muslims into the Indian subcontinent, modes of thinking and living which are a subtle intermixing or synthesis of the world-views and living habits of Muslims and Hindus' (Alam 1999: 29). In *Vivalok Comics*, Rukmini Sekhar presents a new cast of Indian heroes who challenge the dominant formula by demonstrating, as Manik Pir does, that Hindus and Muslims need not be two separate and striving nations of people.

Significantly, as the above examples demonstrate, *Vivalok*'s vision of Indianness presents an active effort to enlarge the common conception of composite culture to entail not only a synthesis of the world-views of Hindus and Muslims, but also a synthesis of the world-views of Indians from various regions, of high- and low-caste peoples, and of men and women. Thus *Vivalok Comics* provides an alternative to *Amar Chitra Katha*'s dominant vision of Indianness in several ways: they present a pluralistic society featuring Hindu and Muslim, high-caste and low-caste, male and female heroes; they focus on local geographies rather than concepts of state and nation; they feature multiple artistic styles rather than a uniform visual aesthetic; and they tell folktales not found in the Sanskrit scriptures of upper-caste Hinduism. And yet as different as these two series are, their creators nonetheless share in common the belief that the comic book medium has the potential to transform young Indians into better, more heroic citizens, and that the true model for Indian heroism can be found not in fictive tales of supermen, but in India's ample corpus of epic literature, folktales and history. It is in this shared approach to comics not as mere entertainment, but as a tool for patriotic socio-cultural transformation, that a uniquely Indian approach to comics can begin to be located.

Acknowledgments

Research for this chapter was made possible by a Fulbright-Hays grant in 2001–02 and grants by the National Endowment for the Humanities and the American Academy of Religion in 2006–07. In addition to the aforementioned granting agencies, the author thanks Anant Pai at *Amar Chitra Katha* in Mumbai for his time and insight; Rukmini Sekhar at the Viveka Foundation in New Delhi for her insight into the *Vivalok Comics* and for her generous permission to reprint images from the comic books here; Kathryn Hansen, Peter Manuel, and Nathan Tabor for their response to an early version of this chapter as presented at the Annual Conference on South Asia in Madison in 2007; and Maria Antonaccio, Paul Macdonald, James Mark Shields, Rivka Ulmer and Carol Wayne White for their comments on an earlier draft.

Notes

1 Quotations from Anant Pai throughout this chapter are from the author's interviews with him at the *ACK* studio in Mumbai in 2001–02.
2 For further information on the making of the *Krishna* comic book, see McLain 2005.
3 Pritchett 1995 provides a useful introduction to the *ACK* series in terms of its overall taxonomy, with careful attention to which historical and mythological figures are included and which excluded. Karline McLain is Assistant Professor of South Asian Religions at Bucknell University. She is the author of the book India's Immortal Comic Books: Gods, Kings, and Other Heroes (Bloomington: Indiana University Press, 2009), which was awarded the Edward Cameron Dimock Jr Book Prize in the Indian Humanities by the American Institute of Indian Studies. Also see McLain 2009.
4 Recent scholarship on visual media (film, television and popular prints) and Hindu nationalism includes: Jain 2007; Pinney 2004; Rajagopal 2001; and Vasudevan 2001. To date, the limited scholarship available on Indian comic books is focused on the long-dominant *ACK* series: Hawley 1995; Lent 2004; McLain 2005, 2007, 2008, 2009; and Pritchett 1995.

5 Quotations from Rukmini Sekhar throughout this chapter are from the author's interviews with her at the *Vivalok* studio in Delhi in 2007.
6 For information on the rise of Hindu nationalism in the 1980s–1990s and the symbolic use of Rama, see Ludden 1996 and Van Der Veer 1994. For an overview on the changing depiction of Rama in the modern period and in Hindu nationalist imagery in particular, see Kapur 1993 and Davis 1996.
7 Hansen 1992 discusses the Indian female heroic ideal of the *pativrata*.
8 For scholarship on women's retellings of the *Ramayana* epic, see Kishwar 2001, Nilsson 2001, and Rao 1991.
9 For further discussion of Anant Pai's interpretation of Goddess Kali in *Tales of Durga*, see McLain 2008. Also, Hawley 1995: 118, discusses Pai's rejection of the snake goddess, Manasa, and the newcomer goddess of satisfaction, Santoshi Ma, because neither goddess belongs to orthodox Sanskrit scripture.

References

Alam, Javed (1999) The Composite Culture and Its Historiography', *South Asia* 22: 29–37.
Davis, Richard H. (1996) The Iconography of Rama's Chariot in Ludden, D. (ed.) *Contesting the Nation: Religion, Community, and the Politics of Democracy in India*. Philadelphia: University of Pennsylvania Press: 27–54.
Hansen, Kathryn (1992) 'Heroic Modes of Women in Indian Myth, Ritual and History: The Tapasvini and the Virangana', in Arvind Sharma and Katherine K. Young (eds), *The Annual Review of Women in World Religions*, vol. II. Albany: State University of New York Press: 1–62.
Hawley, John Stratton (1995) The Saints Subdued: Domestic Virtue and National Integration in Amar Chitra Katha, in Lawrence Babb and Susan Wadley (eds) *Media and the Transformation of Religion in South Asia*. Philadelphia: University of Pennsylvania Press: 107–34.
Jain, Kajri (2007) *Gods in the Bazaar: The Economies of Indian Calendar Art*. Durham and London: Duke University Press.
Kapur, Anuradha (1993) Deity to Crusader: The Changing Iconography of Ram, in Gyanendra Pandey (ed.) *Hindus and Others: The Question of Identity in India Today*. New York: Viking: 74–109.
Kishwar, Madhu (2001) Yes to Sita, No to Ram: The Continuing Hold of Sita on Popular Imagination in India, in Paula Richman (ed.) *Questioning Ramayanas: A South Asian Tradition*. Berkeley: University of California Press: 285–308.
Lent, John A (2004) India's *Amar Chitra Katha*: Fictionalized History or the Real Story? *International Journal of Comic Art* (Spring): 56–76.
Ludden, David (ed.) (1996) *Contesting the Nation: Religion, Community, and the Politics of Democracy in India*. Philadelphia: University of Pennsylvania Press.
McLain, Karline (2005) Lifting the Mountain: Debating the Place of Science and Faith in the Creation of a Krishna Comic Book. *Journal of Vaishnava Studies* 13.2: 22–37.
McLain, Karline (2007) Who Shot the Mahatma? Representing Gandhian Politics in Indian Comic Books, *South Asia Research* 27.1: 57–77.
McLain, Karline (2008) Holy Superheroine: A Comic Book Interpretation of the Hindu *Devi Mahatmya* Scripture, *Bulletin of the School for Oriental and African Studies* 71.2: forthcoming.

McLain, Karline (2009) *India's Immortal Comic Books: Gods, Kings, and Other Heroes.* Bloomington: Indiana University Press.

Nilsson, Usha (2001) Grinding Millet but Singing of Sita: Power and Domination in Awadhi and Bhojpuri Women's Songs, in Paula Richman (ed.) *Questioning Ramayanas: A South Asian Tradition.* Berkeley: University of California Press: 137–58.

Pinney, Christopher (2004) *Photos of the Gods: The Printed Image and Political Struggle in India.* London: Reaktion Books.

Pritchett, Frances W (1995) The World of Amar Chitra Katha, in Lawrence Babb and Susan Wadley (eds) *Media and the Transformation of Religion in South Asia.* Philadelphia: University of Pennsylvania Press: 76–106.

Rajagopal, Arvind (2001) *Politics After Television: Hindu Nationalism and the Reshaping of the Public in India.* Cambridge: Cambridge University Press.

Rao, Velcheru Narayana (1991) A *Ramayana* of Their Own: Women's Oral Tradition in Telugu, in Paula Richman (ed.) *Many Ramayanas: The Diversity of a Narrative Tradition in South Asia.* Berkeley: University of California Press: 114–36.

Richman, Paula (ed.) (1991) *Many Ramayanas: The Diversity of a Narrative Tradition in South Asia.* Berkeley: University of California Press.

Role of Chitra Katha in School Education (1978) Bombay: India Book House Education Trust.

Van Der Veer, Peter (1994) *Religious Nationalism: Hindus and Muslims in India.* Berkeley: University of California Press.

Vasudevan, Ravi (ed.) (2001) *Making Meaning in Indian Cinema.* New Delhi: Oxford University Press.

Specific references

'Akbar' (1979) *Amar Chitra Katha* (no. 200). Mumbai: India Book House/ACK Media.

'Godavari Tales' (2003) *Vivalok Comics* (not numbered). New Delhi: The Viveka Foundation.

'Krishna' (1969) Amar Chitra Katha (no. 11). Mumbai: India Book House/ACK Media.

'Lokamanya Tilak' (1980) Amar Chitra Katha (no. 219). Mumbai: India Book House/ACK Media.

'Rama' (1970) *Amar Chitra Katha* (no. 15). Mumbai: India Book House/ACK Media.

'Rana Pratap' (1971) *Amar Chitra Katha* (no. 24). Mumbai: India Book House/ACK Media.

'Shivaji' (1971) Amar Chitra Katha (no. 23). Mumbai: India Book House/ACK Media.

'Subhas Chandra Bose' (1975) Amar Chitra Katha (no. 77). Mumbai: India Book House/ACK Media.

'The Santhals' (2002) *Vivalok Comics* (not numbered). New Delhi: The Viveka Foundation.

'The Sunderbans' (2002) *Vivalok Comics* (not numbered). New Delhi: The Viveka Foundation.

'Tales of Durga' (1978) *Amar Chitra Katha* (no. 176). Mumbai: India Book House/ACK Media.

'Valmiki's Ramayana' (1992) *Amar Chitra Katha* (no. 10001). Mumbai: India Book House/ACK Media.

12 The gated romance of 'India Shining'

Visualizing urban lifestyle in advertisement of residential housing development

Christiane Brosius

Since the late 1990s I have keep returning and staying in New Delhi. Since that time, many places I have visited or passed by have changed or been demolished; new sites have been built and impacted on the ongoing transformation of urban India in the context of neo-liberalization; some sites have done so more drastically than others.[1] Luxury townships at the outskirts of Delhi's National Capital Region (NCR) have come up, as well as a number of shopping malls, golf courses, gated communities and multi-storey business buildings mushroom across the city. New Delhi has changed in the light of mega-events, such as the Asian Games of 1982 or the upcoming Commonwealth Games of 2010. But by no means are such events the sole force of urban transformation. A megacity and national capital such as New Delhi must constantly attract capital and attention of all kinds in order to be part of the network of global cities and regimes of visibility. Advertisements are a crucial 'aesthetic interface of postcolonial capitalism' (Mazzarella, 2003: 4) and globalizing consumerism of the new cities from the 'globalising South' as they compete for international recognition and investment (e.g. real estate development, retail sector, business product outsourcing).[2]

The images discussed here could not have been found in India ten years ago. They are clearly a product of a flourishing real estate industry as well as a bustling public multi-media culture of 'India Shining'. 'India Shining', a slogan coined by the BJP for their 2004 parliamentary election campaigns, did not get them the expected votes. The elections were lost, but the slogan lived on and climbed new heights in the light of economic liberalization.

Despite the fact that India is changing physically, it is the visibility of prospective and imagined effects of globalization that I am interested in here, that is, the ways in which the images of the world-class city evolve a kind of self-fulfilling prophecy of phantasmagorias of wealth and confidence. It is particularly relevant for this chapter to explore how the globalized imaginary[3] of 'world class' surfaces in those images preceding the urban renewal and development, setting the agenda and designing vistas upon a new world, shaping desires of emerging aspiring middle classes and new social elites.[4] These utopian visions are designed, imagined and circulated through a host of media, many of which are outcomes of media globalization and urbanization: lifestyle magazines, glossy newspaper advertising, street hoardings, real estate magazine and builders' brochures, and even the world-wide web. A substantial number of these images present futuristically shaped buildings or Victorian-style villas amidst green hills and meadows, flamboyantly designed gardens and lakes. These are combined with slogans announcing the construction of a 'new India', 'an ideal land', a 'kingdom for the new maharajas', an oasis in the desert, bringing 'world class' standards to the 'deserving few'. Life in the kind of 'Planet' India designed in front of our eyes through these poster visions simply feels good, comfortable, affluent, meaningful, clean, air-conditioned and safe (see Narayanan, 2006). While we dwell in this world we are encouraged to forget the traffic congestions, the *jhuggi-jhopris* (squatter settlements, partly with proper structures) squeezed into non-places along railway tracks, roads and dirty rivers, switch off those images of children looking through our window while the car waits impatiently at a traffic light. Instead, we seem to move at lightning speed and with great ease between Dubai and Singapore, Kuala Lumpur and New York, like an *avatar* of the Virtual World Second Life (see Figure 12.3).

The focus of this chapter is on how 'India Shining' (Pinney, 2005) is imagined, visualized and sanctioned in and through lifestyle aesthetics that become available in and through the new 2D and 3D spaces. In this process, lifestyle concepts and practices are made 'real', desirable and available for particular experiences of members of the aspiring and affluent urban middle classes in India as well as returning and investment-oriented NRIs. To me, those visions consist of an interesting yet strange assemblage of particular cosmopolitan and folkloristic distinctions. They enhance and inhabit what I term the 'enclave gaze', that is, an inverted gaze, circumambulating itself narcissistically, pretending that it can do without the world outside, in particular signs of poverty.[5] This gaze imbues a particular way of looking at the world and oneself from an insulated perspective. I relate this enclave gaze to the extent public sphere and discourse are altered in this context, for instance through the privatization of public space.[6] I argue that the notion of belonging to world class is crucial to understand the 'efficacy' of the enclave gaze that is generated in the imaginary of the global city. The enclave gaze is part of a selective perception of reality that shapes and legitimizes the lifestyle aspirations and identification of the new middle classes. Furthermore, gaze and associated lifestyle imaginaries call upon and revitalize colonial narratives. Mazzarella has coined this as 'auto-orientalism', that is, a reproduction of India and Indianness as an exotic trope, this time, and particularly visible in advertisement, through self-stigmatization as means of distinction vis-à-vis a modernity declared as Western and foreign. The anthropologist underlines that such a strategy serves the creation of an aesthetic community and cultural identity (2003: 138–44). Likewise, the 'world class' city is conceived as a visual if not multi-sensual, spectacular delight; a fully-fledged sensorial event. Such an experience is eventful, safe, clean and orderly to such an extent that it seems artificially 'out of this world', as if it was located on a strange and distant planet. Likewise, this lifestyle suddenly has come very close to a variety of Indians with flexible careers, access to higher education and private media. The enclave gaze of globalizing India is impacted by display and performance of material affluence and confidence.

It must be seen by others in order to be; it must constantly reassure itself of, and legitimize, its presence. The new script that speaks through the lifestyle images under survey here reassures its beholder that new India has finally freed herself from the stern dogma of Socialist five-year plans, of ration cards and bribing petty bureaucrats for everyday amenities. Conspicuous consumption even seems 'politically correct' because it stimulates economic growth. In the notion of a 'global Indian lifestyle' apparent paradoxes such as tradition and modernity, history and present, family, leisure and work, fuse harmoniously. Thus, we find the familiar beside the new, the 'Indian' next to the 'foreign'. Roman emperors, Egyptian kings and Hindu deities, pillars from Greek antiquity and English landscape gardens promote – and bring sensually close to the viewer – a sense of both national and cosmopolitan identity. They enable a 'vision of the Indian nation based on an idealized depiction of the urban middle classes and new patterns of commodity consumption' (Fernandes, 2000: 612), at the same time both liberalized and enclaved, globalized and Indian.

How are the cities of the future and the lifestyles possible in these visualized projections on poster hoardings and in newspaper advertising? Who has access to this kind of imaginary of the 'beautiful life', is it restricted and if so, by what kinds of distinction and regimes of taste? Can we recognize certain aspirations and worries of the aspiring new middle classes, and even elites, as we explore the vocabulary of metaphors and images of urban space and residential housing of the 'enclave gaze'?

'Gold rush' or 'global living for global Indians'

'There was never a better time to be an Indian and to be in India than now!', tells me of an obviously enthusiastic real estate developer of a firm with head quarters in Greater Noida. This view is shared and declared by many who maintain that India is indeed 'shining'. The 'gold-rush-mood' has turned the real estate market into one of the booming sectors of post-liberalization India. Furthermore, it has become the stage for the negotiation of what, and who, is 'global'. The image of the globalized Indian who 'made it to the top', flexible and mobile in his/her career, confident and beautiful in (life-)style, has become a key figure of globalization. Assotech, a major real estate developer in North India, promises 'truly international lifestyle' for those who buy one of the luxury apartments at Windsor Park in Indirapuram, Greater Delhi. 'Global living for global Indians' is their motto, and the advertisement brochures produced for this display skylines of high-rise apartment buildings (Figure 12.1). Real estate developers are the new promoters of New Delhi's imagined – and partly actual – transformation from Third World, or Third Class, City to what I call First Class, or 'World Class City'. Respectively, categories such as 'second' and 'first' class citizens are invoked in this rhetoric. This envisaged urban transformation places New Delhi and other South Asian megacities right next to Paris, London, New York. Real estate developers, various departments of state governments, investors and the business community assemble to contribute to, and profit from, the image of the world-class city in the

Figure 12.1 'Global living for global Indians.'
Source: Assotech Elegante. Advertisement from a lifestyle magazine, 2005.

making. The visual rhetoric reflects a fairly standardized concept of the 'super-city': a skyline with high-rise buildings, reflecting glass façades (Figure 12.3); an abundance of electricity and water in festively lit-up houses and parks, or the cool elegance of marble floors and golden water taps.

From advertisements by real estate developers such as Assotech we learn that 'A global concept deserves a global audience'. And we see how a young couple, the 'modern maharajas', look out of the grand window of their flat in a high-rise apartment building (Figure 12.2). Their gaze falls onto a cityscape that could be located anywhere from Singapore, to Dubai or Shanghai – places for imagination in transit and montaged. More important than the actuality of the *topos* is that in its appearance, it seems somehow delocalized, 'a place that is truly international!' Then we read that launches of these apartment buildings have simultaneously been held in hubs along what could be called the 'diasporic lifestyle axis', that is, in Dubai, the United States or Canada.

Though they may have never lived abroad, the enclaved gaze of 'world class' standards and goods of living have been shaped and sharpened by satellite television, lifestyle magazines and shopping malls. Its beholders care for both, the 'Indian touch' and 'internationality' or 'world class', the urban and the religious or folkloristic. Imported, 'foreign' commodities, increasingly available after the liberalization of the market economy, are crucial to the discourses and self-esteem of the new middle classes. By now we can sense that the audience is made up of a new 'species' of Indians. Their members represent the ongoing miles-and-more traveller or 'career nomad', who touches ground according to the availability of lucrative jobs and work permits, in India or abroad, with increasingly fluctuating residential addresses and high expectations in adequate lifestyle environments. Many of them might have turned into fairly wealthy employees at high speed – and it is in particular those 'newcomers' who seek

Figure 12.2 'A global concept deserves a global audience.'
Source: Assotech Eleganté, 2005. Advertisement of real estate developer Assotech.

Figure 12.3 'Creating a New India.' Lighted hoarding at Khan Market, New Delhi, October 2006.
Source: Photograph: C. Brosius.

guidance in the vast infrastructure of lifestyle and 'taste' experts. In 2006, Indians were said to have enjoyed the sharpest rise in salaries worldwide. People move and climb up quickly, with their skyrocketing salaries, and the multinational corporations (MNCs) are the ideal place where they can do so. For multinational companies, New Delhi and its immediate surroundings such as Gurgaon are the first places to invest in – even though there is a strong competition for global city status with Bangalore, Hyderabad, Chennai and even Pune. The speed at which lifestyles can change, improve, and have to perform a certain flexibility is evident in the advertisements as well as the conversations with representatives of real estate developers: potential buyers have no time to waste for furniture, therefore the flats come with furniture, or even an interior designer who can be hired ('dial-a-designer'). Fredrick R., an architect in New Delhi, explains in a personal conversation:

> Private high-rise apartment blocks are a relatively new thing to Delhi. Previously, apartment buildings were government-built, subsidized, not more than 4–5 stories high. Increasingly, young people with high salaries, want the most modern space available, move into projections of 'London Lofts' or 'Spanish villas'. Who buys? Multinational corporations who have settled down in Gurgaon in the last five years or so, recruit young people, IT graduates or business students, offering them a good salary, accompanied by a 'packaged lifestyle'.
>
> (April, 2005)

Figure 12.4 A tribute to Bengal by NRIs Developers. Page from an advertisement brochure, Rosedale, Kolkata, 2007.

Clearly, we have new patterns of a consumer culture and subjectivity at work here. The new middle classes indulge in a highly confident form of conspicuous consumption.

Besides young successful career-makers from within India, the NRI has become a key addressee of the real estate imaginary and politics of the world-class city. Some urban developers focus specifically on the NRI market, such as Rosedale Developers in Kolkata. Overseas Indians make up a large section of real estate investors and buyers, since they belong to a stream of temporary or permanent returnees (e.g. for a holiday or even retirement). The Rosedale advertisement of which the above illustration is a part (Figure 12.4) appeals to the alleged desire of NRIs to return to their 'roots', remembering their childhood days, knowing that the idea of home is enforced by memories and the nostalgia of returning to where one grew up, where one originated from:

> No matter where you are, if you have lived in Kolkata, its memories will always remain a part of you. The afternoon cricket matches in the alley, … Think! Why do these memories keep coming back? Because Kolkata is in your DNA. Now you can relive these memories again. By living in Rosedale Gardens. And what's interesting, is that the experiences you'll be gathering here will be packaged better than yesteryears. Because, the changing times have added a fresh perspective to the old ones. The coffee house 'addas' are in the Baristas, the matinee show at Priya cinema has been replaced by movies in the multiplex INOX. In spite of the topsy-turvy times before, the globalization takeover, Kolkata retains its infectious never say die attitudes. So, it's time to rewind those memories and unwind in Kolkata!
>
> (Brochure Rosedale 2007)

Barista is the Indian answer to Starbucks, and a new and rather expensive location used by the globalized Indian, quite distinctly different from the traditional coffee houses (*adda*). The advertisement maintains an essential identity – of belonging to Kolkata – that is imbued in the genes, that only has to be rediscovered and affirmed by 'paying tribute' to memories; possibly memories of a different, not one's own kind.

Life on 'Planet India'

Many advertisements appeal to a beholder and potential customer filled with a certain fascination with India as an exotic and strange country, with Indianness as an orientalized Other (Figure 12.5). By scrolling through newspapers or real estate journals and gazing at the booming satellite cities of megacities such as Kolkata, Delhi or Bangalore, and smaller cities such as Lucknow, Jaipur or Amritsar, the eye of the beholder encounters a plethora of similar depictions that are staged for the pleasure of consumption. The viewer is offered visions and views of a 'five-star life' with the promise of 24-hour security, water and electricity, a club-house, swimming pool, and fitness centre, maybe even a hospital and a school. The items and places on display, catalysing imaginations and desires, are just part of a whole range of new pleasures and spaces that have cumulatively emerged since the 1990s and intensified in this millennium. Some of the visually most eye-catching examples available in 2-D are luxury villas in Gurgaon such as Ansal's Florence Marvel, Gulmohur Greens, and Penthouses, or Negolice's Victoria Gardens.

Seemingly paradoxical, the imagined buyers of such abundance are not only successful businessmen and women clad in Western suits but are often referred to as 'modern maharajas', European kings and queens, heroes of Greek or Roman Antiquity. Colonial India and lifestyle are recurring motifs of real estate advertising, both in image and text. With condominiums such as Windsor Park

Figure 12.5 Hoarding of Gulmohur Greens, SVP Group, located close to East Delhi UP border; January 2007.
Source: Photograph: C. Brosius.

or Victoria Gardens, it almost seems as if the modern Indians of today have been transferred into the imperial era where life (of the ruling elite) was simply better.

The advertisements present festively lit individual villas with huge windows, balconies, and terracotta tiles, possibly topped by a swimming pool. They show blocks of high-rise buildings assembled around a park with green lawns, flowerbeds, lakes or swimming pools, and shady trees. As points of identification, people feature too: we may see a man dressed in a Western suit as he meditates on spacious lawns, or couples and nuclear families enjoying a stroll in a lush and exotic park named after a site in the former colonial capital, Kolkata.

These visual quotations often come to life only after they merge in the viewer's mind and when exhibited along with a plethora of slogans. A newspaper version of an advertisement carries the additional line, '*Inviting those who belong to class. See it, to believe it!*' Underlining these associations is the projection of a competent and self-conscious consumer with 'classic', 'eternal' good taste and global way of life, a true Indian cosmopolitan. The references to golf, jogging, or to people who would regularly host garden or roof terrace parties equipped with the open-air bar on the terrace for regular parties (also indicating the growing acceptance of alcohol as signifier of Westernized sophistication), are suggestive of the luxurious 'high life'. 'Belonging to class' means 'to be special' or 'to have made it', to be part of a trendsetting transnational elite immersed in impression management. As a seemingly distinct style it also indicates that there are certain visible signs and ways of placing them strategically, creating the notion of a clear-cut border between those who belong and those who don't, the haves and the have-nots. In his book on images and lifestyle, Stuart Ewen argues that the notion of 'being special' in particular, the 'feeling' of being exclusive, is crucial to the development of lifestyle aspirations acquired through advertisement images by the middle classes. This requires a distinguishable set of 'images, attitudes, acquisitions, and style'. And even if 'the "life-style" … is not realizable in life, it is nevertheless the most constantly available lexicon from which many of us draw the visual grammar of our lives' (Ewen, 1988). In this context, images of status and style, for example, strategies of distinction, become the social currency and the symbolic and cultural capital in an increasingly mobile and fluid, commercialized and globalized world whose members want all but move downwards or slow down (ibid.: 29).

It seems noteworthy that the new middle class imagined in this and the following advertisements, and its 'visual lexicon' of identification converges with a 'new transnational cosmopolitan class of Indians', a term coined by Ronald Inden (1999: 48). Their Arcadian visions of lifestyle, as Inden argued in his analysis of the Hindi blockbuster *Hum Aapke Hain Kaun…?!* (Who am I to you?!, 1994), are staged in worlds where 'the masses have virtually disappeared. Only the elite are present'. Whether *filmi* heroes and heroines or modern maharajas, they all float playfully in a 'suburbian utopia' (ibid.: 59). Thus, the visual popular language of Bollywood and Gurgaon share the same imaginary, developing a similar 'enclaved gaze' that excludes the majority of Indians who do not (or must not) have any access

Figure 12.6 Victoria Gardens, New Delhi. Negolice.
Source: Advertisement in *Jetwings*, October 2006: 175.

to 'world-class'. The visibility of the Self produces the invisibility of the Other, or, as we shall see below, avails of the latter for exotic consumption and ethnic chic.

To have all the trendy and necessary facilities to live a good and beautiful life, in a centrally located and well-connected place, among others that think and live alike and yet still independent, seems ideal to the aspiring members of 'world class'. This vision is also reflected in the above advertisement that appeals to the affluent and mobile consumers' desire to live 'the way the world lives', like in the case of Victoria Gardens in New Delhi. In the montage, couples with and without children are portrayed walking through an exotic Garden City, with palm trees, lakes, flowers; the skyscraper residential blocks blurred, hardly visible, at the horizon (Figure 12.6). The images of lifestyle in urban India paint a utopian picture in which members of the established and new affluent upper middle classes can safely dwell, without the alleged hassles of everyday life in the chaotic and unsafe city outside. The notion of living abroad becomes a portable item as exemplified in the following excerpt from an advertisement by Opera Garden Luxury Apartments & Penthouses: 'get ready to live abroad in India!' (TOI Property Supplement, January 13, 2007). Such a heterotopic site, or 'privatopia' (Glasze *et al.* 2006: 9), secluded from the everyday garb of the public, is also promised to the potential buyers of a gated township called Vatika City, in Gurgaon:

> For some a Home is more than just an address. It's a statement. ... Live the way the world's jet-set prefers ... [apartments] nestled amidst contemporary townscape architecture and located within the lush settings of Vatika City. Artistically designed for the discerning few, the limited edition apartments

speak of opulence and extravagance. ... Fully air-conditioned. Hermetically sealed, sound proof environs [sic!]. ... State-of-the-art security.[7]

This is a strange combination of desires of the 'world's jet-set' and the 'discerning few', showing how closely tied the aesthetics of fear and security and individual freedom, spatial exclusion and inclusion, the longing for prestige and respectability and social anxieties with respect to 'chaos' and poverty can be. The physical outside world is 'switched off'. Instead, life only happens behind well-guarded walls and under video-surveillance, as in another example of a prime real estate developer and builder. According to anthropologist Caldeira, writing on South American walled communities of middle and upper classes, these people display a longing for independence and freedom 'both from the city and its mixture of classes'. She further writes that 'a new aesthetic of security shapes all types of constructions and imposes its new logic of surveillance and distance as a means for displaying status, and it is changing the character of public life and public interactions' (Caldeira, 2005). Thus, the enclaved gaze of 'hermetically sealed, sound proof environs' is imbued with fear of being disturbed, threatened, if not swallowed up, by a disorderly, uncontrollable public. It seems odd, however, to identify Delhi with a city like Rio de Janeiro or New York; her streets are yet predominantly 'removed from criminality and ghettoization'. Through the enclaved gaze, the integration into the global community seems of more relevance and is perceived as more familiar and 'natural' than the local worlds of the bazaar or the *gali* (alleyway). This rhetoric polarizes outside and inside, shapes notions of 'normal' and 'abnormal': The world 'out there' is a world that must be either successfully disciplined, cleaned and tamed by 'strategic embellishment' (Benjamin, 1999: 23) or ignored by neglect.

Dubaization: staging the city fantastic

Beyond presenting 'worlds en miniature', with shops, hospitals, pools, the advertisements of these new towns or enclaves remind of the nineteenth century 'world exhibition' and phantasmagoria glorifying the commodity fetish (ibid.: 17). The city fantastic must trigger desires, attention, and entertain the beholder by means of a spectacular mega-narrative. Many of these narratives are interlinked with the global city as a theme park, and quite like Dubai has by now become a site of sensual sensations and simulacra (Figure 12.7). A nostalgic projection of a national Golden Age and desire to revitalize this through festive pomp and religious traditions, underlined with historical depth features centrally in the Indian real estate advertisements.

These images and sites are part of the attempt of a new group of experts, that is, 'lifestyle designers' to shape a choreography of 'world-class' and 'international lifestyle'. This kind of lifestyle management concentrates on the display of wealth and self-esteem, claiming that 'good lifestyle' requires care, competence, and know-how. The accumulation of historical items may increase or affirm taste and status of a person choosing to live in one of these compounds. 'Heritage' gives feeling to nationality and cosmopolitanism, even for a nostalgic and romantic encounter with the colonial past. According to the text for the

Figure 12.7 Dubai at Khan Market, lighted hoarding by MGF, October 2006.
Source: Photograph: C. Brosius.

Victoria Gardens advertisement: 'History is blooming once again. Inspired by the Victoria Gardens of Kolkata and the royal lifestyle from the imperial era, comes Victoria Gardens in Delhi.' OMAXE, one of the big real estate names in India, appropriates and interprets Ancient Egypt for one of its latest apartment townships, 'Luxor' in Gurgaon. The advertisement claims that, where more than 400 apartments are situated in nine towers,

> [T]he World's greatest Civilization now comes alive in Gurgaon. LUXOR Apartments and Penthouses. ... The place where Egyptian Grandeur mingles with ultra-modern lifestyle (and) ... Egyptian architecture ... hieroglyphs on walls, coloured sandstone, Egyptian paintings on the wall, and Luxor-inspired domes.
>
> (TOI Online, Rohit Karir: 'Live Life Egyptian-Size')

Text and image reflect the production of transcultural connections, of a 'world-class' history, where the Indian/Hindu culture and Golden Age emerges as a parallel topography to that of Greek Antiquity, the Roman Empire and the Egyptian pharaohs. This is also manifest in the next illustration, taken from an EROS brochure, at Rosewood City, Gurgaon Grand Mansions II (Figure 12.8). The slogan on the front page appeals to the potential buyer to internalize the advice 'seek out a kingdom worthy of thyself', that apparently Alexander the Great has been given by his father. The appeal is superimposed onto a baroque entrance of a huge house that could also be set in the Victorian age. Europe often serves as an index for historical weight and for the visualized distinction of those 'who made it', be it Greek Antiquity, Medieval Baroque, or European Romantic landscape gardens, and late-nineteenth-century English suburban garden cities. It still counts as a luxury label with export quality. But this time, Europe holds as a projection

Figure 12.8 Front page of Brochure for EROS Grand Mansions II, Rosewood City, Gurgaon.

screen for the formerly colonized and new global 'maharajas'. Maybe, one could argue, this is because for so many centuries several of its countries were associated with cultural superiority, successful and powerful imperial and colonial expansion, and international recognition (see Dupont, 2005). However, this fascination with ancient and colonial history is part of a globalized currency through which lifestyles in other megacities under rapid economic liberalization, Shanghai or Moscow, are shaped.

Let us take a closer look at Alexander's appeal to the 'modern maharajas'. The Eros brochure lectures that he was an 'all conquering and free spirit', one of the 'most prolific conquerors of all times', and had even come to north India! The architecture represents 'stately elegance and generous spaces ... classical perfection and grand proportions ... conquering the modern world of lifestyle yet once again ... against constraints of space', the lack of which is so often a given in a megacity like Delhi. We are reminded of Inden's statement of Bollywood's middle classes' Arcadia when the Eros advertisement claims to unveil a 'saga of unparalleled lifestyle', for the 'deserving few', the conquering and the power-hungry: 'finally, couches can be placed far apart ... you can give that big and exquisite Persian carpet its due place'. Likewise, a guide to 'good living' is wrapped up in the next quotation for the Grand Mansions project, where each villa has five bedrooms and imported bath fittings:

> Parthenon-like balconies, stately corridors, magnanimous reception areas with water bodies mingle easily with Jacuzzi, ensuite bathrooms, modular kitchen.... An ancient architecture conquers the modern age constraints of space and economy to broaden your world, while modern lifestyle and privileges make life amidst this glorious architecture a phenomenal experience.

What is meant by 'Parthenon-like' can only be guessed, given the origin of the term in Ancient Greek temple architecture. The eclecticism imbued in this quote mirrors architect Gautam Bhatia's excellent portrayal of popular architectural styles and middle-class attitudes in north India, for which he coined the term 'Punjabi Baroque'. To Bhatia, this style represents a creative attempt to show and produce taste and distinction of aspiring middle-class 'cosmopolitans' by appropriating elements from a vast range of other styles (1994: 32). These visualized and spatialized mosaics are an attempt of the middle classes to avoid being classified as 'provincial' and 'uneducated', to display cultural competence in 'world-class' architecture. Alleged familiarity, one's own as well as world history, qualifies as belonging to 'world-class'.

Themed and tamed nature

There is concern with joining the aesthetics of technological perfection and safety or architectural historicism and exclusiveness with an abundance of tamed nature. In fact, several real estate advertisements and brochures claim that in the light of nature's erosion and scarcity in megacities like Delhi, the condominium comes to replace 'real' nature and even preserve natural diversity for generations to follow, turning Delhi into a 'Green City' (Figure 12.9). The upper middle class and real estate industry thus are presented as environmentalists (see Baviskar, 2003). While exclusiveness is manifest in the advertisements for 'world-class' lifestyle by joining the global Indian with the nostalgia of a grand past, the 'enclaved gaze'

Figure 12.9 Green Delhi, hoarding at roadside in East Delhi.
Source: Photograph: C. Brosius, October 2006.

is also shaped by references to idyllic nature and paradisic solitude, a concept relatively new to an Indian majority and previously associated with asceticism rather than inner-worldly orientation. The ads allow views of Arcadian landscape gardens, visually and metaphorically, suggesting a life where meadows are covered with morning dew; where silent sites for meditation and endless gazing are possible, in the presence of exotic domestic flora and fauna; where evenings are filled with peacock screams and laughter from the pool instead of car and truck noise or the sound of an airplane landing. This feeds into a growing desire among upwardly mobile urban middle classes for the acquisition and consumption of artificially created spaces for withdrawal and recreation from stressful work in the form of themed zones, be it gated communities, fun parks, malls, or golf courses. The pleasure of enjoying nature and silence are often-mentioned attributes of a private enclave. These are positioned against the image of the 'rest' of the city as inhuman and polluted. Tamed and disciplined nature, and the affluence of 'green' and lush gardens underline the idea of an 'unnatural' outside that must be combated: 'In a city full of concrete, a living garden resort to live and breathe. In Delhi. Victoria Gardens. Your Living Garden Resort' (Victoria Gardens, Model Town; Figure 12.6). The more unplanned, ugly, dirty, and noisy the open city in the eyes of the upper and middle classes, the better sells the promise of a gated Eden.

Conclusion: outside the gates of the enclave gaze

Paradoxically, the spaces outside the gated communities of 'India Shining' are equally unreal, in transition, waiting to be called in for transformation. Different images of lived-in environment prevail and shape the everyday lives of the people living there, where meditation on a park bench in order to withdraw from stressful life in manager meetings is probably not even heard of, where new roads have been built in order to allow for smooth movement between the 'islands' or comfort zones. Partly farm land, partly deserted land, possibly waiting to be fenced and turned into another enclave, or shopping mall, the contrast between themed and unrecognized nature could not be more drastic, and yet logical (Figure 12.10).

In conclusion, it could be argued that the iconography of the 'enclaved gaze' reflects the aesthetic and desire of a new affluent and relatively confident Indian middle class and elite for new stages for conspicuous consumption, new sites for both new life-styles and status claims. The visual regime of this popular imagination of cosmopolitan life flaunts the notion that it is possible to distinguish oneself from others by putting on display and thus shaping and participating in a new lifestyle environment, or at least, the idea of what such a life could be like. The pictures discussed are imbued with the desire to 'belong to class', to be 'world class', and for control over the allegedly chaotic, subtly dangerous, uncontrollable 'public'. They provide space to imagine the enclave community as an aesthetic community, united by the inclination to inhabit a beautiful and safe world, with access to uninterrupted flexibility and mobility. This way, the advertisements of a globalizing "India Shining" are part of what King has called the world (class) city becomes a place where the symbolic economy of new cultural meanings and representations takes place' (1995: 228). To me, this is an important remark that connects well with Zukin's (2005) statement about the symbolic economy of the city in which the understanding of what 'culture' is controlled by means of tagging.

Figure 12.10 Gurgaon. March 2006.
Source: Photograph: R. S. Iyer.

It remains to be seen how much localness these new colonies on planet India retain, and how the never-ending flow of citations from other global imaginaries of 'world-class' may work itself into a loop of self-saturation and fatigue.

Notes

1 In 2006, Delhi's population reached 15 million (starting with 410,000 people in 1911), more than 50 per cent living in slum clusters, unauthorized colonies or settlement colonies.
2 Delhi's urbanization responds to that of other megacities in India: Bangalore, one of the top ten new tech cities, Asia's fastest growing city ('Silicon Valley' of India), Pune, ranking amongst the top five Indian cities for IT exports (40,000 professionals), Kolkata, on the threshold of an IT/BPO revolution, with a proactive government, like Pune, and finally Chennai, the IT and BPO-hub of South India (see Heitzman, 2004).
3 The globalized social imaginary has been coined by Gaonkar to define concepts such as glocalization and alternative/multiple modernities, considering the colonial past as well as forces of contemporary global media, migration, and capital (2002: 4).
4 Numbers with respect to the Indian middle classes vary; in 2007, there was an estimation of 250 million members, growing steadily. Varma (1998) distinguishes between 'old' (Nehruvian) and 'new' (post-liberalization) middle classes, between aspiring and established middle classes. Statistics as to how many people (can actually afford to) live in the enclaves of the upper real estate market do not exist. This chapter refers to the imagined membership to gated communities.
5 John Urry (1990) coined the term tourist gaze, a practice involving all senses, and shaping identities and world views discursively and performatively.
6 See Glasze 2006. To what extent the concepts of private and public as well as civil society have different histories and meaning in India, is vital but cannot be discussed within the limits of this chapter (see Brosius 2009).
7 Construction for this township is still ongoing. See http://www.vatikagroup.com/Residential/VatikaCityGurgaon/home.html (accessed on 4 May 2008).

References

Baviskar, Amita (2003) 'Between violence and desire: space, power and identity in the making of metropolitan Delhi', *International Social Science Journal* 55: 89–98.

Benjamin, Walter (1999) 'Paris, capital of the nineteenth century', in *The Arcades Project*, Cambridge, MA and London: Harvard University Press [version of 1935].

Bhatia, Gautam (1994) *Punjabi Baroque and Other Memories of Architecture*, Delhi: Penguin.

Brosius, Christiane (2009) India Shining. Consuming Pleasures of India's New Middle Classes, New Delhi: South Asia Routledge.

Caldeira, Teresa (2005) 'Fortified enclaves. The new urban segregation', in Jan Lin and Christopher Mele (eds) *The Urban Sociology Reader*, London and New York: Routledge, 328–29.

Dupont, Veronique (2005) 'The idea of a new chic Delhi through publicity hype', in Romi Khosla (ed.) *The Idea of Delhi*, Mumbai: Marg, 78–93.

Ewen, Stewart (1988) *All Consuming Images: The Politics of Style in Contemporary Culture*, Basic Books: 20, 58, 62.

Fernandes, Leela (2000) 'Nationalizing "the global": media images, cultural politics and the middle class in India', *Media, Culture & Society*, 22(5): 612.

Gaonkar, Dilip Parameshwar (2002) 'Toward new imaginaries: an introduction', *Public Culture*, 14(1): 1–19.

Glasze, Georg, Chris Webster and Klaus Frantz (eds) (2006) *Private Cities: Global and Local Perspectives*. (=Studies in Human Geography), London and New York: Routledge.

Heitzman, James (2004) *Network City: Planning the Information Society in Bangalore*, New York: Oxford University Press.

Inden, Ronald (1999) 'Transnational class, erotic arcadia and commercial utopia in Hindi films', in Brosius and Butcher (eds) *Image Journeys. Audio-Visual Media and Cultural Change in India*, New Delhi: Sage, 41–66.

King, Anthony (1995) 'Re-presenting world cities. Cultural theory/social practice', in Paul and Peter Taylor Knox (eds) *World Cities in a World System*, Cambridge: Cambridge University Press, 215–31.

Mazzarella, William (2003) *Shoveling Smoke: Advertising and Globalization in Contemporary India*, Delhi: Oxford University Press.

Pinney, Christopher (2005) 'The political economy of gloss', *Bidoun*, 87–9.

Narayanan, Harini (2006) 'Der Schein Delhis. Die luftdicht verpackte Welt der Shopping Malls', in Ravi Ahuja and Christiane Brosius (eds) *Mumbai Delhi Kolkata. Annäherungen an die Megastädte Indiens*, Heidelberg: Draupadi, 157–2.

Urry, John (1990) *The Tourist Gaze: Leisure and Travel in Contemporary Societies*, London: Sage Publications.

Varma, Pavan (1998) *The Great Indian Middle Class*, Delhi: Penguin.

Zukin, Sharon (2005) 'Whose Culture? Whose City?' in Jan Lin and Christopher Mele (eds) *The Urban Sociology Reader*, London: Routledge: 281–9.

13 Advertising in a globalised India

Lynne Ciochetto

Introduction

This study explores the profile of contemporary advertising in India in the wider context of trends in international advertising, recent changes in the Indian economy and society and issues concerning the cultural impact of foreign advertising in India. Findings are complemented with a case study of outdoor advertising collected in three visits to India in 2000, 2001 and 2005. In the 1990s India witnessed a massive expansion of advertising, which was stimulated by the opening of the economy and the growth of the media. Though print is still the dominant media, during the 1990s there was a rapid expansion of television accompanied by television advertising. The advertising industry was quickly overtaken by foreign advertisers and agencies that were affiliated with foreign advertising agencies. Advertising for repeat purchase consumables dominated advertising in India but consumer durable advertising expanded at this time as the disposable income levels of the middle classes rose. There was a change in advertising strategies and increased focus on local cultural references. Another recent trend driven by multinational companies has been the intensification of marketing to the rural sector. Foreign companies were slow to appreciate the market potential of India but in recent years there has been a massive expansion of advertising by foreign companies which plays an important cultural role as the Indian economy increasingly becomes part of the globalised marketplace. The study uses a socio-cultural framework to explore the implications of globalisation on cultural change. Advertising is the key focus because it plays a pivotal role at the junction where the economy and culture interact. Advertising plays an important cultural role which is largely ignored by critical social scientists and economists, while those working in the field of advertising are primarily interested in developing new ideas for attention-getting campaigns, and associated research tends to focus on facilitating better advertising and targeting markets more effectively.

Indian advertising history

There has been a long tradition of advertising in India since the nineteenth century. In the 1970s, advertising began to increase and the first advertising appeared on state television in 1976. In the 1980s, the economy was opened to external influences and the number of alliances with multinational agencies increased. Advertising expenditure grew at nearly 15 per cent a year and reached US$896 million by the end of the decade (de Mooij, 1994: 222). Foreign controlled corporations dominated advertising expenditure, and 80 per cent of these were in the consumer goods sectors. Advertising was also very concentrated and the top 50 advertisers accounted for 80 per cent of advertising spending, with the top 10 advertisers accounting for 32 per cent of the total (Sachdeva, n.d).

In the early 1990s, there was a massive expansion in advertising in India when the government relaxed the regulations on foreign company advertising on television (*Advertising Age*, 4 October 1993). The advertising of foreign products on television was not permitted until 1994 (Pashupati and Sengupta, 1996: 178). At the same time there was a proliferation of television channels including satellite channels. Advertising expenditure increased from US$415 in 1992 to US$1,748 million in 2001, with a slight dip in 1998 after the Asian economic crisis (*Zenith Media* cited in Hargrave-Silk, 2002). The advertising industry has further expanded since 2000 and advertising expenditure in 2006 was estimated at US$4.1 billion (Singha and Suvi, 2007).

Advertising agencies

Advertising in India was dominated by Indian agencies until the 1990s because of government limitations on foreign ownership. By 1992–93, 11 of the top 20 Indian agencies were affiliated with multinational agencies. By 1999, there were about 400 advertising agencies in India employing about 18,000 people and 15 of the top 20 advertising agencies had affiliations or joint ventures with foreign agencies, and 12 of those were with American agencies. These foreign joint venture advertising agencies held more than 75 per cent of the market share, with wholly owned Indian agencies holding the balance. During the decade there was also a growing concentration of agencies and the largest 25 agencies accounted for 75 per cent of the total billings (Srinivas, 1999). Since 2000 there has been further concentration in the industry and the top 5 agencies in 2000–01 earned 47.2 per cent of total revenue (*Emerging Markets Economy*, 2002).

Product profiles

The first foreign companies to move into India were the fast moving consumer goods companies: cigarettes, personal products, cleaning products, soft drinks and pharmaceuticals. In the 1980s, there was a high level of market concentration with the three top brands in 17 selected product groups accounting for over 50 per cent of market share (India Trade Point, 1995). During the 1990s liberalisation policies generated a proliferation of television channels. Rising disposal income levels were reflected in increased advertising for consumer durables. In 1993, 75 per cent of television advertisements were for five major groups of products: toiletries and detergents, cold drinks, foodstuffs, cosmetics and health products. Product profiles differed on private and state television channels.

Leading advertisers

Advertising in India has always been dominated by foreign companies and as the largest global companies expanded into the markets of India in the 1990s competition increased along with takeovers of local brands. The greatest competition was in the key product categories: soap, detergents and soft-drinks. The key competitors in the soap and detergents market were Procter & Gamble, Unilever (HLL) and Colgate Palmolive. The British company Hindustan Lever Limited has been the major advertiser in India for over three decades. During the 1990s, the government increased its spending on advertising and in 1995 The Library of Congress estimated that 50 per cent of newspaper advertising was from government departments (2003). Key sectors which expanded included tourist promotion, army recruitment and aids awareness (Indian Television, 2001). There were changes in the key laundry and detergent market after 2000. Hindustan Lever's dominance was challenged by local manufacturers who had started providing cheaper alternatives and also long-time competitor Procter & Gamble cut their prices (Dinakar, 2005). The soft-drink market is another area of fierce competition between multinational companies Coca Cola and Pepsi.

Media

The development and introduction of new media in the twentieth century has been a great stimulus to the growth of advertising. Overall media usage continues to increase in India. Print is still the dominant advertising medium but after 1990 the proportion of print advertising relative to television advertising declined and by 1999 print accounted for 58 per cent of advertising, while television accounted for 34 per cent (Srinivas, 1999). Television advertising has further expanded since 2000 and the gap in expenditure is narrowing. By 2004, print expenditure was Rs 5,450 crore, US$1.2 billion, while television was Rs 4,860, US$1.1 billion (Adex cited in *The Hindu Business Line, 2005*). Television is an important medium in a market like India where literacy levels are comparatively low. Gallup Polls in the 1990s estimated that 59 per cent of the Indian population had exposure to television (*Euromonitor*, 2001) and by 2004, 37 per cent of Indian households owned a television set (The World Bank, 2005).

The government still controls the main television network Doordarshan but the monopoly of Indian State Owned Broadcasting ended in the early 1990s and there was major expansion in television. New channels were introduced as well as satellite and cable channels. Hong Kong-based Star Television was the first satellite channel to be established in 1992 (Thomas, 2006) but by 1999 there were 60 satellite operated channels. By 1999, 25 per cent of television advertising was on the satellite channels and rising. Cable penetration was estimated at 32 million homes in 2000, and the viewer bases were stabilised and advertisers focused on niche markets (Sehgal, 2000a). By 2006, there were an estimated 250 channels for an estimated 65 million satellite and cable homes (Tungate, 2006). The satellite and cable station audiences were the affluent middle classes.

Outdoor advertising has also been an important medium in major cities and is also common in rural areas, and from 1993–97 averaged about 5.5 per cent of total advertising, which is similar to international trends. Films are another important form of advertising especially for the rural consumers. The latest marketing frontier is the internet. In 2005, the number of internet users in India was 60 million (CIA, 2007), an increase from an estimated 800,000 in 1999 (Subramanian, 1999). Internet users are predominantly male and young (Smita, 2002). Pepsi and Coca Cola are some of the leading marketers targeting this group. Some of the largest advertisers in India are exploring other media to attempt to enter the vast rural consumer market, where even a small percentage of market share amounts to millions of consumers. Media alternatives such as video vans and point of purchase video display were an attempt by major advertisers to communicate to rural purchasers in their local languages, rather than Hindi and English, the main languages on television (Bajpai and Unnikrishnan, 1996; Kilburn, 2000).

Advertising strategies

Advertising strategies used in India have evolved in recent decades in response to a growth in awareness about Indian consumers, especially among international agencies and market researchers. One of the key challenges for foreign marketers in India was to change the pattern of consumer buying from traditional unbranded products to branded products such as toothpaste. A key strategy by the FMCG companies has been to reduce the size of their packages, 'think small', for example, selling tiny sachets of detergent and shampoo. Poorer people will often go without necessities to buy more expensive foreign products that embody dreams and aspirations for affluent lifestyles. During the 1980s, television advertising targeted the top 10 per cent of the population, affluent Indians with significant purchasing power and disposable income for repeat purchase consumables and increasingly consumer durables (Vilanilam, 1989). The elite in India had tended to purchase consumer goods overseas, either because the goods were not available locally or were of poor quality.

Television advertising was seen to play on the foreign obsessions of many Indians in the early 1990s (Bajpai and Unnikrishnan,1996: 305). A cross-cultural comparison between American and Indian magazines (*Life/The Illustrated Weekly of India* and *Newsweek/India Today*) done in the early 1990s concluded from this narrow sample that Western advertising conventions were being transferred cross-culturally along with institutions and technology. Griffin *et al.* clarify that these conclusions are applicable to the smaller segment, the upper- and middle-class elites in India who are the target audience and consumers of these magazines. This group is seen to 'distinguish themselves from the lower social strata by embracing Western manners and style as a sign of "civilisation and prestige". They co-operate in establishing the hegemony of Western practices and forms by their adoption of the consumer culture which transnational corporations sell' (1994: 503).

During the 1990s, advertising changed dramatically in India. There was a growth in the quantity of advertising, an increase in the advertising of international products and the dominance of international agencies. International agencies used imported and standardised advertising strategies in the early 1990s which was partly because emerging markets were low priority (Chandra *et al.* 2002). Prior to 1997, simple and straightforward messages stressing product benefits were seen as the most successful strategies (The Economist Intelligence Unit Ltd., 1997). Research into advertising strategies in India has tended to focus on the viability of importing standardised advertising into India and the focus has been on the middle class and the elite groups that read upmarket magazines and newspapers. A number of studies concluded that using standardised advertising, usually American advertising, was appropriate in elite Indian publications (Chandra *et al.* 2002; Cutler *et al.* 1992; Khairullah and Khairullah, 2002).

According to Sehgal in the 1990s some of the foreign advertising campaigns in India for major companies were unsuccessful including: Nike, Reebok, Johnny Walker, Sony, Panasonic, McDonald's and Coca Cola (2000a). Some of these campaigns lacked sensitivity to local culture or consumer awareness about advertising and reality. In 1997, a television commercial showing a child bungy jumping to get a bottle of Thums Up (owned by Coca Cola), had to be withdrawn after children died trying to imitate the advertisement (*Advertising Age*, 1997a). One of the most dramatically insensitive recent campaigns was that of Cadbury-Schweppes which compared its chocolate to Kashmir: 'Too tempting. Too good to share', which caused a major outrage and had to be withdrawn (*The Economist*, 2002). Failures caused advertisers to look more closely at their strategies and content (Sehgal, 2000a).

During the 1990s the advertising industry in India moved from a focus on demand creation to brand creation and the promotion of specific products (*The Economist Intelligence Unit Ltd.*, August 1997). Smita considered that advertising strategies moved from focusing on product benefits to a focus on values and value change (2002b). By the late 1990s, multinational companies were increasingly customising their advertising to the Indian market. Product endorsement by Indian celebrities and associations with national passions like cricket were some of the strategies used. The Korean company L.G. sponsored the Indian cricket team in the Cricket World Cup in 2003 and Adidas, who had previously made their Indian ads in London, started making them in India in 1999. They used the advertising agency RKSwamy/BBDO and featured Indian cricket star Sachin Tendulkar (Chawla, 1999). L'Oréal increased its sales dramatically by using Diana Haydin, the Miss India who became Miss World, along with its usual models (Fannin, 1999). This trend paralleled changes in the focus of satellite television programming. When Star television was introduced into India in 1992 the Hong Kong owners focused on standardised programming across the region, but in 1994 when the company was taken over by Murdoch's News Corporation they introduced localised and hybrid programming customised for the local market (Thomas, 2006).

During the 1990s, some of the major players in the FMCG sectors, realising the potential profits to be made in the rural sector, launched a massive assault on the Indian rural market. Ogilvie & Mather launched Programme Outreach to target rural consumers and expanded their rural sales force (Kilburn, 2000). Hindustan Lever embarked on a wide range of projects including: Project Shakti (meaning 'power') which supported rural self-help groups with a range of its products and Project Nova which expanded its direct selling network. HLL's profits declined after 2000 with competition from local producers and price-cuts by Procter & Gamble its main foreign competitor (Dinakar, 2005). Other strategies used by multinational companies to target rural communities included the setting up of e-choupals (cybercafes) in villages, and using mobile vans with television screens, games, door-to-door sales, folk dances, placing of tiles in village wells, shoe racks in temples, painting the horns of sacred cows and putting up scarecrows (Kilburn, 2000).

A key area of increased foreign competition was between the soft-drink giants Coca Cola and Pepsi. Coca Cola managed to turn around its 2000 US $400 million loss, by selling smaller bottles in rural markets which resulted in sales increases of 34 per cent in the first quarter of 2002 (Kripalani, 2002). Coke's goal was to make its products available, affordable and desirable. It opened 50,000 outlets in 3,500 villages in the first 3 months of 2002. They also launched other products: a soft-drink concentrate at 4c called Sunfill, Sprite and bottled water. Sprite was launched in 1999 with advertising that spoofed advertising hype and current trends in advertising, targeting youth 'in the process of establishing their identity' (Chawla, 1999).

Cultural change

The expansion of advertising contributes to the processes of social and cultural change that have accompanied the accelerated globalisation of the economy since the 1990s. Advertising contributes to cultural change through the introduction of new values (individualism, definitions of beauty), the intensification of other values such as materialism and consumerism and by diminishing and displacing other key values in society. Many developing nations have expressed concern about the cultural impact of advertising and in 1980 UNESCO compiled a report documenting the key values promoted in advertising. These were identified as: consumerism, materialism, individualism, hedonism, sexuality, stereotyped gender role models and body types (MacBride, 1980), conclusions supported in a similar study by Pollay (1986).

The first study of values in Indian television advertising was made by Vilanilam. He found that television showed an unreal reality of affluence that few could afford. He estimated that television advertising targeted the elite 10 per cent of the population and ignored the majority of the population whose needs were for food, clothing and shelter. Traditional methods of production and products were devalued by omission and one of the key effects of television advertising was to stimulate a revolution of rising expectations among both rich and poor (1989). A decade later Chaudhuri found that the worldview characterising pre-liberalisation India, inspired by socialism and distributive justice, had been displaced by a shift of stereotypes. Peasants and workers were displaced by the modern Indian successful corporate woman, chaste, demure, sexually sanitised and the modern Indian man powerful and successful, rich and glamorous (2001). The traditional icon of the Indian woman as homemaker and mother continued. Advertising was seen to reflect the worldview of the expanding new middle classes in the 1990s.

Srikandath studied the values depicted in television in the late 1980s and concluded that the main values being promoted were technology, modernisation and consumerism. Lifestyles that were promoted were fun, exciting and adventurous, while the promotion of packaged foods and gadgets for the home reflected the emerging trend of nuclear families with working couples not living in traditional extended families supported by servants (1991). In the early 1990s, Bajpai and Unnikrishnan found that television was playing a significant role in the expansion of consumer values in Indian society and that children were effectively being groomed to become future consumers, and the values promoted supported those aims: individualism and the nuclear family (1996: 229–33).

Contemporary advertising for personal products reinforces the decorative roles of women, focusing on image and appearance. The major foreign advertisers in India are the cosmetics and personal products companies (Hindustan Lever, Procter & Gamble, Colgate Palmolive). The beauty industry in its relentless presentation of unrealistic stereotypes creates anxiety and increasing self-consciousness about image and appearance. Products are offered as a remedy (Hamilton and Benniss, 2005). The images of women in advertising play an important role in defining contemporary ideals of beauty and a Eurasian Westernised ideal of beauty is promoted in the media throughout Asia by multinationals largely through the use of standardised advertising (Goon and Craven, 2003; Yu, 2002). Advertisers reinforce narrow stereotypes of female beauty and all images of women have pale skin, what Thapan (2004) calls 'the hegemony of fair skin' (2004) and fine Westernised features. Admittedly pale skin has been a traditional marker of aristocratic heritage and class allegiance in India (Goon and Craven, 2003). Large sections of the population with darker skin and different facial features are currently being devalued by omission. The multinational companies are also well established in the market selling skin whitening cream. Hindustan Lever even ran an advertisement in India in the 1990s that was based on the idea that women would improve their job prospects by having whiter skin and the idea was sold under the guise of removing dark shadows under the eyes. Even what defines beauty in India has been challenged by large companies. Traditionally the eyes, skin and hair were the key features but in the interests of selling lipstick in the 1990s Hindustan Lever embarked on a massive campaign to focus attention on the lips with the slogan 'Who's watching your lips today?' (Smita, 2002a).

The traditional role and status of women have sometimes been challenged by some campaigns from foreign companies. In 1995, J.W. Thompson launched a print campaign for women's rights (Bhandarkar, 1995). Procter & Gamble challenged traditional values and perceptions about privacy in its promotion of Whisper sanitary napkins (a new product in India), supporting their products with information booklets on hygiene and beauty care (Smita, 2002b). However, the majority of advertisements reinforce traditional stereotypes. Srinivas found that traditional Indian sexual stereotypes still play an important role in advertising in India where they are used to attach value to products (1999). Das found that men in Indian magazine advertisements were portrayed as dominant and authoritative while women were portrayed as homemakers (2000). Shoma Munshi's study of the portrayal of women in the 1990s Indian advertising, found that traditional women's roles in the family were being subverted, and often with humour and irony. The traditional roles of women as wives, mothers and daughters-in-law were being modified and changed to reflect social changes in the interests of giving them more consumer power, and liberation was being equated with product purchasing (1998).

One of the characteristics of contemporary advertising in industrialised countries is the continual pushing of the boundaries of intimacy and the promotion of sexuality, but in India regulations continue to be stringent. In April 2001, the new female Minister of Information and Broadcasting had a number of advertisements taken off the national broadcaster Doordarshan for being 'distasteful and degrading for women'. Kissing was banned on television in 2001 (Sehgal, 2001). There seems to be a different standard being upheld in print media. Thapan's (2004) study of advertisements in *Femina*, India's largest circulation English language women's magazine, found a strong emphasis on the body and sensuality in defining the modern Indian woman (2004). Chaudhuri has done a number of studies of gender in advertisements. She found a simultaneous cooptation and backlash regarding feminism in a survey of a number of magazines. Feminism was equated with a narrow framework of liberalisation reflected in the lifestyles of the corporate woman, and the primary focus being on lifestyles and consumption (2000).

Some product groups have been closely tied to certain sets of values. There was a massive expansion in tobacco advertising in the 1990s and the prominent themes for upmarket brands were aspirational, associating cigarettes with success, wealth, achievement, bravery and Western lifestyles. Lower socio-economic groups were targeted with emphases on taste and group allegiance (Bansal *et al.* 2005). There is a tendency for younger women to be represented in Western dress in advertising for high tech products with modernity such as cell phones (Example 1). The majority of men throughout India have adopted Western modes of dress, however high levels of male underwear advertising in rural areas indicate this is a growth area.

The major multinational companies in the fast food, cell phone, clothing and sports shoe markets are heavily targeting the youth market. Cell phone advertising to youth is prominent in outdoor advertising. Western values such as independence, hedonism and self-expression are more common in advertising to youth. A key message is empowerment and the creation of self-identity through branded products and new technology and this is an area of potential cultural change which may contribute to a weakening of the extended family and the arranged marriages that are the norm. Advertising targets these niche markets in certain media, including magazines (Gen X), television channels such as MTV and internet fan sites such as myenjoyzone.com for Coca Cola (Smita, 2002a). The study by Cullity of MTV in India discovered that though MTV had been forced by consumers to Indianise its Western imported programming after it was introduced in 1994, the hybridity of the new cultural images still promoted many Western values notably the beauty ideal of thinness. Women are still defined by the home and the traditional virtues of purity even if they have left the home through education and work (2004). The emphasis on youth was reinforced by findings of a cross-cultural study which found that older people are under-represented in advertising in India, and older women three times less represented than older men (Zhang *et al.* 2006).

Language is another area of cultural impact and advertising on television tends to be in Hindi, English or a blend of the two. This bias means that many groups are excluded and reflects the middle classes who are the primary target audiences of advertisers (Bajpai and Unnikrishnan, 1996). The use of a blend of English and Hindi in Coca Cola advertising, called 'Hinglish', was seen by *Business Week* as reflecting the Indian consumer's preference and it is part of its focus on the youth market (Kripalani, 2003).

Cultural and value change does not occur in isolation but in a dynamic interaction with existing value systems and practices and the result is a hybrid of continuity and change. An increased emphasis on materialism and consumption in contemporary India can actually reinforce traditional practices, such as arranged marriages and dowries (personal comment, 2005). The key cultural institutions of caste and religion are not touched in advertising. The dominant values that are reflected in contemporary advertising both target and reflect recent economic and cultural changes in the middle classes. Ram-Prasad (2007) and Cullity (2004) raise concerns whether the liberalisation of India in the 1990s is reinforcing inequalities between the middle classes and the 700 million in the lower classes and accelerating the separation between the two groups.

Case study: outdoor advertising

I made my first trip to India in 1994, and in recent years I have made three further trips (2000, 2001 and 2005), where I collected images that provide a snapshot view of outdoor advertising at that time. Advertising very much reflected local culture, and regional variations were apparent. The most noticeable feature of the outdoor advertising was the dominance of local advertising and very little evidence of international products or companies. Advertising in the countryside tended to take the form of freestanding billboards, and a large number of advertisements painted on the sides of buildings or on walls. In the cities there were some large billboards along the streets, but the visual landscape was dominated by a proliferation of small advertisements over storefronts and along the top of buildings in public thoroughfares and squares.

The types of products advertised varied in different regions. In the middle of India there was more advertising for agricultural products such as fertiliser, seeds and crops. In Southern India (Kerala, Tamil Nadu, Karnataka) the most advertised product was cement. Underwear for men was also frequently advertised in rural areas (Example 2). The most distinct regional difference in advertising was evident in Kerala which had much more diversity in the range of products which reflected its higher standards of living, while in Tamil Nadu there was a higher proportion of text only advertisements and in Rajasthan a large number of advertisements for agricultural and pumping equipment.

Advertising for product types tended to reflect similar characteristics. Cinema advertising tended to reinforce male and female stereotypes (Example 3). There was a significant amount of advertising for cigarettes which tended to be promoted with lifestyle advertising, cultural and international referents. Some advertising shows simply the packet but others use masculine imagery and lifestyle aspirations (Example 4). There was no evidence of multinational cigarette giants like Marlboro in India. The price-war between the big internationals Coca Cola and Pepsi was the most significant foreign presence on billboards and the strategy used was product illustration.

Political advertising was more common than social service advertising. High technology products and services, including cell phone services, financial services and computers were advertised in the cities, and also in Kerala. New products such as cell phones tended to portray young people, especially women. There was almost no advertising for alcohol.

The profile of outdoor advertising was dominated by local products. There was more advertising for consumer durables and financial and technological services in the cities, for example televisions, refrigerators, fans and automobiles, motorcycles and cell phone services. There were significant amounts of text-only advertising, and where images were used they tended to reflect traditional role stereotypes for men and women. Local culture was reflected in the use of local languages. There was little reference to lifestyles and environment, a dominance of illustration and the use of primary colours.

Conclusion

During the 1990s, advertising changed dramatically in India. The liberalisation of the Indian economy in the early 1990s led to the accelerated entry of foreign business and foreign advertising agencies to sell the products of foreign companies to the vast potential Indian market of over a billion people. There was a growth in the quantity of advertising, an increase in the advertising of international products and the dominance of international agencies. The purpose of advertising is to sell products or ideas, so the massive expansion of foreign companies and advertising, whether coming from overseas or created in India, has meant the massive expansion of the sales of foreign products. In the early 1990s, there were Indian advertising companies in the profile of top advertising agencies but by the end of the decade most had made strategic alliances with foreign agencies. There was a concentration in revenue, both in products, companies (HLL being the largest company and the greatest spender on advertising), and in the fact that 25 agencies accounted for 75 per cent of the advertising revenue in India in 1999 (Srinivas, 1999).

The major competition is in the low end of the market between the cola giants and the personal products and soap markets but there is also an expanding market for electronics, consumer durables and services. Television and satellite television were eroding the market dominance of print advertising in the 1990s, but print is still the largest media sector, including newspapers and magazines, which have expanded considerably in the 1990s. Advertising in the 1990s via television and print focused on the Hindi- and English-speaking population, which was predominantly educated, urban and middle class. In the 2000s however, major companies have been using strategies to target other markets, such as the rural and village market (70 per cent of the population), and the internet user teenage market.

These increases in advertising expenditure and the promotion of foreign products have impacts on culture, through the undermining of traditional habits and behaviours, the creation of new wants and desires, often for products like soft-drinks that have no nutritional benefit, and also by strategies that rework cultural values and beliefs. The roles of men, women and children are changing, traditional roles within home and family, concepts of beauty, identity and personal cleanliness are also undergoing major change. The overall impact of massive increases of foreign company advertising is the acceleration of India into the culture and ideology of consumerism, the expansion of foreign businesses into India and the export of profits to foreign corporations.

References

Advertising Age. (4 October 1993) India permits foreign ads, 64(42): 61.
Advertising Age. (14 July 1997a) Coca-Cola India pulls ad after another child dies. Available online at: http://www.adage.com/news:cms?newid=12466 (accessed 5 August 2002).
Advertising Age. (14 July 1997b) O&M buys Indian shop to aid WPP growth, 68(28): 31.
Bajpai, S. and Unnikrishnan, N. (1996) *The Impact of Television Advertising on Children.* New Delhi: Sage.
Bansal, R., John, S. and Ling, P. (2005) Cigarette advertising in Mumbai, India: targeting different socio-economic groups, women and youth. *Tobacco Control*, 14: 201–6.
Bhandarkar, U. (17 July 1995) India: try to hit the moving target. *Adweek Western Edition*, 45(29): 32.
Chandra, A., Griffith, D.A. and Ryans, J.K. (2002) Advertising standardisation in India. *International Journal of Advertising*, 21(1): 47–66.
Chaudhuri, M. (2000) 'Feminism' in print media. *Indian Journal of Gender Studies*, 7(2).
Chaudhuri, M. (May–August 2001) Gender and advertisements, the rhetoric of globalisation, *Women's Studies International Forum*, 24(3–4): 373–85.
Chawla, I. (12 April 1999) Marketers shift in India. *Advertising Age International*, page 13.
CIA. (2007) *World Factbook* Online. Available online at: cia.gov/library/publications (accessed 20 December 2007).
Cullity, J. (2004) Sex appeal and cultural liberty: a feminist inquiry into MTV India. *Frontiers*. Available online at: BNET.com (accessed 20 December 2007).

Cutler, B., Erramilli, M. and Javalgi, R. (1992) Visual components of print advertising: a five country cross-cultural analysis. *European Journal of Marketing*, 26(4): 7–20.

Das, M. (November 2000) Men and women in Indian magazine advertisements: a preliminary report. *Sex Roles*, 43(9–10): 699–717.

De Mooij, M. (1994) *Advertising and the Globalising of the Economy.* London: Prentice Hall.

Dinakar, S. (8 November 2005) Choice and no choice; Hindustan Lever is being attacked from below and is opting to sacrifice margins to reach choosy Indian consumers of all stripes. *Forbes Magazine.*

Emerging Markets Economy. (28 January 2002) India's advertising industry grows by 23% in 2000–01, Media Properties Trading Limited, 6963464. Available online at: (accessed Business Source Premier 8 July 2003).

Euromonitor. (November, 2000). Consumer lifestyles in India. Global Market Information Database. Available online at: http://www.euromonitor.com.gmidv1/ShowTopic.asp (accessed 9th October, 2002).

Fannin, R. (8 February 1999) Q&A, ask the expert. *Advertising Age International*, 6.

Goon, P. and Craven, A. (2003) Whose debt? Globalisation and whitefacing in Asia. *Intersections: Gender, History and Culture in the Asian Context*, 9.

Griffin, M., Viswanath, K. and Schwartz, D. (1994) Gender stereotyping in the US and India: exporting cultural stereotypes. *Media Culture and Society*, 16: 487–507.

Hamilton, C. and Benniss, R. (2005) *Affluenza: When Too Much Is Never Enough*, Crows Nest, Australia: Allen and Unwin.

Hargrave-Silk, A. (28 August 2002) Privatisation expected to fuel adspend explosion. *Media Asia.*

Indian Television. Available online at: indiantelevision.com/industryresources/adagencies/top50_2001a.htm2001 (accessed 10 September 2002).

India Trade Point, Tradepoint New Delhi. (1995). *Doing Business in India.* UNTPDC Trade Point Server Incubator. Available online at: http://sphere.rdc.pucrio.br/pacierias/untpdc/incubator/ind/tpdel/doingbus.html (accessed 16th October, 2002).

Khairullah, H.Z. and Khairullah, Z.Y. (2002) Dominant cultural values: content analysis of the US and Indian print advertisements. *Journal of Global Marketing*, (16) ½: 47–70.

Kilburn, D. (13 November 2000) Marketing to reach rural India. *Marketing Magazine*, 105(45): 6.

Kripalani, M. (10 February 2002) Finally Coke gets it right. *Businessweek*, (3819): 18.

Kripalani, M. (10 June 2002). Battling for pennies in India's villages. *Business week*, (i3786): p.22.

Pashupati, K. and Sengupta, S. (1996) Advertising in India: the winds of change, in Frith, K. T. (ed.) *Advertising in Asia: Communication, Culture and Consumption*, Ames: Iowa State University.

MacBride, S. (1980) Many voices, one world: communication and society today and tomorrow, Paris: UNESCO.

Munshi, S. (1998) Wife/mother/daughter-in-law: multiple avatars of homemaker in 1990s Indian advertising. *Media, Culture and Society*, (20): 573–91.

Pollay, R.W. (April 1986) Distorted mirror: reflections on the unintended consequences of advertising, *Journal of Marketing*, 50.

Ram-Prasad, C. (2007) India's middle class failure. *Prospect Magazine*, 138.

Sachdeva, S. (n.d) Trends in advertising in the Indian corporate sector. Institute for Industrial Development. Available online at: isid.org.in/pdf/sudha.pdf

Seghal, R. (2001, May). Kiss and sell? Don't try it in India, *Multinational News International*, 7(4): 8–9.

Sehgal, R. (July/August 2000a) India's Renaissance. *Multinational News International*, 6(7): 10.

Sehgal, R. (25 September 2000b) India clamps down on vice, piracy. *Multinational News International*, 21(39): 49.

Singha, A. and Suvi, D. (10 December 2007) Ad industry to grow 61%. *Business Standard*.

Smita, G. (14 June 2002a) Coke and Pepsi take battle to cyberspace. *Media Asia*: 9.

Smita, G. (12 December 2002b) Modern messages told the traditional Indian way. *Media Asia*: 2.

Srikandath, S. (1991) Cultural values depicted in Indian television advertising. *International Journal of Mass Communication Studies*, 48: 165–76.

Srinivas, P. (1999) Advertising services: India. New Delhi: U.S. & Foreign Commercial Service and U.S. Department of State. Available online at: http://www.tradeport.org.ts/countries/isa/isar0012.html (accessed 16 October 2002).

Subramanian, D. (6 September 1999) Economic slowdown fails to dampen adspend by India's top marketers. *Marketing Magazine*, 104(37): 7.

Thapan, M. (2004) Embodiment and identity in contemporary society: *Femina* and the 'New' Indian woman. *Contributions to Indian Sociology*, 38(3): pp 411–444.

The Economist. (24 August 2002) Sticky issue. 364 (8287): 51.

The Economist Intelligence Unit Limited. (August 1997) Growing Up, India Business Intelligence.

The Hindu Business Line (internet edition). (5 January 2005) Print media outpaces TV in advertising. Adex study, *Hindu group of publications* (accessed 12 December 2005).

The Library of Congress. (2003) India: Growth since 1980. Available online at: http://lcweb2.loc.gov/cgi-bin/query/D?cstdy:8:/temp/~frd_7XGG:: (accessed 24 June 2003).

The World Bank. (1 August 2005) India. ICT at a glance. Available online at: www.worldbank.org (accessed 31 March 2006).

Thomas, A. (2006) *Transnational Media and Contoured Markets*. Sage: New Delhi.

Tungate, M. (1 September 2006) Growth prompts consolidation in India's media. *Campaign*, 00082309, 35.

TV in advertising: Adex study, *Hindu Group of Publications*. Available online at: (accessed 12 December 2005).

Vilanilam, J. (1989) Television advertising and the Indian poor. *Media, Culture and Society*, 11(4): 485–97.

Yu, F. (2002) *The tyranny of the brand*. Available online at: http://www.apmforum.com/columns/china-recon2.htm (accessed 20 December 2007).

Zhang, Y.B., Harwood, J., Williams, A. Wadleigh, P. and Thim, C. (2006) The portrayal of older adults in advertising: a cross national review. *Journal of Language and Social Psychology*, 25(3): 264–82.

Part V

Cyberculture – the software industry

14 India goes to the blogs
Cyberspace, identity, community

Pramod K. Nayar

Introduction

On 25 August 2007 two bombs exploded in Hyderabad city. One was in the popular Lumbini Park, opposite the State Secretariat, and the other in a crowded restaurant, Gokul Chat, in Kothi. The total number of casualties 'crossed' 50 over the following week. In a few days personal video blogs were made available on YouTube.com.[1] What was amazing was the coverage and the individual and collective responses. This was the second round of blasts: in May 2007 blasts in the holy Mecca Masjid, in the Old City area, claimed the lives of devotees who had come for their Friday afternoon prayers. Coupled with a frightening collapse of a flyover under construction in the crowded Punjagutta area killing a few passers-by, the explosions had, in September 2007, created a siege condition in the twin cities. Public places and sites of leisure and entertainment suddenly became possible targets, as the law enforcement authorities warned with their customary cheer after the incidents. But to return to the 'blast blogs': to date there are 41 video blogs, with each recording over 2,500 visits and views. People lighting candles in memory of the dead and scenes of the devastation constitute these public sites of grief. 'Januraj', who posted his first (and only) videoblog[2] on 26 August: 'I am dedicating this vdo to thos [sic] who left [sic] their lives in Hyderabad bomb blasts on 25/08'. Paradoxically, as Januraj's blog suggests, these become an interesting mix of space: the private and the public where private sentiments and feelings are expressed for the world to see. The personal blog is suddenly primetime viewing for Internet users – and this is the subject of this chapter.

The blogosphere has suddenly emerged as a popular social space alongside the social networking sites like YouTube, FaceBook or MySpace. The blog is the new site of popular culture, the site of personal diaries, group book discussions and film reviews, and even political debates between people who may never meet in 'real' life.[3] Any study of popular culture must now include the blog because it constitutes one of the most popular dimensions of Internet culture, and because while virtual reality experiments might be a rare experience for most Internet users, the blog is the *popular Internet*. Popular culture that includes Hindi cinema and Harry Potter in a globalized public sphere finds new sites, audience response, alternative news reports, scandals and gossip and even official interventions.

The blog represents a key moment in the widening out of the popular, made possible by globalizing information and communications technology. They have suddenly become, especially for youth, a new *mass* medium, a new social space that cuts across regional, geographical and social barriers. Popular culture studies in India must now accommodate this new form of expression, sociability, cultural exchange.

Ironically, the term 'popular' itself, in fact, seems inadequate to describe the astronomical expansion of the blogosphere. As of 20 October 2007, the time of writing, BlogPulse[4] records 61,653,333 identified blogs, with over 100,690 being added in 24 hours.

I focus on personal blogs produced by Indians, archived at sites such as www.sulekha.com, www.blogstreet.com and the cybermohalla[5] project. Personal blogs and online autobiographies/diaries alter notions of public and private. In India, as elsewhere, autobiographies are written by public figures: *gurus*, industrialists, screen and sport stars and statesmen.[6] Blogging marks a massive democratization of autobiography as a genre. This chapter reads the newest form of Indian popular culture, and demonstrates how we need to move beyond conceptualizing even personal blogs as merely 'personal' to something more/else.

Blogs, prosopopeia, identity

Since 1998 blogging has become simplified enough for anybody to start an online diary. Commercial services such as Blogger and LiveJournal facilitate online diary writing and the Diarist.net awards inspire greater creativity and participation.[7] In this section I explore the 'spirit' of blogging and the strategies through which the self or face is constructed in blogs.

The spirit of blogging

The blog is a genre aligned with online modes of publicizing the self: webcam telecasts, home videos and personal homepages. The ideology of self-disclosure of the blog embodies a 'semi-private environment' (Rak, 2005: 173). For the individual to retain audiences' attention the blog must offer the self, the private and the intimate, become visible in the world.

Adapting apparatgeist theory (Aakhus and Katz, 2003), I suggest that the logic and 'spirit' of the personal blog is: the construction of the hyperlinked private self for public consumption and the resultant creation of a social space. This logic underwrites the presentation software (greater visibility and attractiveness), writing style and evaluative procedures. Blogging and its adjacent networking 'technologies' are designed and imbued with the spirit of perpetual construction of the self for the world – a spirit best captured in YouTube's slogan, 'Broadcast Yourself'.

Blogs are essentially a form of online life-writing.[8] As an active, organic form, blogs represent dialogic life-writing that is perpetually in process. The personal blog is a means of interfacing the self with the world, generating a hyperlinked self where every self/author is a node in a rapidly proliferating rhizome: a whole universe of linked personal blogs/selves. The hyperlinked self of the blog is one that is inherently multiple, fragmented and random. This is the first key feature of the self in blogs: *it is a hyperlinked self.*

As autobiography, the blog is a 'celebration of the self-aware subject' (Kitzmann, 2003: 52), presenting 'the life of a sovereign subject who has a continuous identity and a continuous history' (Reed, 2005: 226). Blogging assumes, like life-writing, that the subject is aware of her/himself and that this subject is worth knowing. It is a means of advertising one's identity but is not limited to it. Blogging also takes on a community role because the self-aware subject writes and publishes blogs in order to share private experiences. This is the online diary's principal difference from the 'regular' one: the online diarist is always irreducibly dialogic, expecting an audience and a response. It accounts for the other, and writes in response to the response of the Other.

Blogs are like cell phones and personal communications technology (where private expressions are imbued with the spirit of public reception/hearing) and the chat room where self-disclosure is central to the formation of an online, and perhaps even offline relationship (Leung, 2002). This is the second key feature of the blog-self: *it is irreducibly dialogic.*

The genre's very design and structure, with links and spaces for 'comments', is explainable as its *apparatgeist* of the construction of the hyperlinked private self for public consumption. This spirit informs the design of the content, the links, the templates, the language and the social response. The cultural and social situation – Indian notions of privacy, the accessibility to public forums – and the available technology determine the individual's behaviour and blog. As the Indian public sphere moves towards greater democratization, technology seeks to make blogging easier. Everyone, theoretically speaking, can now voice an opinion.

The publicness of the private

Blogs extend personal homepages. Homepages themselves constitute online introductions to the self, where the page serves as a threshold: inviting the viewer to go beyond the main door (or, considering the software, 'windows') into the house/self.

Homepages, like the personal essay, break down the distinction between private and public. They advertise the self, or rather those aspects of the self the individual wants advertised.[9] Here the cyberdiary also differs from the print version because they are far more ephemeral than the latter. In the Indian context the blog's dual state of complete anonymity and acceptable public identity has several interesting consequences.

The blog 'Three's Company' posted by 'Sexy Indian Bitch'[10] on 23 October 2006 admits that she is in love with two men at the same time. In this case the blogger is known only by the avatar (and details such as 'situated in New Delhi, age 25 years and is a journalist) presented on the blog. In later blogs she admits that she might be truly lusting for P (23 October 2006). Comments and responses to her post take the form of Agony Aunt columns, with people advising her on what to do. The blog becomes the forum for a community discussion about life, love and lust – all under pseudonyms. What is even more interesting is to see the manifestation of an 'out-law' genre (Kaplan, 1992). Agony Aunt and advice columns in India do not focus directly on the sexual aspects, and rarely do they sprinkle their advice with the word 'fuck'. Here are a few responses to 'Three's Company': http://sexyindianbitch.blogspot.com/2006/10/threes-company.html

> Baby its just tht [sic] tightness inside the panties, go ahead, get it frm him. (Anonymous, 23 October 2006)
> Looking into my crystal ball, I can see you will do him sooner or later. (Anonymous, 25 October 2006)
> You wanna do him babe, just do him, it'll be good!! ('Riche', 27 October 2006)

The author positions her self as an articulate metropolitan professional. Her poise, confidence and comfort level with technology are markers of her self – or the self she presents to the world. Another blogger, this one a London-based bisexual Indian, writes of her shopping experience:

> One of the perks of having a girl friend as opposed to a boy friend is that you can try on clothes together in the fitting rooms & sneak kisses & giggle about it. It's even better if you have the same shoe size, because then you can buy two different shoes and not feel guilty about it.[11]

Responses to the blog included one which was particularly scathing:

> And Girl – stop influencing a desi girl with all your lesbian crap…. Its wrong and its sinful in the eyes of GOD – plant your dirty ideas somewhere alone and leave Indians out of it.[12]

Such blogs are 'out-law' genres, subcultural forms, because their explicitness and their debates about sexuality situate them outside the mainstream genres of agony columns and autobiographies in India. They are 'out-law' genres because they disrupt the literary and cultural conventions in India where sex is not talked about. Such blogs, therefore, constitute tactical acts of resistance.

The woman's dilemma and expressions of desire are made possible not only because of the blog but also because of a community of like-minded 'listeners'. The reader of the blog actively *participates* in the face-making by responding to the confessions. It is interesting to note that she receives a sympathetic hearing, and no reader of the blog raised the 'morality question', with some going out of their way to state: 'I am not one to make moral judgments' (Sofa Warrier, 26 October 2006). http://sexyindianbitch.blogspot.com/2006/10/threes-company.html

For Indians, usually reticent about their sex lives or more personal details in the public sphere, the blog offers great freedom for two reasons. The first is the ephemerality of the genre. Print's permanence makes confessional writing more difficult because it can circulate in the public domain for a greater period of time with little chance of editing and censorship by the author. The second is the unverifiability of the details stated on the blog.

If blogs are to be published as hard copy (as in Blog Print, from Penguin India), then the blogs will alter in style, tone and content so as to win the chance of print publishing. However, this is not a great innovation. The genre's very nature is about face-making: people publish their blogs so that their 'faces' are in the public domain. Unlike the autobiographies of statesmen and celebrities, the individual's blog has to *work* to gain attention and thus involves a high degree of authenticity-building, where details about jobs, desires, fetishes are modes of conveying authenticity. The third key feature of the blog-self is precisely this: *face-making that involves/demands the sharing of the private.*

Face-making in blogs involves a degree of *agential* confession and confusion. The blog, as McNeill (2003) points out, is an extension of the diary which itself was a version of the confession.[13] Like personal diaries the blogs are dated entries (posts). And, like diaries (personal) blogs exhibit a remarkable amount of introspection. It is the ephemerality of the genre that allows the individual the freedom and agency to write and re-write whatever they want and create any face they wish.

However, blogs can also be the source of confusion because the genre blurs the distinction between private and public. The traditional diary is written for one's own private reading pleasure. The blog alters this generic convention where the private diary is what asks for attention from the world. Thus we read a confessional comment like this from a blogger who describes herself as 'twenty-something, single, female, writer', 'Em' (identified later as Meenakshi Reddy Madhavan):

> for me, sex isn't that important unless I have to go without it, in which case I turn into a mixture of Cruella De Ville and Bambi, alternating between long drags of my cigarette and fluttering eyelashes at whatever's closest.[14]

The confessions of intimate desires and tendencies are confessions broadcast to the world. And yet the confession confuses us because we are uncertain as to (i) whether the *avatar* is real and, (ii) whether we ought to be reading this kind of material. The confession is thereby the source not only of knowledge of the blogger but of confusion. The confusion is exacerbated by the fact that the same blogger had also admitted in an earlier post: 'And my life is very fun right now, but full of very intimate personal details that I simply *can't* write about' (Post of 14 September 2007). This blog, which registered over 400 hits a day, became famous enough for newspapers (the UK *Telegraph*, 'Blogger Enraptures and Enrages India', 7 October 2007, URL[15]) to unravel her identity. It was the startlingly intimate form of her writing and her confessions, rarely seen in

Indian writing, that gave her her popularity. It was, in a sense, a subcultural form.

And yet the question of privacy haunts all bloggers, many of whom write under pseudonyms. 'Sexy Indian Bitch' finally shut down her blog because her identity was revealed. Her sign-off post, 19 March 2007, said: 'I can no longer afford to keep writing the way I did when I was assured of my anonymity'.[16] Apparently, bloggers write and modify what they write in response to their audience's reactions. The blogger, especially the woman blogger, simultaneously wishes for an audience, but only an audience in cyberspace. This is the paradox of blogging: bloggers want recognition, identification and listeners without jeopardizing their 'real' identities. This is another feature of the blog-self: *the blurred boundary between private and public that subverts established conventions of writing.*

Everyday in the blog-house

If software companies, corporatized media and technological services constitute 'production' then the question remains as to what the users/consumers *do* with these products and services. Michel de Certeau suggests that within the systems of production, there occurs a hidden 'making' or *poiēsis* (de Certeau, 1988: xii). This 'making' is also production, but an insidious one, and is in fact *consumption* because it is what *users* do with the products of the systems of production. Adapting de Certeau, I suggest that within the system of corporate, monopolistic production of software, technological services and media, there exists a user-production, an *utterance* using the established vocabulary and syntax of the medium and the technology.

This local, vernacular (as opposed to the official one of corporatism, monopoly capitalism and 'First World' technology) utterance or *poiēsis* is not confined to a particular zone but scattered. The blog text lies *between* dominant discourses and production: TV footage, movies, the telephonic conversation, information resources, literature and autobiographical writing. The blog makes *use* of all these 'products'. The *poiēsis* of blogs represents individual *ways of using* the products offered or imposed by the dominant economic order of the new media. This is everyday (literally, in the case of blogs) creativity where, within the organized, dominant grid of official regulation, software and technological services the user indulges in a 'microphysics'. The most sophisticated technologies are appropriated (or 'domesticated', to adapt a term from Haddon and Silverstone, 1996) at the level of the everyday. Where corporations work *strategies* of business moves and monopoly control over technology and the state seeks to regulate their use, blogs and 'native' practices are *tactical*, contingent, fluid, amorphous and insidious. They manipulate events, dominant structures and codes and are inherently heterogeneous. In the case of the blog, the tactical is, in fact the quotidian.

Blogging marks the publicness of the private face, as we have noted in the earlier section. This publicness of the private turns the everyday into the noteworthy or recordable event in the blog: and everyday practices, de Certeau informs us, are tactical in nature (1988: xix) *Blog-selfs make use of the everyday as tactical moves that domesticate and manipulate technologies and services that are monopolistic and dominant.*

Blogs are subcultural forms that subvert 'high' literary standards and generic conventions. Like diaries and the home video, they are mainly about the everyday and the quotidian. Painting the house, a party, a broken love-affair, the pet cat's problems and details of everyday life become subjects of posts. The blog as diary-autobiography suggests that even the ordinary life of the ordinary individual is worth examining, recording and reading.

The lives of individuals change with the arrival and domestication of technologies that facilitate recording everyday events such as travelling through Gurgaon streets.[17] Or, the everyday is now worth recording because the technology allows you to do so.

Celebrity authors, massive hype, awards, profits and high-profile readings constitute the strategy through which 'Literature' is produced and marketed. Within this dominant, restrictive grid, the online blog is a *poiēsis* of a different kind. Using the conventions of the high literary, the movie or the common adventure tale for the purposes of describing an everyday life, the blog is a *tactical* intervention in the social life of texts.

The 'common' individual might consider her/his life significant enough to describe it for the world, but this prosopopaeia must be validated and legitimized by the world. Blogging alters the possibilities of anybody publishing their thoughts, opinions and sentiments for the world to read. The blog is *poiēsis* that, by showcasing the ordinary individual, becomes *tactical* production.

The blog with the 'about me' link reveals much at one go, even though the 'complete profile' is limited to what the author-blogger wishes to reveal. In this sense the blog is based on a certain individualist philosophy: marking freedom of expression for any individual with access to the blogosphere – including individuals who would otherwise be marginalized in a public debate. It is also individualist because it assumes that the individual *has* something to say to the world. And yet, this individualism is what enables the making of a community through blogging.

The diary has been traditionally associated with women (Heilbrun, 1988). It is therefore interesting to know that the cyber-version of diary writing is a predominantly male genre. According to a November 2006 survey 76 per cent of bloggers in India are men. The dominant age group (54 per cent) was of men between 25 and 35.[18]

I propose that, in addition to the hyperlinked self, the technology and feedback mechanism that are integral to the blog's self-representation create an *augmented* self. In the blog the basic database about the diarist-blogger is added to in the form of video, audio, clips from other spaces (even those unconnected with the author, and thus calling into question the very nature of *authorship* or the individual *author-self*; see note 4) and, crucially, *responses* of reader-people. The blog-self is never self-contained, or solitary. With even one 'hit' or response, the blog's self-representation is *augmented* because, in many cases, the self writes back her/his response to the audience's response. With every such interaction the self is revealed, altered and articulated for the world – a process I see as *augmentation*. In terms of the key features of the blog-self, this is the final one: *the blog-self is an augmented self.*

> *The blog self is a hyperlinked, augmented self, in dialogue with the world through the sharing of the private, involving a tactical incorporation of the quotidian, and which (subversively) blurs the distinction between private and public.*

It is in this process of interfacing the private and the public that a new social space emerges in India.

Blogging and the Indian public sphere

Blogging, while marking the democratization of autobiography, also enables the creation of a social space. The blog, while being about the individual, by the individual is not *for* the individual alone. The blog is not simply the home page (the 'root') where the author's self resides. Rather, it should be treated as a link, a *route* to something larger than the authorial self.

Voice and agency

To possess a voice is to possess an agency. Blogging is the online expression of a voice. The voice of the state, embodied in laws and statutes is the voice of authority and authoritarianism. Thus the blocking of blogs is the silencing of a voice because blogs represent a space where personal opinions with political overtones and consequences may be articulated and *shared* – a space that is outside the purview of the state. As Mitra (2004) has pointed out, the 'connection between voice and space becomes particularly critical when such a space is denied in the real life through marginalizing forces and a new space needs to be carved out' (493–4).

In July 2006, *Boing Boing* reported that the Indian government had sought to block several blogs and websites.[19] The 'order' attracted immediate responses – incomprehension, fury and sadness. Some justified the act by arguing that since the Mumbai blasts of 2006 seemed to have been coordinated by using blogs, the state was right in shutting down potential subversion using the new technology. Here is a sampling from one such blogsite:[20]

> Another example of 'what happens if retards run the governments [sic]'
> (Mayhemt, posted 17 July 2006).

> So much for worrying about India as a leader in technology!
> (Davdav, posted 17 July 2006).

still can't figure out why this ban has been brought into place... Is it to stop
terrorists communicating or is it to stop angry Mumbai-ites blogging against
the terrorists...?

(InTeGeR13, posted 17 July 2006).

Some bloggers cited national security concerns as a possible reason for the state
action, while others looked up the Right to Information Act. What is clear is that the
state's action became the subject of politically significant debates about democracy,
information, technology and national identity. The bloggers were demanding the
space to voice their opinions and to be heard.

Linking community

To announce one's private thoughts/fears/desires or to record one's home is to be a
part of the community. MySpace's tag line is 'a place for friends', where it needn't
be offline/real-life friends who come together on this space, but friendships made
entirely through online contact suggests the purpose and spirit of the blog.

Blogging has enabled people to get in touch with each other after several years.
A good example would be the blogging activity of the Mangalore-based doctor
ixedoc on www.sulekha.com (incidentally, the most popular blog on this network).
Having discovered his blog, former students – some from 28 years ago – have
'discovered' him again, and formed a community (www.ixedoc.sulekha.com).
'Connecting Indians Worldwide' – Sulekha's tagline – here creates a community
of those who track old acquaintances.

Face-making and advertising the face to the world also serve particular
political purposes. Juan Cole's controversial Informed Comment blog (http://www.
juancole.com/) with its anti-Iraq war opinions was perhaps instrumental in Yale
denying him tenure – thus demonstrating the public–political consequences of
life-writing. Political blogs such as Cole's or a politician's mark the democratizing
dimension of blogging, as Coleman (2005) has argued.[21] This democratization is
made possible through three key features of blogs. First, blogs constitute a bridge
between the private and civic spaces. Second, blogs allow, unlike speeches and
formal expressions, the articulation of incomplete thoughts and ideas. Finally,
blogs allow access to local, national and global debates for everyone. Unlike
debates in parliaments or special forums, where credentials rather than opinions
govern the legitimacy of speech, blogs allow any one and every one to hold and
articulate political opinions. More importantly, blogs enable politicians and parties
to 'listen' to the groundswell of subjective but politically significant opinions
(Coleman, 2005; Rowbottom, 2006).

What distinguishes blogging from any other (earlier) form of speech or
expression is that, while only select numbers of people can express their opinions on
TV or radio, any number of individuals and organizations (theoretically speaking)
can blog. This is the *political* logic and spirit that drives blogging: that there
is possibly unlimited freedom to express oneself just as there is *potentially* an
unlimited number of readers/listeners possible.

Blogging practices need not be about 'national' issues. In fact one of the most fascinating features of personal blogs by Indians is their focus on very local events and conditions. Thus when citizens in a particular Chennai community (at Velachery) got together, pooled money to repair the road it received wide representation on a personal blog.[22] The blog also called for similar campaigns, thus shifting the focus from the personal to the community and beyond.

Here the blog is less personal than communitarian and therefore political. It takes as its personal theme the political act of civic service. The blog is not simply a 'root' or location for/of the self: it is a *route* to the community, where the links constitute a traversal, a journey rather than a stasis. The 'routes' model that I propose here (following Livingstone, 2003) calls for treating the blog less as a site of the self or self-contained personal page than as a pathway to a community. The fact that almost every blogger provides hyperlinks invites this reading of the personal blog as a route to the community. Bloggers who enjoy reading provide links to favourite authors and elicit responses about particular books (see 'Extempore', Bombay, India, at http://evestigio.blogspot.com/, post dated 4 October 2007. Accessed 8 October 2007. Responses were blogged at URL[23]).

A personal blog becomes the first link in the making of a community. And this is another step towards democratization of the media. Blogging here becomes the means of engaging with the system itself. The detailed responses to these acts on the blogs can even be construed as social protest on the lines of 'letters to the editor' in print journalism. City-centred blogs – such as Bangalore's Metroblogging[24] – serve this purpose of creating a space for the discussion of public issues beginning from the home or personal realms. http://trafficinhyderabad.blogspot.com/, a blogspot dedicated to addressing the horrendous road and traffic conditions in Hyderabad, likewise, serves the purpose of not simply complaining about the chaos but also contributing ideas and suggestions to make city driving safer. Blogs are the opening moments (hopefully) of a social movement, something that is definitely, defiantly political in the face of what is seen as the state's complete disregard for the citizens. That such a social movement that begins in cyberspace can possess considerable real-time power and effect is borne out by the fact that the Deputy Commissioner of Police (Traffic) for Cyberabad area (in Hyderabad) actually met some of the bloggers and discussed ways and means of improving the situation (see post by Sameer, 26 August 2007). And, in addition, software engineers and officers started an initiative to regulate the traffic. In the spirit of blogging, one author who identifies himself as 'hapless in Hyderabad', congratulated the initiative.[25] Hundreds of such posts and we have a social movement!

In the case of the 'Bootle Diaries' Indians working with the Bootle Labs *in* Liverpool or with the Cybermohalla Labs *in* New Delhi, India, responded to posts by their English co-workers. This network built through blogs *in addition to* their professional collaboration often moved across personal terrain. Thus Sara's blog of 14 October 2004 described her witnessing of two women meeting on a street (Bootle Diary 01, URL[26]). 'This text reminds me of an encounter in a tea shop', wrote Lakhmi in her response of 20 October 2004. Sheena Farrell's post of

14 October 2004 describes how she spent her day, overslept, was late for picking up her children and, as a result, had to run all the way to the school (Bootle Diary 05). Rakesh's response to this personal diary 'entry' is to request a description of the places she passes by on the way to the school. The sharing of a personal experience enables a person sitting across the world to participate in the experience and be elsewhere while doing so. Once again the telecasting of a personal experience enables the making of a community/network.

There is what Jean Baudrillard (1984) called the 'strategy of the real' in blogging. It is the 'amount' of reality and authenticity inscribed into the blog entry that facilitates readership interest, popularity and community formation. Photographs, personal details, verifiable information render the private blog 'real'. This is the irony of the Internet – cyberspace avatars have to be 'real' (enough) for the author to acquire a readership. The blog thus alters the *public* sphere through the insistence on accurate, authentic and reliable *personal* details. In a democratizing space created by the Internet, readers look for trustworthy 'voices' (Mitra, 2004: 495), and therefore demand strategies of the real.

In addition, blogs such as those at Cybermohalla, where locals are interviewed and their recorded responses recorded (in audio, text and video) become an important form of the popular 'glocalization' of the digital realm, a nativization of global technologies by the use of *local* slang, the *vernacular* (Compu*ghars* and 'cyber*mohalla*') and local practices (Nayar, 2007, 2008).

Traditional media freedom debates focused on the audience reached, with little discussion of the speaker's role. Online expression shifts the focus on to the speaker, or blogger. Blogs are central to the debate about media freedom because these are expressions of individual's opinions that appear online *without mediation by others* (Rowbottom, 2006). The significance of the blog is not the size of the audience reached but in the freedom it accords the individual speaker to express her/himself or connect with a small community of people. Very often this facilitates politically edged discussions among people who would otherwise not be able to air their views.

On 19 September 2007 IBN Live reported how the Uttar Pradesh police in Muzaffarnagar paraded a girl after she was caught with her male friend in a hotel.[27] 'Just Jo' blogged his responses to this incident, using it as a starting point to discuss moral policing, the state of the Indian police force and society ('Indian Police Force – Time for A Change', URL[28]). This blog, ranked 254th on Blogstreet.com elicited just two responses, even though the issue was topical. Clearly there is a hierarchy of blogging, where some bloggers are read more widely than others. Blogging and the Internet also possess a certain amount of media elitism, where such blogs as Just Jo's do not become central in terms of the network.

Reviewing Shah Rukh Khan's *Chak De India*, Rashmi Bansal on her blog launched a series of comments on the attitudes to women, women in/and sports and the Indian family ('Chak De Kudiyan', posted 22 September 2007, http://youthcurry.blogspot.com/, accessed 28 September 2007). Her comments elicited responses that discussed the institution of marriage, the gendered nature of Indian sport and patriarchal social structures.[29] One post (Liza Varghese) shifted the terms of the debate by referring to the film's theme of a Muslim's allegiance to his country. Here the personal response to a popular film enables men and women to debate feminism, the role of women and the structure of Indian society. It created a 'Thirdspace' for debates.

Tactical media, third space

The debates on blogs may not be cast in high academic lingo or written with the theoretical sophistication of celebrity feminist critics (such as Susie Tharu or Tejaswini Niranjana). It is in opposition to such high academic discourses that the woman in the street offers her versions of feminist interpretations of texts, movies and social life. Further, where academic debates are confined to conference rooms or, to a lesser extent, the classroom, and occasionally the court of law, blogging makes the debate more open. It is here that the community gets a chance for greater participation in public debates, via a personal blog. Rashmi Bansal's face-making as a feminist elicits responses that suggest the presence of other feminists in the community of bloggers. A personal view structures a *community of vernacular feminists* (and I use the term 'vernacular' to signal the local and native) – indeed many of the responses to Rashmi Bansal mixed individual-personal experience with public issues. Face-making is also, here, community formation and freedom of expression dovetails into the freedom of association.

With such associations, the personal space of the blog leads onto the public sphere through linkages and networking with other bloggers. After the disastrous tsunami of 2004, bloggers networked to start relief operations, collect funds and generate a global awareness about the catastrophe.[30] Social space's two key realms – the private and the public – merge precisely through this networking of the personal (Zalis, 2003: 95). And this is how the blog goes political: it becomes a part of a community. This is the paradox of blogging: the intimate is what enables the making of a social network, the local is what takes the blog global. Reading the Velachery pothole programme, for instance, commentators residing in other cities in India immediately recognized the significance, and began wondering whether the effort could be replicated in their own cities. Here a local act engenders a pan-region debate and perhaps action. The blog literally connects Indians, albeit over potholes.

The blogosphere constitutes 'tactical media'. They are 'digital micro-politics' (Lovink, 2003: 254), even though they work within the parameters of global techno-capitalism. Tactical media introduces an element of uncertainty, 'locality' and alternative thinking within mainstream internet cultures. The blog is a hybrid form that combines the personal diary, the intimate letter, the public forum into one space, especially when personal blogs undertake tasks such as consciousness-raising or political mobilization (as I write in late 2007, the number of blogs seeking support for the monks in Myanmar multiply). While such a mobilization may occur only through virtual calls, it cannot be denied that the distinction between 'real' action and directed publicity is increasingly untenable. The virtual, in fact, is what constitutes political action *as* support-mobilization.

The blog constitutes a specific kind of social space here because it brings together people on the basis of *similarity*. Respondents to blogs are those who are interested in the same things as the blogger, whose politics are more or less on the same plane and whose abilities to debate are compatible with the rest of the blogging community. The keywords listed at the top of the blog tell potential readers of the contents of the entries. Blogging brings together people with similar social values, ideas and often, social concerns. Blogging thus constructs a new Indian public sphere, or at least a social space through the genre.

Examples of such tactical media and media activism in blogging are aplenty. Blogs exist in a 'thirdspace', somewhere between the state and the monopolistic marketplace of software and techno-capitalism. The responses to calls for action, support and even funding that blogs elicit suggest a media activism. This media activism, driven by the attention to the other marks the emergence of a new public sphere. This public sphere, ironically, is often without the face-to-face interaction and *rational* debate that Jürgen Habermas (1989) identified as its key feature.

The blog is where individuals *respond* to the Other. The media is what Roger Silverstone (2007) has aptly termed 'the space of appearance': it is where the world appears to us, becomes proximate, visible to us. Thus the media constructs and expands our imaginary, where the elsewhere, the Other, is also *here*. In the individual's response to the Bihar lynchings, Myanmar or Kashmir genocides within the thirdspace of the blogs, the Other is responded to, responsibly. When the blogger responds in such a way – let us, for want of a better term and with a nod to Emanuel Levinas, call it the 'ethical' way – to the trauma of the Other, the media has become tactical in its fullest sense. It suggests alternatives to state responses, a new politics where non-governmental, non-recognized actors gain a voice and muster support.

Understandably, blogging is very different from political responses in the public sphere. Yet, as Silverstone (2007: 34) emphasizes, a space where only reason determines the viability of discourse (as is the case with the Habermasian conceptualization of the public sphere) undermines and limits the possibilities of human communication. Not all human communication is about 'reason'. Blogging, with its emphasis on highly subjective ('I hate', or 'I love' are standard elements in blogging discourse), sentimental responses, provides a new kind of social space where sentimentality is also politically inflected and effective. Campaigns built on emotional responses are no less valuable *as campaigns*.

It is in this response to the Other within the blog that we recognize its potential as a social rather than a personal space, a *route* rather than a root, a path rather than a home.

As more and more of India goes to the blogs, a new *tactical* deployment of cyberspace and its monopolistic technologies emerges where the everyday is supreme. It is within this new 'mediapolis' (to return to Silverstone for the last time) that a new politics of connectivity, action and responsible action can perhaps be effected. The blog is the route to a better community.

Notes

1 http://www.youtube.com/watch?v=Cyx9gi7RbDE
2 http://www.youtube.com/watch?v=iZngtb1MmkI, accessed 23 September 2007.
3 The blog is a short form for web logging. It is a personal homepage with chronological entries that resemble a diary. It is essentially a personal form, but is available for public consumption because it is published on the WWW.
4 http://www.blogpulse.com/
5 http://www. http://www.sarai.net/practices/cybermohalla
6 According to a November 2006 survey 42 per cent of online users read blogs to stay informed about world events, and 49 per cent for entertainment. Blogs are on their way to becoming the new fourth estate, according to the survey (http://www.ciol.com/content/news/2006/106112703.asp, accessed 25 September 2007).
7 The first online diary is attributed to Carolyn Burke for her posting of 3 January 1995. For an account of online diary writing and its pioneers see Online Diary History Project at http://www.diaryhistoryproject.com/. Penguin India now plans to print publish blogs.
8 The term 'writing' itself now means the inclusion of multimedia, visual texts and audio. While readymade images and software tools (like Dreamweaver) for 'writing' constrain the nature and degree of multimedia writing on blogs (one can pick digital objects to be inserted into one's own 'text', but one cannot create that object – that is, one inserts the image of that object, not the object itself), it alters significantly the elements that can be used. Recombination, the key feature of 'writing' software, thus problematizes the notion of 'author' itself: if the blogger uses objects, images and texts from cyberspace, what is the nature of authorship? Does authoring include this incorporation/recombination? And therefore what is the nature of the author-self? For the problem of authorship see Gillespie 2003.
9 Studies have shown that most home pages do not necessarily reveal the author's personhood at all (Killoran, 2003). Whether the blogs actually reveal their author's complete details is a matter of debate and dispute (see Qian and Scott, 2007).
10 http://sexyindianbitch.blogspot.com/2006/10/threes-company.html, accessed 23 September 2007.
11 http://closetconfessions.wordpress.com/, posted 6 October 2007, accessed 7 October 2007.
12 http://closetconfessions.wordpress.com/2007/09/18/to-the-girl-yes-theres-more/#comments, Anonymous URL, 18 September 2007, accessed 23 September 2007.
13 Julie Rak (2005) argues that the blog is not comparable to the diary at all. Rak suggests that the blog is a specifically Internet genre. People were writing online diaries even before blogs but it is with cheaply (even freely) available software that publishing blogs became a phenomenon.
14 http://thecompulsiveconfessor.blogspot.com/, posted on 17 September 2007, accessed on 25 September 2007.
15 http://www.telegraph.co.uk/news/main.jhtml?xml=/news/2007/10/07/wblog107.xml, accessed 17 October 2007.
16 http://sexyindianbitch.blogspot.com/, 25 September 2007.
17 Neha Viswanathan, 2 September 2007, http://www.withinandwithout.com/index.php?paged=4, accessed 7 October 2007.
18 http://www.ciol.com/content/news/2006/106112703.asp, 25 September 2007.
19 http://www.boingboing.net/2006/07/17/report-indian-gov-bl.html, accessed 25 September 2007.
20 http://digg.com/tech_news/Indian_Government_Blocks_Blogs
21 Employee blogs have also resulted in serious repercussions for the bloggers – indeed many have lost their jobs for what the company regards as unseemly conduct, either making disparaging comments about the company or even for their self-representation on personal blogs (Negroni, 2004). The phenomenon is now common enough for

commentators and etiquette trainers in India to warn bloggers about 'writing with care'. See, for instance, Payal Chanania, 'Company Blogs – Write with Care', *The Hindu*, 'Opportunities', 21 February 2008, p. 1.
22 http://www.kiruba.com, posted 13 September 2007, accessed 25 September 2007.
23 https://www.blogger.com/comment.g?blogID=13539110&postID=3211123116204652903
24 http://bangalore.metblogs.com/
25 https://www.blogger.com/comment., post of 29 August 2007, accessed 29 September 2007
26 http://www.sarai.net/practices/cybermohalla/, accessed 28 September 2007.
27 http://www.ibnlive.com/news/caught-in-hotel-with-beau-girl-paraded-around-town/48942-3.html, accessed 28 September 2007.
28 http://jocalling.blogspot.com/, posted 26 September 2007, accessed 28 September 2007.
29 https://www.blogger.com/comment.g?blogID=9605787&postID=8094140897190287679, accessed 28 September 2007.
30 See, for instance, http://www.abdulqabiz.com/blog/archives/general/tsunami_victims.php; sites such as http://www.bethechange.org/ and their blogs.

References

Aakhus, M.A. and Katz, J.E. (2003) 'Making Meaning of Mobiles: A Theory of Apparatgeist', in J.E. Katz and M.A. Aakhus (eds) *Perpetual Contact: Mobile Communication, Private Talk, Public Performance*, Cambridge: Cambridge University Press, 301–18.
Baudrillard, J. (1984) 'The Precession of Simulacra', in Brian Wallis (ed.) *Art After Modernism: Rethinking Representation*, New York: New Museum of Contemporary Art, 253–81.
Coleman, S. (2005) 'Blogs and the New Politics of Listening', *Political Quarterly* 76.2: 272–80.
De Certeau, M. (1988) *The Practice of Everyday Life*, trans. Stephen Randall. Berkeley: University of California Press.
Gillespie, T. (2003) 'The Stories Digital Tools Tell', in Everett, A. and Caldwell, J.T. (eds) *New Media: Theories and Practices of Digitextuality*, London and New York: Routledge, 107–23.
Habermas, J. (1989) *The Structural Transformation of the Public Sphere: An Inquiry into a Category of Bourgeois Society*, trans. Thomas Burger, Cambridge, MA: MIT Press.
Haddon, L. and Silverstone, R. (1996) 'Design and the Domestication of Information and Communications Technologies: Technical Change and Everyday Life', in Mansell, R. and Silverstone, R. (eds) *Communication by Design: The Politics of Information and Communication Technologies*. Oxford: Oxford University Press, 44–74.
Heilbrun, C. (1988) *Writing a Woman's Life*. New York: Ballantyne.
Kaplan, C. (1992) 'Resisting Autobiography: Out-law Genres and Transnational Feminist Subjects', in Smith, S. and Watson, J. (eds) *De/Colonizing the Subject: The Politics of Gender in Women's Autobiography*, Minneapolis: University of Minnesota Press, 115–38.
Killoran, J.B. (2003) 'The Gnome in the Front Yard and Other Public Figurations: Genres of Self-Presentation on Personal Home Pages', *Biography* 26.1: 66–83.
Kitzmann, A. (2003) 'That Different Place: Documenting the Self Within Online Writing Environments', *Biography* 26.1: 48–65.
Leung, L. (2002) 'Loneliness, Self-Disclosure, and ICQ ("I Seek You") Use', *Cyberpsychology and Behavior* 5.3: 241–51.

Livingstone, S. (2003). *Young People and New Media: Childhood and the Changing Media Environment*. London: Sage.

Lovink, G. (2003) *Dark Fiber: Tracking Critical Internet Culture*. Cambridge, MA: MIT Press.

McNeill, L. (2003) 'Teaching an Old Genre New Tricks: The Diary on the Internet', *Biography* 26.1: 24–47.

Mitra, A. (2004). 'Voices of the Marginalized on the Internet: Examples From a Website for Women of South Asia', *Journal of Communication* 54.3: 492–510.

Nayar, P.K. (2007) 'The Digital Glocalized', *Writing Technologies* 1.1, www.ntu.ac.uk/writing_technologies.

Nayar, P.K. (2008) 'New Media, Digitextuality and Public Space: Reading "Cybermohalla"', *Postcolonial Text*. http://journals.sfu.ca/pocol/index.php/pct/article/view/786/521

Negroni, C. (2004) 'Fired Flight Attendant Finds Blogs can Backfire', *New York Times*, 16 November 2004, http://www.nytimes.com/2004/11/16/business/16pose.html. 21 February 2008.

Qian, H. and Scott, C.R. (2007) 'Anonymity and Self-Disclosure on Weblogs', *Journal of Computer-Mediated Communication* 12: 1428–51.

Rak, J. (2005) 'The Digital Queer: Weblogs and Internet Identity', *Biography* 28.1: 166–82.

Reed, A. (2005) ' "My Blog is Me": Texts and Persons in UK Online Journal Culture (and Anthropology)', *Ethnos* 70.2: 220–42.

Rowbottom, J. (2006) 'Media Freedom and Political Debate in the Digital Era', *Modern Law Review* 69.4: 489–513.

Silverstone, R. (2007) *Media and Morality: On the Rise of the Mediapolis*. Cambridge: Polity.

Zalis, E. (2003) 'At Home in Cyberspace: Staging Autobiographical Scenes', *Biography* 26.1: 84–119.

15 The Indian software industry

Cultural factors underpinning its evolution

Florian Taeube

The setting: the Indian IT industry

Bangalore is known worldwide for its achievements in the high technology domain. Almost every multinational company has located some of its global activities in one of the technology parks around the city thereby integrating Bangalore in their global value chains. Moreover, many indigenous software firms that sprouted during this process over the last decade or so have themselves developed capabilities and reached reputation levels rather uncommon to Indian companies before.

The Indian IT industry mainly consists of a broad spectrum of software development enterprises. The figures for software exports show an astonishing annual growth of roughly 50 per cent p.a. for the 1990s. Having started with basic programming, India now delivers services and products on a globally competitive level that has not been witnessed in any other industry since independence. There are several factors contributing to this extraordinary development and there is hardly any uncertainty pertaining to the purely economic aspects. Over the last few years a number of studies have analysed the Indian software industry ranging from perspectives focused on innovative capabilities (D'Costa, 2002) and quality considerations (Banerjee and Duflo, 2000), emphasizing the involvement of multinational firms (Patibandla and Petersen, 2002) as well as an eventual development impact (Arora and Athreye, 2002).

The historical evolution of Indian IT can be visualized as illustrated in Figure 15.1. Note the deliberate absence of an explicit ordinate; possible measures include variables like number of IT firms or software exports. Moreover, phase 3 is not terminated with the start of phase 4, because foreign multinational companies (MNCs) continue to flock to India opening up Indian subsidiaries. Lastly, 'going global' refers to corporate strategies, mainly cross-border acquisitions (which are not part of this study, but rather of future research). On an operational level this industry has been highly global since its inception with its basic business model based on the so-called body-shopping – the physical sending of software programmers to clients' premises mainly in the United States.

However, the most advanced software centres continue to cluster in Bangalore. Overall, one finds an uneven distribution of the software industry locations which

224 *Florian Taeube*

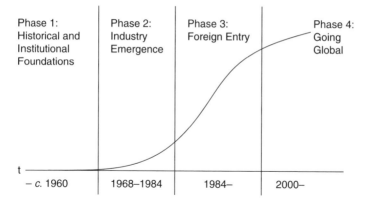

Figure 15.1 Historical evolution of the Indian IT industry.

are clustered in the South (Bangalore, Hyderabad and Chennai), West (Mumbai and Pune), and around the capital New Delhi in the North.

Most studies claim to cover the entire software industry without *explicit* treatment of the geographical concentration in South India, mainly Bangalore. Thus, the question addressed in this chapter is why some regions are more successful than others? Given the relatively even distribution (or lack of) capital, infrastructure and other input factors for industrial development I am particularly interested in potential cultural factors facilitating such a development first and foremost in the South. Therefore, this chapter is mainly concerned with analysing the above-mentioned development in the case of Bangalore, based on original fieldwork and extant literature. In the following this case will be illustrated by discussing the main developments that took place which are summarized in Table 15.1.

Early foundations: a culture of learning and knowledge

Initial historical conditions leading to path-dependencies that evolved later on can be traced back at least to colonial times, and even before the arrival of foreign (political) powers. An extensive study of anthropological literature revealed considerable differences between North and South India in terms of appraisal of education. This led to a number of college formations under Sir M. Visweswaraiah, a well-known South Indian engineer. After early retirement he became Divan (first Minister) of the Kingdom of Mysore, an important autonomous Princely State under the British Empire and pursued his vision of broad-based education witnessed by the early foundation of the Indian Institute of Science (1909), University of Mysore (1916), the sixth oldest in India and modelled after Chicago, Oxford and Cambridge, and the important Regional Engineering College of Bangalore (1917).

There had been a strong research base, in particular in electrical engineering and manufacturing of machine tools even before independence. With early location

Table 15.1 Important milestones in the development path of the Bangalore IT cluster

Period	Innovation system factor	Main events (italics denote national level)
Colonial time	Educational Institutions	1909 – Indian Institute of Science, IISc 1917 – Viswesvaraya College of Engineering
Independence	Research Institutes	1940 – Hindustan Aeronautics, HAL
late 1960s–early 1980s	Indigenous private sector IT firms	1973 – Process System India (Bangalore)
Mid-1980s–early 1990s	Policy shift/ First MNCs	*1984 – Rajiv Gandhi: New Software Policy* 1984 – Texas Instruments
Since 1990s	MNC wave	*1991 – Liberalization*

Note own representation.

of military, hence defence research Hindustan Aeronautics (HAL) (1940), and later space research (1972), that is, concentration of research-intensive technology industries, led to Bangalore becoming the prime location for high-tech equipment in an economy rather left behind in terms of technological development due to a prohibitive import tariff structure. Co-evolution of these research and training institutions best reflects the systemic character of what led to initial competitive advantage (cf. Murmann, 2003).

Many employees of these research institutions later trained the graduates of the numerous engineering colleges in the city and the state. The number of these graduates has been much higher than in other Indian regions since the late 1970s, when the privatization of higher education in the state of Karnataka witnessed a first boost. It has been the first state to privatize higher education, several decades back. Many of these privately funded colleges received not only the regular fees, but also a capitation fee for a quota of the student intake. These funds enabled the establishment of computer labs required for teaching students in IT.

Openness

Interestingly, one apparently striking feature which was revealed very clearly during fieldwork interviews concerns the social composition of the IT industry. Virtually no one found the industry to be really dominated by South Indians or any other social group. On the contrary, most interview partners even argued in the opposite way. They claimed it is very much the cosmopolitan nature of the city and the historical and traditional openness towards foreigners, both Indian and from abroad which had a high impact on the IT industry. Compared to other states in India, the investment climate has eventually been much more hospitable to foreign direct investment. The city has grown even more cosmopolitan due to the central government's policy to locate national institutions there. These national institutions were staffed with people from the Indian Administrative Service (IAS) or researchers employed after nationwide job announcements and recruitment processes. The following relocation of many Indians from other parts of the country after independence and a realignment of state boundaries in 1956 enhanced the already established cosmopolitan nature of the city. More recently, due to the prospects of a booming economy and job market there has been a continuous inflow of foreigners (for non-economic factors motivating migration in India see Gidwani and Sivaramakrishnan, 2003). Therefore, it was no surprise to find a similar pattern in my primary data collection with a total of 54.5 per cent among the randomly sampled respondents not being from Bangalore. Apparently Bangalore has reached a level of diversity that allowed benefiting more from the positive effects thereof than suffering from its negative impact.

The impact of policy: benign neglect?

Interestingly, initial decades of the Indian IT industry were characterized by a complete absence of targeted policy measures. But despite many scholars arguing for a benign neglect the Government of India (GOI) did introduce a couple of – theoretically – stimulating policies. As early as 1971, India established a Department of Electronics particularly addressing electronics production, which was larger than (South) Korea's at that time. The underlying philosophy of Indian polity, however, until at least 1984, or even 1991, was import-substitution led industrialization (ISI) that culminated in 1978 with the expulsion of MNC's that did not want to conform to minority ownership regulations for their Indian operations such as Coca-Cola and, more importantly, IBM. At that time, no effective Indian software *industry* existed.

In 1984, Rajiv Gandhi, introduced the first measures to stimulate the software industry, which was also formally recognized as an industry through the 'Computer Policy'. These measures included easing of imports and exports by lowering tariffs and other incentives explicitly encouraging software exports as a priority. This helped attracting investment such as Texas Instruments in Bangalore mentioned earlier. In 1988, software firms themselves formed an industry association to further their interests. This quickly resulted in the establishment of the Software Technology Parks (STPI) of India, as export-processing zones with dedicated satellite links, other service provisions and incentives. Bangalore was among the first three STPI units set up (1990) – again resulting in a first-mover advantage of Bangalore over comparable locations in other cities.

The role of transnational linkages

Following a macroeconomic crisis in 1991 further liberalization policies led to the inflow of MNCs that located primarily in Bangalore which had already gained some international reputation. There is no agreement in the literature about the role of international or foreign influences on the development of the Bangalore cluster. However, for successful cluster development entirely localized network structure seems not sufficient, for it might lead to a lock-in or suboptimal equilibrium (March, 1991). Hence, clusters need some form of external linkages in order to provide a continuous inflow of knowledge (Chiarvesio *et al.* 2004; Wolfe and Gertler, 2004; Yeung *et al.* 2006).

An important related characteristic is the increasing significance of transnational networks, primarily between the US-American high-tech cluster of Silicon Valley and Bangalore, although in the Silicon Valley the influence of culture seems negligible. Saxenian (1999) found Indians in Silicon Valley share a common Indian identity that transcends boundaries of caste or ethnicity and try to integrate into the US business mainstream. However, the geographical origin or ethnicity seems to play a very important role as regards the flows through transnational networks that are directed towards South India. This positive feedback process increases the regional concentration of the Indian software industry. This process seems to be already well under way providing in particular Bangalore, and to a lesser extent diffusing to Hyderabad and Chennai, with the competitive advantage in knowledge-intensive industries.

The importance of local social networks itself has not been estimated by many respondents as highly as expected from cluster and network literatures. Since they often spin off from leading MNCs, they have accumulated necessary technological (but less business) know-how in order to access the more advanced Western markets. Since major clients are located overseas, local networking makes less sense for these companies. They normally do not interact with captive development centres in India, but rather with headquarters or other research units directly.

However, there have been a couple of reports of local networking in the Indian IT industry. Right from the start it was even at the highest levels and quite informal. But, with the growing industry, it becomes more formalized, and it diffuses to different, lower levels. Those participating in such networking events report mostly positive experiences. And those who do not have the time regret not being able to spend some time for socializing. However, local networking is far from a level found in Silicon Valley. It seems to be rather the cultural and professional proximity to (Indians in) the leading Western markets than the spatial proximity to other Indian companies, that allows for an innovative environment in Bangalore. More than inter-firm collaboration, university–industry relationships and a regional culture of learning seem to play an important role. Some of the interview partners, on the contrary, suggested that indigenous firms were responsible for the growth of the Indian IT industry without much involvement of overseas Indians at all.

How could these indigenous firms achieve such a development? Given the importance of learning, the following section takes a look at the antecedents of education emphasizing regional culture of south India.

A regional culture of knowledge, innovation and entrepreneurship

'Indian' economic culture

This section is a theoretical exercise to outline the basic features of an 'Indian' economic culture and the role of Brahmin and South Indian background, respectively.

The question is whether there exists a regional culture of innovation resembling the one of Silicon Valley (Gertler, 1997; Saxenian, 1994.

Broadly speaking, for the Indian society the cultural framework can be interpreted as 'Hinduism', which provides rather an all-encompassing philosophy than 'merely' a religion. But what is commonly known as belonging to 'Hinduism' is only part of the more complex Hindu civilization – it is embedded in an all-encompassing worldview (e.g. Stietencron, 1995). Albeit the differences within that composite of religious beliefs are too subtle to be explored here, the broader cultural view allows for the observation of several regularities.

Is there anything that makes the Indian economy a peculiar object of analysis, something that precludes a conventional economic study? Presumably it is, given the unique phenomenon of caste as the characteristic feature of the Indian society. On the other hand there are those who downplay the influence of caste and, moreover, the institution as such is an invention of 'orientalist' scholars. The most compelling argument is that some social structure similar to the caste system existed long before the arrival of the British, but only for their desire for rationally understanding the Indian society with the support of Indian elites they hierarchically institutionalized the rather informal norms (Bayly, 1999). While the issue whether there is a system of caste is heavily disputed in the anthropological literature, it is quite safe to assume a certain influence of caste. That is why it is taken as one of the proxies for culture in this analysis.

However, the term caste is used in two different contexts. First, it is used to describe the jati, hierarchically ranked endogamous kinship groups with a regional base centring around the performance of traditional occupations (such as leatherworkers, priests, merchants, or tailors) in an interdependent relationship with other jatis. Second, it depicts the more aggregate societal structure of a class-like division, the varnas (Bayly, 1999).

Describing the caste system as consisting of a four-fold hierarchy of varnas plus the so-called untouchables, mistakenly referred to as outcastes (Dumont, 1980),[1] is a gross oversimplification[2] that does not do justice to the complexity of this perhaps most refined institution extant today. Except for the highest varna of the Brahmins the remaining ones consist of numerous jatis. But it is useful in the sense that the categories so derived allow for a pan-Indian examination of issues related to caste. It can be seen as the conceptual framework for the actual practice of the society stratified by jati.

Although very prominent, and studied both intensively and extensively by anthropologists, predominantly in field studies, but also on a theoretical level, its meaning for development has not been scrutinized thoroughly by economists. It is predominantly both the alleged stability of this unique institution and in connection with that fatalism, the presumed tendency of the poor to ascribe everything to their karma, which led many economists to the conclusion that the caste system impedes modernization of the Indian economy (most notably Marx, 1971; Myrdal, 1968; Weber, 1958). They blurred both concepts with the resulting lack of an adequate picture of Indian reality as known through anthropological fieldwork. In order to establish through economic theory the rigidity and drawback of the caste system, they overlook that it has always been much more open, flexible and adaptable.

The actual meaning of karma is action or deed, and that it also influences current and future lives, but is often (mis-)interpreted simply as fate, which defies the ability of the individual to influence his/her present life, which is inconsistent with the actual Hindu philosophy as understood, for instance, by Thapar (1990).

Parry (1996), firmly rejecting Weber's thesis of the 'spirit of capitalism' being absent in India, states that the ethical preconditions for the emergence of capitalism have been much more hospitable in India than they actually were in Europe. This might be seen as implicitly subscribed to by Lal (1988) who argued that the caste system initially was a highly efficient institution and very much in favour of economic development, embodied quite early in a high-level equilibrium which then was maintained at stable conditions over millennia by still encrusted hierarchies. The recognition of commerce, trade and other sources of accumulating wealth being in conformity with the religious doctrines, which are definitely culturally determining, on whichever element the emphasis is placed, allows to identify a climate in traditional India, be it in ancient times or in remote areas today, which was unmistakably favourable to generate a capitalist spirit.

There is a prolific misconception of the Indian or better 'Hindu' attitude towards secular affairs, at least if one tries to locate the source of fatalism and 'accommodation', to use Galbraith's (1979) notion, in the roots of the cultural and religious traits as manifested in the ancient scripts. This inference has been initially proposed by Weber[3] and is known also as the karmic view on the Indian society. This picture erroneously propagates the pursuit of religious duties and the outright rejection of material wealth as the basic components of the 'Hindu' belief. From these, according to this perspective, supposedly originates the ignorance of the, indeed, very religious Indian population of (technical) change and innovations that could otherwise bring progress to and enhance the welfare or well-being of the deprived population. The presumption underlying this image is a traditional society with a well-balanced power structure in which innovations of whatever nature are deemed as a threat to the existing equilibrium. These scholars ascribed the stagnation in what Lal calls a 'high level equilibrium trap' (1998: 34) mono-causally to the extant ideologies of 'Hinduism'.

Upper-caste groups, such as Brahmins and merchant and ruling groups, have traditionally discriminated against lower-caste groups, but the ranking of upper- and lower-caste groups has varied by region and through time.

> If the stability of the caste order could not hinder property differentiation, it could at least block technological change and occupational mobility, [E]ven today, the very fact that new skills and techniques actually lead to the formation of new castes or subcastes strongly handicaps innovation. It sustains tradition no matter how often the all-powerful development of imported capitalism overrides it.
>
> (Weber, 1958: 104)

Although there has always been upward (and downward) mobility, one could say that the principal varna providing economic services like merchants or entrepreneurs was that of the Vaishyas (Rutten, 2002), complemented, of course, by the minority communities of Parsis, Jains and Sikkhs (see e.g. Tripathi, 1992).

Brahmins, on the other hand, were traditionally seen as priests, teachers or in related professions. These related professions comprise all the tasks necessary to perform the various religious rituals. This consists mainly of studying, reciting and handing down the sacred texts, but includes auxiliary sciences such as grammar or astronomy, as well as mathematics and geometry (in order to construct optimally the altar for sacrifices) (Stietencron, 1995). Moreover, the Hindu-Brahminical education system envisaged medicine, literature, philosophy and logics (Das, 2000). Hence, there are many disciplines that are very useful for intellectually challenging professions in the so-called knowledge economy such as sciences or research-related pharmaceuticals, biotechnology or software. Being handed down from one generation to the next for decades or even centuries would place descendants in a privileged position regarding such professions and, thus, be an example for (economic) culture as summarized in the previous section. Therefore, even if Brahmins have monopolized learning, as some argue, there might be a positive impact on the Indian economy in the 'knowledge age' (Das, 2000: 153).

Especially with regard to traditional professions like artisans, this division of labour seems to be still perfectly in place. There is evidence from various field studies, both economic as well as sociological or anthropological that this holds true.[4] Moreover, such a network of interdependent producers and traders adhering to their customary occupation can be described as a cluster. In the traditional footwear cluster of Agra a major factor for the successful mastering of crises is the extent of vertical relationships (Knorringa, 1999).

However, with regard to the urban, and more so in the metropolitan, areas of India, this traditional aspect of the culture derived from religion is being undermined by various factors, most notably industrialization and occupational diversification in general (Srinivas, 1978). In particular, caste is being superseded by issues of class (and ethnicity), more among the upper castes than among the lower (Béteille, 1996).

Whatever might be the importance of these moral values today, it is noteworthy how they are supposed to have spread during the past millennia in a process described as 'Sanskritization' of the lower castes, that is, the imitation of customs and rites as followed by the Brahmins, to an extent possible in terms of ability to perform these rites (Srinivas, 1978).

As already said, the most widespread inference made is the one which does not take into account the internal dynamics of caste and its adaptability and tolerant attitude towards external institutional changes, be they political or legislative or anything else. Nevertheless, this stance is usually taken by economists who ignore the insights from history and anthropology evidently showing the opposite. They do neither account for the upward mobility of previously lower castes through economic success nor for the process of Sanskritization as inherent to caste. Instead it is seen as inseparably interrelated with the Hindu religion, despite the fact that it is hosting other religions and sects, too, albeit as subdivisions, jatis, being ranked according to the prevailing circumstances like, for instance, economic success.

Closely related to the flexibility of the system with regard to the mobility of castes, or better jatis, almost as a precondition, is the emergence of new occupational activities. The jati-dharma has been almost fixed for ancient castes and jatis through scriptural tradition. But there cannot be prescriptions for all the newly evolving sub-castes as there cannot be explicit contracts specifying every contingency. Thus, in the modern Indian society there is some indeterminateness concerning the future adherence and obedience to dharma, because there is no (religious) authority legitimated to declare such a social code of conduct. Furthermore, the developments observed reveal a certain tendency to reverse the process Max Weber has described as 'the transformation from ethnicity to caste' (Fuller, 1996: 22), which Dumont labelled 'substantialisation of caste' (quoted in Béteille, 1996: 172; Fuller, 1996) and anthropologists more broadly have named ethnicization. It might be particularly meaningful in India as it dissociates class from caste (Béteille, 1996; Fuller, 1996).

Recently, there is evidence that the structure of new Indian enterprises is determined not only by Vaishyas, the traditional merchant caste, but also Brahmins and others (Taeube, 2004). It might result from the fact that Brahmins have been involved not only with the profession of priesthood but more generally with activities relating to knowledge and wisdom. In earlier times Brahmins had a much more negative attitude towards business, trade and commercial castes in general.

South India: a regional culture of knowledge and innovation

With regard to South India there are a few notable, somehow contradictory deviations. First, caste has been perceived to be imported by the (Brahmin) Indo-Aryan-speaking migrants from the North.[5] Therefore, the position of the Brahmins as representatives of this hierarchical order seemed to be more exposed in the Southern states, particularly in Tamil Nadu, but also in the neighbouring Karnataka and Andhra Pradesh. However, there has also been an indigenous Dravidian culture with its own languages, symbols and sacred texts as well. These South Indian cultural elements had to be balanced against their own Sanskritic ones by the Brahmins. First, there have always been high-caste non-Brahmins pertaining to the indigenous Dravidian population who were not only engaged with the learning of the Dravidian texts but 'who were adept in Sanskrit learning as well' (Stein, 1999: 52). Hence, Brahmins are to be seen as mediators who provided for the diffusion of Sanskritic knowledge rather than monopolists. Thus, apparently the foundations for a knowledge-based society have always existed in South India ever since and, moreover, have been much more diffused throughout the whole society. Moreover, political movements in favour of the backward groups of Indian society started much earlier in the South and led to a more equal pattern there as opposed to the more traditionally dominated Northern states (Jaffrelot, 2002).

Second, the indigenous population of the South is said to be much more homogeneous and not displaying the two middle-caste groups of Ksatriyas and Vaishyas to the same extent as in the North (Stein, 1999). There was a further distinction between so-called 'right hand' and 'left hand' divisions in at least three of the four Southern states, adding to the complexity of a hierarchy. Both Brahmins and high-caste non-Brahmins have been excluded from the occupations of these two caste groups, which included different kinds of traders and merchants, both agricultural and non-agricultural occupations. The absence of the warrior castes of the Ksatriyas in particular resulted in a generally more peaceful and contemplative society, one reason often cited for the higher political stability of South Indian states (Stein, 1999).

This greater emphasis for learning is reflected by the higher than proportionate share of all the South Indian states in institutions of tertiary education and a higher proliferation of higher education. This is particularly revealing when taking into account the lower economic status of these states compared to the North Indian ones (Chalam, 2000). Generally, mathematics and other pure sciences are said to confer a high status to people proficient in them, since they are intellectually the most demanding.

What is particularly striking is the large number of technical or engineering colleges in the four southern states. Although there are varying numbers according to the definition of a college used by different sources, the shares remain relatively stable. Arora and Athreye (2002) report as percentages for South India roughly 50 per cent of all Indian engineering colleges and enrolment as well as 79 per cent for privately financed colleges as against the national average of 69 per cent (Table 15.2).

They find the latter startling and hypothesize that it might relate to cultural and political factors. Chalam (2000) more explicitly links this fact to social and cultural movements (see previous section) that tried to break away from the traditional and superstitious customs in order to arrive at more humanitarian values.

Table 15.2 Number of engineering colleges and enrolment

Region	No. of engineering colleges	National share in engineering colleges	Enrolment (sanctioned capacity)	National share enrolment	Per cent share of national population	Share of self-financed colleges
Central	50	7,54%	9,470	6,05%	–	52%
East	25	3,77%	4,812	3,07%	25,8%	26%
North (incl. north-west)	140	21,12%	25,449	16,26%	31,3%	42%
West	140	21,12%	34,165	21,83%	19,6%	74%
South (incl. South-west)	308	46,46%	82,597	52,78%	23,2%	79%
Total	663	100,00%	156,493	100,00%	100,00%	69%

Arora and Athreye, 2002.

Taken together, the Southern part of India seems to exhibit a more intensive regional culture not only of learning, quite literally, but also of innovation (see Vijayabaskar and Krishnaswamy, 2004). Apparently, this attitude is a solid foundation for the absorptive capacity necessary in order to adapt to new technologies.

Concluding remarks

Lessons from this regional culture of knowledge and innovation for other states or countries include that co-evolution of research and industry perhaps best reflects the systemic character of what led to the initial competitive advantage (Murmann, 2003). But, apart from these well-known components of an innovation system (e.g. Nelson, 1993), the openness and diversity seem to have played a substantial role. With this line of reasoning from diversity to innovation being reflected not only in interview data, but also in official figures, it seems to be worthwhile doing further research in this direction.

One specific implication for policy-makers would be to make education and technological change better accepted among the population. This is not a new result for development policy, especially when looking at East Asia, but its relevance cannot probably be overemphasized. Another important implication is to create an environment hospitable for the return of emigrants and actively encourage entrepreneurship – for instance, by trying to provide an atmosphere that is rich in amenities, which seems to be one key determinant for inward migration (cf. Glaeser and Saiz, 2004).

Notes

1 Dumont (1980) regards as the most outstanding feature of the caste system that nobody is excluded from the societal structure, contrary to (medieval) Western class conceptions.
2 M.N. Srinivas (1978) mentions an earlier 'calculation' by Ghurye 'that there are 2000 sub-castes (*jatis*) in every linguistic area'.
3 'Ever since Max Weber's analysis of Indian society, many Western (and Indian) social scientists have interpreted social institutions such as caste and the extended family as oppressive, in the sense of hindering the growth of such personality traits as "independence", "initiative", "persistence" and "achievement motivation" in the individual' (Kakar, 1981: 10).
4 See Nafziger (1986) for economic studies conducted in the southern state of Andhra Pradesh; Rutten (2002) for a sociological perspective on the western state of Gujarat; and Reiniche (1996) for an anthropological field study of a merchant caste in south Indian Tamil Nadu.
5 Stein (1999) points out that there is no evidence for such an invasion or migration of substantial dimensions.

References

Arora, A., V.S. Arunachalam, J. Asundi and R. Fernandes (2001) The Globalization of Software: The Case of the Indian Software Industry, A Report submitted to the Sloan Foundation, Carnegie Mellon.

Arora, A. and S. Athreye (2002) The Software Industry and India's Economic Development, Information Economics and Policy, Vol. 14, Issue 2, 253–273.

Banerjee, A.V. and E. Duflo (2000) Reputation Effects and the Limits of Contracting: A Study of the Indian Software Industry, *Quarterly Journal of Economics*, August, 989–1017.

Bayly, S. (1999) *Caste, Society and Politics in India from the Eighteenth Century to the Modern Age*, Cambridge: Cambridge University Press.

Béteille, A. (1996) Caste in Contemporary India, in C.J. Fuller (ed.), *Caste Today*, Delhi: Oxford University Press, 150–79.

Chalam, K.S. (2000) Human Resources Development in South India, *Journal of Social and Economic Development*, II(2), July–Dec, 291–313.

Chiarvesio, M.E., Di Maria and S. Micelli (2004) From Local Networks of SMEs to Virtual Districts? Evidence from Recent Trends in Italy, *Research Policy*, 33, 1509–28.

D'Costa, A. (2002) Export Growth and Path Dependence: The Locking-in of Innovations in the Software Industry, *Science, Technology & Society*, 7(1), 13–49.

Das, G. (2000) *India Unbound – The Social and Economic Revolution from Independence to the Global Information Age,* New York: Anchor.

Dumont, L. (1980) *Homo Hierarchicus: The Caste System and its Implications*, Chicago and London: The University of Chicago Press.

Fuller, C.J. (1996) Introduction: Caste Today, in C.J. Fuller (ed.), *Caste Today,* Delhi: Oxford University Press, 1–31.

Galbraith, J.K. (1993 [1979]) *The Nature of Mass Poverty,* London: Penguin.

Gertler, M. (1997) The Invention of Regional Culture, in R. Lee and J. Wills (eds), *Geographies of Economies*, London: Arnold, 47–58.

Gidwani, V. and K. Sivaramakrishnan (2003) Circular Migration and the Spaces of Cultural Assertion, *Annals of the Association of American Geographers,* 93(1), 186–213.

Glaeser, E. and A. Saiz (2004) The Rise of the Skilled City, (joint with A. Saiz), *Brookings-Wharton Papers on Urban Affairs* 5, 47–94.

Jaffrelot, C. (2002) The Subordinate Caste Revolution, in A. Ayres and P. Oldenburgh (eds), *India Briefing: Quickening the Pace of Change*, Armonk NY: M.E. Sharpe, 121–15.

Kakar, S. (1981) *The Inner World: A Psycho-analytic Study of Childhood and Society in India,* Delhi: Oxford University Press.

Knorringa, P. (1999) Agra: An Old Cluster Facing the New Competition, *World Development*, 27(9), 1587–1604.

Lal, D. (1988) *The Hindu Equilibrium: Cultural Stability and Economic Stagnation,* New York: Oxford University Press.

Lal, D. (1998) *Unintended Consequences: The Impact of Factor Endowments, Culture, and Politics on Long-Run Economic Performance,* Cambridge: The MIT Press.

March, J.G. (1991) Exploration and Exploitation in Organizational Learning, *Organization Science*, 2, 71–87.

Marx, K. (1971 [1872]) *Das Kapital: Kritik der politischen Ökonomie, Band I: Der Produktionsprozeß des Kapitals,* Frankfurt: Verlag Ullstein.

Murmann, J.P. (2003) *Knowledge and Competitive Advantage: The Coevolution of Firms, Technology, and National Institutions,* Cambridge and New York: Cambridge University Press.

Myrdal, G. (1968) *Asian Drama – An Inquiry into the Poverty of Nations*, Vol. 3, New York: Pantheon.

Nafziger, W. (1986) *Entrepreneurship, Equity, and Economic Development*, Greenwich, Connecticut and London: JAI Press.

Nelson, R. (ed.) (1993) *National Systems of Innovation: A Comparative Study*, Oxford: Oxford University Press.

Parry, J. (1996) On the Moral Perils of Exchange, in J. Parry and M. Bloch (eds), *Money and the Morality of Exchange*, Cambridge: Cambridge University Press, 64–93.

Patibandla, M. and B. Petersen (2002) Role of Transnational Corporations in the Evolution of a High-Tech Industry: The Case of India's Software Industry, *World Development*, 30(9), 1561–77.

Reiniche, M.L. (1996) The Urban Dynamics of Caste: A Case Study from Tamilnadu, in C.J. Fuller (ed.), *Caste Today,* Delhi: Oxford University Press, 124–49.

Rutten, M. (2002) A Historical and Comparative View on the Study of Indian Entrepreneurship, *Economic Sociology,* European Electronic Newsletter, 3(2), 3–16.

Saxenian, A. (1994) *Regional Advantage: Culture and Competition in Silicon Valley and Route 128,* Cambridge (MA): Harvard University Press.

Saxenian, A. (1999*) Silicon Valley's New Immigrant Entrepreneurs,* California: Public Policy Institute of California.

Srinivas, M.N. (1978) The Caste System in India, in A. Béteille (ed.), *Social Inequality*, Harmondsworth *et al.*: Penguin, 265–72.

Stein, B. (1999) *Peasant State and Society in Medieval South India,* Delhi: Oxford University Press.

Stietencron, H.V. (1995) Die Erscheinungsformen des Hinduismus, in D. Rothermund (ed.) *Indien: Kultur, Geschichte, Politik, Wirtschaft, Umwelt*, München: C. H. Beck, 143–66.

Taeube, F. (2004) Culture, Innovation, and Economic Development: The Case of the South Indian ICT Clusters, in S. Mani and H. Romijn (eds), *Innovation, Learning and Technological Dynamism of Developing Countries,* New York: United Nations University Press: 202–28.

Thapar, R. (1990) *A History of India – Volume One*, London: Penguin.

Tripathi, D. (1992) Indian Business Houses and Entrepreneurship: A Note on Research Trends, *The Journal of Entrepreneurship*, 1(1), 75–97.

Vijayabaskar, M. and G. Krishnaswamy (2004) *Understanding Growth Dynamism and its Constraints in High-Technology Clusters in Developing Countries: A Study of Bangalore, Southern India.* Paper presented at Cornell Conference June 10–12.

Weber, M. (1958) *The Religion of India: The Sociology of Hinduism and Buddhism*, Glencoe, IL: The Free Press.

Wolfe, D. and M. Gertler (2004) Clusters from the Inside and Out: Local Dynamics and Global Linkages, *Urban Studies*, 41(5/6), 1071–93.

Yeung, H.W., L. Weidong and P. Dicken (2006) Transnational Corporations and Network Effects of a Local Manufacturing Cluster in Mobile Telecommunications Equipment in China, *World Development*, 34(3), 520–40.

Part VI

Sports – tourism

16 Opiate of the masses or one in a billion[1]

Trying to unravel the Indian sporting mystery

Boria Majumdar

Until very recently, as K. A. Sandiford has argued,

> [S]ocial historians neglected sport because in their view as well as that of
> laymen, it merely involved forms of play. History was a much more serious
> business, involving work, industry and worship. This narrowness of approach
> was not confined to historians; it was at one time characteristic of all social
> science.[2]

This attitude has been true for India/South Asia than most places.

Worldwide, however, there has been noticeable change since the early 1990s.
There is today a substantial corpus of literature on the sociology, history and
anthropology of sport. As Sandiford writes, 'Historians now know that it is hardly
possible to write intelligibly about work without also dealing intelligently with
play; and it is universally recognized that sport is one of the most important features
of any society's culture'.[3]

Yet, Indian history writing remained immune to this trend until lately.[4] In
fact, sport continues to be a marginal presence in Indian/South Asian history
writing. Sports history is still considered a 'fun thing'[5] and the challenge
confronting sports scholars is to demonstrate that sport is far from being 'mere
leisure' or 'entertainment' as has been argued or continues to be argued in the Indian
historical context. A study of Indian cricket, more than any other Indian sport, it
will be evident from the following pages, is central to an understanding of India's
colonial and postcolonial encounters, long-standing engagements of Indian/South
Asian history writing.

Why histories of Indian sport?

> Cricket is a fascinating subject but Indian cricket is more so because of the
> peculiar traits of the Indians who play it ... To point this out is not to extol
> the Indian at cricket as against others, just as Gandhiji's loin cloth does not
> necessarily constitute the ideal in the Indian national dress nor an example to

the rest of the world. Yet, both are significant; they reveal the nation through the game or through the kit – for the better or for the worse.[6]

In modern India, no hyperbole is sufficient to capture the importance of cricket in the country's national life. This is because India, the most populous nation in the world, is a rather insignificant presence globally once we account for the export of software professionals to the Middle East and the West. This marginality is especially prominent in sports. In the Sydney Olympics of 2000 India won a solitary bronze medal.[7] The country continues to baffle with the panoply of anomalies it produces. Consider the fact that 44 per cent of Indians still spend less than dollar a day and 70 of a thousand Indian children die before their first birthday. In world politics, India remains a peripheral presence, communal and caste conflict continues to be a looming spectre and 'Brain drain' is one of the biggest threats that confront the nation.

However, when we turn our attention to a very particular arena of Indian sport – cricket – the narrative of 'backwardness' and 'gloom' ends. Cricket is the only realm where the Indians can flex their muscles on the world stage; it is her only instrument to have a crack at world domination. It is, to put it simply, much more than a 'game' for Indians, demonstrated most recently by the Indian Premier League.

Indian Premier League – India's crack at world domination

What the Indian Premier League (IPL) drives home, once and for all, is the reality that the nerve centre of the game has firmly shifted to the subcontinent. That this 'shift' is atypical of modern international sport is perhaps the most important of all developments. Most, if not all, Olympic sports are still controlled by the West. While the Greeks claimed during the Athens games in 2004 that the flame will travel to every country of the globe, they, confidently and with indifference, had initially left out the second most populous nation in the world. The Chinese too had issued a threat in April 2008 that India will miss out on the Olympic flame unless Delhi curbed possible Tibet protests. India caved in because she is aware that hosting the Olympics is still a far cry. What we can get at best is the flame because the Chinese had kindly consented to take it past Delhi.

India, which hardly produces an Olympic champion, does not figure in the Western schema of a sporting nation. This opinion of India is not unusual. Rather, it is also the accepted view in the Americas, evident from the following description in the ESPN magazine on Indian sport in December 2003:

> But that's India, a place where numbers, and most everything else, can make your head spin. From 20 million or so temples to 3 million or so Hindu gods; from hundreds of millions of desperate poor people to hundreds of thousands of free ranging cows; whatever you count, big numbers abound. But there are much smaller numbers, more precise and no less bewildering,

especially to sports fans. Olympic medals won by India: 16. Medals won at the 2000 games: 1. And here's a round number for you: Indian Athletes most Americans could name on Jeopardy! If the category was Indian Athletes you have heard of even once: 0.

In sharp contrast, when we turn our attention to cricket, this discourse of 'catching up' ceases. Cricket is the only realm where the Indians can dictate to the West. It is an arena where after an Australian creates a world record, he has to run to the Indian market to reap dividends. It is one, which inspires English players to revolt against their own board and for which the Australians can contemplate giving up the coveted baggy green cap. An Indian domestic tournament now results in 'windfall' for the West and India is, all of a sudden, thanks to cricket, the most coveted land to visit. It is this radical potential of cricket that IPL underlines.

Salve for a troubled nation

Indians have played cricket since at least the late nineteenth century. The Indian Cricket Board was formed in 1928, and India played its first Test match at Lords, in London, on 25 June 1932. But it was only after India's triumph in 1983 that the game came to be perceived as a viable path to fame and income for middle- and lower-middle-class Indians. All it took was the excitement and energy following one victory: India's World Cup win on 25 June 1983. That evening, what used to be a mere sport was converted into a lucrative career option, and cricketers into default national icons. And from then on Indians – and along with them, the rest of the region – began to look to cricket as both a relaxant and something into which to channel their energies, patriotic and otherwise. Soon enough, the corporate world would take note – and the rest of the world would follow. That one victory paved the way for corporate sponsors to invest in cricket, in anticipation of rich dividends. It also gave the media events for it to build hype around, and cricket proved a salve for a troubled nation.

In the two decades since 1983, the craze for cricket has become a veritable mania. In the contemporary sporting world, few would argue with the assertion that, economically at least, India is the new cricketing superpower. As a consequence, cricket has become integral to defining the culture of postcolonial India, a country anxious to define its position in a world rapidly changing and characterized by globalization and growing interdependence. As was evident during the Indian Premier League, cricket mania completely dominated the country. During the six weeks of the tournament between 18 April and 1 June, all other news seemed to melt into the background as millions of Indians sat glued to their television sets, following their team's every move.

As was to be expected, cricket commerce was also at an all-time high during the tournament. Given the amount of attention focused on it, the soaps and serials, staple of Indian homes in the evening had gradually lost their stranglehold. This is because cricket encapsulates the story of postcolonial India in microcosm: a tapestry woven around the performance of 11 men, who carry the hopes and demands of millions.

Hockey and football – distant seconds at best

The Indian madness for cricket does not transfer to other sports. Indeed, the popularity of the country's two other popular games, football and hockey, does not compare, even though the latter is technically India's national game. Since the mid- to late-1970s, Indian teams have fared poorly in these games at the international level. In hockey, India performed miserably in the Olympics and the Champions Trophy tournaments during the 1980s and 1990s; in the eight-country tournament held in the Netherlands in August 2005, the Indian hockey team finished a dismal seventh. Though it did win India bronze medals in the 1968 and 1972 Olympics, hockey's popularity has notably diminished over the past three decades – during which time cricket's ratings have skyrocketed.

From gold to dust – the story of Indian hockey

Interestingly, the years 1980–2008, which witnessed cricket's spectacular rise, also witnessed the sliding down of hockey from its position of pre-eminence. Sadly for hockey, every major cricketing achievement has followed a singular hockey disaster. The 1983 Prudential Cup Triumph followed India's disastrous 1–7 defeat at the hands of Pakistan in the 1982 Asian Games. Again, the failure to make the semi-finals at the Los Angeles Games of 1984 was followed by the 1985 Benson and Hedges win in Australia. More recently, a disappointing seventh place showing at the Sydney Games in 2000 ensured that hockey was unable to take advantage of cricket's match-fixing phase. Again, India's world cup final showing at South Africa 2003 and the away series win in Pakistan in 2004 was followed by a seventh place showing at Athens. And the defeat to Great Britain recently, which resulted in India not qualifying for the summer Olympics for the first time in her hockey history, came immediately after Dhoni's men had made history down under defeating the Australians in a one-day series after two decades.

Finally, the recent muddle in Indian hockey resulting in the sacking of President KPS Gill and suspension of the Indian Hockey Federation (IHF) has come at a time when the IPL had captured the nation's imaginary. Also, it is of interest to note that the current muddle is an exact replication of events dating back to the 1970s.

It is to this exact similar situation of turmoil in the 1970s we can trace the beginning of the decline of our national sport. While the disorder looked to be temporarily resolved with the suspension of the IHF, as appears the case now, further chaos was only days away with the ousted President of the IHF dragging the Indian Olympic Association to court.

The moot point is that the work of the Indian Olympic Association has only begun with the sacking of KPS Gill. If it has to rescue Indian hockey from its miseries, it must brace itself for a long and acrimonious battle ahead.

Regionalism and decline

The story of sports administration in 1970s India was but a small theatre of a far more important story of regional assertion, of the contest for supremacy between lobbies associated with the north and the south of India.

Things had been going reasonably well for Indian hockey until 1973 when Ashwini Kumar, president of the Indian Hockey Federation, was forced to step down from his post due to burgeoning opposition against him. His resignation was followed by a long spell of anarchy within the ranks of the IHF and conflict between the north and south blocs as P.N. Sahni and M.A.M. Ramaswamy engaged in a bitter struggle for the presidency.[8]

The feud turned murky when the group led by Sahni made every effort to stall Ramaswamy's assumption of the IHF presidency, so much so that government had to appoint a reputed Supreme Court judge to oversee the hockey federation's elections. With the dispute at its height in 1974, the IOA cancelled the affiliation of the IHF and took over the administration of hockey in the country. This decision by the IOA is evident from a confidential letter written by Raja Bhalindra Singh, then president of the IOA, to Rene Frank, president of the International Hockey Federation. In his letter, Raja Bhalindra Singh expressed deep resentment over the actions of the Ramaswamy faction in taking the IOA to court and suggested that such actions might have prevented the Indian Olympic Association from selecting a team for the forthcoming Teheran Asian Games.[9]

A year after participating in the Asian Games at Teheran, the Indian hockey team, still under the stewardship of the IOA, won the Hockey World Cup for the first and only time in its history at Kuala Lumpur under the coaching of Balbir Singh Jr. So bad was the administrative situation by now that the coaching camp before the tournament and the tour itself had to be funded by the Punjab government in the absence of funding from a dysfunctional IHF. Interestingly, on such vagaries was Indian sporting success scripted!

Internal squabbling within the IHF temporarily seemed to end in 1975 when Ramaswamy won an acrimonious election against Sahni. But the angry losers would not back off. There were numerous affiliated units that were opposed to the move and thus refused to participate in activities of the IHF. In fact, the fight between the IOA and the IHF flared up again in mid-1977 on the eve of the IOA general assembly meeting. At a meeting on 2 July 1977, members of the IOA general council expressed dissatisfaction with the working of the IHF and it was 'desired that the IOA must make concerted moves to remedy the situation and if necessary place the entire situation before the Government'.[10]

Not surprisingly, the IOA executive council, which met on 24 September 1977, expressed deep resentment at the conduct of the IHF and its president and in its next meeting on 14 January 1978 suspended the functioning of the IHF. The IHF responded by dragging the IOA to court and claimed, as KPS Gill had already done, that the resolution suspending the IHF was illegal. On this basis the Madras High Court on 18 January 1978 granted a temporary injunction against the suspension. The suspended IHF drew upon support from the international hockey federation, which declared that 'as far as the suspension of the IHF by the IOA is concerned, we fully disapprove it'.[11]

While the administrators argued and jostled, the game continued to suffer. The immutable fact is that international officials always saw vicious infighting as endemic to the Indian situation. Writing to Rene Frank in 1978, the IOC president, Lord Killanin noted, 'Your federation is not the only one, which has had trouble in India of a fairly similar nature…'[12]

If Indian hockey was to have an epitaph, this was it.

The story since has been one of persistent decline and gloom. Whether or not the Suresh Kalmadi led IOA can reverse the trend and come out of the present imbroglio with credibility will decide if a resurrection is possible or if the 1970s epitaph was a permanent one.

Goalless: the story of Indian football

The last time that Indian football performed decently was at the Bangkok Asian Games in 1970, where the team won a bronze. Since then, the tale of football in the country has been one of continuous decline; in rankings for June 2007 compiled by the Federation Internationale de Football Association (FIFA), India was placed at a dismal 161st. Football infrastructure in the country is such that FIFA's president, Sepp Blatter, argued during a recent visit that India should not hope to enter the sport's big league anytime in the next two decades.

In the valedictory session of the 'Conference of Indian Football' held in March 2003 at New Delhi, Dato Peter Velappan, General Secretary, Asian Football Confederation (AFC), exuded confidence in India's future potential: 'The time to act is now, for yesterday was past, tomorrow is the future and the present is the transition. Decide where you wish to be in the Asians Cup final or the World Cup?'[13] The immediate antecedent of this confidence is important. Velappan presented in the same conference a paper titled, 'Vision India – The Way Forward', which when implemented was expected to revolutionize football in the country. He said 'if there is a will then blessings begin to shower. A nation of over one billion population with 33 per cent of them in the U-14 years category presents a vast segment of potential footballers who need to be tapped, moulded and brought up on the right lines.'[14] He also highlighted the 11 elements, like 11 men of a team on a football field, which need to be looked into for a way forward: National State Associations, Marketing, Youth Development, Coaches Education, Referees, Sports Medicine, Men's Football, Women's Football, Futsal, Media & Communications and Fans.[15] Later on the project started, as he had affirmed, with the building of a permanent headquarters of the All India Football Federation (AIFF) in the capital, and would be followed by football offices in various states and expertise at every step.

Urs Zanitti, Head of the Development Division of Federation Internationale de Football Association (FIFA), who was a delegate in the conference, lamented a few months later: 'It's a scandal from an outsider's point of view. FIFA's job is to provide the money but, in countries like India, we are forced to deal directly with the people to whom the money is paid eventually.'[16] Pointing to the FIFA House project – the plan to build a permanent office and much more for the AIFF in New Delhi's Dwarka area, he exclaimed: 'We are dealing directly with the architects and contractors, because nothing seems to get done otherwise. It was supposed to have been built a year or so ago, but it's still not in functioning condition'. His experience with the AIFF top brass has been more revealing: 'They seem interested enough but where's the administration? Where are the administrators? You have some people in Delhi. Some in Kolkata. Some in Goa. There are no people. The human resource is very poor. The financial resources are poor also, but that's where we come in. But here we need to take part in creating the human resource also.'[17]

Both football and hockey have long-standing histories in India, and the reasons for their decline are many. The Indian Olympic Association, the All India Football Federation and the Indian Hockey Federation have all recently accused the corporate world and the media of what they perceive as unfair treatment of these two sports. While there is a kernel of truth to these contentions, poor marketing strategies, internal politicking and the myopic views of the officials who run these institutions have also accounted for their sports' stagnation.

Given India's history of failure in other team sports, the Indian public has grown accustomed to leaning on the cricket team. Somewhere along the way, appreciation of individual performance came to be drowned out by the clamour for national victory. Players are now lauded not for great innings so much as for those performances, however brief they may be, that have proven decisive. After his penultimate ball four against Pakistan in the final of the Independence Cup in Dhaka in January 1998, Hrishikesh Kanitkar was as much a star as Saurav Ganguly or Robin Singh, both of whom had scored very high in the same match. Stars are made on the basis of last-minute saves. Thus, a young Sachin Tendulkar, a relative newcomer in 1993, whose meagre score of 15 runs had been a disappointment in that year's Hero Cup semi-final against South Africa, was catapulted to stardom when he conceded only three runs while bowling the last over. The crowd hailed a saviour who had brought victory by two runs; Tendulkar's sad 15 was soon forgotten.

The post-colonial game

Cricket today provides India a feel-good space, where nearly all differences can be overcome. The assertion of an Indian 'identity', the expression of cultural nationalism or the feeling of a common emotion – these are no longer confined to the stadium and post-match activities. For instance, a poll conducted a few years back found that more than 50 per cent of India's youth would prefer to live in another country. However, as journalist Sandipan Deb has observed: 'Even when they do go away to some other country, they have a live cricket scorecard open surreptitiously on their computer monitors throughout their working day, and they turn out in daunting numbers at the stadium whenever India's playing in their adopted country. The global Indian wants simultaneously to escape his country and to embrace it. Clearly, cricket is no longer a mere 'national' obsession.

Anthropologist Robert Foster has offered similar analysis of the role played by the Papua New Guinean rugby star Marcus Bai in stirring the Papuan national consciousness. Similar to Bai's role vis-à-vis his countrymen, cricket in India is no longer a vehicle for merely imagining the nation, but has become one by which to transcend the nation – to escape the troubled country, even, through a form of 'imagined cosmopolitanism'.[18] Foster says that such imagining conjures a utopian vision for the future, one where a Papuan, or an Indian, can engage with the world on a level playing field. In India, however, cricket provides far more than an opportunity for imagination. The sport allows post-colonial India to assert itself on the world stage.

For a short while, India's craze for cricket succeeded in hiding the grim realities confronting many of the region's countries, particularly with regards to poverty. Retired cricketers faced destitution, and it was, and to some extent still is, commonplace to hear of former players being rescued from inhumane conditions by human-rights workers and the most ardent of fans. If this was the fate of once beloved sportsmen, there was little wonder about the circumstances of much of the rest of the population. Since the turn of the millennium, things have begun to change. In 2004–05, the Board of Control for Cricket in India (BCCI) formally started a pension scheme, converting cricket into a proto-industry. Any player who has represented the country now qualifies to receive a monthly pension of at least INR 25,000 from the cricket establishment, for as long as he lives. Players' widows are also part of the scheme. Perhaps most significantly, however, a proposal is now under discussion to extend the pension scheme to India's roughly 50,000 national-level, interstate players, known as Ranji Trophy cricketers. Doing so would suddenly allow for a relatively large constituency to see cricket on a national level as a realistic, stable, life-long career.

Even as it finally begins to look to the well-being of its non-international players, Indian cricket has felt confident enough to turn its attention to its would-be competitors – namely, other sports. Take a look at the following Press Trust of India news release, from May 2006:

> The Indian cricket team will play a match every year to raise around Rs 45 crore to promote other games in the country. 'It is not only cricket the BCCI is worried about. It will spend rupees fifty crore every year on training the country's top-ranking junior player of any individual game played in the Olympics', BCCI president Sharad Pawar said. He concluded saying, 'It is not good for the country that we are not winning golds in the Olympics. Cricket has people's cooperation and the board's finances are improving. It is appropriate for the board to assist other games.

Indeed, through the pension scheme and through these new efforts to give players of other sports a boost, Indian cricket has undertaken an important programme of ensuring that sport is, for the first time, able to directly benefit a significant and growing group of people in the country. During the course of what may be seen as a decade-long transition, cricket has become the first South Asian example of what could be called a 'postcolonial' sport. As recently as the 1990s, despite its vast popularity and increasing financial might, national-level cricket was still essentially just a game – a game that rich people played while poor people worked. Several factors during the past decade led to the establishment of cricket as an institution, one in which several groups of participants – cricketers themselves, but also administrators, fans and sponsors – have a stake.

Eastern colonialism

The opening up of the Indian economy during the 1990s, coupled with the role of the new media, stimulated the solidifying of a commercialized, and increasingly jingoistic, cricket culture. Until a 1995 judgment by the Supreme Court, the state-owned television channel Doordarshan had monopoly rebroadcast rights over Indian cricket. Following the decision, however, the BCCI suddenly found itself able to sell telecast rights of cricket matches in India to any private broadcaster. What followed was a phenomenal influx of corporate finance to Indian cricket.

Soon, and just as the Indian public was being drawn into the global economy, names like Sachin Tendulkar and Rahul Dravid began promoting various brands of products. Indeed, cricket became inseparable from brand names. Though an indulgence for most Indians, Adidas, Nike, Reebok and other cricketer-endorsed brands found a place in the cricket enthusiast's participation in the game. Off-field, drinking a particular soft drink became importantly symbolic of participation in national triumphs. The 1996 World Cup hosted in India, Pakistan and Sri Lanka, for example, is remembered as much for being an organizational success as for the advertising war that took place between Pepsi and Coke.

For their part, cricketers went from being mere glamour icons to becoming integral parts of the entertainment/advertisement economy. Soon, in India at least, they were able to directly influence the day-to-day lives of the masses, whether in generating active patriotism, inadvertently inducing destruction following failure in matches, or building and fashioning a consumer culture. Cricket stars began shaping lives.

As India's cricketers rose in stature, the country was increasingly able to disengage itself from its colonial past. This is visible in particular by the ease with which the Subcontinent has been able to overpower Western countries to win rights to host World Cup competitions.

Cricket's iconic status within the South Asian diaspora underlines the region's transformation into the new centre of global cricket. One simple example from 2004 is enough to prove the point. During the inaugural match of the Champions Trophy in Birmingham, England, not a single hoarding board at the event advertised for a local company – they were all from the Subcontinent. And South Asia (or at least India, Pakistan, Sri Lanka and Bangladesh), despite being a tardy entrant into the contest to win the rights to host the 2011 World Cup, was eventually the runaway winner.

The dark side

While the cricket picture does allow for some hope, what dims such optimism is the old reality that a politician or a bureaucrat controls virtually every Indian sporting body, and once entrenched most manage to stay on for years, if not for decades. The list is long: Congress MP Suresh Kalmadi, President of the Athletics Federation since 1989; BJP MP VK Malhotra, President of the Archery Federation since 1972; Congress MP Priyaranjan Dasmunshi, President of the Football Federation since 1989 and former Congress MP KP Singh Deo, President of the Rowing Federation for 24 years.[19] In addition, BJP leader Yashwant Sinha has been running the Tennis Federation since 2000, VK Verma has been in charge of Badminton since 1998, the INLD's Ajay Chautala runs Table Tennis since 2001 and Samata Party's Digvijay Singh has headed Shooting since 2000.[20] Little wonder then that one of the forgotten initiatives of the late Sunil Dutt, as Sports Minister in 2004, had been to try and act against long-serving association heads. At the time, Congress leader Jagdish Tytler had been the chief of the Judo Federation for about 12 years and Himachal Congress chief Vidya Stokes had been heading the Indian Women's Hockey Federation for 12 years.[21] This is apart from the complete dominance of cricket bodies by politicians. To name just a few, at the time of writing, the NCP's Sharad Pawar is head of the BCCI, the BJP's Arun Jaitely runs the Delhi Association, former Congress MLA Narhari Amin heads the Gujrat Cricket Association, former Kolkata police commissioner Prasun Mukherjee heads the Bengal body, National Conference leader Farooq Abdullah is in charge of Jammu and Kashmir cricket and the RJD's Lalu Prasad Yadav headed the now de-recognized Bihar cricket association.

So why are politicians or bureaucrats attracted towards sport? Is the pre-eminence of the politicians yet another example of Indian exceptionalism, deeply linked to the cultural forces that shape Indian society or is this a management system that has dangerously veered out of control, at variance with its avowed aims of sporting excellence?

The answer to this key question lies in the early history of Indian Olympism and the attributes needed by sports administrators, as identified by Sir Dorabji Tata, the founder of the Indian Olympic Association. In 1927, when the IOC pressed Tata for recommending an Indian successor, he pushed for the Maharajah of Kapurthala, citing one major reason: that Kapurthala had the personal means and influence to visit Europe frequently. Tata was a man whose commitment to Indian sport accrued directly out of a deep commitment to Indian nationalism. Yet, he argued in favour of a prince with the resources and the leisure to network with European society. This, in his view, was considered crucial to keep a tab on international developments and to coordinate with the IOC. Sir Dorabji Tata repeatedly emphasized that a regular presence in Europe was a necessary precondition.[22] Tata's arguments were revealing because they pointed to the fact that sporting structures were initially set up by political and moneyed elites. Only someone with the influence and power of a Tata or a prince in pre-independence

India had the means to incur the expense required for running a national sporting body. India's emerging sporting structures were part of a fast-emerging global sporting arena that was weaved together in inter-locked networks of power and patronage and by the very nature of this arrangement only the elites could apply in the initial years.

After independence, as Nehruvian India grappled with the challenges of welding together a polyglot nation state many princes sought to integrate themselves even more with sporting governance. Deprived of their kingdoms, the princes saw sport as one of the few arenas of power and social capital still open to them. While many princes became power-brokers or direct participants in the new game of democratic elections, many continued to see sport as a simultaneous site of social dominance. This, for instance, is why Patiala continued its pre-independence patronage of Olympism with an even greater vengeance and the house of Patiala has had an almost permanent presence in the higher structures of the IOA since 1947. The corollary to this argument is the fact that no one but the princes could have fulfilled this role in the early years of independent India. At a time when sport was a low governmental priority and a significant middle class was still emerging – largely consisting then of nascent governmental cadre – no one but the princes or the few handful of philanthropic Indian industrialists had the resources to devote themselves to sport. The middle class was still to emerge as a major social category and the post-liberalization monetary avenues its emergence opened for popular games like cricket, for instance, were still in the distant future.

Echoing Dorabji Tata's argument in favour of princes in 1927, VK Malhotra in 2004 was to argue for politicians citing precisely the same reasoning: means, power and influence. 'Being a politician helps in getting things done … It's easier to organize sponsors and get clearances from government since we are influential,' says Malhotra.[23] This is an argument also echoed by former hockey player Zafar Iqbal, 'The cost of running a federation is high. And players have to run to netas to get things done. Since they are influential and can get things done faster, politicians are preferred as federation heads'.[24] He did not, of course, mention that in the true traditions of the license-permit raj system, sporting control has also come to be seen as yet another avenue for the perks of office, influence, hogging the limelight and international travel.

Finally, while political parties are subject to five-yearly performance reviews by the electorate, which unleashes its own internal dynamics, there is no such mechanism to temper the behaviour of those who control sporting bodies. They operate in splendid isolation, as private bodies, answerable only to the rules and strictures of the global bodies they are affiliated with. To illustrate this point further, the BCCI, responding to a Public Interest Litigation against its functioning, famously argued in court that it was a private body and did not represent India. It is impossible for the government to intervene – and its intervention may be worse than the problem – because all Olympic sporting bodies are governed by the Olympic charter, which fiercely espouses the amateur cause and mitigates against any form of governmental intervention. This is why the IOA had to intervene in the affairs of Indian hockey. Had the Government of India done so, Indian hockey could well have been disaffiliated from the global hockey clique.

Conclusion

The cardinal question then is: Is the current scenario impossible to change? Are we condemned to a sporting system that will remain locked in place with no hope for change? The optimist in me is still hopeful, for sport, as this chapter has shown, is a mirror that reflects societal change and Indian societies, as evident from the other chapters in this book, have witnessed unprecedented change in the last decade.

Notes

1 Finally, Abhinav Bindra won India's first ever individual gold medal at the Beijing Games. This article written before Bindra's feat has not been able to analyse its significance. Suffice to say though that he remains an exception and a flash in the pan in the current Indian sporting scenario.
2 Sandiford, K. A. (1994) *Cricket and the Victorians*, London: Scolar Press.
3 Ibid.
4 Ibid.
5 This view was reiterated by OUP India representative Nitasha Devasar at the BASAS conference at Balliol College, Oxford on 7 April 2003. Speaking of academic publications on sport, she made it clear that sports history remains a ghetto in India with publications on sport considered objectionable by most academic publishers in the field.
6 Sarbadhikary, B. (1945) Indian Cricket Uncovered, Calcutta: *Illustrated News*, p. 1.
7 Karnam Malleswari won a bronze in the 63-kilogram category in women's weightlifting at Sydney. In the 1996 Atlanta Olympic Games also India had won a solitary bronze medal. Leander Paes won the bronze in men's tennis at Atlanta.
8 For details see chapter 8 in Majumdar, B. and Mehta, N. *Olympics: The Indian Story*, New Delhi: HarperCollins (Forthcoming).
9 Ibid.
10 Ibid.
11 Ibid.
12 Ibid.
13 'Report on the Conference of Indian Football', in Proceedings of the *All India Football Federation Annual General Meeting,* 10 January 2004, New Delhi: AIFF, p. 86, housed in IFA Archives. I am grateful to the IFA officials for access to this document.
14 Ibid., p. 85.
15 Ibid.
16 Dasgupta, S. (2004) 'India is loser, AIFF scoring the own-goal of corruption. Football: FIFA official slams unprofessional, corrupt system', *Indian Express*, 13 January.
17 Ibid.
18 Robert Foster articulated this concept at a conference organized on 'Muscular Christianity and the Postcolonial World' at the University of Chicago in May 2005.
19 Sharda, U. (2004) 'Track Record of Shame', *India Today*, 21 June.
20 Ayaz Memon (2008) 'KPS Gill is not the only exception', *DNA* Mumbai: 12 March.
21 Pandey, V. (2004) Why a political head for sports? *The Times of India*, 24 July.
22 For most of his letters see; IOC Archives, ID Chemise 7334 CIO 3535 MBR-TATA-CORR, Correspondence de Dorabji Tata 1926–30.

23 Pandey, V. (2004) 'Why a political head for sports?', *The Times of India*, 24 July.
24 Ibid.

References

Dasgupta, S. (2004) India is loser, AIFF scoring the own-goal of corruption. Football: FIFA official slams unprofessional, corrupt system. *Indian Express*, 13 January.
ESPN Magazine, New York, ESPN, December 2003, pp. 40–41.
Majumdar, B. and Metha, N. (forthcoming) *Olympics: The Indian Story*, New Delhi: HarperCollins.
Memon, Ayaz (2008) K. P. S. Gill is not the only exception. *DNA*, Mumbai 12 March.
Pandey, Vineeta (2004) Why a political head for sports? *The Times of India*, 24 July.
Sandiford, K. A. (1994) *Cricket and the Victorians*, London: Scolar Press.
Sarbadhikary, B. (1945) Indian Cricket Uncovered, Calcutta, *Illustrated News*, p.1.
Sharda, U. (2004) Track Record of Shame, *India Today*, 21 June.

17 Going places

Popular tourism writing in India

Anna Kurian

Travel features regularly in Indian newspapers, usually in the Sunday papers, but also in other supplements. Travel columns constitute an important component of Indian popular culture for the sheer volume of work produced which supplements blogs, TV shows and specialized magazines such as *Outlook Traveller*. Newspaper columns range across various kinds of tourism: from adventure to urban, rural India to foreign locales. Travel columns are usually impressionistic, and are at other times akin to tourist guidebooks in their information content (travel writing is a notoriously hard-to-define and amorphous genre, as Jan Borm has argued, 2004).

Contemporary Indian travel (as in travel *by* Indians) itself has changed remarkably – from pilgrimages to summer family trips and now travels for pleasure. There does not appear to be any adherence to a 'tourist season' in these articles. Though 'best times to visit' are sometimes mentioned, it also becomes apparent that some of these visits are undertaken at other times: the Himalayas (Swahilya, 2008: 8) or the wine country (Karthikeyan, 2008: 4) in winter. Whether this is a personal choice so that the tourist crush can be escaped or whether these trips are offshoots of other primary trips made for non-'touristy' purposes remains unclear. It is striking that much of this travel is voluntary, and we can increasingly discern a class of Indian traveller who is (a) willing to travel and (b) at ease travelling anywhere in the world.

I focus on newspaper articles on travel from July 2007 to February 2008 in two English language newspapers: the national daily, *The Hindu*, and the Andhra Pradesh-based local daily, *Deccan Chronicle* (hereafter *DC)*. My rationale for this choice is simple: one is a widely circulated, and highly regarded national newspaper and the other is the largest circulating regional daily in my state of residence and work.

Tourism writing in newspapers does not focus on any one type of tourism alone: people travel to a variety of destinations, to indulge in an assortment of activities. The *Hindu* organizes its travel columns thus:

- 'heritage', about Indian destinations with a historical flavour;
- 'travel' implying foreign travel;
- 'environment', about wildlife sanctuaries and eco-tourist destinations.

While both newspapers have a 'celebrity travel' column (*DC* on Sundays and Metroplus, the *Hindu* supplement, on Thursdays), the *DC*'s Travel page in addition to essays by travellers, features,

• travel guides (factual accounts);
• travel blogs (in print);
• occasional boxes titled 'Travel tips' and 'News you can use'.

Destinations include small towns (Dey, 2007: 4), villages (Venkatesh, 2007: 5) and well-known tourist destinations worldwide: Paris, Rome (Narayanan, 2007: 8; Sinha, 2007: 5), Mexico (Bharadwaj, 2007: 5), the Arctic (Krishnan, 2007), the celebrity circuit (Balachandran, 2008: 8) and Angkor Wat (Padmanabhan, 2008: 8). From adventure through celebrity to culture and heritage to urban tourism most tourism genres are covered in the newspapers.

I would use the term 'tourism writing' for this kind of popular writing about travel, for reasons that will emerge throughout what is essentially a series of meditative observations (rather than an essay) on travel columns.

The writers of the travel articles in these newspapers are usually not professional travellers or writers: they include singletons, mother and son teams and friends travelling together. The spread is varied but what emerges is, curiously enough, not one full-blown personality or even details regarding these individuals which would render them 'real'. They remain nebulous and intangible, people who do not come to life in their words. Some details find their way in occasionally, such as Pushpa Chari's vegetarianism which is contrasted to her son's love of fish (Chari, 2008) or the writer who while writing about Buddhist monks at Mirik, speaks about his Andamans home (Dey, 2007). But the people who write appear to focus on the *place* they have gone to with a single-mindedness which consequently makes them disappear from their words. The tourist spot is well delineated but the person who is writing, though (s)he starts with an 'I' or a 'we' fails to personalize him/herself. In fact, the extremes to which this is taken are seen in many pieces, both in *DC* (Dighe, 2008: 5; Sequeira, 2007: 5, among others) and in *Hindu* (Podder, 2008), wherein there is no 'I' whatsoever. This raises the question as to whether these are pieces written by individuals who have travelled to these places, or whether they are well-researched, informative pieces written as 'travel guides'.[1]

My thesis from reading newspaper essays on travel is: there is a new kind of traveller, the elite Indian in the First World travel spot, or what I call the 'global Indian'.[2] What I am calling the 'global Indian' is apparently a favourite of tourism businesses the world over, and countries are trying to woo her/him (Tripathi, 2004).

I unpack four key elements in the 'tourist gaze' in these newspaper essays.

The impersonal traveller

If travel writing enables the creation of the self through the encounter and engagement with the Other, and the merging of the private and public worlds

(Dyson, 1978: 3; Quadflieg, 2004: 29) then one is struck by the complete absence of the seeing self or the private world in these travel articles. Travel implies a sustained interaction with the Other, with the new and with the strange. Tourism, on the other hand, is fleeting, superficial and fragmented.

The traveller's gaze presupposes a conscious, observing subject, which is then the voice of the narrator. However, most of the articles that appear in these pages lack personality. Exceptions include the Beatles/Liverpool article by Indu Balachandran (2008: 8): 'we felt we were devotees on a pilgrimage'; 'the goose bumps had set in'; 'we found a place to inscribe our names on the wall': here the travellers are as visible as the place they go to. The Valentine's Day special issue in the *DC* is another exception where all the three articles on the page repeatedly call attention to the writer-traveller couples: 'Beach babies as we are' (Chakrabarti, 2008: 5); 'Ira and I spent most of the day lazing on the beach' (Merani, 2008: 5) and 'you will realize, as we did, that Paris is one hedonistic delight after another' (Kaji, 2008: 5). In spite of the 'I' or 'We' that these pieces start with, they are, mainly, addressed to the reader: 'If you crave something more exotic' (Balaji, 2007: 5); or 'if you like experimenting ...' (Nadkarni, 2007: 5). Though this style is occasionally seen in *The Hindu* (Pillai, 2007: 8) it is more a feature of the *DC*. Some of these pieces do not incorporate a first person narrative at all (Raghavendra, 2007: 5) nor do they give 'personal impressions' of the places they describe and advertise, preferring the retelling of associated historical details (Rao, 2008: 8) or listing the 'must-see sights' (Iyengar, 2007a: 8). In most of these essays therefore, we do not get a sense of a perceiving 'gaze'. This is the reason why I describe such essays as 'tourism writing' rather than 'travel writing'.

The self-effacement, I suggest, is an essential component of the 'global Indian'. Minus any markers of Indianness they 'fit in' into the world's cultures easily. The 'global Indian' absorbs, observes everything because s/he refuses to 'be' any particular identity.

The quest for the authentic

The traveller in these columns is one who is searching for an Indian experience that is both 'authentic' and 'original': preferably a lesser known destination, a place which if not unfamiliar, is at least a little off the beaten track or rendered unfamiliar by being visited in the off-season.[3] The emphasis in articles on Indian tourist destinations is usually on remoteness, distance and the unknown.

> A relatively unknown but exotic summer getaway, declares one writer (Raghavendra, 2008b: 5).
>
> Rural India gets explored very rarely. This holiday season you could probably take some of the lesser traveled roads ... a quaint village with houses in a row, with cows tied outside, and people going about their business – depicting a typical village scene.
>
> (Venkatesh, 2007: 5)

Another asks us to explore a 'Road Less Travelled' (RLT): 'A scrub forest for an RLT outing may not be appealing. Yet I am off'. Through the article we are introduced to the doubtful joys of walking through a forest where '(w)ild grass and groves of bamboo, thistles and bramble, thorny trees and shrubs surround you' (Basu, 2008: 4). Even as the writer-tourist hammers home the point that 'RLTs are meant to be different, sometimes exotic and fun, at times tough and unique' we are also told that 'I really can't say whether scrub forests make for a good picnic spot' (Basu, 2008: 4). The option to finding a 'new' destination is to visit a well-known place in the off-season: thus there are those who visit Pushkar, but *not* at the time of the Pushkar Mela (Nair, 2007: 4), or those who choose to go for a mini trek in the Himalayas in the winters (Swahilya, 2008: 8). We are persuaded to step back in time and participate in a lifestyle which is set in remote India.

This search for the real and the authentic in India, which is located in the lesser-known, is however not carried on abroad. The foreign destinations and trips that figure in the papers are mostly the well-known tourist routes. Thus the Indian tourist travelling abroad does the 'given', on the whole: Bali (Choudhary, 2007: 5; Mahalingam, 2008: 8), Singapore (Muthalaly, 2007: 7; Nadkarni, 2007: 5), Zurich (Kanchi, 2007: 5), France (Karthikeyan, 2008: 4; Singha, 2007: 5) and Scotland (Muthuraman, 2007: 7). And as they move through these thronged places they frequently mention the other tourists whom they encounter, the mix of nationalities and races: thus in Liverpool, celebrating the Beatles Indu Ramachandran speaks of a 'busload of Beatle-struck tourists that included Japanese, Bolivians, Croatians and even a girl from Brunei' (Balachandran, 2008: 8). The presence of other tourists appears to *confirm* the authenticity and significance of these destinations. So in Angkor Wat, Mukund Padmanabhan makes 'a list of nationalities from appearances, accents, dress and behaviour: English, German, French, Spanish, Italian, Arab, American, Thai and the ubiquitous Japanese' (Padmanabhan, 2008: 8). But even as he mourns the crowds, he asks 'will Angkor survive the invasion of tourists?' The move which entails what Padmanabhan terms 'escap[ing] the tourists' also means seeing oneself as authentic and native, belonging to, and hence superior to the average run-of-the-mill tourist:

> There is virtually nobody around and I think I have my first *real* Angkor experience, sitting amidst the rubble in the dim green light of a temple complex totally consumed by the jungle. This is what Angkor was not so long ago. And this, I couldn't help thinking, is what it should be. (emphasis added)

Yet even as a 'real' Angkor experience is sought and undergone the real is located in the absence of tourists, not in the search for an RLT. This of course elides the fact that the person is himself a tourist!

This elision is visible in articles which detail the writers' experiences in major tourist spots in India as well. So they point out that though they may be at a popular tourist destination they are not really tourists: that is a category that includes only foreigners. As in Pushkar: 'Foreigners are more visible than locals ... Indian tourists are few' (Nair, 2007: 4). Or Jaisalmer: '500 other awestruck tourists ... it is quite a sight to see tourists sunning themselves under canopied tables on a rampart here, a parapet there' (Kumar, 2008). The attempt to distance oneself from the tourists is apparent in statements such as 'at a spot further away from the conventional one, we had the entire place to ourselves' (Manmadhan, 2007: 4). The irony here is that Indians who do not see themselves as tourists in India see certain spots as tourist-y only due to the presence of foreigners there.

So the Indian in search of the tourist experience heads out of the country or into the remote recesses of India. The negative connotations (McCabe, 2005: 98–100) usually associated with being a 'tourist' (one who is more concerned with the tour guide and itinerary) as opposed to being a 'traveller' (one who searches for the local and the authentic and does not seek fleeting impressions) are ones which disappear in these newspaper columns as the writers revel in doing the 'touristy' routes while appearing in print under the heading 'travel'.

The paradox of authenticity is that in India the traveller looks for the remote and the unknown as truly 'authentic'. Abroad, the authentic is the regular (i.e. crowded) tourist spot.

The exotic

The search for the new and the strange, something that sets a place apart from the familiar is the essence of travel. The exotic is the 'realization of the fantastic beyond the horizons of the everyday world' (GS Rousseau and Roy Porter's definition, cited in Nayar, 2008: 135). Therefore, the exotic is something that charms, fascinates, even frightens *because* it is unfamiliar.

In the Indian tourism narrative, one is struck by the celebratory tone when speaking of foreign places. It is almost as though the exotic is something prepared for, and therefore the real edge of the exotic – the shock of the strange – has been eroded. Thus the tone is usually approving and eager-to-be-pleased (not shocked) with everything that the tourist destination has to offer. However, the few deviations that occur from this uniformly celebratory tone are found in pieces, not on European or other Western destinations but on those in the East or India. Thus speaking about Bali the writer comments on the Hinduism practised there: 'their rituals seem to be a world away from the Hindu rituals we see in India'. Taking issue with the offerings made to the Gods the writer says, 'And every Balinese, whether shopkeeper or hotelier, makes these offerings everyday with such touching earnestness' (Mahalingam, 2008: 8). The good intent of the people is not what is seen as faulty, rather the version of Hinduism being practised, which is not quite 'right'. Again while Angkor Wat might be huge in terms of scale the temples there 'lack the sculptural detail of their Indian counterparts' (Padmanabhan, 2008: 8). In the Pushkar piece also there is carefully worded disapproval regarding the preponderance of foreign tourists and the way in which the local culture is selling out to them (a point about host cultures and tourism contested in Joseph and Kavoori, 2001), seen in the easy availability of German baked goods and signboards in Hebrew all of which testify to 'selling out' (Nair, 2007: 4).

In contrast to these are the articles on European, American and Australian destinations which are unvaryingly laudatory. So 'Milan showcases some of the best things Italy has to offer' (Mallah, 2007: 8), Ireland is 'a picture-seeking person's paradise', full of 'astonishing cathedrals' (Balachandran, 2007: 8); Bologna 'has a mesmerisingly seductive air that captivates your mind' (Kaji, 2007: 5) and so on. It is difficult to find any criticism in these and other similar articles, and even cautionary notes are worded humorously and eventually, dismissively: thus overcrowded tourist spots can be seen positively as in 'hundreds of fans and car enthusiasts from all over the world … land up … and the tracks turn into one hot party zone' (Sequeira, 2007: 5).

Where then, does the Indian go for an exotic locale if the exotic is something already familiar? The exotic is, by definition, something foreign. Yet, when the foreign is familiar, the exotic is something one seeks *within* India. The exotic's 'traditional' discomfort – by virtue of its strangeness and difference – is carefully glossed over in favour of its pleasures and appeal. The exotic is domesticated as something pleasurable.

It appears as though the only truly exotic is interior, remote India, untouched by travellers, unspoilt by tourists. The sheer number of Indians who seek hidden, out-of-the-way places in India seems to suggest a 'native exotic', to coin a term.

I see this as an interesting reversal of the tourism paradigm: foreign tourists are lured to the main tourist sectors (New Delhi–Agra–Jaipur continue to be the most prominent), and Indian travellers (never 'tourists', it must be remembered) seek interior India.

What I am pointing to here is that the exotic is no more a truly exotic for the Indian traveller, who has, in a sense, always already travelled ('been there, done that!'). Charles Forsdick has argued that, in the postcolonial era, exoticism stands for transculturation (2001: 24). Such a 'version' of exoticism-as-transculturation is, to me, the most striking feature of popular tourism writing. It marks the rise of what can only be called a 'global Indian'.

The global Indian

What is fascinating about these travel pieces is that no Indian traveller seems out of place (literally) in any part of the world – from the busy London streets to the quiet vineyards of France. It is as if the contemporary Indian is at home in the world, possessing a 'global soul' (to borrow the title of Pico Iyer's travelogue; Iyer, 2000). If travel entails an encounter with the Other and 'transculturation' (Pratt, 1995 [1992]), Indian travellers arrive at the tourist zone *already* transculturated.

The significance of being a tourist (and that too from the Third World) in a foreign land is glossed over in these pieces. Writers on travel have pointed out that, for the Westerner, travel is almost a civil right. In other, Asian cultures (say, Vietnam), it becomes a sign of upward social mobility (Alneng, 2002: 133). The argument applies equally to India in the 1990s and after.

Tourism has generally been a phenomenon marked by a uni-directional flow in keeping with global inequalities of power: First World/centre to Third World/periphery (Huggan, 2001: 177). Theorists have argued that the term 'tourist' itself seems to denote only Westerners, and cannot be applied to 'Third World' travellers (Alneng, 2002). It seems as though the postcolonial reversal of this politically loaded term is now at hand, at least as evidenced by the travel columns.

Contemporary Indians reverse the trend of tourism as a First World phenomenon.[4] However, more than the sheer number of foreign travel pieces by Indians, one is struck by their attitude. The familiarity with, and comfort levels in, New York or London indicates that these are individuals who are truly 'citizens of the world'. Thus celebrities going 'berserk shopping' in New York (Anand, 2008: 5; Dwivedi, 2008: 5), 'lov(ing) New Zealand for its energy' (Gadde, 2008: 5) or enjoying 'family trips to London' (Sripriya, 2008: 4) are all 'ordinary'. *But* – and this is crucial – these travel pages increasingly feature non-celeb writers: comfortable in the world and knowledgeable about it. So from the Havelis of Gujarat (Kapur, 2007: 8) to the eleventh century high rises of Gimignano (Roye, 2007: 8) they enjoy the travel, they know the history and other legendary details and they do not betray, at least in their writing, their Third World origins.

This is evidenced in many spheres: their thorough knowledge and appreciation of Western art, sculpture, painting, music and literature (Balachandran, 2007: 8; Narayanan, 2007: 8); their willingness to delve into the mysteries of wine and whisky tasting (Karthikeyan, 2008: 4; Muthuraman, 2007: 7); their purchasing power and their touristy-shopping activities: single malt in Scotland (Muthuraman, 2007: 7) and 'two plates and a tile' at the Royal Delft Porcelain factory in Holland (Mitra, 2007: 8); and even in their refusal to pay much attention to the cuisine in these foreign parts.

One way of establishing themselves as 'global Indians' is by refusing to acknowledge food 'troubles'. Food-related problems, arguably among the most common hassles faced by Indians travelling abroad, are rarely focused on. Most articles mention food in passing, and this is true whether travelling in India or abroad (except for the few 'food guides'). Occasionally one gets suggestions on where it is most likely to find 'home style food' (Ganesh, 2008: 4; Manmadhan, 2007: 4). Very rarely is there a reference to the difficulty in procuring vegetarian food (Chari, 2008). Interestingly, with various culture-specific taboos on meats and alcohol, the variety of meat is not specified. Instead the articles focus the readers' attention on the ways in which these travellers/writers fit into the culture of their destinations. Kishore and Smita Iyengar state openly: 'We felt *at home* in this outstanding icon of world class dining where seductive tangos ... added zest to a truly great evening' (Iyengar, 2007b: 7, emphasis added). Similarly in Zurich Swarna Kanchi speaks of buying food at the weekly farmers' market (2007: 5).

Even when in non-English speaking countries these travellers appear effortlessly at ease. Indeed the comfort levels with Western cultures and mores are such that even as these travellers encounter the strange and the new at their tourist destinations the comparisons are usually with other Western images, artifacts, geographical landmarks. Thus '(t)he Pedestrian High Street is to Canterbury what the Piazza is to Italian cities' is how Sadhana Rao clarifies the significance of the street to her (un)informed reader (2008: 8). 'For those of us who've glimpsed the cavernous, dust-filled and eerie crater of Mt. Vesuvius, Bali's volcanoes come as a delightful surprise' writes Sudha Mahalingam (2008: 8), a statement which might be demystificatory to some, but to some alone! The traveller thus exhibits good taste, knowledge and a practical wisdom in negotiating so-called 'foreign places', a feature of contemporary elitism (Thurlow and Jaworski, 2006: 102–3). The taste and erudition are 'shown off' to good effect by these travellers, and become a mode of self-attribution (Thurlow and Jaworski, 2006: 103) that inserts them into the rank of 'elite'. In many of these cases it is possible to argue for a *pre-tourist*, where English-speaking, metropolitan Indians, educated in the cultures of the world via promotional materials, news, documentaries – in general mass media representations – seem to be prepared for the surprises of foreign places which are, ironically, not foreign enough since they do not surprise. There are comparisons to Indian images, cities and cultural customs but these are generally in articles that deal with Indian/Asian/Eastern tourist destinations. So Bangkok is described as a city 'that towers well above your average Indian skyscraper' (Chakrabarti, 2008: 5), the café at Nathu La is compared to hangout joints on Park Street, Kolkata (Vittal, 2008: 4) and the enormity of Angkor Wat elicits the question 'why isn't there anything in India even remotely as big as this' (Padmanabhan, 2008: 8).

Having said all this there still remains the crucial issue: what are the demarcating characteristics of these travellers? Do we come to know them at all? Though individual identities remain blurred and indistinct, seen collectively, they possess a composite character. For one they are rarely aggressive travellers, not out to emblazon their mark on the destinations they travel to, not even out to distinctively stamp their essays with their personalities. Even their personal reactions to the people they meet are couched in general terms. Thus the individuals they encounter are named but no personality traits emerge apart from complimentary generalities: 'Our charming hostess, Cledy' (Roye, 2007: 8) or 'the courteous staff' (Raghavendra, 2008a: 5). There are no details as to how the 'natives' (non-Indian 'hosts'/host-cultures) react to these tourists (Indians) either: so that each becomes a generic type: 'the tourist', rather than specifics like 'Indian' or 'woman' or anything else and the 'host'. In fact it is also curious that all these travel pieces are silent on the subject of gender. Even though more than half are written by women, many of whom appear to be travelling alone (an assumption provoked by the use of the singular pronoun 'I') not one specifies what it is like to be a female, often single, third-world traveller.

The self-effacement apparent in these narratives is so pervasive as to be almost un-noticeable: the attempt to 'fit in' into the world they are visiting, to not disrupt or unsettle the 'natives', and the recourse to established stereotypes. Thus travelling through Rome the writer takes the proverb literally: 'When thou art at Rome, do as they do at Rome. Roman warriors are who we decided to be like' (Narayanan, 2007: 8). Writing about a trip to Scotland Chitra Phadnis echoes commonly held views about the Scots and their 'legendary parsimony' (Phadnis, 2008: 8), while another stereotypes the ignorant rural folk: 'None of these children had any idea of Andaman, Delhi or even Kolkata [...] Geography, politics or modern science, were still distant subjects from their curricula' (De, 2007). In thus stereotyping the 'host' (whether Indian or Scottish), the Indian traveller fits into the image of the 'tourist'.

Thus the socially produced 'tourist gaze' (to adapt John Urry's formulation, 1998 [1990]) proceeds from that of a well-informed Indian traveller, a 'global soul' at home in the world. My reading of popular tourism writing suggests – as I have already proposed at the beginning of the chapter – that this is the new 'type' of Indian abroad.

Notes

1 The function of guidebooks, as John Vaughan (1974) and Inderpal Grewal (1996) have noted was to render the strange and the new into something familiar through a supply of readily understandable information, and usually through a depersonalized tone. These travel essays seem to function in much the same way when they 'depersonalize' their writing.

2 If all travel by choice is elite, as Zygmunt Bauman has suggested (cited in Thurlow and Jaworski, 2006: 100), then this certainly makes many of the Indian travellers elite. However, as we shall see towards the conclusion of this chapter, this is not the only mark of elitism.

3 Chris Ryan suggests that we speak in terms of 'authorization' rather than 'authenticity', 'posing a number of questions: Who has authorized a given representation? For what purposes has it been authorized? And under what limits, and for whom has it been authorized?' (2002: 9–10).

4 According to news reports, many countries in the world love Indian tourists because 'Indians splurge on shopping' (Tripathi, 2004. Also see 'Britain steps up efforts to woo Indian tourists', *Hindu Business Line*, 9 March 2006, www.thehindubusinessline.com/2006/03/09/stories/2006030901001900.htm. Accessed 15 May 2008. For a differing view, based on a survey of European hoteliers, which says that American tourists are preferred over Indian, Chinese and others see a nondescript boxed item in *Foreign Policy* 163 (2007): 21. Statistics show that India itself has been the beneficiary of the growth in tourism. According to *Incredible India* statistics, India saw an increase of 20.2 per cent in its foreign exchange earnings (in dollar terms) through tourism ('India Tourism in 2005', *Incredible India*: 1, http://www.incredibleindia.org/, Accessed 15 May 2008).

References

Alneng, V. (2002) 'The modern does not cater for natives: Travel ethnography and the conventions of form', *Tourist Studies*, 2 (2): 119–42.

Anand, S. (2008) 'Goa tops my choice', *Deccan Chronicle*, 17 February: 5.

Balachandran, I. (2007) 'Ireland un-Corked', Magazine, *The Hindu*, 30 September: 8.

Balachandran, I. (2008) 'A sing-along around Liverpool', Magazine, *The Hindu*, 6 January: 8.

Balaji, Y. (2007) 'Bewitching Brestagi', *Deccan Chronicle*, 7 October: 5.

Basu, S. (2008) 'Walk through, if you can', Metroplus, *The Hindu*, 10 January 2008: 4.

Bharadwaj, S. (2007) 'Top of the world', *Deccan Chronicle*, 12 August: 5.

Borm, J. (2004) 'Defining travel: On the travel book, travel writing and terminology', in G. Hooper and T. Youngs (eds) *Perspectives on Travel Writing,* Aldershot: Ashgate. 13–26.

Chakrabarti, S. (2008) 'Thailand, love at first sight', *Deccan Chronicle*, 27 January: 5.

Chari, P. (2008) 'Expectations and experiences', Magazine, *The Hindu*, 10 February. http://www.thehindu.com/thehindu/mag/2008/02/10/stories/2008021050220800.htm (accessed 9 May 2008).

Choudhary, S. (2007) 'Hit Bali this new year', *Deccan Chronicle*, 2 December: 5.

De, S. (2007) 'Sabbatical of the fugitive', Magazine, *The Hindu*, 30 December. http://www.thehindu.com/thehindu/mag/2007/12/30/stories/2007123050310700.htm (accessed 9 May 2008).

Dey, U. K. (2007) 'Sandakphu is all surprises', *Deccan Chronicle* 11 November: 4.

Dighe, S. (2008) ' Melbourne magic', *Deccan Chronicle* 20 January: V.

Dwivedi, N. (2008) 'London never fails to charm Nikhil', *Deccan Chronicle* 20 January: 5.

Dyson, K. K. (1978) *A Various Universe: A Study of The Journals and Memoirs of British Men and Women in the Indian Subcontinent, 1765–1856,* Delhi: Oxford University Press.

Forsdick, C. (2001) 'Travelling concepts: postcolonial approaches to exoticism', *Paragraph* 24 (3): 12–29.

Gadde, S. (2008) 'Nothing beats New Zealand', *Deccan Chronicle*, 24 February: 5.

Ganesh, D. (2008) 'Ferry me to Langkawi', Metroplus, *The Hindu*, 24 January: 4.

Grewal, I. (1996) *Home and Harem: Nation, Gender, Empire, and the Cultures of Travel*, Durham and London: Duke University Press.

Huggan, G. (2001). *The Postcolonial Exotic: Marketing the Margins*, London and New York: Routledge.

Iyengar, K. and Smita (2007a) 'Lingering magic of Oz', Magazine, *The Hindu*, 12 August: 8.

Iyengar, K. and Smita (2007b) 'Culinary chic', Magazine, *The Hindu*, 28 October: 7.

Iyer, P. (2000) *The Global Soul: Jet Lag, Shopping Malls and the Search for Home*, London: Bloomsbury.

Joseph, C. A. and Kavoori, A. P. (2001) 'Mediated resistance: tourism and the host community', *Annals of Tourism Research* 28 (4): 998–1009.

Kaji, S. (2007) 'Bewitched in Bologna', *Deccan Chronicle*, 25 November: 5.

Kaji, S. (2008) 'Rekindle romance by the Seine', *Deccan Chronicle*, 27 January: 5.

Kanchi, S. (2007) 'Wish you a white X'mas', *Deccan Chronicle*, 16 December: 5

Kapur, M. (2007) 'Fading grandeur', Magazine, *The Hindu*, 9 December: 8.

Karthikeyan, A. (2008) 'The city that cheers', Metroplus, *The Hindu*, 14 February: 4.

Krishnan, K. V. (2007) 'Dance of the Auroras', Magazine, *The Hindu*, 23 December. http://www.thehindu.com/thehindu/mag/2007/12/23/stories/2007122350240800.htm (accessed 9 May 2008).

Kumar, S. (2008) 'Sands of time', Magazine, *The Hindu*, 3 February. http://www.thehindu.com/thehindu/mag/2008/02/03/stories/2008020350180800.htm (accessed 9 May 2008).

McCabe, S. (2005) ' "Who is a tourist?": A critical review', *Tourist Studies* 5 (1): 85–106.

Mahalingam, S. (2008) 'Bali: tropical and timeless', Magazine, *The Hindu*, 20 January: 8.

Mallah, I. K. (2007) 'Mystique of Milan', Magazine, *The Hindu*, 11 November: 8.

Manmadhan, P. (2007) 'Rock empire', Metroplus, *The Hindu*, 13 December: 4.

Merani, V. (2008) 'Let Mauritius work its magic', *Deccan Chronicle*, 27 January: 5.

Mitra, S. (2007) 'Vermeer's town', Magazine, *The Hindu*, 12 August: 8.

Muthalaly, S. (2007) 'Weekend getaway', Magazine, *The Hindu*, 19 August: 7.

Muthuraman, V. (2007) 'The mysterious ways of malt', Magazine, *The Hindu*, 9 December: 7.

Nadkarni, R. (2007) 'A foodie's guide to Singapore', *Deccan Chronicle*, 18 November: 5.

Nair, N. (2007) 'Song of the road', Metroplus, *The Hindu*, 13 December: 4.

Narayanan, H. (2007) 'When in Rome…', Magazine, *The Hindu*, 16 December: 8.

Nayar, P. K. (2008) *English Writing and India, 1600–1920: Colonizing Aesthetics*, London and New York: Routledge.

Padmanabhan, M. (2008) 'The last stand', Magazine, *The Hindu*, 17 February: 8.

Phadnis, C. (2008) 'Highlands mystique', Magazine, *The Hindu*, 6 January: 8.

Pillai, M. D. (2007) 'The flavours of the Riviera', Magazine, *The Hindu*, 23 September: 8.

Podder, T. (2008) 'Mad about Macau', Magazine, *The Hindu*, 3 February. http://www.thehindu.com/thehindu/mag/2008/02/03/stories/2008020350080800.htm (accessed 9 May 2008).

Pratt, M. L. (1995 [1992]) *Imperial Eyes: Travel Writing and Transculturation*, London and New York: Routledge.

Quadflieg, H. (2004) ' "As mannerly and civill as any of Europe': Early modern travel writing and the exploration of the English self', in G. Hooper and T. Youngs (eds) *Perspectives on Travel Writing*, Aldershot: Ashgate. 27–40.

Raghavendra, S. (2007) 'Revel in the magic of marble rocks', *Deccan Chronicle*, 5 August: 5.

Raghavendra, S. (2008a) 'Take a trip back in time', *Deccan Chronicle*, 6 January: 5.

Raghavendra, S. (2008b) 'Cool off at the Gokak falls this summer', *Deccan Chronicle*, 20 January: 5.

Rao, S. (2008) 'The making of a spiritual city', Magazine, *The Hindu*, 20 January: 8.

Roye, J. (2007) 'Medieval skyscrapers', Magazine, *The Hindu*, 2 December: 8.

Ryan, C. (2002) 'Stages, gazes and constructions of tourism' in C. Ryan (ed.) *The Tourist Experience*, 2nd edn, London: Continuum. 1–26.

Sequeira, R. (2007) 'Strike gold at Gold Coast', *Deccan Chronicle*, 2 December: V.

Singha, S. (2007) 'France is not just about fashion', *Deccan Chronicle*, 5 August: 5.

Sinha, A. (2007) 'Paris is where the action is', *Deccan Chronicle*, 12 August: 5.

Sripriya. (2008) 'My kind of place', Metroplus, *The Hindu*, 24 January: 4.

Swahilya. (2008) 'Himalayan trek', Magazine, *The Hindu*, 24 February: 8.

Thurlow, C. and Jaworski, A. (2006) 'The alchemy of the upwardly mobile: symbolic capital and the stylization of elites in frequent-flyer programmes', *Discourse and Society* 17 (1): 99–135.

Tripathi, S. (2004) 'Why the world loves Indian tourists', 23 October. http://www.rediff.com/money/2004/oct/23spec2.htm (accessed 15 May 2008).

Urry, J. (1998) *The Tourist Gaze: Leisure and Travel in Contemporary Societies*, London: Sage.

Vaughan, J. (1974) *The English Guidebook c. 1780–1870, London: Newton Abbot.*

Venkatesh, S. (2007) 'Explore rural getaways in India', *Deccan Chronicle*, 16 December: 5.

Venkatesh, S. (2007) 'Take a break this winter', *Deccan Chronicle*, 9 December: 5.

Vittal, B. (2008) 'On top of the world', Metroplus, *The Hindu*, 10 January: 4.

Part VII
Food culture

18 The discreet charm of Indian street food

Bhaskar Mukhopadhyay

What does globalization mean in terms of the quotidian? Of course, built into this question is a certain notion of the quotidian or the customary derived from Hegel's well-known discussion of spirit which starts from what he calls '*Sittlichkeit*' (customary or conventional). Since social life is ordered by customs we can approach the lives of those living in it in terms of the patterns of those customs or conventions themselves – the conventional practices, as it were, constituting specific, shareable *forms of life* made actual in the lives of particular individuals who had in turn internalized such general patterns in the process of acculturation. The more recent concept of the everyday, defined by one of its ablest exponents as 'a transformational process by which macro-structural categories are ongoingly translated into manageable structures of sense at human scale' (Frow, 2002: 633), goes a long way towards rehabilitating Hegel's *Sittlichkeit*. The only problem is that it is very difficult to remain faithful to a certain notion of 'custom' at a time of rapid social change, if by custom one means something unchanging. Under late-capitalism, everyday life does indeed change even in the not-so-long-run – say a lifetime – and the recent theoretical shift towards micro-sociology of the Tardeian variety has been rather enabling in thinking out my project of rethinking the street culture in Calcutta. What I want to do here is to study the ensemble of practices associated with street food in Calcutta, the broader aim being the discernment of the recent mutations in these practices which could be connected, however tenuously, to 'globalization'.

Antecedents

In Calcutta, street food as such is a sign of modernity because touch had (and still has) a complex phenomenology in caste-based cosmology. Cooked food is unlikely to cross the *jati*-barrier while roasted nuts and other assorted *bhajas* (roasts) were somewhat more mobile across *jatis* because these did not contain any 'meal' element (in the Bengali cosmology, cooked rice, lentils, vegetables and fish formed the core of the 'meal'). However, there is no evidence in those picturesque *nakshas*[1] of the nineteenth century that street food of any kind was a popular practice in the halcyon days of the Bengali *babu*. *Kantalaler Kolikata Darshan* (Daschowdury, 1924–25), a moralistic, colourless upper-caste view of

Calcutta which delves deep into street-culture and mentions the then novelties like tea shops and the sale of French pornographic picture postcards on Calcutta streets, does not mention street food vendors. The inescapable conclusion is that street food is a rather recent phenomenon whose flowering could not have taken place before a certain atrophy of caste and its attendant institutions.

If I have written on Calcutta street food in recent past (Mukhopadhyay, 2004: 37–50), the point in that writing was not amusing the globally mobile Bengali chattering classes whose members sent me dozens of e-mails, including some hate mails. The point was to demonstrate that the 'modern', official Bengali culture is highly regimented and sometimes blatantly reactionary, the complacent Bengali *bubu*'s (including the poco *babus*) self-image as vanguard of 'modernity' notwithstanding. And food and taste were the twin axis through which the nationalist 'disciplining' of the tongue was effected. I will reiterate the main contours of that argument in a minute but the argument of this chapter has less to do with the historical ontology of street food than its current ramifications. In terms of lived experience, one of the major shifts in late twentieth century life in Calcutta (this period coincides with my youth) has been the gradual emergence of consumption as the leitmotif of everyday life. In terms of food intake and eating, this has led to a certain dematerialization of food. All that was solid melts into the air – meaning that erstwhile solid and somewhat 'heavy' lives of our parents gave in to a lifestyle which lacks depth and density: from the early or mid-1980s onwards, we woke up to a certain bearable lightness of being brought about by the culture of tape-recorders (a metonymy for electrical and electronic gadgets) (Rajadhyaksha, 1990: 34–52), television soaps, synthetic fibres (first 'Terilyn' and later, 'Tericot' – as the Bengali would have it), the invasion of brands, the gradual emergence of the idea of 'flat' or apartment as dwelling (instead of the erstwhile house – *badi*) and, above all, eating food that is standardized (Leidner, 1993). This 'small' history of 'our' (non-metropolitan) late modernity is yet to be written but the larger politics of the country also took a distinctive turn at this point: the collapse of the Congress hegemony, the rise of caste, region and religion-based 'ethnic' politics and what Partha Chatterjee has called the rise of 'political society': a certain penetration of the institutions of the State in the everyday life of the poor. Rajadhyaksha has astutely noted the gradual erosion of the control of the nation state on the everyday life of the people as a marker of this transition. The arrival of McDonalds and various metropolitan brands of Pizza in Calcutta in recent times completed the circle.

Street food, conduct, government

In my earlier work, I have studied the trajectory of modern Bengali food and delineated three moments in the construction of the national *haute cuisine*. First, high-nationalism and its disavowal of 'archaic' Bengali food culminating in Bankimchandra's and Vivekanada's denunciation of the erstwhile staple meal – 'rice and fish cooked in tamarind sauce' – as crude, impure and barbaric. This is correlated with the inception of a certain notion of 'culture' as 'cultivation' or 'spiritual exercise' (Bankimchandra's *anusilan*) aiming at a certain 'education of desire' which I read in a Foucaultian spirit, referring to Foucault's notion of *police*. It now occurs to me that Hegel's notion of culture (*Bildung*) in *Phenomenology*, as self-alienation through acquired cultivation, might have had some relevance in understanding the moment of Bankimchandra's invention of culture qua *anusilan*.

The second moment was the post-*swadeshi* (post-1920s) scienticization (as opposed to Bankim's semioticization) of food which acknowledged, quite explicitly, food as an arena of reform and nationalist 'regeneration'. This is visible in Vivekanadna too, but it did not take the shape of an avowed project. Besides, the accent is now entirely on 'hygiene', 'nutrition', 'vitamin', 'protein' and so on – things that crept into the Bengali vocabulary from the second decade of the last century. And by that time, culture qua a post-Tagorian *sanskriti* (a way of life) has already acquired a certain momentum. Culture as exercise/cultivation has borne fruit and ripened into *sanskriti*.

The third moment comes in the post-independence period (1960s onwards) and can be related to a collapse of the erstwhile meal ontology (Douglas, 1975: 249–75) and the rise of a 'youth culture'. Living in a still Nehruvian India, the middle-class Indian youth lacked the consumerist accoutrements (blue jeans, popular music, mass-produced hamburger) available to the post-Beat generation of the 'free world', but the spirit was willing even when the flesh could not partake in the pleasures of consumerism. The origin and rise of the mass-mediated teenage and youth culture in India must be dated during this period. Unlike South East Asia, whose tryst with the destiny of mass-culture began much later, India's mass culture (youth culture included) of those days had very distinct vernacular elements. *Our late modernity was not simply a pale reflection of metropolitan postmodernity, we modified it to suit our customs, needs and aspirations.* The best exemplars of this business of 'recycling' are 'Indian cricket' and of course, the culture of Bollywood (which was called 'Hindi cinema' until recently).

Street food is a much less spectacular manifestation of this phenomenon of the emergent vernacular mass-culture (I am aware of the oxymoronic nature of this nomenclature) and I am in no position to offer a pan-Indian perspective on it. As an anthropologist of 'manners' (the word understood in its widest connotations), I have to restrict myself to the locality and the milieus I know best and this happens to be the middle-class Bengali culture centred around Calcutta in the present state of West Bengal. But I am quite sure that similar narratives could be written on Bombay, Hyderabad or Delhi street food.

Calcutta's pavements offer a range of street foods and this range is unlikely to be matched by any other city in the world. From freshly roasted peanuts to *jhalmuri* (puffed rice mixed with various condiments and garnishes), from *telebhaja* (deep-fried vegetables in batter) to *desi* ice-creams and *kulfis*, from Anglo-Indian *chop-cutlet* (bears little or no relationship with the metropolitan lamb chop or cutlet) to Chinese *chowmein*, from candy-floss to roasted maize, from *fuchka* to *ghugni* – the repertoire is truly mind blowing. Much of this comes from the diasporic non-Bengali populations (Gujaratis, Biharies, Marwaris, Chinese and upper-Indian Muslims) living in Calcutta for generations now. They have a far more variegated snack-culture than the Bengalis who seem to be wedded to what Mary Douglas called the sacrosanct 'meal'. The *roll* (*kebab* wrap) – Calcutta's handy youth food par excellence – came into existence during the late 1970s (this the period when the influence of the North Indian, especially Mughlai cuisine, came to be felt on Bengali eating at large) and was invented by *Nizam*, the famed Muslim restaurant of New Market.

For Bengali adolescents or young adults, the ingestion of 'dematerialized' street foods like *fuchka*, *alukabli* or *hojmi*, which have little or negative use-value (nutrition, nourishment), is pleasurable. Their consumption leads to what can be called *furti* (fun) as opposed to *masti* (jouissance), which is reserved for things more serious: alcohol, sex, heavy dancing or a combination of all these. Street food is valued not because of its nourishing qualities but because of its vicious, electrifying taste (a surfeit of very sour tamarind and red-hot chillies) and its symbolic significance *qua* 'junk' or 'anti' food. I have demonstrated elsewhere that historically, in the construction of Bengali *haute cuisine*, a historic repression (in the Freudian sense) was operative which disavowed these tastes – *katu* (hotness) and *amla* (sourness) (occupying the extreme positions in the traditional East Indian taste hierarchy) – as archaic, as subaltern and therefore, unfit for polite cuisine. So, what the genteel adult taste despises is invested with prestige in youth culture. It is the cultural image around this genre of (anti)food – its exchange rather than use-value in the symbolic economy – that is important. Eating these anti-nutritious 'trash' foods that break the code of diet and 'meal', entails the membership of a loosely defined cultural group and confers on the eater a certain non-conformist identity. These foods exude non-conformist values like youth, vigour, sexiness, humour and fun times. The lurid names of these totemic anti-foods (*fuchka*, *current* etc.), the manner in which these are eaten, involving finger-licking, exaggerated chewing, gulping, blowing of nose, the places where these are eaten, busy, dusty street corners and mostly in groups often exploding in giggles and using cult language and argot, all these serve as a disorderly and carnivalesque counter to the sober and anodyne world of grey, restrained, constipated *bhadralok* Bengali adulthood.

The upshot of all these is that the rise of street food in the urban Bengali context is strictly correlated with the decline of the familial meal as a ritual activity and the emergence of non-meal eating (snacks) directed at sensuous stimulation rather than assuaging hunger pangs. I remember my mother calling my craving for street food '*dustu khide*' (naughty hunger) as opposed to hunger proper, to be satisfied by cooked food at home. I have demonstrated elsewhere, with archival evidence, that the 'civilizing' project of Bengali nationalism tried to eliminate what they perceived as *excess*, the extremes in the spectrum of Bengali taste hierarchy, namely tamarind and chilly. The incitement to civilize the tongue (as part of the larger nationalist casuistry) came from a certain desire to mimic the mild flavours of European cuisine. In the new Bengali *haute cuisine* which emerged in the late nineteenth century, these two items were considered as taboo, as unfit for polite cuisine, and increasingly came to be recognized as markers of the subaltern (the peasant – *chasa*) and the archaic. However, as these extreme tastes were repressed and prohibited in the dominant discourse, simultaneously, these were also made alluring. To prohibit something is also to invite people to transgress the prohibition; this is how the economy of pleasure has always worked. Repugnance and fascination are the twin poles of the process in which a political imperative to damn the debasing low conflicts powerfully and often unpredictably with a desire for the other. The net effect of prohibition has thus been to make chilli and tamarind tempting 'transgressions' to certain sensitive sections of the population: young girls, adolescents, pregnant women and social subalterns. Today's Bengali street food, which uses tamarind and chilli in plenty, inheres the subalternity inscribed historically on the two tastes constitutive of the Bengali palate: *katu* (hot) and *amla* (sour). As for their quality of being tempting to young people, I want to hazard a certain homology between sexual flowering, raging hormones, adolescence and the burning hot and vicious sourness of a certain genre of street food. The connection has been exploited recently by a top-selling Bengali teenage magazine whose advertisement ran as follows: Teenage mane *fuchka*, *jhalmuri*, *adda*, cricket and *Anadamela* (roughly: Teenage means *fuchka*, *jhalmuri*, *adda*,[2] cricket and Anadamela – the magazine). This establishes decisively the cultural locus of these anti-foods as lifestyle of status food.

Street food as a sign of dematerialization

In recent post-Marxist discussions of late-capitalism, 'dematerialisation' and 'immaterialisation' have often been invoked as tropes for capturing the qualitative transformation in the nature, form and organization of labour (Dowling *et al.* 2007). This putative transformation in the nature of labour has been necessitated by what Toni Negri calls 'informatisation' of capitalist production (Hardt and Negri, 2000). In my usage, immaterialization or dematerialization is used in a much more encompassing – one could say, in almost a metaphysical or poetic – sense. I do think that the idea of 'immaterialisation' can have a much wider purchase if taken out of its narrow economic context and viewed in more general and even epochal terms.

The collapse of the 'meal-ontology' and the triumph of a generalized 'snack-ontology' take place under the larger script of this dematerialization. There is even room in all this for a certain moralizing and nostalgia. Clinging to a certain sociological positivism, writers such as Pasi Falk have written that the postmodern 'alienated' person seeks a certain oral stimulation from junk food to fill the empty space (s)he perceives inside: this 'oral' urge is not the manifestation of 'oral security' but on the contrary, a symptom of its absence (Falk, 1994). The narrative strategy of positing an erstwhile plenitude in order to lament its subsequent loss, is fairly well known.

The interesting thing about the contemporary history of India is that it telescopes a long series of developments in a relatively short span of time. The pace of the process of dematerialization in the realm of food and cuisine is truly breathtaking. Between the 1970s and the 1990s, I myself have witnessed the gradual transition from coal and cow dung operated clumsy, smoky *chulas* to today's sleek electric or gas ovens. This must have taken at least a good 200 years in Europe. And it is well-known that food is the most resilient part of culture and cultural identity. And yet, the kind of flux that the Bengali food culture underwent in the last 30 years is truly astonishing: who could imagine a *dhoti*-clad Bengali *babu*, standing on the pavement in front of the *Writers Building*, stuffing himself with greasy noodles served on a *sal*-leaf plate?

If dematerialization is indeed the process that is taking place in the realm of food, leading to the preponderance of snacks and ready-to-eats (street foods), its nature and trajectory in India are somewhat different from the West. The absence of an organized retail trade industry and the incredible ability of the so-called 'informal sector' to seize opportunities and offer commodities at prices much lower than the organized sector, would lead to a scenario where 'dematerialization' (hitherto understood as a metonymy for monopoly capital and the colonization of everyday life by the forces of commodification) would, paradoxically, mean a shot in the arm of the informal sector (this has already happened in the larger cities of South East Asia). This has also to do with the peculiarities of the Indian palate and its resistance to the kind of bland food offered by the McDonald's, KFC and the various metropolitan pizza brands. India's ability to appropriate other's foods is legendary: the adaptation of the noodle in the 1980s and the 1990s was accompanied by its indigenization through spices, oils and chillies. Nestlé made a valiant attempt to capture the emergent segment with its ready-to-eat noodle brand, Maggie. The reason why Maggie and the other branded noodles did not succeed has to do with their blandness. With respect to taste, their noodles, though hygienic and posh, would come nowhere near the stuff sold by the numerous vendors in the streets of Indian cities and towns. And it is doubtful if the Indian tongue, whose proclivity for spices and chillies is well-established, would ever accept the kind of standardized, mass-mediated, bland (almost tasteless) food offered by McDonald's, for example. Price will be an important factor too.

In effect, we would have in India, 'dematerialization' notwithstanding, a kind of vernacular or folk version the global, dematerialized, street food culture. It is already happening in the streets of the larger cities of India. The surveys carried out by the WHO and other international agencies in collaboration with the local bureaucratic organization like the *All-India Institute of Hygiene and Public Health* in the 1990s, whose purpose was to governmentalize street food, clearly demonstrated that it is impossible to regulate, let alone eliminate, the small man from the street food sector of urban India. This is how the third-world multitude defers the project of a unified empire.[3]

Notes

1 The best known of this genre is Kaliprasanna Sinha's *Hutom Pancher Naksha* (1861); see Nag (1997) and Roy (2007).

2 The unique Bengali institution of *adda* (irreverent chatting) has recently been the subject of a celebrated essay by Dipesh Chakrabarty (Chakrabarty, 2000, 180–21).
3 Although a great admirer of Ashis Nandy's pop-sociological writings, I am not entirely in agreement with his pessimistic arguments put forward in Nandy (*1994a) and Nandy (*1994b).

References

Chakrabarty, Dipesh, 2000, '*Adda*: A History of Sociality', *Provincializing Europe: Postcolonial Thought and Historical Difference*, Princeton: Princeton University Press, 180–213.

Daschowdhury, Yogendra, 1924–25, *Kantalaler Kolikata Darshan*, Calcutta: Published by the author himself.

Douglas, Mary, 1975, 'Deciphering a Meal', *Implicit Meanings: Essays in Anthropology,* London: Routledge and Kegan Paul, 249–75.

Dowling, Emma, Rodrigo Nunes and Ben Trott (eds), 2007 (February), *Ephemera* [Theme issue: Immaterial Labour], 7:1.

Falk, Pasi, 1994, *The Consuming Body*, London: Sage.

Frow, John, 2002, ' "Never Draw to an Inside Straight": On Everyday Knowledge', *New Literary History*, 33:1, 623–37.

Hardt, Michael and Negri, Antonio, 2000, *Empire*, Harvard: Harvard University Press.

Leidener, Robin, 1993, *Fast Food, Fast Talk: Service Work and the Routinization of Everyday Life*, Berkeley: University of California Press.

Mukhopadhyay, Bhaskar, 2004, 'Between lite Hysteria and Subaltern Carnivalesque: The Politics of Street food in the City of Calcutta', *South Asia Research,* 24:1, 37–50.

Nag, Arun, 1997, *Satik Hootum Pancher Naksha*, Calcutta: Subarnarekha.

Nandy, Ashis, 1994a, 'Sugar in History: An Obituary of the Humble Jaggery', *Times of India* 16 July.

Nandy, Ashis, 1994b, 'Philosophy of Coca-Cola: The Simple Joy of Living', *Times of India,* 27 August.

Rajadhyaksha, Ashish, 1990, 'Beaming Messages to the Nation', *Journal of Arts and Ideas* 19, 34–52.

Roy, Swarup, 2007, *The Observant Owl: Hootum's Vignettes of Nineteenth-century, Calcutta*, Delhi: Permanent Black.

Conclusion

Popular culture, as a field of inquiry, has made rapid progress during the past two decades, marching relentlessly forward and conquering new territory. It has achieved the dubious distinction of becoming one of the most popular disciplines in the academe. However, in a certain sense, it has fallen victim to its own success. On the one hand, it has become amorphous and protean; and on the other, in its obsession with theory, it has become more and more Eurocentric, an issue strongly endorsed by Denzin (2007) in his Foreword to 'A Cultural Studies that Matters' (Cameron Mc Carthy *et al.* 2007). One of the objectives of this volume is to free popular culture from its European theoretical clutches and return it to questions of history, social formation and local tradition, an understanding of which is crucial. This is also a way of thinking through the disjunctures and differences that are clearly evident in globalised cultures. We have sought to accomplish this by focusing on diverse aspects of popular culture and lived realities of India.

One formidable challenge for scholars of popular culture is the critical engagement with history and the recognition that popular imagination is a social practice deeply grounded in history and cultural memory. It is becoming increasingly evident that popular culture scholars have begun to pay less attention to the imperatives of history. One of our aims, in putting together this volume, has been to bring the topic of history back into the discussions of popular culture in a central way. Many of the chapters in this volume (for example, Chapters 5, 6, 7, 9, 11, 16 and 17) are informed by a deep sense of Indian history. History can most profitably be understood as a discourse, as a signifying system, constructed by human beings living at a specific time and place in response to specific social experiences. How this history is inscribed in the public imagination, through popular culture, is a topic that demands careful and sustained analysis.

The concept of experience, too, seems to be getting short shrift in contemporary popular culture. This is indeed ironic since when Cultural Studies as a discipline had its origins at the University of Birmingham, the intersecting concepts of experience and social formation were of paramount importance to the early researchers. It looks as though the concept of experience has become suspect in modern western theory and in cultural studies. The current post-phenomenological thinking has served to de-valorise the concept of experience as being ideologically suspect, a product of discourse and marginal to theoretical exploration. The writings of such thinkers as Lyotard, Derrida and Althusser tend to reinforce this line of thinking. However, inspirers of cultural studies such as Raymond Williams recognise the importance of the concept of experience while being sensitive to its fraught nature. Williams is of the view that experience involves an appeal to the whole consciousness, the whole being, as against dependence on more specialised or more restricted faculties. Therefore, experience is perceived as a general movement which underlies the growth of culture. We have been, in our emphasis on experience in this book, guided by this mode of thinking.

Chapters 3, 5, 6, 7, 9, 16 and 18 inter alia in this volume address the question of tradition both directly and obliquely. The concept of tradition, like the term culture, admits of a plurality of definitions, depending on the interpretive space that one occupies. It is connected in complex and interesting ways with terms such as the past, history, customs, cultural memory, modernity and ideology. It is vitally linked to the notions of authority and legitimacy, and Max Weber was of the view that tradition is one of the sources of authority and legitimacy. In the past, tradition has been understood as a means of handing down ideas, concepts, practices, assumptions and values from generation to generation; there was a sense of authenticity linked to it. With the publication of the influential book, the invention of tradition by Eric Hobsbawm and Terence Ranger, the idea of tradition as something invented, fabricated gained wide circulation. The idea of the manipulability of tradition became important. This is indeed the view of tradition entertained by many modern cultural studies scholars. In this volume, we are making the case that this is an unduly restrictive view of tradition and that tradition needs to be seen as something that has deep roots and is of indubitable value to the people concerned.

Some chapters (e.g. 2, 3, 4, 5, 7, 14) advance the view that tradition needs to be understood as a critical historical practice; it is a site where *meanings* are made, unmade and remade. It is importantly and complexly interconnected with ideas of community and locality. Traditions are reaffirmed, challenged and re-negotiated on the basis of community experience. Pierre Bourdieu's concept of habitus and Michael Polanyi's concept of tacit knowledge shed useful light on the concept of tradition. The writers included in this book, whether they are discussing Indian folk theatre or religious performances or television shows, invoke this dynamic notion of tradition in interesting ways. We have sought to move beyond the notion of tradition as something invented to a more complex and nuanced understanding of it. The way tradition intersects with the idea of nationhood as an inescapable site of identity politics is indeed important and is reflected in, for example, chapters 9 and 15 in this volume.

Any discussion of tradition invariably gives rise to the concept of modernity; in some sense, they are two sides of the same coin. Any book on popular culture has to confront the dynamics of modernity, and ours is no different. Going beyond the standard comprehension of modernity as a universal phenomenon, we have sought to focus on the culture-specific nature of diverse modernities and their local faces as manifested in India. Many chapters (such as, for example, 2, 3, 4, 8, 10, 12, 13, 14, 15, 16, 18) in this book point to the intricate ways in which modernity takes shape in non-Western contexts through popular culture. One interesting point about modernity is that it produces its own past, and through the instrumentalities of expressive cultural performances in theatre and cinema, we can, as demonstrated in the essays on cinema and theatre, see how this is occurring in India. The construction of new subjectivities through film, television, advertising and marketing is an important facet of this phenomenon; how these subjectivities are inflected by cultural memory becomes an important problematic for some of the scholars represented in this volume.

One useful way of re-understanding the importance and function of popular culture is by examining the complex ways in which it enables citizens whether they are from India or anywhere else to make sense of their quotidian lives. Here the concept of the social imaginary, as formulated by the eminent philosopher Charles Taylor, can be of great heuristic value. In Taylor's view, the idea of the social imaginary encompasses something much broader and deeper than conceptual categories and analytical schemes that scholars deploy when anatomising social reality. According to him, it refers to the ways in which ordinary people imagine their social existence and how they fit together with fellow citizens, and how interactions take place among them, the expectations which are aroused and the assumptions which underlie them, hence the concept of relationality mentioned in the Introduction. It is a way in which average citizens re-imagine the social context of their existence. Popular culture provides us with a productive way of defining and articulating this social imaginary. We can go a step further. As chapters 1, 4, 10, 11, 13, 14, 15, and 17 clearly demonstrate, the idea of social imaginary can lead to what we refer to as the demotic sensibility. The demotic sensibility points to the images, symbols, narratives, visualities that animate a given culture (in our case, Indian culture), and therefore enabling us to enter into the discourse of historical and political meanings of culture. We feel that our volume goes some way towards focusing on this issue.

There is a general tendency in discussions of art culture and popular culture to invoke the concepts of auteurship and genre. Art cultural products bear the imprint of the author while popular cultural products have to be understood in terms of the imperatives of genre. Filmmakers who represent the artistic tradition of filmmaking in India such as Satyajit Ray, Adoor Gopalakrishnan and Mrinal Sen have to be examined in terms of auteurship while filmmakers associated with the popular cinema such as Raj Kapoor, Manmohan Desai and Ram Gopal Varma have to be studied in terms of genre. This, we feel, is an inadmissible oversimplification, and chapters 1, 8, 9 and 10, for example, in this book give reasons for its untenability. How the concept of genre functions in popular cinema needs to be examined at a deeper level of cultural apprehension. It is important to recognise that genre can become an important site of meaning-making; it is not an outwardly imposed category but a vital strategy for communicating with readers, spectators, listeners in an idiom readily understood by them. Genre, it needs to be stressed, mediates between the cultural product and the cultural discourses that surround it, and establishes vital connections with texts that preceded it. Although the chapters that address this issue have not categorically made these assertions, they move in a direction that serves to validate them.

When we discuss the significance of popular culture and its role in contemporary society, a topic that cannot be evaded is that of the aesthetics of popular culture. This is, to be sure, a vexatious and complex topic. When it comes to elite cultural products, artistic cinema, there is a pretty general consensus among the aesthetic norms and criteria that we should bring to bear on our discussions of them. However, in the case of popular culture no such consensus exists. We are pretty much agreed about the aesthetic criteria we should apply to the works of Satyajit Ray or Adoor Gopalakrishnan. However, there is a great measure of confusion to the criteria we should apply in assessing the work of Raj Kapoor or Manmohan Desai. Although we have not, in this volume, tackled this issue head on, a number of useful insights have been set in motion. As students of popular culture, it is of the utmost importance that we focus on this salient issue.

Let us, for example, consider Indian popular cinema. It is a total cinema that is animated by a poetic of excess, often requiring a willing suspension of disbelief in which narrative, spectacle, action, didacticism, song and dance come together in a loose union to constitute a filmic experience whose very constructedness is foregrounded. When we attempt to come up with a poetics of Indian popular cinema, it is vitally important that we focus on the signifying possibilities of the diverse constituent elements and the manner in which they both construct and subvert familiar understandings. In seeking to understand the true dimensions of popular culture in India we need to pay close attention to its aesthetics. Similarly, the aesthetics of television demands close consideration, since television is becoming increasingly important in the popular consciousness in India. The poetics of television drama should be different from that of cinema. In television drama, the cumulative effect of the series as opposed to the individual episode and repetition becomes a defining element; this is indeed a point that Umberto Eco has made in relation to the poetics of cartoons. Similarly, the nature of visual registers in television dramas is different as, for example, the frequent deployment of close-ups would indicate. The context of the appreciation of television is also different; as Raymond Williams has suggested, the idea of flow, the intermeshing of programmes and commercials, is an important part of the televisual experience. All these elements need to be worked purposively into the construction of an aesthetic of television. What we have sought to do in this book is to offer the merest of indications.

Chapters 1, 5, 6, 8, 9, 11 and 16 address the question of performance, and it is indeed a crucial element of popular culture. The idea of performance, whether it be in the folk-theatre or in television or in music, has to be understood in terms of physical action, cultural communication, symbolic meaning, semiotics of entertainment, the cultural construction and display of emotion. A probing into the idea of performance, and its deep roots in Indian cultural memory, is vital to a deep understanding of theatre, rituals, television, music, advertising, fashion, dance and sports in India. How performances are imbricated with issues of identity, social roles, power, resistance merit closer investigation in terms of the dynamics of popular culture.

As we broach the question of the aesthetics of popular culture, and how best it could be re-conceptualised and re-imagined, we would like to invoke Martin Heidegger. This might seem like an act of intellectual recklessness, because he was not interested in cinema or popular culture; he discussed aesthetics and art in terms of Greek temples and Holderlin's poetry and Van Gogh's paintings. However, his general approach seems to have some validity in our way of re-understanding popular culture. Heidegger's considered view was that art not only reflects the style of a given culture but that it reincarnates it. Art works, according to him, generate a commonly experienced perception and understanding of our social lives and the world we inhabit. This ontological approach to art, we believe, holds great promise for the understanding of popular culture.

The question of globalisation permeates almost all the chapters (e.g. 2, 12, 13, 14, 15, 16 and 18) in this volume in diverse ways. It is evident that the local is constantly transforming itself and reinventing itself as it seeks to reach beyond itself and engage the global, an issue often referred to as glocalisation. The writers gathered in this book have demonstrated this fact from their diverse vantage points. What is interesting about the issue of globalisation is that while it introduces new elements such as blogging and the software industry into diverse popular cultural practices of India, it also re-emphasises what is distinctly and characteristically local and place-bound in fascinating ways. This dialectic is crucial to a proper understanding of the nature and significance of popular culture in India.

Along with globalisation, the question of commodification becomes a salient issue in the re-description of popular culture. In contemporary capitalist societies, popular culture operates within the space of consumerism. Therefore, the manifold relations that exist between consumption and popular culture need to be recognised and explored; chapters 12, 13, 17 and 18 in this book have done so in interesting ways. It is a fact that in modern societies, the texture of desires and forms of imaginations of citizens are shaped largely by marketing forces and advertising strategies as in the case of food and tourism. Our identities and subjectivities are constructed by what we consume. These have great implications for the understanding of popular culture; understanding popular culture necessitates the comprehension of the materialities of discourse and their relations to power. How cultural objects inhabit social horizons of meaning is vividly demonstrated through the activities of popular culture. As one reads the chapters collected in this volume, these facets of exploration need to be kept in mind.

At the beginning of this Conclusion, we made the critical observation that popular culture is becoming too Eurocentric. One way of counteracting this tendency is to draw on indigenous conceptualisations without falling into a kind of cultural essentialism. For example, in discussing Indian cultural performativities, one turns productively to the vocabularies inscribed in classical texts such as the 'Natyashastra', 'Dasharupa' and 'Sangita Ratnakara' as well as the performative syntax of folk entertainments. Similarly, one can press into service concepts such as that of 'rasa' (aesthetic emotion). The effort that we call for, to be sure, demands careful investigation.

In putting together this volume, we were motivated by a desire to capture the complex operations of popular culture in India in a rapidly globalising age. Because we were concerned with the overly Eurocentric nature that popular culture has begun to assume in recent times, we decided to focus on questions of Indian history, tradition and social formations in a significant way. This edited volume is by no means the most comprehensive – it is difficult to capture the totality of India in a single volume – missing, for example, are studies on Fiction, Print Journalism, Radio, Gay and Lesbian Cultures, Youth Cultures, Festival Cultures, Caste, Secularism. But in dealing with many aspects of popular culture in a globalised India, we hope this edited volume will contribute in some way to the ongoing theoretical discourse about popular culture in the academe – both about its strengths and its deficiencies – and provide the stepping stones for others to build on.

Bibliography

Barker, C. (2004) *The Sage Dictionary of Cultural Studies*. London: Sage.

Barker, C. (2008) (3rd edn) *Cultural Studies*. London: Sage Publications.

Baudrillard, J. (1988) *Selected Writings*. M. Poster (ed.) Cambridge: Cambridge University Press.

Bauman, Z. (1989) 'Sociological Responses to Postmodernity', in *Thesis Eleven*, 23 35–63.

Binford, M. R. (1989) *Indian Popular Cinema Quarterly Review of Film and Video*, Vol II, 1–9.

Bounds, P. (1999) *Cultural Studies*. Trowbridge: The Cromwell Press Ltd.

Bourdieu, P. (1977) *Outline of a Theory of Practice*, trans by R.N. Nice, Cambridge: Cambridge University Press.

Branston, G. and Stafford, R. (4th edn) (2006) *The Media Student's Book*. London: Routledge.

Callinicos, A. (1989) *Against Postmodernism*: *A Marxist Critique*. Cambridge: Cambridge University Press.

Castells, M. (1996) *The Rise of the Network Society*. Oxford: Blackwell.

Castells, M. (2000) 'Information Technology and Global Capitalism', in W. Hutton and A. Giddens (eds) *On the Edge: Living with Global Capitalism*. Cape: London.

Clifford, J. (1988) *The Predicament of Culture: Twentieth Century Ethnography, Literature and Art*. Cambridge MA: Harvard University Press.

Debord, G. (1984) *Society of the Spectacle*. Detroit: Black and Red Press.

Denzin, N. (2007) Foreword in Cameron McCarthy *et al. Globalising Cultural Studies*: *Ethnographic Interventions in Theory, Method and Policy*. New York: Peter Lang.

Dharwadker, V. (2007) *The Greenwood Encyclopedia of World Popular Culture, Volume 6 Asia and the Pacific Oceania*. Westport CT: Greenwood Press.

Fiske, J. (1989) *Understanding Popular Culture*. Boston: Unwin Hyman.

Foucault, M. (1980) *Power/Knowledge Selected Interviews and Other Writings 1972–1977*, in C. Gordon (ed.). Brighton: Harvester Press.

Gains, R. and Cruz, O. Z. (eds) (2005) *Popular Culture: A Reader*. London: Sage.

Garga, B. D. (1996) *So Many Cinemas*. Mumbai: Eminence Designs Limited.

Gilroy, P. (1982) *The Empire Strikes Back Race and Racism in 70s Britian*. London: Roultedge.

Gilroy, P. (1992) *There Ain't any Black in the Union Jack*. London: Routledge.

Gokulsing, K Moti (2004) *Soft-Soaping India the World of Indian Televised Soap Operas*. Stoke-on-Trent: Trentham Books Ltd.

Gray, A. (2003) *Research Practice for Cultural Studies*. London: Sage.

Guha, R. (2007a) Great Expectations in *FT Magazine*. April 7/8 26–27.

Guha, R. (2007b) Tarnished jewels in India's crown, *THES (Times Higher Education Supplement)* (27/04) 14.

Hall, S. (1981) 'Cultural Studies: Two Paradigms', *Media Culture and Society* 2.1.

Hall, S. and Du Gay, P. (eds) (1996) *Questions of Identity*. London: Sage.

Harriss, J. (2005) How and Why Does Culture Matter? *Economic and Political Weekly*, January 8, 113–14.

Hills, H. (1993) Review, *The Sociological Review*, 41(2) 377–81.

Hoggart, R. (1957) *The Uses of Literacy*. London: Chatto and Windus.

Jones, A. (2006) *Dictionary of Globalisation*. Cambridge: Polity Press.

Kasbekar, A. (2006) *Pop Culture India!* California: ABC:CLIO.

Landes, D. (1998) *The Wealth and Poverty of Nations: Why are Some So Rich and Others So Poor*. New York: WWW Norton.

Lyotard, J. F. (1984) *The Postmodern Condition; A Report on Knowledge*. Minneapolis: University of Minnesota Press.

McCarthy, C., Durham, A. S., Engel, L. and Filmer, A. (2007) *Globalising Cultural Studies: Ethnographic Interventions in Theory, Method and Policy*, New York: Peter Lang.

McQuail, D. (ed.) (2005) *McQuail's Reader in Mass Communication Theory*. London: Sage.

McRobbie, A. (1980) Settling accounts with subcultures; a feminist critique, *Screen Education*. 34 Spring 23–43.

Milner, A. and Browitt, J. (3rd edn) (2002) *Contemporary Cultural Theory: An Introduction*. London: Routledge.

Mukhopadhyay, B. (2006) Cultural studies and politics in India today, *Theory, Culture & Society*, 23(7–8) 270–92.

O'Sullivan, T. *et al.* (2nd edn) (2001) *Key Concepts in Communication and Cultural Studies*. London: Routledge.

Rao, V. and Walton, M. (2004) *Culture and Public Action*. Stanford: Stanford University Press.

Sen, A. (1993) 'Pluralism', *Monsoon*, 20(3) 27–46.

Storey, J. (1993) *An Introductory Guide to Cultural Theory and Popular Culture: A Reader*. Hemel Hempstead: Prentice Hall/Harvester.

Strinati, D. (2nd edn) (2004) *An Introduction to Theories of Popular Culture*. London: Routledge.

Thompson, E. P. (1963) *The Making of the English Working Class*. Harmondsworth: Penguin.

Thwaites, T., Davis, L. and Mules, W. (1994) *Tools for Cultural Studies: An Introduction*. Australia: Macmillan Publishers.

Turner, G. (1996) *British Cultural Studies: An Introduction*. Sydney: Routledge.

Williams, R. (1963) *Culture and Society 1789–1950*. Harmondsworth: Penguin.

Williams, R. (1965) *The Long Revolution*. London: Penguin.

Williams, R. (1976) *Keywords: A Vocabulary of Culture and Society*. London: Fontana.

Index